Garden and Landscape History

COMMON LAND IN BRITAIN

Garden and Landscape History
ISSN 1758-518X

General Editor
Tom Williamson

This exciting series offers a forum for the study of all aspects of the subject. It takes a deliberately inclusive approach, aiming to cover both the 'designed' landscape and the working, 'vernacular' countryside; topics embrace, but are not limited to, the history of gardens and related subjects, biographies of major designers, in-depth studies of key sites, and regional surveys.

Proposals or enquiries may be sent directly to the editor or the publisher at the addresses given below; all submissions will receive prompt and informed consideration.

Professor Tom Williamson, School of History, University of East Anglia, Norwich, Norfolk NR4 7TJ, UK.

Boydell & Brewer, PO Box 9, Woodbridge, Suffolk, England, IP12 3DF, UK.

Previous publications are listed at the back of this volume.

COMMON LAND IN BRITAIN

A HISTORY FROM THE MIDDLE AGES TO THE PRESENT DAY

ANGUS J. L. WINCHESTER

THE BOYDELL PRESS

© Angus J. L. Winchester 2022

All rights reserved. Except as permitted under current legislation no part of this work may be photocopied, stored in a retrieval system, published, performed in public, adapted, broadcast, transmitted, recorded or reproduced in any form or by any means, without the prior permission of the copyright owner

The right of Angus J. L. Winchester to be identified as the author of this work has been asserted in accordance with sections 77 and 78 of the Copyright, Designs and Patents Act 1988

First published 2022
The Boydell Press, Woodbridge
Paperback edition 2024

ISBN 978-1-78327-743-8 hardback
ISBN 978-1-83765-132-0 paperback

The Boydell Press is an imprint of Boydell & Brewer Ltd
PO Box 9, Woodbridge, Suffolk IP12 3DF, UK
and of Boydell & Brewer Inc.
668 Mt Hope Avenue, Rochester, NY 14620–2731, USA
website: www.boydellandbrewer.com

A CIP catalogue record for this book is available
from the British Library

The publisher has no responsibility for the continued existence or accuracy of URLs for external or third-party internet websites referred to in this book, and does not guarantee that any content on such websites is, or will remain, accurate or appropriate

The author and publisher gratefully acknowledge the support of the Marc Fitch Fund and the Open Spaces Society in making grants towards the cost of illustrations.

CONTENTS

List of Illustrations ix
Acknowledgements xii
List of Abbreviations xiv

INTRODUCTION 1

PART I: COMMON THREADS

Chapter 1 COMMONS IN THE BRITISH LANDSCAPE 9

Chapter 2 CUSTOM AND LAW: THE GENESIS OF COMMON LAND 21

Chapter 3 MANAGING COMMUNAL RESOURCES 51

Chapter 4 COMMONS AS COMMUNAL SPACES 83

Chapter 5 LIVING ON THE EDGE: COMMONS AND THE POOR 111

Chapter 6 THE AGE OF 'IMPROVEMENT': PRIVATISATION AND THE RECONFIGURATION OF COMMON LAND 129

Chapter 7 THE COMMONS REINVENTED 153

Chapter 8 THE CHANGING FACE OF COMMON LAND SINCE 1860 183

PART II: A KALEIDOSCOPE OF COMMON LANDSCAPES: EIGHT CASE STUDIES

Chapter 9 NORTH ASSYNT COMMON GRAZINGS, SUTHERLAND 207

Chapter 10 NETHER WASDALE COMMON, CUMBERLAND 215

Chapter 11	COCKFIELD FELL, CO. DURHAM	223
Chapter 12	ISLE OF AXHOLME TURBARY ALLOTMENTS, LINCOLNSHIRE	229
Chapter 13	LLANLLECHID MOUNTAIN AND ABER MOUNTAIN, CAERNARVONSHIRE	235
Chapter 14	BRINGSTY COMMON AND BROMYARD DOWNS, HEREFORDSHIRE	245
Chapter 15	IBSLEY COMMON AND ROCKFORD COMMON, NEW FOREST, HAMPSHIRE	255
Chapter 16	WIMBLEDON COMMON AND PUTNEY HEATH, SURREY	265
	CONCLUSION: COMMON GROUND	275
	Select Bibliography	283
	Index	303

ILLUSTRATIONS

Figures

1	Upland commons: the high fells of the central Lake District	2
2	An Oxfordshire common: Kingwood Common, Rotherfield Peppard (image courtesy of Rod D'Ayala and the Nettlebed & District Commons Conservators)	2
3	Common land in Britain today (map courtesy of Graham Bathe)	10
4	Common land and parish boundaries near Wymondham, Norfolk	13
5	Common land in relation to farmland and settlement	16
6	Eden Valley, Cumbria: extent of common land before enclosure	18
7	Coldingham Moor, Berwickshire: a 'shire moor'	24
8	Parish boundaries and former common land, central Lincolnshire	47
9	Plan of Exmoor, 1675 (TNA, MPB 1/54)	48
10	Boundary markers across open common land, Newby manor, near Ingleton, Yorkshire (Image (a) courtesy of Valerie Winchester)	49
11	'Pains' from Cumwhinton, near Carlisle, Cumberland (CAS, D/AY/3/2; reproduced by kind permission of Susan Aglionby)	53
12	Sheepwalks, Cwmdeuddwr Common, Radnorshire	62
13	Sheep ear marks from mid-Wales (reproduced by kind permission of Erwyd Howells)	65
14	William Stewart MacGeorge, 'A Galloway peat moss', 1888 (National Galleries of Scotland. Bequest of Dr Samuel Murdoch Riddick 1975)	70
15	Harvesting bracken, Eskdale (Cumb.), probably in the 1920s (photograph by Mary Fair, courtesy of Cumbria Libraries: Carlisle Local Studies Library; reproduced by permission of CWAAS)	78
16	Early medieval meeting places on common land: Moota (Cumb.) and Mootlaw (Northumb.)	84
17	'Ground Plot of Wey Hill Faire', 1683 (Queen's College Archive 3V165, courtesy of The Provost and Fellows of The Queen's College, Oxford)	92
18	Racecourse on the common at Lyndhurst (Hants) (extract from *A Plan of His Majesty's Forest, called the New Forest, in the County of Southampton ... from surveys undertaken by Thos. Richardson, Wm. King and Abm. and Wm. Driver ... MDCCLXXXIX* (2nd edn, 1814))	98

19	Chartist meeting at Basin Stones, Todmorden, in 1842, by Alfred Walter Bayes (Bankfield Museum, Halifax: Acc. No. 1998.907; reproduced by permission of Calderdale Museums Service)	103
20	'Fox's Pulpit', Pardshaw Crag, Cumberland	105
21	Covenanter monument and communion stones, Skeoch Hill, Kirkpatrick Irongray, Kirkcudbrightshire (image courtesy of Nick Addington @ToTheObelisk)	107
22	Gorsley Common (OS Six-Inch map: Herefordshire 47SE, surveyed 1883–87)	117
23	Edgerley township, Shropshire, in 1771 (Shropshire Archives, 6001/2482)	122
24	Botany Bay gardens, Wheeler End Common, West Wycombe (Buckinghamshire Archives, Tithe/420)	126
25	Oxenhope Moor (Yorks. W.R.): a landscape of Parliamentary enclosure (image courtesy of Steven Wood)	137
26	Commonty at Wilton, near Hawick, 1764 (NRS, RHP 181)	140
27	Partial enclosure: Bassenthwaite Common, Cumberland	141
28	Bassenthwaite Common: improved land and stinted pasture	142
29	Chipping Norton, Oxfordshire: enclosure of common land since 1770	144
30	Barnham Broom, Norfolk, enclosure plan, 1812 (Norfolk Record Office, C/Sca2/15)	149
31	Wandsworth Common: land lost between 1768 and 1865	170
32	Tablet at Baptist Chapel, Rushmere Heath, Suffolk (image courtesy of www.ipswich-lettering.co.uk)	173
33	Samuel Henry Alken, 'Farriers of the 17th Regiment of (Light) Dragoons (Lancers) shoeing a horse from a mobile forge, Chobham Camp, 1853' (image courtesy of the National Army Museum, London)	174
34	Second World War radar station, Barrow Common, Brancaster, Norfolk	176
35	'The Squatters', *Punch*, 9 February 1945 (image courtesy of Punch Cartoon Library/TopFoto)	178
36	Peat restoration at Buckstones on Marsden Moor, Yorkshire (image courtesy of Penny Anderson)	189
37	Nettlebed Common, Oxfordshire (image courtesy of Valerie Winchester)	195
38	Roydon Common, Norfolk (image courtesy of *Lynn News*)	197
39	Town Moor, Newcastle upon Tyne (OS Six-Inch map, Durham 2, revised 1913–14)	199
40	Kennington Park, London (OS 1:2,500 plan, London 55, surveyed 1871)	201
41	Location of case study commons	206
42	Stoer common grazing, Assynt, Sutherland	208
43	North Assynt, Sutherland: (A) farm boundaries in 1774; (B) modern common grazings	209
44	Herdwick sheep on Nether Wasdale Common, Cumberland	216

45	Nether Wasdale Common	217
46	Cockfield Fell, Co. Durham (image courtesy of Valerie Winchester)	224
47	Cockfield Fell: LIDAR image, 2018 (courtesy of Stephen Eastmead, altogetherarchaeology.org; contains public sector information licensed under the Open Government Licence v1.0)	225
48	Cockfield Fell in 1857 (OS Six-Inch map, Durham 41, surveyed 1857)	227
49	Isle of Axholme, Lincolnshire: turbaries and extent of former common land	230
50	Epworth Turbary, Isle of Axholme	232
51	Aber Mountain with multicellular sheepfold beside Afon Anafon	236
52	Llanllechid Mountain: Elias Owen's map of 'ancient remains' on the common, 1866 (image courtesy of Bill Britnell)	237
53	Llanllechid and Aber Mountains, Caernarvonshire	238
54	Lower slopes of Llanllechid Common	240
55	Bringsty Common in 1885 (OS Six-Inch map, Herefordshire 21NE, published 1885)	246
56	Bromyard Downs in 1885 (OS Six-Inch map, Herefordshire 21NW, published 1885)	248
57	Cottage on Bringsty Common	249
58	Bromyard Downs in July	250
59	Ibsley Common, Hampshire	256
60	Ibsley and Rockford commons	257
61	The New Forest: bee gardens recorded in 1635	260
62	Ponies grazing on Rockford Common	262
63	Putney Heath in the 1890s (OS Six-Inch map, Surrey 7NW, published 1899)	271
64	Wimbledon Common (image courtesy of Natalie Winchester)	272

Tables

| 1 | Changes in number of ewes grazing selected Lake District commons following the introduction of agri-environment schemes | 186 |
| 2 | North Assynt common grazings | 212 |

Figures 22, 39, 40, 48, 55, 56 and 63 are reproduced under a Creative Commons Attribution-NonCommercial-ShareAlike 4.0 International (CC-BY-NC-SA) licence with the permission of the National Library of Scotland.

The author and publisher are grateful to all the institutions and individuals listed for permission to reproduce the materials in which they hold copyright. Every effort has been made to trace the copyright holders; apologies are offered for any omission, and the publisher will be pleased to add any necessary acknowledgement in subsequent editions.

ACKNOWLEDGEMENTS

RESEARCHING THIS BOOK, I have met with much kindness and generosity and it is a pleasure to be able to record my thanks to some of the many people who have given help and encouragement across the years. The bulk of the book was written during the Covid-19 pandemic in 2020–21, when access to libraries and record offices was severely limited. I have necessarily relied heavily on material available online, so, before singling out individuals, I should like acknowledge the debt that all historians now owe to the unseen army of web designers and software engineers whose labours have transformed research in recent years.

My debts to individuals are many, and the greatest thanks go to Graham Bathe (formerly Common Land Project Manager at Natural England) who read the body of the book in draft and offered very full, penetrating and constructive comments, drawing on his great depth and breadth of knowledge about the history of commons. The book is the better for Graham's thoughtful criticism, though I take full responsibility for its final form.

Across the years I have learned much from colleagues who share an interest in common land. Especial thanks go to Eleanor Straughton, my fellow historian on the Arts & Humanities Research Council-funded 'Contested Common Land' project in 2007–10, and to our colleagues then in Newcastle Law School, Christopher Rodgers and Margherita Pieraccini. Julia Aglionby and Andrew Humphries of the Foundation for Common Land have shared their deep knowledge and understanding of commons over many years. Paul Warde, Tine De Moor and José Miguel Lana-Berasáin, among others, opened my eyes to the history of commons in continental Europe, and my former research students, James Bowen, Frances Kerner and Bill Shannon, have introduced me to commons in different parts of England. I should also like to record my thanks to the following for their generosity over specific matters as the book was in preparation: Penny Anderson, John Blair, David Crouch, Simon Draper, Andrea Jarman, Blue Kirkhope, Jamie Lund, Sharolyn Parnham, Roger Pearce, Jane Platt, Julia Sandison, Brian Short, Chris Short and Annie Tindley.

Speedy efficiency has been the hallmark of those who provided images, and permissions to use them, as credited in the list of illustrations. It has been a pleasure to work with Sheila Ripper who drew the maps with her usual care and eye for detail. Library and record office staff have been particularly helpful in trying

ACKNOWLEDGEMENTS

circumstances and I owe special thanks to Guz Gonzalez (Surrey History Centre), Annwen Jones (Gwynedd Archives), Chloe Phillips (Norfolk Record Office), Lorna Standen (Herefordshire Archives) and Jan Wood (Devon Archives). Likewise, the Commons Registration officers – Svetlana Bainbridge (Cumbria), Naomi Boyd (North Lincolnshire), Scott Hutchinson (Co. Durham) and Jane Norton (Herefordshire) – who provided copies of commons registers, and Lynne Hendry and Claire Mackintosh of the Crofting Commission and Andrew Johnstone of the Scottish Land Court, who supplied copies of grazing regulations from Assynt.

I owe particular thanks to those who helped me to understand the recent histories of the case study commons, namely: Jeanette McCarthy and Carol MacRae in Sutherland; David Diamond, Julius Manduell, Simon Webb and Julia Wrigley in Cumbria; Joanne Bainbridge and Stuart Heddle (Cockfield Field Reeves) and Brian Roberts in Co. Durham; Dave Bromwich (Lincolnshire Wildlife Trust) in the Isle of Axholme; Gethin Evans of The National Trust in Gwynedd; Derek Brookes, Tom Fisher, Catherine Fuller, Linda James, Nigel Shaw and Noëlle Wilson in north-east Herefordshire; and Richard Deacon, Mike Osborne, Gareth Owen and Sue Westwood (Clerk to the Verderers) in the New Forest.

Finally, I should like to acknowledge the enthusiastic encouragement of Tom Williamson and Caroline Palmer and the friendly efficiency of all involved at Boydell & Brewer, especially Christy Beale, in bringing the book to publication.

My wife, Val, who has shared my journey into the history of common land over many years, had no escape from my single-minded focus on the subject during lockdowns. As ever, I thank her for her love and her unwavering support.

Angus Winchester
Chapel-le-Dale
March 2022

ABBREVIATIONS

AgHR	*Agricultural History Review*
Ashdown Forest	B. Short (ed.), *The Ashdown Forest Dispute 1876–1882: Environmental Politics and Custom* (Lewes, 1997)
BL	British Library
CAS	Cumbria Archive Service
CCD	Commons Commissioners' Decisions, available at https://www.acraew.org.uk/commissioners-decisions. County, place and CL unit number are given, followed by the reference number of the original typescript decision.
Contested Common Land	C. P. Rodgers, E. A. Straughton, A. J. L. Winchester and M. Pieraccini, *Contested Common Land: Environmental Governance Past and Present* (London, 2011)
CL	Common Land unit number in registers compiled under the CRA
CPS	Commons Preservation Society (forerunner of The Open Spaces Society)
CRA	Commons Registration Act 1965
CWAAS	Cumberland & Westmorland Antiquarian & Archaeological Society
DB	Domesday Book. Reference is to folio number, followed in parentheses by county and entry number in the Phillimore edition, ed. John Morris (35 vols, Chichester, 1973–86)
Eversley	Lord Eversley [George Shaw Lefevre], *Commons, Forests and Footpaths* (London, 1910)
Gadsden	E. F. Cousins with R. Honey, *Gadsden on Commons and Greens* (London, 2012)
HARC	Herefordshire Archive and Records Centre, Hereford
Harvest	A. J. L. Winchester, *The Harvest of the Hills: Rural Life in Northern England and the Scottish Borders, 1400–1700* (Edinburgh, 2000)
HER	Historic Environment Record

ABBREVIATIONS

HLE	Heritage List for England: https://historicengland.org.uk/listing/the-list/ (followed by site number)
Hoskins & Stamp	W. G. Hoskins and L. Dudley Stamp, *The Common Lands of England and Wales* (London, 1963)
HRO	Hampshire Record Office, Winchester
IBG	Institute of British Geographers
NLS	National Library of Scotland, Edinburgh
NRS	National Records of Scotland, Edinburgh
NYCRO	North Yorkshire County Record Office, Northallerton
OE	Old English
OS	Ordnance Survey
RCCL Rep.	*Report of Royal Commission on Common Land 1955–1958* (Cmnd. 462, 1958)
RO	Record Office
TNA	The National Archives, Kew
Town Commons	M. Bowden, G. Brown and N. Smith, *An Archaeology of Town Commons in England: 'A very fair field indeed'* (Swindon, 2009)
Trans CWAAS	*Transactions of the Cumberland & Westmorland Antiquarian & Archaeological Society*
Trans IBG	*Transactions of the Institute of British Geographers*
VCH	*Victoria County History*, cited by county set, volume and page number
Wimbledon Ct R.	[P. H. Lawrence (ed.)], *Extracts from the Court Rolls of the Manor of Wimbledon extending from 1 Edward IV to AD 1864* (London, 1866)

Places are identified by historic county, using standard county abbreviations.

Technical and obsolete terms are explained in the text when first mentioned; these explanations are signalled in bold in the Index, for ease of reference.

Website URLs cited in the footnotes and Bibliography were accessed on 22 December 2021 to confirm that they were then live.

INTRODUCTION

COMMON LAND – WHETHER MOUNTAIN, moorland, heathland or marsh – holds an enduring fascination for many people. Both its untamed ecological character and the existence of shared interests set it apart in a world dominated by private property. It touches a deep place in the collective historical memory, especially in England, where, in popular imagination, commons were 'stolen' from the poor during the enclosure movement of the eighteenth and nineteenth centuries. Yet the nature of common land is often poorly understood, recurrent misconceptions being that commons belonged to no one or, conversely, to everyone and that they are untouched, 'natural' landscapes. In reality, commons have a rich history as public-private space; they are not 'natural' environments but the product of interaction between humanity and nature over many centuries.

This book aims to survey the history of common land in all three nations of Great Britain from the Middle Ages to the present day, casting the net wide in order to explore the intersections between how commons have been viewed and valued across the centuries, how they have been used, and how the landscapes and vegetation of common land have changed. The bulk of the book (Part I) provides an overview, based largely on published literature, while eight case studies of individual commons (Part II) present detailed local histories drawing on archival research.

A mention of common land conjures up a range of images in twenty-first-century Britain. To a hill shepherd, it means whistling his dog onto the back of his quad and heading off to the open grazings of moor or mountain to find their flock. To many in the English countryside it means walks through scrubby woodland, bracken and gorse, criss-crossed by footpaths. To a young couple in London, loading their sleeping baby into a pushchair, to get some fresh air on paths winding past ponds echoing to the calls of ducks, as the traffic rumbles and planes roar overhead. What binds these snapshots together is that, though the environments differ, they share two features. Each is a tract of uncultivated country and a haunt of wildlife; the land is not fully tamed. They are also shared spaces: the shepherd's ewes share the hill with other flocks; the walkers on the heath meet volunteers repairing paths for the local wildlife trust; the young couple join joggers, dog-walkers and other families on the urban common. These twin characteristics – being untamed land and shared space – lie at the heart of the land with which this book is concerned. Commons are landscapes of

Figure 1. Upland commons: the high fells of the central Lake District from Buttermere Common, Cumberland.

Figure 2. An Oxfordshire common: Kingwood Common, Rotherfield Peppard.

INTRODUCTION

semi-natural vegetation (in Alan Everitt's memorable phrase, 'half-wild country')[1] and also shared land, in which resources are not controlled or fully appropriated by any one individual.

This duality – a type of landscape; but also land with a distinctive legal status – means that defining 'common land' for the purposes of this book is not straightforward. The legal definition of common land in English law excludes some communally used resources which would be considered 'common land' in lay parlance. On the other hand, some landscapes of semi-natural vegetation are private property and not subject to the shared use inherent in common land. As a result, both the legal and the ecological characteristics of commons must be considered further.

In English law, common land can be defined as private property over which third parties possess legal rights allowing them to make use of produce from the land. These common rights are what lawyers term 'incorporeal hereditaments', giving commoners the right to 'take or use some part of the natural produce of ... the land of another person'. To be true common land, part of the benefit of the land in question must remain with the owner of the soil, so that 'there is a community of use, or commonality, between owner and rights holders'.[2] This is a definition which is at once too wide and too prescriptive for my purposes. It is too wide because the focus of this book is on the 'half-wild' commons described above, while, historically, the legal definition also included the open fields and meadows of pre-improvement times, over which common rights were exercised for part of the year after the crop had been taken. In terms of landscape character, the nature of common rights, and their place in the agrarian economy, the open fields and meadows were quite different from common land as defined for this book and are not discussed in the following chapters.

The English legal definition is also too narrow for my purposes. Not only has it never applied to Scotland, but it also excludes some categories of land in England and Wales, such as stinted pastures, which are used communally but fall outwith its strict legal parameters.[3] Moreover, by focusing on property rights, legal concepts had only limited bearing on the many informal aspects of common land in local culture. The sheer range of activities which have taken place on common land (from fairs and horse races to military training) and the assortment of people using commons without a formal legal right (squatters, gypsies, field preachers, for example) show that the legal niceties of the law of commons were often irrelevant and that commons were communal spaces in which many could claim a sense of 'ownership' beyond the letter of the law.

The commons discussed in this book are therefore the left-over, unimproved land, beyond the limits of actively managed farmland. They embrace a broad spectrum of landscapes, including mountain, hill and heather moorland, scrubland and heath, fen and salt marsh. They encompass the ice-scoured 'cnockan and lochan' terrain of the north-west Highlands; the rocky fells and heather moorlands of northern England; the grassy uplands of mid-Wales; the granite moors of the south-west; the heathlands of

---

[1] A. Everitt, 'Common land', in J. Thirsk (ed.), *The English Rural Landscape* (Oxford, 2000), p. 210.
[2] *Gadsden*, §§ 1-01, 1-24. See below, Chapter 2.
[3] For stinted pastures, see below, pp. 57–8, 143–5.

the New Forest, Surrey and East Anglia; the wetlands of the Fens and the Somerset Levels; mosslands in southern Lancashire and northern Shropshire; and coastal marshes flanking the Humber and Solway estuaries and the north Norfolk coast.

Such 'left-over' land was far from unproductive. Commons were – and in upland Britain remain – an integral part of livestock farming, providing essential grazing, especially in summer, for sheep, cattle and horses. Historically, the grazing of livestock on common land was ubiquitous and was generally of greater economic importance than other common rights, though grazing intensity and patterns of use changed over time. Keeping pigs in woodland ('pannage'), important in medieval times, disappeared from most commons in later centuries, for example. The grazing of cattle and horses continued, but patterns changed, and most upland regions saw increasingly intensive use of hill commons by flocks of sheep from the eighteenth century.

Until the twentieth century, many commons also yielded other resources essential to pre-modern life. Of these, the right to take fuel was the most valuable, the type of fuel being determined by local ecology.[4] Sticks and wood for the fire and gorse for bread ovens could be collected on many commons; turf and peat were cut from upland moors and from fens and mosses in the lowlands. It is easy to forget the importance of communal sources of fuel, now that, unlike grazing, the fuel resources of common land in Britain are little used. Commons also provided building materials, including sand and clay, stone and turf, and thatching materials, such as heather, bracken and reeds. Food could be gathered in the form of nuts and berries, fish and wildfowl, and (sometimes illegally) game. Managing the exploitation of resources on common land was a perennial challenge to local communities, as they sought to regulate demand and to resolve tensions between competing uses.

Regulating use lies at the heart of much of the literature on commons. Common land in Britain is but one manifestation of a global phenomenon which was much more ubiquitous in the past – the sharing of resources by communities, rather than their appropriation by individuals. Commons offer an alternative model of land ownership, and the existence of shared interests lies at the heart of the enduring interest in them and the strong opinions, both negative and positive, they evoke. Common land has sometimes been viewed, by both contemporaries and modern scholars, as 'left-over land' in another sense: an anachronistic hangover from the pre-modern world, characterised by multiple interests which sit uncomfortably with norms of private property. That negative view drove the concerted attacks on common land during the age of enclosure in the eighteenth and nineteenth centuries and floats in the background in the international literature on commons, which concentrates on resource exploitation and sustainability. In the rich history of common land the challenge of balancing private interests with the common good never lies far below the surface.

One of the most influential discussions of these issues was Garrett Hardin's paper, 'The tragedy of the commons' (1968), which used common land as a metaphor in an

---

[4] See P. Warde and T. Williamson, 'Fuel supply and agriculture in post-medieval England', *AgHR*, 62 (2014), pp. 61–82.

essay on the perils of unchecked population growth. To Hardin, it was self-evident that communal resources were unsustainable. On 'a pasture open to all', he wrote, the 'rational herdsman' will graze more and more animals, in order to maximise his return – but so will all his fellow commoners, so that the resources of the pasture become exhausted. As Hardin put it, 'Freedom in a commons brings ruin to all'.[5] It was pointed out long ago that Hardin's basic premise that there would be a free-for-all on a common was ahistorical and certainly false as far as the history of common land in Britain and Europe was concerned,[6] yet his paper, summarising as it did the essence of longstanding negative attitudes to common land among those who championed private property, continues to haunt the literature.

A major correction came with the 'new institutionalist' approach to the understanding of common resources, spearheaded by the economist Elinor Ostrom. Her seminal work, *Governing the Commons: The Evolution of Institutions for Collective Action* (1990), demonstrated that communal resources were not doomed to Hardinesque failure; the issue was not communal property rights *per se*, but rather success in developing effective means of regulating the use of commons. Drawing on numerous studies of contemporary common pool resources (forests, fisheries, irrigation systems, for example), Ostrom identified a set of design principles which were needed to ensure their sustainable management over the long term. These included clarity over who had access to a common's resources; the formulation of appropriate rules to regulate communal use; and the presence of effective monitoring systems with sanctions for those who broke the rules.[7]

Ostrom's ideas have been influential in relation to contemporary 'global commons' (such as oceans and sea beds, or the Antarctic) and sustainable environmental management of local communal resources in many different countries.[8] Her design principles have also served as a tool for historians seeking to understand the evolution of European commons over time.[9]

The approach taken in this book is to survey the history of commons on a wider front, rather than to focus solely on regulatory systems. The overarching aim is to explore the interplay between evolving conceptions of common land and the use and

---

[5] G. Hardin, 'The tragedy of the commons', *Science*, new ser. 162 (3859) (1968), p. 1244.
[6] S. J. B. Cox, 'No tragedy on the commons', *Environmental Ethics*, 7 (1985), pp. 49–61.
[7] E. Ostrom, *Governing the Commons: The Evolution of Institutions for Collective Action* (Cambridge, 1990), pp. 90–101. See also below, p. 79.
[8] See, for example, S. J. Buck, *The Global Commons: An Introduction* (Washington DC, 1998); T. Murota and K. Takeshita (eds), *Local Commons and Democratic Environmental Governance* (New York, 2013). The 'Digital Library of the Commons' (https://dlc.dlib.indiana.edu/dlc/) and the open access *International Journal of the Commons*, published by the International Association for the Study of the Commons, founded in 1989 (https://iasc-commons.org/), demonstrate the vibrancy of international research springing from Elinor Ostrom's work.
[9] For example, by the contributors to M. De Moor, L. Shaw-Taylor and P. Warde (eds), *The Management of Common Land in North West Europe, c.1500–1850* (Turnhout, 2002). They are addressed more fully by T. De Moor, *The Dilemma of the Commoners: Understanding the Use of Common-Pool Resources in Long-Term Perspective* (Cambridge, 2015).

ecology of the landscapes of commons in Britain. In pursuing that objective, Part I traces the changing cultural meanings of common land across time, taking a broadly chronological approach. After a survey of the extent and character of common land in the British landscape (Chapter 1), four chapters focus on the medieval and early modern periods, exploring the distinctive legal status of common land and the management regimes regulating the exercise of common rights (Chapters 2 and 3), then moving on to consider the role of commons as communal spaces and as a resource for the poor (Chapters 4 and 5). The second half of Part I traces the history of commons since the seventeenth century: their loss (but also their persistence) during the 'age of improvement' (Chapter 6), the changing conceptions of the value and right use of commons since the nineteenth century (Chapter 7), and their changing ecological character (Chapter 8). Part II (Chapters 9–16) illustrates something of the variety of common landscapes and the richness of their history at local level, through eight brief case studies of individual commons from across Britain.

I have drawn evidence from the histories of both surviving commons and common land which remained in shared use in the early modern period but was later enclosed. The history of commons has often been told through the lens of enclosure, concentrating on the processes of their destruction and disappearance from the landscape, as shared usage was abolished and they were converted into private property. The following chapters seek to redress the balance by examining common land on its own terms, as an economically and culturally important element in the British landscape from the medieval period to the present day.

PART I: COMMON THREADS

CHAPTER 1

COMMONS IN THE BRITISH LANDSCAPE

ACCORDING TO MODERN LEGAL definitions, common land covers more than 2.7 million acres (1.1 million ha) of Britain. In England, 986,000 acres (399,040 ha) or 3 per cent of the land area is registered common land (a figure which includes 62,900 acres (25,470 ha) of commons in the New Forest, the Forest of Dean and Epping Forest, which were excluded from the Commons Registration Act 1965). The bulk of common land in England lies in the uplands, as it does in Wales, where registered commons amount to 428,387 acres (173,366 ha) or 8.4 per cent of the land area. In Scotland 1.46 million acres (591,900 ha) of common grazings in the north-west Highlands, Western Isles and Shetland are registered under the Crofting Acts, amounting to 7.4 per cent of the country.[1]

At the macro-scale, the distribution of common land can thus be said to be environmentally determined. The largest stretches of common land are found in the uplands, from the Highlands and Islands of Scotland, through the Pennines, the North York Moors and Lake District fells, to Snowdonia, the Brecon Beacons and the moorlands of Dartmoor and Bodmin Moor (Figure 3). Over half of the area of common land in England lies in the two northern counties of Cumbria (31 per cent of the total) and North Yorkshire (21 per cent) and, when Devon (12 per cent) and Co. Durham (8 per cent) are added, over 70 per cent of all England's common land is found in just those four counties. In lowland England, commons are numerous. Some wetlands and heaths cover large areas but many lowland commons are very small – half of all registered commons in England contain less than one hectare. Lowland common land is most frequent in the southern counties and East Anglia and across the Welsh Marches; few commons survive in the 'Central Province', the heartland of former open-field farming.[2]

Assessing the extent of common land in a historical context poses several difficulties, not least because it was a shifting acreage which shrank over time as a result of enclosure. The chronological starting point for this book is the early medieval period, during which the framework of the rural landscape (its villages and territories, manorial and administrative boundaries) was laid down. By comparison with later

---

[1] *Gadsden*, § 1-21; Scottish Government, *Economic Report on Scottish Agriculture* (2010 edn), p. 96.
[2] *Gadsden*, § 1-21; J. Aitchison *et al.*, *The Common Lands of England: A Biological Survey* (Aberystwyth, 2000), pp. 14–16. For the 'Central Province', see B. K. Roberts and S. Wrathmell, *Region and Place: A Study of English Rural Settlement* (London, 2002).

9

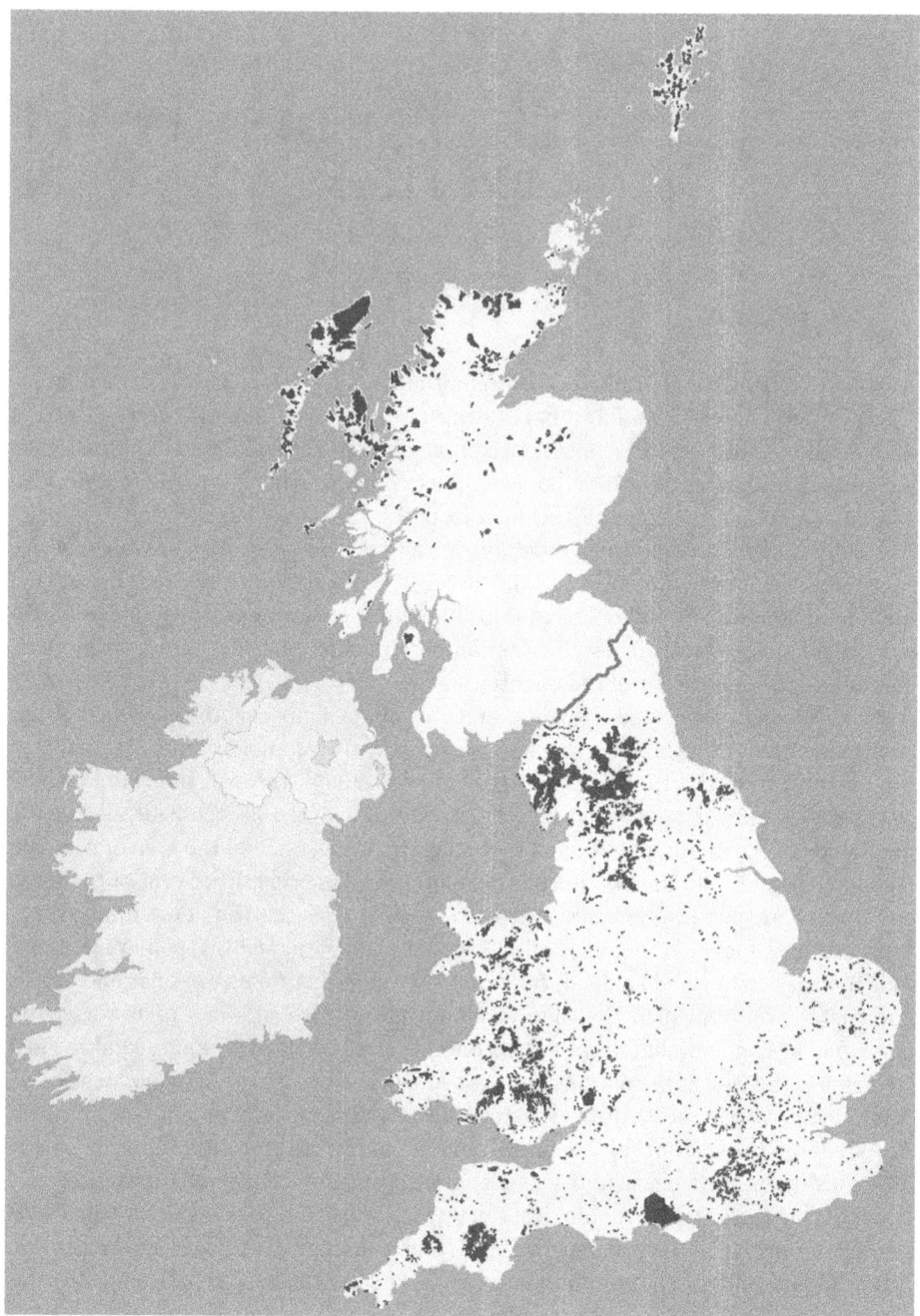

Figure 3. Common land in Britain today. The map shows registered common land in England and Wales (and other areas of common exempt from registration under the Commons Registration Act 1965) and registered common grazings in Scotland.

times, large stretches of country remained unreclaimed and unappropriated when the documentary record shedding light on common land begins in earnest around 1100. Commons were reduced substantially through colonisation during the land hunger of the thirteenth and early fourteenth centuries, and encroachment along their margins continued to reduce their extent between the fifteenth and nineteenth centuries. Wholesale enclosure took place from around 1600, culminating in the 'age of improvement' between c.1750 and c.1860, when millions of acres of mountain, moorland, heath, scrubby grassland, marsh and fen were enclosed and to a greater or lesser extent reclaimed across Britain.[3]

By far the bulk of the common land which existed in the medieval period was converted into private property as a result of these processes but there were striking regional variations in the chronology and extent of enclosure, which are reflected in the modern distribution of commons. Most improvable common land was swept away, resulting in the wholesale disappearance of commons from large parts of lowland England and from Scotland outside the Highlands and Islands. Surviving commons are mostly on land which was not susceptible to reclamation for more intensive agricultural use.

Reconstructing the extent of common land in the past involves adding the acreage of enclosed commons to the common land which survives. Various estimates have been made.[4] Alan Everitt suggested that perhaps 25 per cent of the land surface of England as a whole was manorial waste in the late seventeenth century, compared with 3 per cent today, meaning that around 85 per cent of the common wastes which survived to the early modern period are now enclosed. He concluded that Gregory King's estimates from the 1690s that there were 8 to 9 million acres (c.3.5 million ha) of wastes and commons in England and 5 million acres (2 million ha) in Wales, were not far off the mark.[5] Within England, there were striking regional contrasts, reflecting topography and different agrarian systems. In the Central Province, amounts of common land were often small: around 6 per cent of the land surface in parishes near Solihull (Warw.) c.1700; around 7 per cent in the Buckinghamshire Chilterns in the century 1650–1750; approaching 10 per cent in Northamptonshire.[6] In Oxfordshire less than 20 per cent

---

[3] The chronology of enclosure is discussed below, principally in Chapter 6.
[4] The figures proposed by Gregory Clark and Anthony Clark (G. Clark and A. Clark, 'Common rights to land in England, 1475–1839', *Journal of Economic History*, 61 (4) (December 2001), pp. 1009–36) are not considered here as they almost certainly greatly under-estimate the amount of common waste. Proprietary rights in manorial waste are largely invisible in their source, the records of charitable land endowments: unless a charity held the lordship of a manor, its only interest in waste would be common rights, most of which will be invisible, being appurtenances treated as integral parts of a holding of land. Although their definition of waste excluded stinted grazings, their estimate that 'no more than 5 per cent of land was "waste" in England in 1750, or even in 1600' (p. 1032) is simply not tenable.
[5] Everitt, 'Common land', pp. 220–4.
[6] V. Skipp, 'The evolution of settlement and open-field topography in North Arden down to 1300', in T. Rowley (ed.), *The Origins of Open Field Agriculture* (London, 1981), p. 166; F. Kerner, 'Enclosure and survival: common land in the Buckinghamshire Chilterns c.1600–c.1900' (PhD thesis, Lancaster University, 2016), p. 65. The Northamptonshire figure is based on Neeson's

of most parishes remained common pasture on the eve of enclosure, the mean figure being 13.5 per cent where precise acreages were recorded.[7] In Norfolk, over 12 per cent of the county's surface was common or heath in the later eighteenth century.[8] In the southern part of the Vale of York, between one-tenth and one-third of most townships remained as common land on the eve of enclosure.[9]

Estimates from further north in England suggest that the figures there were higher, with around half of the land area surviving as waste in the early modern period: figures of 58 per cent have been proposed for Co. Durham in 1625, 55 per cent for Westmorland and 49 per cent for Cumberland in the late medieval period.[10] However, such global figures obscure marked differences between upland and lowland areas. Commons accounted for around 70 per cent of the land surface in the Pennine and Lakeland hills but perhaps 25–30 per cent in the northern lowlands. Comparable proportions of common probably survived in lowland Scotland before the later eighteenth century,[11] whereas in the Highlands the land was largely waste, farmland consisting of islands in a sea of moorland and peat moss, which accounted for between 81 and 96 per cent of the wilds of Assynt in Sutherland in 1774 and 76 per cent on the Lovat estates in the gentler glens behind Beauly, Inverness-shire, in the 1750s.[12] The history of common land is thus the history of a significant proportion of the British landscape, and of the majority of the land surface in the uplands.

At a local level, environmental factors have also played a large part in determining which areas remained as common land. As most commons were marginal land unsuitable for ploughing, their distribution reflects their origin as residual land, often forming 'edgelands' on the margins of village territories and between settlements, beyond the limits of farmland (Figure 4). Until the era of improvement, the edge of the common often lay where the interplay between gradient and soil (whether thinning soils upslope or waterlogging in low-lying territory) defeated the farmer – in these areas, tracts of rough hill grazing or watery fen or marsh stretched out beyond the fields. Even where such obvious environmental factors were absent, common land often

---

estimated figure of 62,500 acres of waste, which represented 9.7 per cent of the total county area: J. M. Neeson, *Commoners: Common Right, Enclosure and Social Change in England, 1700–1820* (Cambridge, 1993), pp. 96–7.

[7] Calculated from acreages for forty-six townships given in H. L. Gray, *English Field Systems* (Cambridge, Mass., 1915), pp. 536–42.

[8] Calculated from the figure of 160,012 acres (64,756 ha) of waste given in A. Macnair and T. Williamson, *William Faden and Norfolk's 18th-Century Landscape* (Oxford, 2010), pp. 102–3.

[9] B. Waddell, *Landscape and Society in the Vale of York, c.1500–1800*, Borthwick Paper 120 (York, 2011), p. 32.

[10] H. M. Dunsford and S. J. Harris, 'Colonization of the wasteland in County Durham, 1100–1400', *Economic History Review*, 2nd ser. 56 (2003), pp. 39–40; C. Newman, 'Mapping the late medieval and post medieval landscape of Cumbria' (PhD thesis, University of Newcastle upon Tyne, 2014), pp. 41–2, 311–13.

[11] The existence of 'outfields' complicates any assessment of the extent of common land in lowland Scotland (see below, pp. 14–15).

[12] NLS Estate Plans: Peter May's plans of the annexed estates of Lovat, 1757, 1760 (Lovat 355, Lovat 021, Lovat 350); John Home's Survey of Assynt, 1774 (Dep. 313/3585).

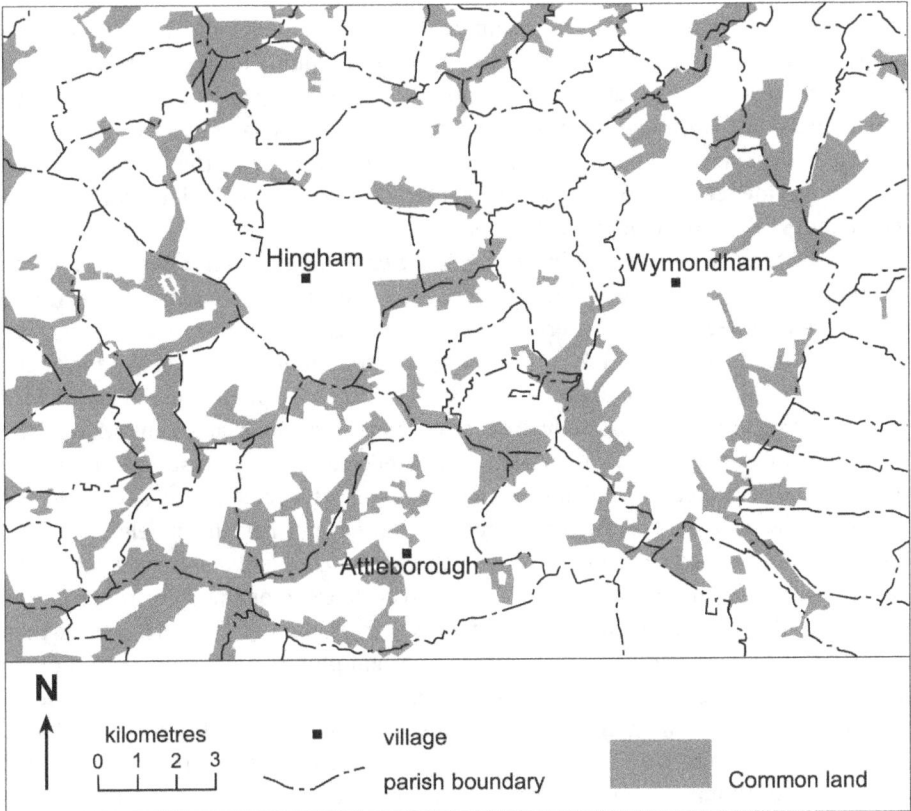

Figure 4. Common land and parish boundaries near Wymondham, Norfolk. The commons are those shown on William Faden's *Map of Norfolk*, published 1797.

took the characteristic form of fragmented patches of rough ground or heath along a parish boundary. On clay lands, many commons were in origin woodland around the edges of cleared farmland, used by medieval times as wood pastures, where livestock grazed in open woodland. Over time, depending on how the common was managed, the trees might disappear as a result of grazing pressure, or active protection and management might preserve the common's wooded character.[13]

Environmental determinism ought not to be overstated, however. This book treats commons as an element in the historic landscape of the medieval and post-medieval centuries, yet there is ample evidence of earlier, prehistoric land use where settled, farmed landscapes covered areas which later became common land. Abandoned Bronze Age settlement sites, field systems and clearance cairns, on Dartmoor and on Lake District commons, for example, show that some commons had been appropriated and exploited by prehistoric societies and were not an untouched wilderness beyond the

---

[13] O. Rackham, *The History of the Countryside* (London, 1986), pp. 141–4.

limits of the medieval fields.[14] Environmental change, notably climatic deterioration during the late Bronze Age/early Iron Age, probably accounts for the abandonment of many of these prehistoric landscapes, as podsolisation (leaching of nutrients from the upper layers) and waterlogging of the soils restricted future land use. The absence of land clearance and cultivation on most surviving commons since the Middle Ages has preserved evidence of earlier use, giving common land its particular importance as the location of visible archaeological remains.

In the historic landscape, grazing for livestock was essential, even where the agrarian economy was tilted towards arable production. Retaining land as common grazing was thus driven by need and not merely by environmental constraint. Indeed, shortage of pasture has been identified as one of the drivers behind the development of the Midland three-field system, the retention of one-third of the ploughland as fallow each year providing untilled land on which livestock could graze in a landscape where little waste remained.[15] The boundary between farmland and common waste was ultimately the product of choice, as individuals and communities decided where to place the limit of reclamation. In East Anglia, some wetter areas may have been deliberately set aside as common grazing grounds, where sufficient grass could be ensured across the parched summer months. The name 'Tye' (OE *teag*, 'a close or small enclosure'), used of small commons in Essex and southern Suffolk, perhaps suggests that, rather than being 'left-over' land, these commons were in origin plots intentionally fenced off to be used for communal grazing.[16] A comparable early and active choice to preserve wetter open land as common has been proposed in the Bourne valley (Cambs.) There, commons called 'Offal' or 'Offil', which can be shown from thirteenth-century sources to derive their names from 'old *feld*' (*feld* having the sense of open country), have been interpreted as poorly drained, open areas in pre-Conquest woodland, used as communal pastures in Anglo-Saxon times.[17] Human agency in determining the pattern of common land was probably of greater importance than has sometimes been admitted.

Furthermore, the boundary between farmland and common land in the historic landscape was not necessarily clear-cut. That was especially true where sections of common land were cultivated periodically, as in the 'infield-outfield' system found in

---

[14] A. Fleming, *The Dartmoor Reaves: Investigating Prehistoric Land Divisions*, 2nd edn (Oxford, 2008); J. Quartermaine and R. H. Leech, *Cairns, Fields and Cultivation: Archaeological Landscapes of the Lake District Uplands* (Lancaster, 2012).

[15] H. S. A. Fox, 'Approaches to the adoption of the Midland system', in T. Rowley (ed.), *The Origins of Open Field Agriculture* (London, 1981), pp. 100–1; D. Hall, *The Open Fields of Northamptonshire* (Northampton, 1995), pp. 82–94. For a wider perspective, see T. Williamson, 'Joan Thirsk and "The Common Fields"', in R. Jones and C. Dyer (eds), *Farmers, Consumers, Innovators: The World of Joan Thirsk* (Hatfield, 2016), pp. 35–48.

[16] T. Williamson, *Shaping Medieval Landscapes: Settlement, Society, Environment* (Macclesfield, 2003), pp. 161–3; E. Martin, 'Greens, commons and tyes in Suffolk', in A. Longcroft and G. Jobey (eds), *East Anglian Studies* (Norwich, 1995), pp. 167–9.

[17] S. Oosthuizen, *Landscapes Decoded: The Origins and Development of Cambridgeshire's Medieval Fields* (Hatfield, 2006), pp. 51–9.

lowland Scotland and parts of England. Outfields formed an intermediate category of land, part of the waste tilled in sections on a long rotation, the bulk of which remained as common rough grazing in any one year.[18] Even in the absence of a 'system' of outfield cultivation, pieces of waste were sometimes tilled on an ad hoc basis, as on the flanks of Dunkery Hill, Exmoor, and in Staffordshire, in the sixteenth century,[19] or at Yardley (Warw.), where part of the common was ploughed temporarily in the 1610s, with the lord of the manor's consent, to grow corn in a 'tyme of dearth'.[20] There was also a chronological dimension, as the boundary between farmland and waste could ebb and flow. Marginal land which had been cultivated in the era of population growth and colonisation in the twelfth and thirteenth centuries sometimes reverted to waste in the late medieval period. Medieval plough ridges on the slopes of the Cheviot Hills and Lammermuirs, for example, provide physical evidence of a fluctuating moorland edge.[21] In the history of common land, change was by no means inexorably in the direction of loss through enclosure.

COMMON LANDSCAPES

Today, the entrance to common land is often marked by a cattle grid, where field boundaries peel away and a road or track, to that point hemmed in by hedges or walls, runs on, unfenced, across open ground. The boundary between farmland and common usually marks an abrupt transition from managed fields to the 'half-wild' ecology of the unenclosed common. Functionally and in terms of property rights, that boundary (the 'head-dyke', to use the Scottish term) formed the primary division of the rural landscape, separating the farmland from the communal resources of the waste, which were complementary to ploughland and meadow in the traditional agrarian economy.

The inter-dependence of farmland and common land is reflected in the relationship between commons and the settlement pattern. In areas of dispersed settlement, farmsteads often lay along the edge of the common, giving them immediate access to both farmland and waste. Where steadings were concentrated in a nucleated village, a tongue of common land frequently penetrated the farmland, bringing the common right into the settlement and demonstrating that many village greens were in origin an integral part of the common grazings (Figure 5).

The shapes of many commons – particularly smaller commons in the lowlands – reflect their evolution. Their margins tend to be ragged and irregular, having been nibbled away by enclosures around the edges. Fields abutting on a common typically have convex boundaries, giving it a scalloped edge or even a star shape; there are

---

[18] For outfields, see A. R. H. Baker and R. A. Butlin (eds), *Studies of Field Systems in the British Isles* (Cambridge, 1973), pp. 63–7 (north-west England), 300–3 (East Anglia), 550–67 (Scotland).

[19] M. Aston (ed.), *Aspects of the Medieval Landscape of Somerset* (Bridgwater, 1988), pp. 85–7; J. Thirsk (ed.), *The Agrarian History of England and Wales, Vol. IV, 1500–1640* (Cambridge, 1967), p. 183.

[20] V. Skipp, *Crisis and Development: An Ecological Case Study of the Forest of Arden, 1570–1674* (Cambridge, 1978), p. 37.

[21] M. L. Parry, *Climate Change, Agriculture and Settlement* (Folkestone, 1978), pp. 112–23.

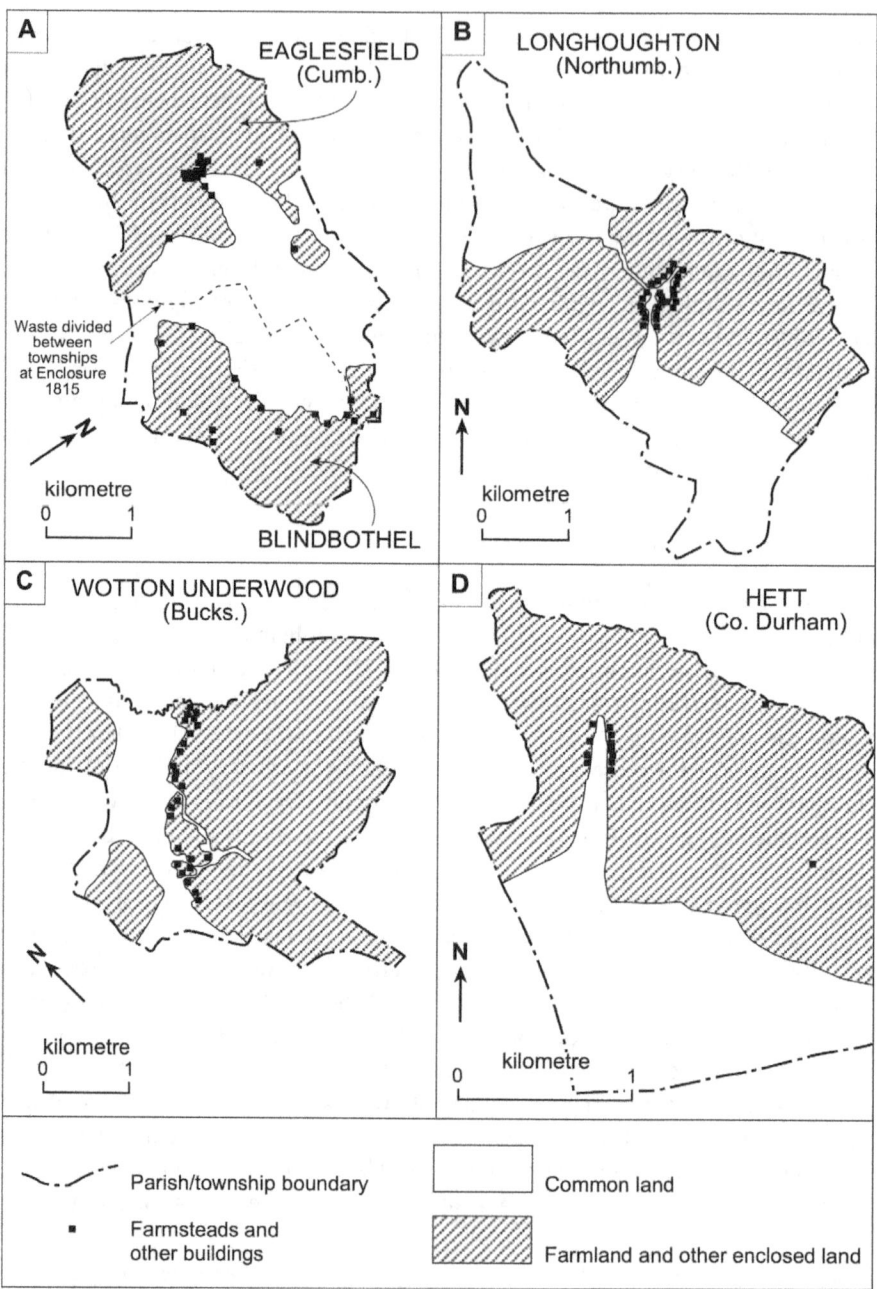

Figure 5. Common land in relation to farmland and settlement, illustrating two recurrent patterns: (i) funnels of common land reaching through farmland to a nucleated village, as at Eaglesfield (A), Long Houghton (B) and Hett (D); (ii) dispersed settlement along the boundary between common and farmland, as at Blindbothel (A) and Wotton Underwood (C). Sources: A: CAS, Q/RE/1/33; B and C: A. R. H. Baker and R. A. Butlin (eds), *Studies of Field Systems in the British Isles* (Cambridge, 1973), pp. 115, 352; D: Durham Cathedral Archives, DCD/E/AA/20/1).

islands of enclosure surrounded by common land, and funnels where the common projects into the farmland, narrowing to become a lane between fields where the cattle grid marks the transition.

Commons belonged to communities, even if property rights in them were vested in individuals. Thus, parish and township boundaries run out to embrace sections of common land which continue to be linked by name on the modern map to the settlements which used them. When mapped, it is striking that peripheral patches of common in one parish not infrequently abut on the commons of neighbouring parishes, so that their combined extent can form a considerable stretch of open land; indeed, almost one-quarter of surviving commons in England are contiguous with at least one other common (see Figure 6, for example). The largest concentration of common land in England, on the hills of Cumbria and the northern Pennines, is a tract of no fewer than 150 contiguous commons; that in Wales comprises thirteen separate commons in the Brecon Beacons.[22] Before enclosure in the eighteenth and nineteenth centuries, such tracts were more numerous in lowland areas. When historic landscape patterns have been reconstructed at regional level, stretches of contiguous common land have been identified, particularly along watersheds, reinforcing their role as cultural boundaries.[23] Along the Lincolnshire/Leicestershire border, south-west of Grantham, for example, a belt of limestone heath remained as rough pasture until the 1770s.[24] In Norfolk, 'great strings of commons, linked end to end, rambled across the clay interfluves' in the late eighteenth century;[25] while in the Buckinghamshire Chilterns thin strips of common aligned to form a series of discontinuous tracts of open land trending towards London.[26]

Across England, runs of names record the link between commons and the villages to which they belonged: Newbiggin Fell, Croglin Fell and Renwick Fell on the north Pennine edge in Cumbria; Helperby Moor, Tholthorpe Moor and Aldwark Moor on the floor of the Vale of York; Dunsby Fen, Haconby Fen and Morton Fen, part of a series of seventeen such names along the western edge of the Lincolnshire Fens. In Wales, sections of mountain pasture (*mynydd*) are linked to specific farms in such hill names as Mynydd Dolgoed, Mynydd Hendre-ddu and Mynnydd LLwydiarth in Dovey Forest in the Merionethshire hills.

Place-names also record the ecological characteristics of common land, conveying an immediate impression of topography and landscape. Beyond the generic 'Common', a handful of terms were used to describe most commons from the medieval period. The most widespread was 'moor' or 'muir' (OE *mōr*), which had associations with wetness but also barrenness. It was used both of 'low-lying marsh', as in the Weald Moors

---

[22] Aitchison *et al.*, *Common Lands of England*, p. 16; J. W. Aitchison and E. J. Hughes, 'The common lands of Wales', *Trans IBG*, 13 (1) (1988), p. 98.

[23] See C. Phythian-Adams, 'Introduction: an agenda for English local history', in C. Phythian-Adams, *Societies, Cultures and Kinship, 1580–1850: Cultural Provinces and English Local History* (Leicester, 1993), pp. 1–23.

[24] A. W. Fox, *A Lost Frontier Revealed: Regional Separation in the East Midlands* (Hatfield, 2009), p. 24.

[25] Williamson, *Shaping Medieval Landscapes*, pp. 93–6.

[26] Kerner, 'Enclosure and survival', map.

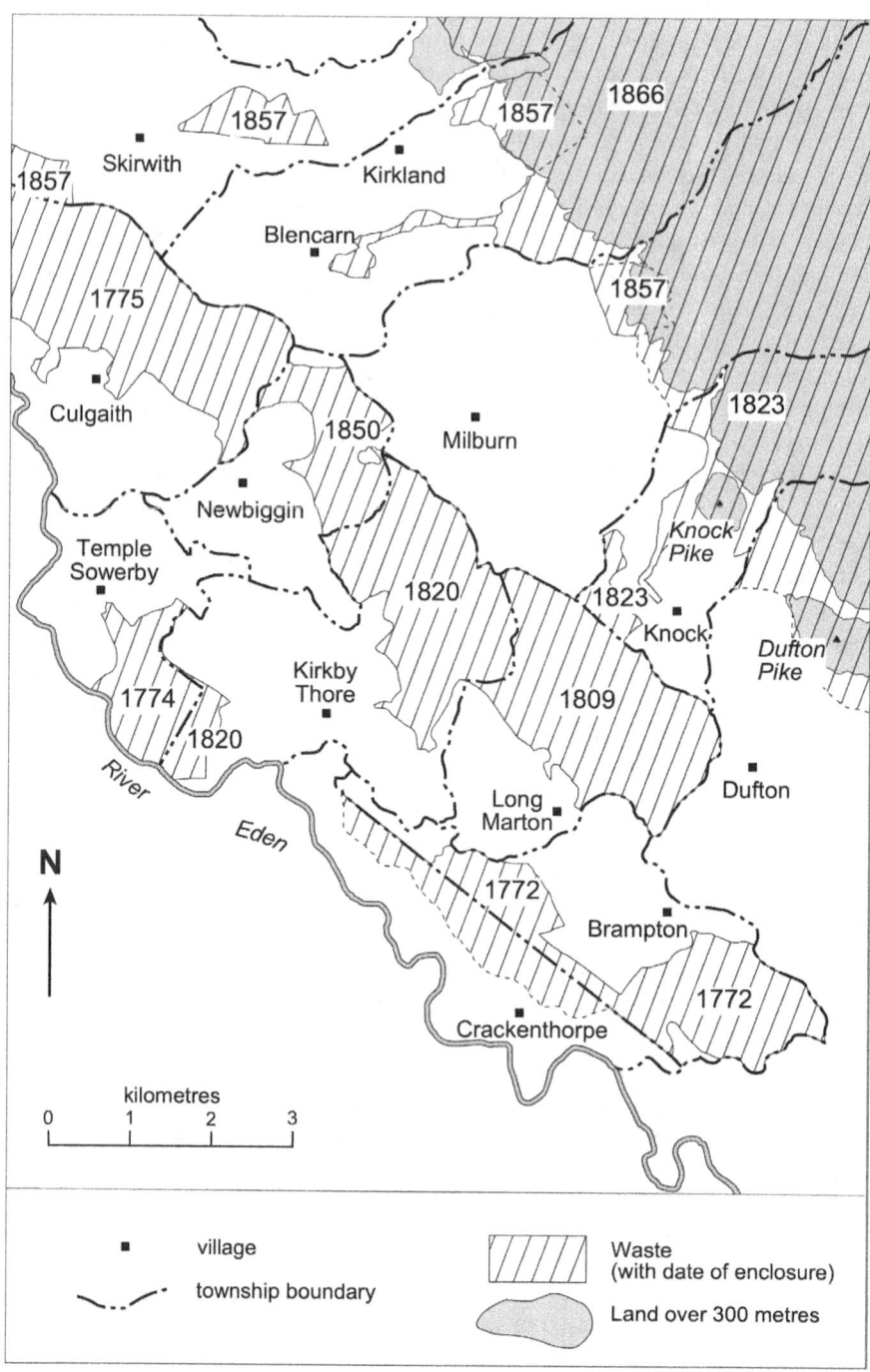

Figure 6. Eden Valley, Cumbria: extent of common land before enclosure, reconstructed from enclosure awards. As well as the fell commons on the Pennine scarp, a belt of contiguous lowland moors separated the fell edge villages (from Skirwith to Knock) from those on the valley floor (from Culgaith to Brampton).

(Shrops.) and Sedgemoor (Som.), and of 'barren upland' (as in Dartmoor, Stainmore and Lammermuir) and was frequently used of lowland commons as well. 'Moors' tended to be wetter commons than 'heaths' (OE *hǣth*), the name given to many drier lowland commons where the vegetation was dominated by heather. True wetland commons were termed 'fen' (peaty wetlands) or 'moss' (bog, specifically peat bog dominated by sphagnum and other species of moss).[27] Hill commons, if not termed 'moor' or 'hill', were generally named from the local term for 'mountain' ('fell' (ON *fjall*) in northern England; *mynydd* in Wales).

Despite the 'half-wild' nature of commons, they are far from natural environments. Their ecology has not been static, as changing patterns of use have resulted in significant changes in vegetation. W. G. Hoskins overstressed continuity when he wrote that, watching livestock grazing a hill common, 'we are contemplating a scene that has been repeated each year without noticeable change for some thousands of years and we are in the presence of an impressive antiquity'.[28] While it is true that elements of pastoral commoning are deeply traditional and changed comparatively little until touched by modernity in the later twentieth century (with the advent of the quad bike and agri-environmental schemes, for example), the use and management of common land, and the conceptions surrounding it, have by no means remained static since the Middle Ages.

As levels of resource exploitation have varied, so has the ecology of commons. Quarrying for stone, digging sand or clay, stripping turf and digging peat all had a direct, destructive impact on the ecology of common land, and when those practices ceased, allowing natural processes of colonisation by plants and animals to return, the ecology was rarely as it had been before exploitation took place. Of far greater, if less obvious, impact have been changes in the intensity of livestock grazing across the centuries. Heathlands, the ecological category characteristic of so many lowland commons, were particularly susceptible. If they were to be maintained as open heath, carrying the characteristic variety of heathland vegetation – heather, gorse, broom and bracken – on dry, acidic mineral soils, they had to be actively managed and grazed. As grazing declined on many heathland commons in southern England from the nineteenth century, the open heaths were replaced by scrub, then trees, often birch and pine, converting open landscapes into woodland.[29] Conversely, overgrazing has affected many hill commons, reducing species diversity and causing erosion. Despite the vulnerability to change, some commons contain important ecological survivals, including relics of ancient woodland such as Wistman's Wood on Dartmoor, the Keskadale oaks in the Lake District and the yews on Merrow Downs, near Guildford (Surrey). The increasing value placed on such precious remnants of the natural world

---

[27] M. Gelling, *Place-Names in the Landscape: The Geographical Roots of Britain's Place-Names* (London, 1984), pp. 40–1 (fen), 54–6 (*mōr*), 56–7 (moss), 245 (*hǣth*); Rackham, *History of the Countryside*, pp. 282–327 (heathland and moorland), 374–82 (wetlands).

[28] Hoskins & Stamp, p. 28.

[29] Rackham, *History of the Countryside*, pp. 282–304; T. Williamson, 'How natural is natural? Historical perspectives on wildlife and the environment in Britain', *Transactions of the Royal Historical Society*, 29 (2019), pp. 294–6. See below, pp. 191–7.

means that many commons are now protected for their high conservation value: over three-quarters of all common land in England and Wales lies in either National Parks or Areas of Outstanding Natural Beauty (AONBs).[30]

Such landscapes were described as 'waste' in medieval and early modern sources, bracketing all commons under a single heading which fails to do justice to the diversity and richness they contain. They were 'waste' in the sense of being to at least some extent wilderness, land untouched by civilisation. By the modern period, unchecked exploitation of some commons had led them to become 'waste' in the second sense of the word, land which had been 'ruined and defiled', 'consumed and exhausted' by humanity. What binds these contradictory meanings together, Vittoria Di Palma has suggested, is that the concept of wasteland provided 'the antithesis, the absolute Other, of civilization'.[31] In these terms, common land was wild land, out there beyond the fields.

Across the centuries, common land has carried multiple meanings and associations in British culture, the dominant views shifting over time. In the medieval and early modern centuries commons provided essential resources to rural communities; from the seventeenth century, they came to be viewed as unallocated land awaiting reclamation and improvement; from the 1860s, as open spaces to be preserved for recreation, acting as the lungs of an increasingly urban population; and by the later twentieth century as ecosystems which were intrinsically valuable, contributing to biodiversity, water quality and carbon capture. Some perceptions persisted: common land was marginal land (in terms both of its peripheral location and its economic potential) and was associated with marginal groups in society – commons could be 'edgy' places on the fringes of civilisation, untidy places where undesirables lurked, or even places of dangerous encounters, of murders and gibbets and of witches on the 'blasted heath'. As the following chapters demonstrate, perceptions were not always uniform. Multi-layered conceptions of the value of common land continue to co-exist, so that the wide-open spaces of fresh air and exercise for the general public are also a valuable grazing resource for farmers or a protected ecosystem for conservationists. Sometimes pulling in opposing directions, potentially conflicting claims over common land, both past and present, mean that common landscapes have often been contested spaces.[32]

---

[30] *Gadsden*, § 1-21. See also below, p. 157.
[31] V. Di Palma, *Wasteland: A History* (London, 2014), pp. 2–4.
[32] A theme explored in *Contested Common Land*.

CHAPTER 2

CUSTOM AND LAW: THE GENESIS OF COMMON LAND

SHARED USE LAY AT the heart of common land and required mutual understandings between users and an agreed framework to structure the exploitation of resources. The law relating to commons developed from a bedrock of custom and tradition, which had deep roots and common characteristics but was essentially local in its particularities. No single set of legal concepts has underpinned all commons in Britain. Common land, as it is generally conceived, was in origin an English construct without a direct equivalent in the different legal traditions of Scotland or medieval Wales.

In teasing out the complexities of custom and law, this chapter begins by considering evidence for the organisation of common land in the pre-feudal societies of early medieval Britain. The bulk of the chapter then outlines the legal framework of property rights over common land since the medieval period – who owned common land, the nature of common rights and how these were determined – identifying recurrent themes but also considering patterns of rights and use which diverged from the legal norms. A final section examines the manifestations of legal frameworks on the ground, in territorial boundaries separating the common land belonging to one community from that of its neighbours.

PRE-FEUDAL COMMONS: EXTENSIVE LORDSHIP

Taking a very long chronological view, it can be postulated that settlements existed at an early date as islands in an ocean of unappropriated waste, the resources of which could be drawn upon freely. Population growth and expanding numbers of settlements would place increasing demands on the resources of untamed land, prompting claims to exclusive use by individual settlements or groups. Boundaries would evolve through custom and practice, defining the limits of a group's rights. By the early medieval period, patterns of customary use had already drawn wastes into the institutional structures of society, converting wilderness into common land 'belonging to' communities.

Folk memories of the process were recalled on the expansive wetlands of eastern England in the thirteenth century. Fen land in the Pinchbeck area of Lincolnshire had been 'common to all of the countryside (*patria*) desiring to use it' until the 'first habitation of Holland', when it was divided between vills.[1] Further south, around Sawtry, competing claims were backed by stories about the division of the fens in the time of Thurkil the Dane or in the time of Cnut. Some fens remained undivided, shared by adjacent communities in the twelfth and thirteenth centuries.[2] It was said of the Humber levels c.1237 that 'the moor is spacious and large and they do not know of any boundaries [to show] how much belongs to one vill and how much to another'.[3]

Which settlements shared a tract of wetland was determined not solely by geography; groups of communities sharing a common tended to correspond with early administrative territories. In Lincolnshire, the vills in the soke of Bolingbroke shared the East Fen and West Fen, and three sokes had shared the 'Wildmoor' in the same vicinity.[4] All the vills in Wisbeach hundred (Cambs.) intercommoned on 'Heyefen' and a comparable hundredal pasture existed in Suffolk, where Domesday Book recorded a pasture 'common to all the men of [Colneis] hundred'.[5] The correlation between patterns of grazing rights and early institutional structures appears to have been a feature of pre-feudal arrangements.

Intercommoned wastes were thus a key feature of these early arrangements. This was true intercommoning, where the shared waste lay *between* vills, rather than the situation where flocks and herds shared a tract of moorland by straying across a manorial boundary, a practice recognised in English law as common *pur cause de vicinage* and sometimes acknowledged by payment of a sum of money in recognition of 'overleap' across the boundary.[6]

Fleeting glimpses of intercommoned wastes appear occasionally in early charters, such as the 'common marshland meadow' (*ymene morlese*) near the source of the Thames, on which four vills near Cirencester (Glos.) had common rights in the tenth century, or the moor in the Vale of Pickering (Yorks. N.R.), shared by three vills in the 1160s.[7] Other intercommoned wetland wastes persisted: the hundredal fens, noted above; Wallingfen and Bishopsoil (Yorks. E.R.) in the Humber lowlands; the low-lying common at Burton Agnes (Yorks. E.R.), intercommoned by five townships; and the 'hundredal' peat mosses of lowland Lancashire, where the boundaries between townships ran 'up to the edge of the waste and not across it'.[8]

---

[1] N. Neilson (ed.), *A Terrier of Fleet, Lincolnshire, from a Manuscript in the British Museum* (London, 1920), p. xxiv.

[2] Ibid., pp. x–xii, xxxvii–xxxviii, xlvii.

[3] P. Vinogradoff, *Villainage in England* (Oxford, 1892), p. 264, n. 3.

[4] Neilson, *Terrier of Fleet*, pp. x–xii, xviii.

[5] Ibid., p. xlvii; DB, f. 339b (*Suffolk*, 7–78).

[6] Gadsden, § 2.27. For 'overleap', see A. J. L. Winchester, *Landscape and Society in Medieval Cumbria* (Edinburgh, 1987), pp. 90–1.

[7] S. E. Kelly (ed.), *Charters of Malmesbury Abbey*, Anglo-Saxon Charters XI (Oxford, 2005), no. 46; D. E. Greenway (ed.), *Charters of the Honour of Mowbray, 1107–1191* (London, 1972), nos. 247, 252.

[8] D. Crouch and B. McDonagh, 'Turf wars: conflict and cooperation in the management of Wallingfen (East Yorkshire), 1281–1781', *AgHR*, 64 (2016), pp. 133–56; *VCH Yorks. E.R.* X, part 2, pp. 140–53; B. McDonagh, 'Landscape, territory and common rights in medieval East Yorkshire', *Landscape History*, 40 (2) (2019), pp. 80–5; W. D. Shannon, 'The survival of true

In the absence of documentary evidence, the legacy of earlier patterns of rights is sometimes preserved in parish boundaries, notably in detached portions, which often appear to be the ghosts of intercommoning on former shared wastes. Parish boundaries divided parts of the Fens and the coastal marshes of Essex into fragments assigned to the parishes which had shared grazing rights over them.[9] The pattern of detached portions on the Dengie peninsula (Essex), for example, suggests that both the Danbury Hills and the coastal marshes were shared grazings for settlements within an early territorial entity, the *regio* called 'Deningei', recorded in an eighth-century charter.[10] Detached pieces of territory in the woodlands of Arden in Warwickshire, on the wolds along the Nottinghamshire–Leicestershire border, in the Weald in Sussex and Kent, and in the wetlands of the Norfolk Broads also point to rights in sought-after resources being exploited by groups of settlements from a distance.[11]

Where early evidence survives, it often suggests that rights were organised within a framework of extensive lordships covering multiple settlements. In origin, these may have been early folk territories, shadowy units which Anglo-Saxon charters sometimes term *regiones* or *pagi*.[12] They were defined by networks of obligation which bound the inhabitants of the settlements within them to an estate centre, but they were also resource territories, providing within their bounds all the necessary landed resources for the communities they embraced. Such territories were based, as John Blair has put it, on access to resources across 'broad ecological zones', rather than the more intensive exploitation seen later within the boundaries of township and manor.[13] The roots of these territories lay deep, probably in pre-Anglo-Saxon times, as the recurrence of similar renders and services in England, Scotland and Wales points to common foundations.[14] The change to more concentrated exploitation within smaller territories is generally associated with what has been termed a shift from the 'landscape of obligation' of pre-feudal times to a 'landscape of ownership', as manorial lords increased their control in the two centuries from *c*.950.[15]

---

intercommoning in Lancashire in the early-modern period', *Agricultural History*, 86 (2012), pp. 182–3.

[9] H. C. Darby, *Domesday England* (Cambridge, 1976), pp. 157–9.

[10] S. Rippon, *Kingdom, Civitas and County* (Oxford, 2018), pp. 215–17.

[11] H. Fox, *Dartmoor's Alluring Uplands: Transhumance and Pastoral Management in the Middle Ages* (Exeter, 2012), pp. 134–7; H. Fox, 'The people of the Wolds in English settlement history', in M. Aston, D. Austin and C. Dyer (eds), *The Rural Settlements of Medieval England* (Oxford, 1989), pp. 87–9.

[12] Rippon, *Kingdom, Civitas and County*, pp. 215–19; S. Bassett (ed.), introduction to *The Origins of Anglo-Saxon Kingdoms* (Leicester, 1989), pp. 17–19.

[13] J. Blair, *Building Anglo-Saxon England* (Princeton, 2018), pp. 4–5.

[14] The literature is summarised and discussed in R. Faith, *The English Peasantry and the Growth of Lordship* (London, 1997), especially pp. 1–14; and B. K. Roberts and P. S. Barnwell, 'The multiple estate of Glanville Jones: epitome, critique, and context', pp. 25–128 in P. S. Barnwell and B. K. Roberts (eds), *Britons, Saxons and Scandinavians: The Historical Geography of Glanville R. J. Jones* (Turnhout, 2011).

[15] Faith, *English Peasantry*, p. 10; Blair, *Building Anglo-Saxon England*, pp. 4–5.

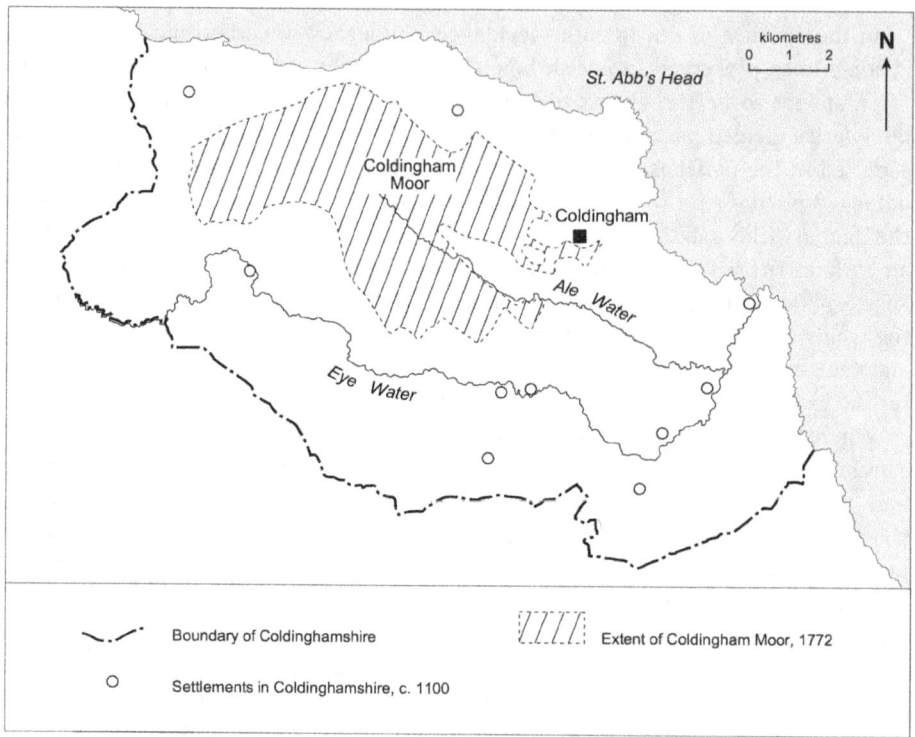

Figure 7. Coldingham Moor, Berwickshire: a 'shire moor'. Source: Plan of commonty of Coldingham, 1772: NLS, EMS.s.45A.

Much of the evidence for the organisation of common land within the framework of pre-feudal estates comes from the Northumbrian 'shires' of northern England and southern Scotland. Work by J. E. A. Jolliffe in the 1920s, extended by Geoffrey Barrow in the 1970s, identified a model in which each shire had a 'shire moor', a central reserve of pasture on which the stock of all the communities within the shire might graze. Barrow concluded that it was 'an essential, probably a very primitive, characteristic'.[16] In Northumberland the eponymous Shiremoor was intercommoned by the seven townships in the manor of Tynemouth, for example; Shildon Great Moor by the parishes of Corbridge, Bywell and Ovingham. North of the border were Coldingham Moor (Berwickshire), common to the shire of Coldingham (Figure 7), and Gladsmuir and Dunbar Common (East Lothian), serving Haddingtonshire and the shire of Dunbar, respectively. Further north, a waste called *Cotken* or *Cathkin* (probably Gaelic *coitcheann*,

---

[16] G. W. S. Barrow, 'Pre-feudal Scotland: shires and thanes', in his *The Kingdom of the Scots: Government, Church and Society from the Eleventh to the Fourteenth Century*, 2nd edn (Edinburgh, 2003), pp. 7–56 (quotation p. 43). For shires in Scotland north of the Forth, see D. Broun, 'Statehood and lordship in "Scotland" before the mid-twelfth century', *Innes Review*, 66 (1) (2015), pp. 1–71, who rejects the idea of the shire as an 'unchanging unit of royal lordship' in that area.

'common'), near Muir of Orchil (Perthshire), described c.1250 as having been beyond memory 'free and common pasture for all the men living around the said pasture', may have been common to the shire of Muthill in Strathearn.[17]

In northern England other areas of moorland on the fringes of the uplands probably served a similar function. Rombaldsmoor (Yorks. W.R.), the Pennine outlier between Wharfedale and Airedale, may have been a shire moor for the pre-Conquest estate centred on Otley, the constituent vills of which encircled it. The names of Whillimoor (Cumb.), arguably a shire moor for Copeland barony, Spennymoor (Dur.), and Gunolfsmoors (Lancs.) indicate that they had identities separate from the settlements surrounding them, perhaps suggesting comparable early patterns of use.[18]

A different dimension of grazing arrangements under extensive lordship is seen where grazing rights were granted throughout a 'shire' or an equivalent wider territorial unit. Examples include grants of common pasture to the monks of Brinkburn Priory (Northumb.) 'through all my land within *Feltonschyre*' and to May Priory across the shires of Kellie and Crail (Fife). Byland Abbey had land at Warcop (Westmld) with common pasture in the hills 'anywhere to the furthest boundary of the common pasture which pertains to Westmorland', suggesting that the whole barony of north Westmorland shared that tract of Pennine moorland.[19] Evidence from other upland areas points in a similar direction. In the hills of mid-Wales Strata Marcella Abbey had pasture rights across whole commotes (*provinciae*) of Cyfeiliog and Mochnant (Montgom.) and Penllin on the slopes of Berwyn mountain (Denb.).[20] Again, they suggest that pasture rights across the whole of a superior lordship were still in the gift of overlords in the decades around 1200.

These grants to monastic houses clearly point to grazing rights across a wide area but they do not necessarily imply the presence of a single shire moor. The phrase 'common pasture in the shires of Kellie and Crail' could equally well refer to a general right across all the wastes of the shire, and perhaps the farmland as well. Nevertheless, taken alongside the evidence for separate shire moors, they point to the survival of elements of earlier extensive lordship, in which some wastes were vested in the overlord, rather than in the lord of an individual vill or manor.

The transition to feudal society and the rise of the manor led to the demise of earlier arrangements. Across the medieval centuries the unity of intercommoned wastes tended to fragment, as sections were claimed by adjacent lords and boundaries across them came to be defined. The division of the intercommoned fens began in the twelfth century and accelerated in the thirteenth, when disputed claims were resolved by agreement and at law.[21] On the putative shire moor of Whillimoor (Cumb.),

---

[17] A. J. L. Winchester, 'Shielings and common pastures', in K. J. Stringer and A. J. L. Winchester (eds), *Northern England and Southern Scotland in the Central Middle Ages* (Woodbridge, 2017), pp. 282–3.
[18] Ibid., pp. 284–5.
[19] Ibid., pp. 283–4.
[20] G. C. G. Thomas (ed.), *The Charters of the Abbey of Ystrad Marchell* (Aberystwyth, 1997), nos. 15, 34, 41.
[21] H. C. Darby, *The Medieval Fenland* (Newton Abbot, 1974), pp. 74–8.

the rights of the overlord waned after the twelfth century and the moor had been appropriated by the lords of adjacent vills by the mid-fourteenth.[22] In some instances, uncertainty over the balance of rights rumbled on. The division of the estate at Burton Agnes (Yorks. E.R.) between two heiresses in 1199, along with later sub-infeudations, created a complex manorial structure which cut across the unity of Burton Moor, intercommoned by the parish's five townships. Competition between the manors spawned disputes over common rights in the later fifteenth and sixteenth centuries and eventually led to the division of the moor between the townships.[23] Disputes in the early modern period over Gunolfsmoors (Lancs.) and Masham Moor (Yorks. N.R.) turned on whether adjacent lords had rights over defined sections of the moor or whether it was jointly owned or claimed by a feudal superior, questions which were probably echoes of the age of intercommoning in pre-manorial times.[24]

PROPERTY RIGHTS OVER COMMON LAND FROM THE THIRTEENTH CENTURY

By the later Middle Ages, major differences had developed between the legal frameworks of common rights in different parts of Britain. English and Scottish law differed, as English common law gave greater weight to custom, and the English Statute of Merton of 1236 accentuated the differences in legal thought between the two nations. In Wales, to which the English legal system applied from 1536, rights in common land rested on a bedrock of native Welsh concepts. It is necessary to examine the legal framework to common land in each of the three nations separately.

England: The Statute of Merton and Manorial Waste

In England, most common land had the status of manorial waste, a legal category confirmed in the thirteenth century by the Statute of Merton (1236).[25] It established a balance of rights which continued to underpin the use of common land until the later twentieth century: the lord of the manor owned the wastes; the manorial tenants held use rights which allowed them to take resources from it. Most common land in England was thus neither a 'no man's land', nor land owned communally, nor land vested in the Crown, but private property over which third parties held use rights.

The central focus of the Statute of Merton was 'approvement', the power of manorial lords to enclose land from the waste. The preamble noted that many lords had complained that they were unable to exploit fully 'the residue of their manors', defined as 'wastes, woods and pastures', because of objections from their tenants who claimed pasture rights. Merton allowed lords to approve the waste as long as sufficient pasture was left for their tenants. The statute (confirmed by Westminster II in 1285, which

---

[22] Winchester, *Medieval Cumbria*, pp. 85–7.
[23] McDonagh, 'Landscape, territory and common rights', pp. 80–5.
[24] *Harvest*, p. 27; Shannon, 'Survival of true intercommoning', pp. 171–2.
[25] Statute of Merton: 20 Hen. III, c.4. The date of the statute is sometimes given as 1235 but the assembly at Merton took place on 23 January 1236: H. R. Luard (ed.), *Matthaei Parisiensis, Monachi Sancti Albani, Chronica Majora, Vol. III* (London, 1876), p. 341.

extended the lord's approvement rights against neighbouring landowners)[26] formalised and strengthened the concept of 'manorial waste', confirming that ownership of 'the residue of the manor' belonged to the lord of that manor. That it was confirming existing conceptions of property rights over wastes, rather than establishing something new, is clear from earlier evidence. Domesday Book records lords taking renders from the resources of common land – swine renders from woodland or payments for eels from wetlands, for example[27] – and appurtenance clauses in some twelfth-century charters confirm that lordship extended to the wastes surrounding settled areas. The grant of Middlethorpe (Yorks. W.R.), near York, to Byland Abbey (c.1154 x 1175), for example, included 'pastures, turbaries, moors, wastes and all other things pertaining to the said vill and manor of *Thorp*, as is clearly shown by ancient boundaries (*metas*), namely dikes (*fossata*) and old perambulations'.[28] Such grants make it clear that acknowledged boundaries ran across the wastes, dividing them between lordships, decades before Merton. Nor was the requirement that lords should leave sufficient common when approving land an innovation: in a lawsuit of 1221 concerning enclosures in a common at Yardley (Warw.) it was claimed that local custom ('the law in Arden') allowed lords to enclose from the waste only if commoners' pasture rights were not infringed.[29]

A common right under English law was 'the legal right of one or more persons to take or use some part of the natural produce of … the land of another person'.[30] Common rights were generally ancillary rights, attached to a holding of land. They were said to be 'appendant' or 'appurtenant' and were conceived of as an integral part of the holding, giving the tenant rights which were exercised communally with others.[31] Although rights separate from land ('rights in gross') were found, an understanding that common rights were attached to land lay at the heart of the English law of commons.[32]

English law traditionally recognised six categories of common right. By far the most widespread was common of pasture, the right to 'take grass by the mouths of cattle'. At its heart was the need to provide pasture to keep the plough beasts and other livestock vital to the medieval agrarian economy safely away from the growing crops across the summer months. The other rights were common of pannage (a subset of common of pasture, allowing pigs to graze in woodlands in autumn); common of estovers (the right to take wood and other vegetation for fuel and other necessary uses); common of turbary (the right to dig peat or turf); common of piscary (the right to take fish); and rights in the soil (which allowed a commoner to extract sand, gravel, stone, etc.). In some places a seventh category of right, that of taking wild animals from the common,

---

[26] Statute of Westminster II: 13 Edw. I, c.46.
[27] Darby, *Domesday England*, pp. 159, 175–8, 352.
[28] Greenway, *Charters of the Honour of Mowbray*, no. 55.
[29] D. M. Stenton (ed.), *Rolls of the Justices in Eyre* (Selden Society 53, 1934), pp. 448–9.
[30] *Gadsden*, § 1-01.
[31] The technical distinction between 'common appendant' (a freehold tenant's right to graze plough beasts) and 'common appurtenant' (a right by prescription to graze a wider range of livestock) was largely irrelevant to the day-to-day use of common land: see *Gadsden*, §§ 2-17, 2-19.
[32] Ibid., §§ 2-17–2-25.

was also treated as a common right.³³ Grazing rights were ubiquitous, but the nature of other rights varied depending on the local environment. For example, common of estovers on the Cornish moorlands near Redruth was described in 1388 as the right to take peat, heather, fern and gorse, whereas in the wood of Barnby (Notts.) in 1235 it was 'common of ferns (*feuger*) and of dry branches fallen to the ground through wind or age'.³⁴

Comparatively few common rights were recorded in specific grants; most were rights by prescription, the product of custom and practice over many years. Custom carried legal weight in English law and formed the bedrock of the local agrarian law administered in manorial courts. It arose out of day-to-day experience and resided, ultimately, in 'the memory of the people', transmitted orally across the generations.³⁵ When it came to common land, patterns of use, etched in local memory through repeated practice, became part of the custom of the manor, which, as one seventeenth-century lawyer put it, 'being continued without interruption time out of mind ... obtaineth the force of Law'.³⁶ Local customary law, fleshing out wider principles, gave common land and common rights in England their unique legal character, which structured the history of commons from the later medieval period to the twentieth century.

Wales: *Cytir*

Since the 1530s, the legal basis of common land in Wales has, in theory, been identical to that in England but it overlay a native tradition in which commons were tribal land, shared by groups of kinsmen. Common wastes were *cyd-tir* or *cytir*, literally 'joint land', ownership being vested in a group of hereditary heirs of a clan (*gwely* or *gafael*). In 1561 the tenants of Arwystli and Cyfeiliog (Montgom.) claimed that both the wastes and the enclosed lands of each commote were divided into 'gavell' (that is by gavelkind, or partible inheritance) and that the rent paid was 'as well for the one [the wastes] as for the other [the enclosed land]'.³⁷ In other words, the wastes were an integral part of the tenants' farms, rather than belonging to the lord, as in the English concept of manorial

---

33 Ibid., §§ 2.34–2.49. Most of these categories were recognised by the thirteenth century: see H. Bracton, *De Legibus et Consuetudinibus Angliae*, book 3, p. 167.
34 *Catalogue of Ancient Deeds*, IV, no. A8698; R. T. Timson (ed.), *The Cartulary of Blyth Priory* (London, 1973), nos. 255, 260.
35 For the interface between custom and law, see R. Houston, 'Custom in context: medieval and early modern Scotland and England', *Past & Present*, 211 (2011), pp. 35–76; D. Ibbetson, 'Custom in medieval law', in A. Perreau-Saussine and J. B. Murphy (eds), *The Nature of Customary Law* (Cambridge, 2007), pp. 151–75; L. R. Poos and L. Bonfield (eds), *Select Cases in Manorial Courts, 1250–1550: Property and Family Law* (Selden Society 114, 1998), pp. xxvii–xxxv; L. Bonfield, 'What did English villagers mean by "customary law"?', in Z. Razi and R. Smith (eds), *Medieval Society and the Manor Court* (Oxford, 1996), pp. 103–16. For custom in local communities, see E. P. Thompson, 'Custom, law and common right', in his *Customs in Common* (Harmondsworth, 1993), pp. 97–184; A. Wood, *The Memory of the People: Custom and Popular Senses of the Past in Early Modern England* (Cambridge, 2013), esp. pp. 94–111.
36 Sir John Davies, 1612, quoted in Wood, *Memory of the People*, p. 96.
37 E. Evans, 'Arwystli and Cyfeiliog in the sixteenth century: an Elizabethan inquisition', *Montgomeryshire Collections*, 51 (1949–50), pp. 26, 35.

waste. Sections of the wastes were allocated to the exclusive use of individual clans, as suggested by the phrase *Cytir Gafael Waring* ('the common of clan Waring') encountered in a fifteenth-century rental of an estate at Conway.[38] When manorial lords attempted to impose English notions of manorial waste, Welsh tenants determinedly claimed that the wastes were not manorial common land but shared *cytir*. At Bryncoch in 1637 the *cytir* was said not to be common but to be shared by five adjoining landowners as 'coparceners in gavelkind'.[39] Surveying the lordship of Oswestry (Shrops.), hard on the border of Wales, in 1602, John Norden was exasperated by the concept of *cytir*, under which the tenants claimed liberty to enclose sections of the wastes: 'they stand upon a frivolous terme Kyttyr which they will have to be as much as inheritance undivided … the word importeth common in Welsh and they have no other word in Welsh to expresse comon'. As an English lawyer, he saw 'Kyttir' as a 'vayne conceyt', and an 'antient dreame'.[40]

As in England, common rights in Wales were appurtenances to land. Rights on *cytir* were determined according to 'the fraction of heritable interest' in the waste allocated to the clan (*gwely*) of which the holding formed a constituent part.[41] Thus, the rights attached to holdings in the hills of mid-Wales in 1199–1200 were 'as much as belongs from the hills to those lands' (*quantum pertinent de montibus ad terras illas*) and 'in hills, in grazing lands (*pascuis*), in pastures and in all other conveniences belonging to the said land' (*ad dictam terram spectantibus*).[42]

Scotland: Commonty and Common Grazings

Scotland possessed no direct legal equivalent to manorial waste, so the balance of rights inherent in English common land was largely absent. Nevertheless, Scotland's many thousands of acres of communally-used, 'half-wild' land were functionally almost identical to common land south of the border. Almost all Scottish commons in the lowlands, in the uplands south and east of a line from Elgin to Kintyre, and in Orkney disappeared during the age of improvement in the eighteenth and nineteenth centuries. Surviving common grazings in the crofting districts of the Highlands, the Western Isles and Shetland are, in their current legal form, a creation of late nineteenth-century crofting legislation.[43] The focus here is on the medieval and early modern legal frameworks of common land across Scotland as a whole.

The Scottish legal framework differed from that in England, largely as a result of what Rab Houston has called 'the stark clarity of rights of property in Scotland'. A Scottish landowner or 'heritor' had absolute right over their land: as a court judgment

---

[38] T. Jones Pierce, *Medieval Welsh Society* (Cardiff, 1972), pp. 106–7, 225n.
[39] Barnwell and Roberts, *Britons, Saxons and Scandinavians*, pp. 162, 212, 260–1; J. Thirsk (ed.), *The Agrarian History of England and Wales, Vol. IV, 1500–1640* (Cambridge, 1967), pp. 380–1.
[40] W. J. Slack (ed.), *The Lordship of Oswestry, 1393–1607* (Shrewsbury, 1951), pp. 59, 65, 71, 72, 79, 88.
[41] Jones Pierce, *Medieval Welsh Society*, p. 50.
[42] At Rhoswydol (Montgom.) and Dolwen: Thomas, *Charters of Ystrad Marchell*, nos. 20 (pp. 162–3), 23 (pp. 165–6).
[43] See below, pp. 159–60.

put in in 1744, 'It is a privilege of property that the proprietor can be put under no restraint'.[44] The provisions of the Statute of Merton to limit a landowner's freedom on common waste would have been unthinkable in Scotland. Heritors were free to remove access to communal resources, including grazing.

Access to the waste was attached to holdings of land as 'rights of servitude'. Though expressed in different legal language and lacking the legal protection of common rights in England, these were analogous to the most prevalent common rights south of the border. Common pasturage, 'the servitude by which one may pasture his cattle on another's ground', was ubiquitous; the servitudes of 'fewel, feal and divot' were equivalent to common of turbary, allowing the commoner to take peat for fuel and turf for roofing and other necessary uses. Rights of servitude could be explicitly granted in writing but could also arise by prescription on proof of forty years of uninterrupted use – but they could also be removed at the whim of the heritor.[45]

Wastes within the bounds of an estate were thus under the absolute control of the proprietor. However, many of the hills and muirs of Scotland had the status of 'commonty', a legal term for a stretch of common land held in shared, undivided ownership.[46] The owners of adjacent estates used such land as a shared resource, allowing their tenants to graze livestock and take other produce from it, but they could not claim any distinct section as their exclusive property; the commonty remained in joint ownership between them. Intercommoning was thus implicit in the concept of commonty: the livestock of a proprietor's tenants and those of neighbouring heritors shared the grazing of the whole common. As a lawyer commented in 1739, the term commonty 'supposed more proprietors than one; in the language of the law there was no commonty where there was only one proprietor', even where the resources were used by numerous commoners.[47]

In Shetland, commonties were referred to as 'scattalds', a term which originally applied to all the land used by a group of farms paying tax ('scat') as a single unit. As such, the scattald was a primary social unit and administrative division, covering both the arable lands and the common grazing shared by a group of settlements and running from the hill pastures to the shore – 'fra the heast [highest] stone in the hill to the lawest in the eb', as it was put. By the eighteenth century, use of the term had come to be restricted to the common grazings, which were in many cases shared by neighbouring proprietors as commonties.[48]

---

[44] Houston, 'Custom in context', pp. 45, 55.

[45] A. MacDowall Bankton, *An Institute of the Laws of Scotland in Civil Rights, Book II* (Edinburgh, 1751), pp. 682–4; A. L. Jarman, 'Customary rights in Scots law: test cases on access to the land in the nineteenth century', *Journal of Legal History*, 28 (2) (2007), pp. 212–14.

[46] See I. H. Adams, 'The legal geography of Scotland's common lands', *Revue de l'Institut de Sociologie*, 2 (1973), pp. 259–332.

[47] W. Maxwell Morison, *The Decisions of the Court of Session from its first institution to the present time* (Edinburgh, 1801), vol. 3, p. 2472.

[48] For scattald, see B. E. Crawford, *Scandinavian Scotland* (Leicester, 1987), pp. 149–50, 181; Adams, 'Legal geography', pp. 268–9; S. A. Knox, *The Making of the Shetland Landscape*

On the common grazings of the crofting communities in the Highlands and Islands the legal framework created in the late nineteenth century built on earlier patterns of use. The vast scale of many Highland estates meant that large tracts of moor and mountain were in single ownership, rendering the concept of commonty less relevant there. What is more, vestigial notions of tribal ownership survived in the ill-defined concept of *duthchas* ('heritage') whereby tenants were linked to their landlord by theoretical ties of kinship deriving from the clan system. Land was held without security other than the obligation of the chief towards his clansmen and distant echoes linking the land to lineage groups.[49] Such hazy ideas of tribal ownership presumably extended to common land, suggesting parallels with the ideas of shared tribal land found in Wales.

Despite the different legal framework, much of the day-to-day activity on the common lands of Scotland corresponded to that on the manorial wastes of England. As in so many aspects of agrarian history on either side of the border, 'Different structures existed, but similar processes occurred.'[50] Differences in law and the language of rural society sometimes obscure commonalities in the history of common land in England and Scotland.

* * *

Common rights were but one aspect of the legal exploitation of resources on the wastes. Landowners continued to exercise their rights as the owners of the soil, retaining absolute control in Scotland, and access to common land could also be by licence, whereby a person taking produce from the common paid the owner for the privilege of doing so. Even in England, where the law required that the rights of commoners were not infringed, owners could graze their livestock on the common (or license others to do so), enclose sections of it, and they retained monopolies over resources unaffected by common rights, such as game, timber and minerals, which they could exploit directly or by licensing. Mineral rights are a case in point. Although common in the soil allowed commoners in some manors to take stone, clay, sand or gravel from some commons, quarrying was generally undertaken under licence from the lord. For example, potters digging clay on Selby East Common (Yorks. W.R.) paid licence fees in the later seventeenth century, as did those quarrying building stone at Myddle (Shrops.), where inhabitants of the manor benefited from a preferential rate compared to outsiders.[51]

(Edinburgh, 1985), pp. 22–8; B. Smith, *Toons and Tenants: Settlement and Society in Shetland, 1299–1899* (Lerwick, 2000), pp. 37–57.

[49] See R. A. Dodgshon, *From Chiefs to Landlords: Social and Economic Change in the Western Highlands and Islands, c.1493–1820* (Edinburgh, 1998), pp. 44–6; Houston, 'Custom in context', pp. 58–9.

[50] J. Goodare, 'In search of the Scottish agrarian problem', in J. Whittle (ed.), *Landlords and Tenants in Britain, 1440–1660: Tawney's* Agrarian Problem *Revisited* (Woodbridge, 2013), pp. 100–16, at p. 115.

[51] B. Waddell, *Landscape and Society in the Vale of York*, p. 33; R. Gough, *History of Myddle*, ed. D. Hey (Harmondsworth, 1981), p. 62.

Whereas a common right was part of a bundle of rights attached to a holding, licensed use was not necessarily linked to land. In the thirteenth century, Bracton drew a distinction between a right of common and a right of herbage, the former attached to a holding of land, the latter involving payment for the right to graze.[52] From the late Middle Ages, most common rights were treated as integral parts of a holding, for which no separate rent or service was paid over and above that for the holding as a whole. However, the distinction was not always clear-cut. A common right could entitle its holder to the benefits of a resource even though payment might be required in order to exercise the right so acquired. This was the case with common of pannage, where the payment of a fee to the lord of the manor, typically 1d per full-grown pig, was the norm in medieval times.[53] Payments for common pasture were less common, though agistment on forest wastes (discussed below) constituted an important exception. Elsewhere, renders paid by tenants for *herbagium* are sometimes recorded, as at Glastonbury (Som.), for example, where the tenants paid 1d for each animal put to graze on their common pasture in the thirteenth century.[54] Commoners' rights and licensed use thus co-existed. An individual might exercise both, like the holder of a life lease at Skelton in Cleveland (Yorks. N.R.) in 1356, who held a house and land with quantified common rights of pasture, turbary and estovers but also a licence to cut forty packs of heather on the moors of Skelton, which was clearly separate from his appurtenant rights.[55]

More frequently, local commoners would share the common with outsiders who used it by licence, as in the numerous grants of grazing rights to religious houses, some of which were independent of a holding of land in the manor. Where a grant of a very small acreage of land was accompanied by common pasture for a considerable number of livestock, it seems likely that the patch of land was merely a means of paying lip service to the concept of appurtenant rights and that the grant was, in reality, licensing external use.[56] In a different context, a distinction was drawn in the Fens between 'intrinsec' vills, which held common pasture rights without payment, and 'forinsec' settlements which paid for grazing. It extended to turbary rights, with the result that sales of turves, over and above the common turbary rights of the 'intrinsec' vills, yielded substantial income in the later thirteenth and fourteenth centuries. By the thirteenth century the balance between the two was changing as lords sought to increase their income by accepting larger numbers of paying beasts or increasing sales of turbary. In consequence, the rights of the commoners became more strictly controlled.[57] Multiple interests thus existed over common land, so that by no means all users of a common were commoners.

---

[52] Bracton, *De Legibus*, book 3, p. 167.

[53] J. Birrell, 'Common rights in the medieval forest: disputes and conflicts in the thirteenth century', *Past & Present*, 117 (1987), pp. 38–40.

[54] N. Neilson, *Customary Rents* (Oxford, 1910), pp. 75–6.

[55] H. Warne (ed.), *The Duke of Norfolk's Deeds at Arundel Castle: The Dacre Estates in Northern Counties* (Chichester, 2006), p. 208.

[56] For examples, see Winchester, 'Shielings and common pastures', p. 279 and the sources there cited.

[57] Neilson, *Terrier of Fleet*, pp. xiii–xv, lii–liii.

DEFINING COMMON RIGHTS

The existence of common rights immediately raised questions. How much of a resource might a commoner take? Which members of a community had access to the common? Customary usage and legal principles, evolving across the medieval and early modern centuries, created a framework which delimited the exercise of rights.

Quantifying Common Rights

Since most common rights were ancillary to the holding of land, under English law they could only be used to support that house or farm; the amount of produce taken had to be 'reasonable' and was restricted to 'necessary use'. It had to be a fair share of the quantity of the produce in question on the common and also, crucially, a share appropriate to the size of the holding. It followed from this basic framework that produce from the common could not be taken out of the manor, nor could it be sold.[58]

Quantifying the most valuable common right, common of pasture, involved expressing 'necessary use' as an equitable and sustainable figure for the number of animals which might be put to graze on a common. Many grazing rights were 'without number' but that did not mean that they were unlimited. Although rarely stated explicitly before the late medieval period, rights were generally determined by a principle recorded widely across western Europe as the 'rule of hay and straw' and in English law as the rule of 'levancy and couchancy', which stated that a commoner could put to graze on the common in summer only as many animals as he could keep over winter on the produce of his holding.[59] It was also found in Wales, where it was described as 'an old custom ... used amongst themselves' by the inhabitants of Nantconwy (Caern.) in 1552, and in Scotland, where numbers on the 'outgerss' of the common grazings were limited to those kept on the 'ingerss' within the head-dyke in winter.[60] An important consequence of the rule was that it prohibited bringing livestock in from elsewhere by way of agistment. Sometimes this was stated explicitly, as in thirteenth-century charters from South Brent (Devon) which granted common of pasture 'for all ... livestock which can be sustained in winter, without agistment'.[61]

Even where explicit references to levancy and couchancy are absent, it is clear that local custom placed limits on pasture rights. Notions of shareholding underpinned common rights across Britain and articulations of equitable quantity are found widely spread across space and time. Some lay stress on customary use and tradition. In

---

[58] *Gadsden*, §§ 2.66–2.68.
[59] The phrase 'levancy and couchancy' can be traced back to legal judgments in the fifteenth century: *Contested Common Land*, p. 195; *Gadsden*, §§ 2.69–2.75. For the 'rule of hay and straw', see M. De Moor, L. Shaw-Taylor and P. Warde (eds), *The Management of Common Land in North West Europe, c.1500–1850* (Turnhout, 2002), pp. 132, 158, 212; A. J. L. Winchester, '"By ancient right or custom": the local history of common land in a European context', *The Local Historian*, 45 (4) (2015), p. 273.
[60] W. O. Williams (ed.), *Calendar of the Caernarvonshire Quarter Sessions Records, Vol. I, 1541–58* (Caernarvonshire Historical Society, 1956), p. 97 (no. 164); R. A. Dodgshon, *Land and Society in Early Scotland* (Oxford, 1981), p. 170.
[61] Fox, *Dartmoor's Alluring Uplands*, p. 85.

Scotland, rights in the commonty were for 'as many cattle as is customary in the township for so much land' (*pastur for sa mony katel in the common ... as consuetude is of the toun to sa mekil land*) (Keithick, near Coupar-Angus, 1475), or were those 'pertaining to the said lands by use and wont' (Meigle (Perthshire), 1661).[62] Others imply a sharper definition. Common 'belonging to so much land' (*quod ad tantum terram pertinet*) (Wormley (Herts.), late twelfth century) or 'after the raytte and costom' of the township (Thornes (Yorks. W.R.), 1535)[63] suggest clear and known limits, as do presentments for overcharging the common with animals 'beyond the quantity of their land' (Wimbledon (Surrey), 1464) or 'over the nombre assessid to his tenor' (Windermere (Westmld), fifteenth century).[64] Such wording may imply 'stinting', an alternative to levancy and couchancy, which restricted grazing rights by placing a numerical limit on the number of animals an individual could put to the common. Where this was the case, the number of stints belonging to an individual was again underpinned by the concept of shareholding and determined by reference to the size of their holding of land, whether expressed in the traditional language of fiscal assessment or in the amount of rent or tax paid. Stinting became increasingly widespread on English commons across the post-medieval centuries.[65]

Access to Common Rights

Another persistent issue in the legal framework around common rights in England was the need to determine which members of the local community should have access to the resources of a common. Was it the tenants of an estate or all the inhabitants of a settlement? The latter would include sub-tenants, lodgers, servants and labourers, for example, who might not appear on a manor's rent roll. The question gained importance as pressures grew on common land from the sixteenth century to the eighteenth, focusing minds on the rights of the landless in a time of population growth, when the resources of common land became increasingly important to the poor.

Holding land to which common rights were attached conveyed an undisputed right to resources on the common; the grey area lay in the rights of landless cottagers and undertenants. In practice, local custom dictated who had access to commons and often blurred the distinction between manorial property rights and wider understandings of community use based on residency.[66] There seems to have been considerable variation

---

[62] C. Rogers (ed.), *Rental Book of the Cistercian Abbey of Cupar-Angus* (London, 1880), vol. I, p. 203; J. H. Ramsey, *Bamff Charters AD 1232–1703* (Oxford, 1915), p. 297 (no. 261). Comparable wording is recorded elsewhere: Rogers, *Rental Book*, vol. II, p. 82 (Inverarity (Angus), 1550); Ramsey, *Bamff Charters*, p. 316 (no. 285) (Creuchies (Perthshire), 1670).

[63] R. Ransford (ed.), *The Early Charters of the Augustinian Canons of Waltham Abbey, Essex, 1062–1230* (Woodbridge, 1989), no. 397; Leeds University Special Collections, YAS/MD225/1/260A (I am grateful to Murray Seccombe for this reference).

[64] *Wimbledon Ct R.*, pp. 15–17; *Harvest*, p. 156 (no. 1.32).

[65] Stinting is discussed further below, pp. 56–61, 143–5, 165. See also A. J. L. Winchester and E. A. Straughton, 'Stints and sustainability: managing stock levels on common land in England, c.1600–2006', *AgHR*, 58 (2010), pp. 30–48.

[66] As noted by Houston, 'Custom in context', p. 54.

between manors in England, reflecting in part, no doubt, differences in the extent of common land and the pressure on its resources. On some manors, poor cottagers were protected: an agreement over the commons at Banham (Norf.) in 1630 explicitly allowed cottagers to keep ten sheep and two cows or one horse on the common 'for maintenance of their famylyes', because 'equalitye is the first part of equitye'.[67] On the Shropshire manor of Prees in 1585, newly-built cottages were allocated one day's turf-digging a year to enable them to have a supply of fuel, in effect creating a turbary right attached to the cottage.[68] At Church Lawton (Ches.) questions arose in 1640 about the common rights attached to cottages on freehold properties within the manor. The court confirmed that established cottages ('aunycent Cottages under the Free tenants') had 'usually' kept geese and swine on the manor's wastes.[69] Such largesse was by no means universal, however. Common rights at Great Bentley (Essex) and Ewyas Lacy (Heref.), for example, were restricted to freeholders and copyholders (and at the latter, 'antient leasehold tenants' as well), implicitly excluding cottagers,[70] while the restriction of furze-cutting rights at Great Milton (Oxon.) to those paying rates also effectively excluded the poor.[71]

By the early seventeenth century a distinction was often drawn between 'commonable' cottages and others which did not have common rights attached to them, the latter generally being those erected more recently. The language used to describe cottagers' common rights at Holme-on-Spalding Moor (Yorks. E.R.) in 1621 probably reflected wider norms: the custom was that only 'such howses as have bene Auncyent toft and croft' had access to the common as of right; other houses had common 'by composition' (presumably by paying for the privilege), while 'new erected howses ... ought to have noe common at all'.[72] As late as 1831, a dispute over fuel rights at Chippenham (Cambs.) centred on whether the rights had been restricted to ancient cottages or were for all the poor cottagers in the parish.[73] It is sometimes possible to quantify 'commonable' cottages. In parishes with rights on Geddington Chase (Northants), for example, less than half (43 per cent) of over 350 households had formal common rights in the eighteenth century, but the proportion of commonable cottages varied widely, ranging from over 80 per cent in one parish to around 35 per cent in others. More generally, it has been suggested that perhaps

---

[67] Wood, *Memory of the People*, p. 326.
[68] J. P. Bowen, 'Cottage and squatter settlement and encroachment on common waste in the 16th and 17th centuries: some evidence from Shropshire', *Local Population Studies*, 93 (2014), p. 19.
[69] G. Lawton (ed.), *Church Lawton Manor Court Rolls, 1631–1680* (Record Society of Lancashire & Cheshire, 147, 2013), p. 42.
[70] Wood, *Memory of the People*, pp. 324–5; J. Moir '"A World unto Themselves"? Squatter settlement in Herefordshire, 1780–1880' (PhD thesis, University of Leicester, 1990), p. 67.
[71] L. Shaw-Taylor, 'The management of common land in the lowlands of southern England circa 1500 to circa 1850', in De Moor *et al.*, *Management of Common Land in North West Europe*, p. 76.
[72] Wood, *Memory of the People*, p. 168.
[73] J. M. Neeson, *Commoners: Common Right, Enclosure and Social Change in England, 1700–1820* (Cambridge, 1993), p. 76.

half of all cottages were 'commonable'.[74] Whatever the legal definitions, numerous poor householders made use of common land, claiming customary rights which might not be seen by lawyers as formal common rights but were nevertheless essential to their livelihood.[75] Notwithstanding the concept of 'commonable cottages', in practice almost all residents of the parishes around Geddington Chase exercised what they claimed to be common rights.[76]

In his influential essay on 'Custom, law and common right', E. P. Thompson noted the increasing acrimony of disputes over common right in the eighteenth century as legal minds attempted to achieve precision in the area, both to settle disputes and when enclosure was mooted. Gateward's Case of 1607, a landmark judgment which ruled that residents of a manor who did not have a legal interest in the houses they occupied did not have an interest in the common, limited the common rights of the landless. Thompson commented that the case 'drew an expert knife through the carcass of custom, cutting off the use-right from the user'. By defining an interest in the common in terms of landholders and customary tenants, it 'altogether disqualified indistinct categories of small users'. In theory, it stripped rights from the landless when cases came to court, though some jurors ignored it, giving greater weight to custom, and the continuing use of commons by the landless suggests that its impact on the reality of access by the poor may not have been great.[77]

The limits of what constituted formal common rights were challenged by custom as late as the 1870s in Ashdown Forest (Sussex). A prolonged dispute over common rights there centred on local farmers' claims to the right to cut litter (defined as 'anything that falls to the scythe', including bracken, heather, gorse, broom and coarse grass) as bedding for their livestock, and also extended to rights to take turf, peat, gravel, loam and sand from the forest commons. Access to these resources had been long tolerated by custom, even if it was sometimes challenged ineffectually by the lord. By being integral to the local economy and working culture, customary uses such as these gained weight through repeated practice across the generations, becoming jealously guarded 'rights'.[78]

A tension between local custom and the letter of the law is a theme running through the history of common land, as will be seen. As one Victorian lawyer, Philip Lawrence, a leading light in the Commons Preservation Society, put it, customs 'existed before, and not in consequence of, the legal maxims which are current respecting them' and

---

[74] Ibid., pp. 55–80; Shaw-Taylor, 'Management of common land', pp. 71–3; S. Hindle, '"Not by bread only"? Common right, parish relief and endowed charity in a forest economy, c.1600–1800', in S. King and A. Tomkins (eds), *The Poor in England 1700–1850: An Economy of Makeshifts* (Manchester, 2003), pp. 39–75. Figures quoted are from p. 49.

[75] See Neeson, *Commoners*, pp. 64–70; and comments on the relationship between customary practice and 'legalistic formulations' in Wood, *Memory of the People*, pp. 162–6. See also below, pp. 112–13.

[76] Hindle, '"Not by bread only"?', p. 49.

[77] Thompson, 'Custom, law and common right', p. 134; C. W. Brooks, *Law, Politics and Society in Early Modern England* (Cambridge, 2008), p. 342.

[78] *Ashdown Forest*, esp. pp. 41–3.

the law 'gave a rigid form to custom, previously elastic and variable'.[79] The history of common land cannot be told in terms of legal frameworks alone.

FURTHER DIMENSIONS OF COMMON RIGHT

The tidy legal edifices outlined above, defining property rights over common land in relation to landholding and lordship, did not sit easily with agrarian reality in several respects. First, rural society had deep roots, at the heart of which lay the community of the vill or township, whose members shared a resource territory which might bear little relation to patterns of lordship. Seasonal movement of livestock to distant pastures could also cut across manorial boundaries, while further shades of difference were found in common rights on land designated as hunting forest in the medieval period and on commons belonging to urban communities. Each of these dimensions of common right affected how commons were used in the medieval and post-medieval centuries.

Township and Vill

In England the concept of manorial waste was moderated by the enduring thinking that common rights were attached to vills or townships, rather than manors. The phrase 'the common pasture of the vill' was ancient and widespread. It is implied in the tenth-century laws of Edgar (959–75) which required anyone purchasing livestock when on a journey to bring them home to the common pasture (*gemænre læse*) and to do so openly, before neighbours – 'with the witness of his township' (*mid his tunscipes gewitnyse*).[80] In the eleventh century, the Domesday survey of Cambridgeshire, Hertfordshire and Middlesex regularly records 'pasture for the livestock of the vill' (*pastura ad pecuniam villae*),[81] strongly suggesting that the vill was the organisational unit for grazing rights from an early date in those areas. Likewise, intercommoning rights in the shared wetlands of the Fens were said to belong to vills, not manors.[82]

The 'common pasture of the vill' was integral to the shareholding principles which lay beneath the ancient fiscal assessment of settlements. Holdings measured in hides and virgates, oxgangs (bovates) and ploughlands (carucates), included rights to all the vill's communal resources, not just its arable fields.[83] Such thinking underpinned the appurtenance clauses found in twelfth- and thirteenth-century charters from northern England and southern Scotland, which granted 'as much common pasture as belongs to so much land in the vill'.[84] What was meant by the 'common pasture of the vill' was

---

[79] *Wimbledon Ct R.*, p. ix.
[80] Edgar IV, clause 8: F. Liebermann (ed.), *Die Gesetze der Angelsachsen I* (Halle, 1903), pp. 210–11. The phrase 'witness of his township' is rendered 'witness of his neighbours (*vicinorum*)' in the Latin version of the text.
[81] Darby, *Domesday England*, p. 149.
[82] Neilson, *Terrier of Fleet*, p. li.
[83] See P. Vinogradoff, *The Growth of the Manor* (London, 1905), pp. 150–98; R. A. Dodgshon, 'The landholding foundations of the open-field system', *Past & Present*, 67 (1975), pp. 3–29; Faith, *English Peasantry*, p. 147.
[84] Winchester, 'Shielings and common pastures', pp. 276–7.

sometimes spelt out. At Milverton (Som.) tenants were granted 'common in pasture and in ploughland' (*communiam in pastura et in ganneto*) in 1195;[85] a thirteenth-century charter from Northumberland granted common 'both in cultivated land and in wastes'; another from South Hailes (East Lothian) expressed the same idea more fully, 'both in arable land once the grain has been carried and in all other pasture belonging to the vill'.[86]

The 'common pasture of the vill' thus comprised two complementary rights: grazing in the fields after harvest and pasture on the wastes. Grazing rights on fields and meadows after the arable and hay crops had been taken were exercised during the 'open season' across autumn and winter, when the vill's livestock could graze throughout the farmland within the head-dyke, until the fields were closed for sowing. Even in the uplands and in areas characterised by enclosed fields in northern England, the concept of an 'open season' is recorded in later medieval sources.[87] Pasture rights on the waste provided grazing in spring and summer, when fields and meadows were closed to protect the growing crops.

This seasonal rhythm of moving stock between fields and waste underpinned farming in most parts of Britain in the medieval and early modern centuries. The area of waste over which a grazing right could be exercised was rarely specified, suggesting that the boundaries of the waste belonging to the vill in question were recognised and known. By formalising a manorial framework which labelled wastes as the 'residue of the manor', the Statute of Merton also presupposed that clear manorial boundaries existed – and implicitly assumed that manor and vill were coterminous, which was by no means always the case. Where vill and manor did not coincide in Midland England, it is clear that decisions concerning the organisation of pasture rights fell to the community of the vill in the late medieval centuries.[88]

That notions of community 'ownership' of commons persisted is suggested by tensions between lords and commoners over seigniorial fold courses on common land in sixteenth-century East Anglia. Among the articles drawn up during Kett's Rebellion in 1549 was the demand that 'no lord of no manor shall common upon the Comons'. Echoes of such thinking resurfaced at Mildenhall (Suff.), where a witness recalled being told by aged men in the 1630s that they 'never suffered any Lord or Lords of the said Mannor to feed any beasts ... upon the Comon or to take any Turffe or Fodder out of the said wasts', as the lord 'had noe right thereunto'.[89] In a region in which many vills contained more than one manor, it could be difficult to reconcile the provisions of the Statute of Merton to reality on the ground. One might even say that, from its inception, Merton contained a fiction, namely that the manor was invariably the organising unit through which property rights on common land were acquired.

---

[85] N. E. Stacy (ed.), *Charters and Custumals of Shaftesbury Abbey 1089–1216* (Oxford, 2006), pp. 51–2.

[86] Winchester, 'Shielings and common pastures', p. 278.

[87] Winchester, *Medieval Cumbria*, pp. 60–1; *Harvest*, pp. 54–6; at Cockerham (Lancs.) orders of 1483 forbade tenants from holding closes in severalty across winter from Michaelmas to Candlemas: R. Sharpe France, 'Two custumals of the manor of Cockerham, 1326 and 1483', *Transactions of the Lancashire & Cheshire Antiquarian Society* 64 (1954), p. 50.

[88] W. O. Ault, 'Village by-laws by common consent', *Speculum*, 29 (1954), pp. 384–5.

[89] Wood, *Memory of the People*, pp. 326, 333.

Forest and Chase

On the large tracts of Britain which had the status of hunting forest in the medieval period, special considerations affected the use of the wastes. Royal forests in England, Wales and Scotland were subject to forest law, protecting deer and their habitats, and restrictions also applied to the private forests (or 'free chases') which covered large parts of the uplands of all three nations.[90] Some lay outside the structure of vill and township, like the forests in the lordship of Rhuddlan (Flints.) in 1086, which 'do not pertain to any vill in the manor',[91] and the royal forests of Dartmoor and Exmoor, which each consisted of a central block of Crown moorland, flanked by the manorial wastes of the settlements around their edges.[92] Most forests contained extensive tracts of untamed land, by no means always wooded, which were in practice used communally by communities within and around the forest. The provisions of the Statute of Merton did not apply in English forests (as forests were not manors) but the Charter of the Forest (1217) had confirmed common rights in royal forests 'to those who were before accustomed to have them'.[93] Ancient prescriptive rights were therefore claimed by settlements within a forest's bounds.[94] Intercommoning was often a feature of forest wastes, not only by communities within the forest but also by surrounding settlements. In Whittlewood Forest, for example, six 'in-towns' had common grazing from 25 March to 1 November each year, and a further nine 'out-towns' from 25 April to 25 September.[95]

However, forest status was often accompanied by grazing restrictions that did not apply outside the forest boundary. In English royal forests, these theoretically included seasonal restrictions when grazing was forbidden – the 'fence month' during the fawning period in the summer, and a longer closed season across the winter – and restrictions on the livestock which could be grazed: cattle and horses were commonable but swine, sheep, goats, asses and geese were not.[96] The earliest forest laws of Scotland, possibly dating from the reign of David I (1124–53), contained similar stipulations: grazing was restricted in pannage time and in the fence month, livestock were to be closely herded and were not to remain in a forest overnight.[97] Even the lord

---

[90] For forests in England and Wales see http://info.sjc.ox.ac.uk/forests/ForestMapTiles.html; for upland forests see Winchester, 'Shielings and common pastures', pp. 273–97.

[91] DB, f. 269a (*Cheshire*, FT 1-1, FT 2-1).

[92] Fox, *Dartmoor's Alluring Uplands*, pp. 22–7; E. T. MacDermot, *The History of the Forest of Exmoor*, revised edn (Newton Abbot, 1973), p. 346.

[93] Charter of the Forest, cited in J. Langton, 'Medieval forests and chases: another realm?', in J. Langton and G. Jones (eds), *Forests and Chases of Medieval England and Wales, c.1000 to c.1500* (Oxford, 2010), p. 29.

[94] In Ashdown Forest and the Forest of Dean, for example: *VCH Sussex* II, p. 314; C. E. Hart, *Royal Forest: A History of Dean's Woods as Producers of Timber* (Oxford, 1966), p. 37.

[95] R. Jones and M. Page, *Medieval Villages in an English Landscape: Beginnings and Ends* (Macclesfield, 2006), pp. 141–2.

[96] B. Harris and G. Ryan, *An Outline of the Law Relating to Common Land* (London, 1967), §§ 1-54–1-60; P. A. J. Pettit, *The Royal Forests of Northamptonshire: A Study in Their Economy 1558–1714*, Northants Record Society XXIII (1968), p. 153.

[97] J. M. Gilbert, *Hunting and Hunting Reserves in Medieval Scotland* (Edinburgh, 1979), pp. 105–7, 291–2.

of a free chase could restrict grazing to those to whom he had granted permission and there are other indications that sections of forest land might be closed to livestock as 'preserved forest', in which grazing was strictly controlled.[98]

Many grazing rights in forests were technically by agistment, whereby livestock were licensed to graze on payment of a fee. In origin, agistment meant 'the opening of a forest for a specified time to livestock'. It permitted grazing while enabling the lord to maintain control over the number of livestock entering a forest.[99] In the case of pannage, the common right to graze pigs in woodland, there was an almost complete overlap between the right and agistment – payment for pannage on a per capita basis was ubiquitous.

Customary access to grazing grounds on forest wastes came to be formalised as agistment in some forests by the payment of sums of money. The fixed customary rents paid by tenants in the lordship of Arwystli and Cyfeiliog in the hills of mid-Wales for pasture in the lord's 'forests or frithes' suggest this.[100] In the northern Pennines and the Lake District, separate payments for pasture rights, combined with numerical limits (stints) on those rights, also suggest that tenants in those forests had been granted licence to graze their livestock in return for payment on a per capita basis and that, over time, the origin in licensed agistment was forgotten and it was assumed that the right to graze was a normal common right.[101]

Longstanding customary use by adjacent communities was also based on agistment. Devon parishes abutting Dartmoor forest paid 'venville' rents, which, significantly, originated as fines for trespassing with livestock on the forest, suggesting that agistment might represent a licensing of livestock which were technically grazing a forest without right.[102] More widely, inhabitants from across the county of Devon (except Totnes and Barnstaple) possessed a customary right to summer their cattle on central Dartmoor, which can be traced back to 1204, but for this they paid a fee, set at 1½d per beast by 1296. Custom defined the limits of access to the summer pastures but those whose beasts joined the annual 'red tide' making its way up to the moor paid for the privilege.[103]

Similar payments are recorded elsewhere. In the New Forest (Hants), a render termed 'hafhorsis' (or 'hafforsis') was paid for pasture by 'strangers' whose animals were found in the forest in the 1290s.[104] On Fforest Fawr in the lordship of Brecon in south Wales

---

[98] See Winchester, 'Shielings and common pastures', p. 289.

[99] See, for example, *Harvest*, pp. 94–6; A. J. L. Winchester, 'Vaccaries and agistment: upland medieval forests as grazing grounds', in Langton and Jones (eds), *Forests and Chases of Medieval England and Wales*, pp. 116–18.

[100] Evans, 'Arwystli and Cyfeiliog', pp. 25–6, 28, 30, 31.

[101] This is discussed further in Winchester and Straughton, 'Stints and sustainability', pp. 37–9; cf. *Harvest*, p. 94.

[102] J. Langton and G. Jones, 'Deconstructing and reconstructing the forests: some preliminary matters', in their *Forests and Chases of Medieval England and Wales*, p. 9, n. 94; see also Fox, *Dartmoor's Alluring Uplands*, pp. 52–4.

[103] Fox, *Dartmoor's Alluring Uplands*, pp. 49–51, 55–73.

[104] D. J. Stagg (ed.), *Calendar of New Forest Documents, 1244–1334* (Hampshire County Council, 1979), nos. 372, 375, 377–8, 381, 393, 395, 400.

the inhabitants of the eight parishes which had grazing rights on the forest wastes paid 3d per beast (reduced to 1d in 1484) which was termed *cyfrif* (literally 'number; tally'), clearly pointing to an origin as agistment.[105] Comparable rents were paid for grazing rights on the forest of High Peak (Derby.) and on Clee Forest (Shrops.).[106] At Molland (Devon), on the edge of Exmoor, the Domesday survey recorded a render 'from the pasture of the moors' (*pascua morarum*), suggesting that the large-scale agistment on Exmoor in later centuries (over 30,000 sheep were agisted there in 1736) had deep roots.[107] Communities just outside the bounds of Cannock Chase (Staffs.) made payments for pasture on the Chase in the early fourteenth century, while settlements within the Chase did not.[108] The herbage tolls found in forests in Scotland in the fourteenth and fifteenth centuries were similar renders.[109] Thus, forest wastes often provided common grazing for communities over a wide area, outside the framework of manorial rights.

Transhumance

One particular aspect of this involved seasonal transhumance, by which livestock were moved to summer grazing grounds, sometimes accompanied by herds who lodged in seasonal dwellings (shielings) on the pastures.[110] The practice, which enabled communities on the fringes of the hills to make use of upland grazings during the summer months, also cut across the tidy concept of manorial waste. It survived until the sixteenth century in the north Pennines and the seventeenth along the Anglo-Scottish border and continued in Highland Scotland into the nineteenth century.[111] Comparable practices are recorded in Wales, where distant hill grazings (*hafodydd*) were exploited using temporary summer houses or 'dairies' (*hafoty* or *lluestau*) in the sixteenth and seventeenth centuries.[112]

In Scotland and northern England, transhumance was a communal event. The dates at which communities were to go to the summer shielings were laid down by manor courts in those parts of the north Pennines and Border hills where transhumance

---

[105] W. Rees, *The Great Forest of Brecknock: A Facet of Breconshire History* (Brecon, 1966), p. 10; J. Lloyd, *The Great Forest of Brecknock* (London, 1905), pp. 5–6.

[106] Winchester, 'Vaccaries and agistment', p. 117; R. C. Purton (ed.), 'A Description of ye Clee, ye L'dships, Comoners and Strakers adjoined, made about 1612, 10 Jac.', *Transactions of the Shropshire Archaeological Society*, 2nd ser. 8 (1896), pp. 195–8. The adjacent manors paid 'Clee Rent' for their use of the common.

[107] DB, f. 101 (*Devon*, 1–41); M. Siraut, *Exmoor: The Making of an English Upland* (Chichester, 2009), p. 88.

[108] Birrell, 'Common rights in the medieval forest', p. 39.

[109] Gilbert, *Hunting and Hunting Reserves*, pp. 106–9.

[110] The following section draws on Winchester 'Shielings and common pastures', pp. 291–5. For an overview of transhumance in Britain, see Fox, *Dartmoor's Alluring Uplands*, pp. 27–40.

[111] *Harvest*, pp. 85–90; A. Bil, *The Shieling 1600–1840: The Case of the Central Scottish Highlands* (Edinburgh, 1990).

[112] E. Davies, 'Hafod, hafoty and lluest: their distribution, features and purpose', *Ceredigion*, 9 (1) (1980), pp. 1–41; R. Suggett, *Houses and History in the March of Wales: Radnorshire, 1400–1800* (Aberystwyth, 2005), pp. 249–55; *Contested Common Land*, pp. 142–4.

survived in the later sixteenth and early seventeenth century, and individuals were sanctioned if they did not go.[113] Each community had its own shieling ground, thus linking settlements in the lowlands to summer pastures in the hills. The communal basis of transhumance can be traced back to an early date, when we hear of communities in Scotland going to the shielings as a group in the decades around 1200.[114] In the Lammermuir Hills, both twelfth-century documents and place-names indicate links between settlements near the coast and shieling grounds in the hills, a pattern reflected in the parish boundaries of the area, where long, narrow, interlocking territories reach far inland from the shore.[115]

The legal context of transhumance varied. In some cases, shieling grounds were, like common rights in general, appurtenances to holdings of land. In parts of Scotland, the right to erect shielings was sometimes explicitly included in twelfth-century charters, implying that shielings on moorland were by then an integral part of the agrarian system. In a dispute over a shieling on a common on the English side of the border in 1279, it was claimed that 'by the custom of the region' a lord could build shielings wherever he wished, without regard to the common rights of others, a claim perhaps reflecting earlier practices, before the increasing pressure on waste land during the thirteenth century.[116]

However, not all shieling grounds were appurtenances. In medieval northern England, grants of and income from *scalinge* (a term which often referred to summer pastures, rather than simply the herdsmen's huts) make it clear that shieling grounds could form a distinct source of income with a separate rental value. In Redesdale (Northumb.), where shieling practices survived in the early seventeenth century, the tenants paid 'summer farm' for their shieling grounds, separate from the rents paid for the farmland (the 'wintersteeds') lower down the valley. At Kidland in the Cheviot Hills, where grazing rights were let independently of holdings of land, income from summer shielings in the mid-sixteenth century was described as 'small agystemente', a telling phrase suggesting that grazing rights on these shieling grounds were not common rights as such, but a form of licensed agistment.[117] Like the evidence from Dartmoor, this reinforces the view that it is not always possible to draw a simple distinction between transhumance as an appurtenant common right, on the one hand, and as agistment, on the other.

Urban Commons

Urban communities required access to the resources traditionally provided by common land, not only for pasture (as farming remained part of the economy of many medieval towns and grazing was needed for the horses on which the urban

---

[113] *Harvest*, pp. 88–90.
[114] Winchester, 'Shielings and common pastures', p. 292.
[115] Barrow, *Kingdom of Scots*, p. 236.
[116] K. J. Stringer, 'Lordship and society in medieval Cumbria: Gilsland under the Moultons (c.1240–1313)', in K. J. Stringer (ed.), *North-West England from the Romans to the Tudors: Essays in Memory of John Macnair Todd* (Kendal, 2014), p. 148.
[117] *Harvest*, pp. 85–90.

economy relied), but also for fuel, on which even a modest-sized town could make heavy demands. Many towns possessed their own common pasture, the 'town moor', which was usually in the hands of the community of burgesses or free men of the borough, embodied in corporate towns in a formal institution, the corporation.[118] Where an urban community was a distinct legal entity, this impinged on the evolution of rights over its common land.

The communal basis of the rights enjoyed by the inhabitants of even a small, unincorporated town is illustrated by the case of the seigniorial borough of Cockermouth (Cumb.). Under a charter of c.1210, confirming the borough's privileges, the community (*villata*) of Cockermouth paid 8 lbs of wax yearly for their liberties. By the sixteenth century, the wax payment had come to be associated specifically with 'ther fredome and lybertyes upon the Commons and Moores of Cockermouth'.[119] Disputes over the extent of the borough's common rights (principally the right to take turf, peat, gorse and 'flawghts' (sods) for fuel) and the uncertain boundaries with neighbouring villages across adjacent moorland flared up in 1583 and again on the eve of enclosure in the nineteenth century.[120]

Corporate ownership resulted in a sense of communal right quite distinct from the rights of individuals on rural common land. From this stemmed an understanding that urban commons, both in England and Scotland, were there for the common good of the town community and could be used to raise income. On many commons, the town charged those exercising grazing rights, thus generating funds for the public purse.[121] At Newcastle upon Tyne the burgesses petitioned the Crown in 1357 for the right to mine coal on the Town Moor to help pay the borough's fee farm of £100. The mines were not operated on a fully commercial basis, but rather to ensure a supply of coal at a modest price to the borough's inhabitants – the communal benefit thus cut two ways.[122] Elsewhere in England by the eighteenth century some corporations leased out their common pastures to tenant farmers, applying the income to support poorer freemen and widows.[123] Partial enclosure was sometimes seen as a means of solving civic financial difficulties in English towns from the fifteenth century, though such attacks on common rights could provoke rioting, as at Coventry (on several occasions

---

[118] The town moors discussed here were only one aspect of common rights granted to boroughs: see H. R. French, 'Urban agriculture, commons and commoners in the seventeenth and eighteenth centuries: the case of Sudbury, Suffolk', *AgHR*, 28 (2) (2000), pp. 173–6; *Town Commons*, pp. 5–7.

[119] R. Hall, 'An early Cockermouth charter', *Trans CWAAS*, new ser. 77 (1977), p. 77; Cockermouth Castle Muniments, box 314/39, f. 20.

[120] Cockermouth Castle Muniments, box 103, lawsuit papers 1583; CAS, DBEN, box 227, 553h, plan of disputed ground, post-1814.

[121] H. R. French, 'Urban common rights, enclosure and the market: Clitheroe Town Moors, 1764–1802', *AgHR*, 51 (1) (2003), pp. 46–7; French, 'Urban agriculture, commons and commoners', pp. 179–82; S. Stevenson, *Anstruther: A History* (Edinburgh, 1989), p. 38.

[122] E. M. Halcrow, 'The Town Moor of Newcastle upon Tyne', *Archaeologia Aeliana*, 4th ser. 31 (1953), pp. 150–1, 156.

[123] H. French, 'The governance of urban common lands in England, 1500–1840', working paper (December 2017), https://www.researchgate.net/publication/321685425.

between 1429 and 1525) and York (after a proposal to enclose part of the Knavesmire in 1536).[124] At Malmesbury (Wilts.), conflict over access to the King's Heath, a 500-acre (200-ha) common, said to have been granted to the town by King Athelstan in the tenth century, erupted in the early seventeenth century, when it was claimed that the aldermen and burgesses, the town's wealthy elite, had sought to exclude poorer inhabitants, enclosing part of the Heath in 1607 and driving off the cattle of poorer households.[125] Henry French has concluded that town commons tended to survive where the body of free burgesses was large, so that a concentration of control in the hands of a small group was less likely.[126]

On urban commons in England, the basis of use rights varied from town to town. Access sometimes extended to all householders in the borough; sometimes it was restricted to freemen (or often, by the eighteenth century, to resident freemen). Elsewhere, rights were attached to property held by burgage tenure, though the accumulation of burgage property in comparatively few hands and a trade in stints could break the direct link between property and grazing rights, as had occurred at Clitheroe (Lancs.) by the later eighteenth century.[127]

In Scotland, town muirs were part of the 'common good' of royal burghs, granted by charter when a settlement was given burgh status. By the sixteenth century, burgh authorities were exploiting their common lands commercially to raise income for the burgh coffers, a practice which could lead to competition with the use of the common by the inhabitants. An act of 1593 regulated the raising of private profit from burgh lands but did not outlaw it, with the result that many burgh muirs in Scotland were lost by the nineteenth century, having been divided or feued away.[128]

Where commons did survive, some burghs succeeded in balancing communal use and corporate profit. At Anstruther (Fife), the common lands were being leased by the mid-eighteenth century but the rights of the inhabitants – grazing beasts, steeping flax in pits on the muir, bleaching cloth, digging turf and cutting gorse – were protected.[129] Elsewhere, tensions between commercial and communal uses were never far below the surface, as in the well-documented case of St Andrews, where commercial use of

---

[124] *VCH Warw.* VIII, p. 203; Thompson, *Customs in Common*, pp. 122–3; *VCH Yorks. City of York*, p. 501.

[125] A. Wood, 'The loss of Athelstan's gift: the politics of popular memory in Malmesbury, 1607–1633', in Whittle, *Landlords and Tenants in Britain*, pp. 85–99.

[126] French, 'Governance of urban common lands'.

[127] French, 'Urban common rights, enclosure and the market', pp. 41–2.

[128] N. Reid, 'Five centuries of dispute: the common lands of St Andrews', *Scottish Archives*, 21 (2015), p. 32; A. C. Loux, 'The Great Rabbit Massacre: a "comedy of the commons"? Custom, community and rights of public access to the Links of St Andrews', *Liverpool Law Review*, 22 (2000), pp. 129–30; Jarman, 'Customary rights in Scots law', especially pp. 209–10. Although commons belonging to royal burghs were exempt from the Commonties Act 1695, that did not prevent division and enclosure: Adams, 'Legal geography', pp. 270, 299–300.

[129] Stevenson, *Anstruther*, pp. 37–9.

the common links as a rabbit warren generated long-running disputes with the burgh community which rumbled on from the sixteenth century to the nineteenth.[130]

In Scotland, the legal basis of use rights differed between royal burghs, where the corporation could claim rights of servitude over the common on behalf of the inhabitants, and burghs of barony, where rights on the commons were servitudes attached to individual properties rather than to the burgh as a body. In the eighteenth century, legal wrangling broke out over whether the use of common land near burghs as bleaching greens for drying linen (a necessity in the economy of many Scottish towns) constituted a legal right of servitude. By the mid-nineteenth century, a run of lawsuits had determined that it was, indeed, a community right.[131]

Thus, the legal framework of town commons in both England and Scotland increasingly separated them from rural commons across the early modern centuries. Control tended to become concentrated in the hands of an urban oligarchy acting as a town council or corporation and it was increasingly acknowledged that urban commons should be used to raise income for the common good of the urban community, as well as (or instead of) being exploited by conventional common rights.

THE LEGAL FRAMEWORK ON THE GROUND: BOUNDARIES OVER COMMON LAND

The legal scaffolding outlined in this chapter divided tracts of open waste into commons belonging to communities. Property rights required recognised boundaries. If the resources of a stretch of unenclosed hill, heath or marsh were to be exploited amicably, both lords and commoners needed to know where their common land ended and their neighbours' commons began. As touched on in several places in this chapter, the process of ascertaining and negotiating boundaries across common land was protracted. The break-up of intercommoned shire moors and the numerous disputes over boundaries during the colonisation of the twelfth and thirteenth centuries settled many boundaries across common land, but some remained contentious and some commons continued to be shared between communities well into the post-medieval age.[132] Where neighbouring communities jostled to appropriate sections of waste, place-names sometimes preserve memories of disputed boundaries, as in the frequent pairing of 'threap' (from OE *þreapian*, 'to dispute or argue over') with 'moor'/'muir', 'moss' and 'hill' across lowland Scotland.[133]

---

[130] Reid, 'Five centuries of dispute'; Loux, 'Great Rabbit Massacre'. See below, p. 100.

[131] A. L. Jarman, 'Urban commons: from customary use to community right on Scotland's bleaching greens', in A. Lewis, P. Brand and P. Mitchell (eds), *Law in the City: Proceedings of the Seventeenth British Legal History Conference, London 2005* (Dublin, 2007), pp. 319–45. See also Jarman, 'Customary rights in Scots law'.

[132] E.g. Burton Moor (Yorks. E.R.): McDonagh, 'Landscape, territory and common rights', pp. 82–5.

[133] G. W. S. Barrow, 'The uses of place-names and Scottish history – pointers and pitfalls', in S. Taylor (ed.), *The Uses of Place-Names* (Edinburgh, 1998), pp. 68, 71.

In England, after 1236, the provisions of the Statute of Merton would have encouraged the definition of manorial boundaries across the waste, as lords sought to be free to enclose tracts of rough grazing under their rights of approvement. Uncertain boundaries persisted in places, however, until tidied up during the process of Parliamentary enclosure or under the Tithe Commutation Act 1836, which empowered commissioners to determine disputed or ill-defined boundaries.[134] Yet the parcelling out of wastes between communities remains incomplete, as the label 'Lands common to the parishes of X and Y' on modern Ordnance Survey maps testifies.[135] In Scotland, by contrast, where lords lacked the statutory encouragement provided by Merton to divide shared wastes, creating new boundaries was deferred until commonties were divided between estates, mainly in the eighteenth and nineteenth centuries.

Once defined, the boundaries between commons were defended jealously, through periodic perambulations and by committing details of the boundary line to paper, especially in cases of challenge or dispute. Periodic boundary ridings by manorial and parish authorities also occurred, fixing the boundary in communal memory and passing this knowledge down the generations.[136] In Shetland, communal 'hagries' (literally 'pasture rides') under the auspices of the seigniorial courts played an identical role in reinforcing the boundaries of scattalds across moss and hill.[137]

Topography might almost dictate the pattern of boundary lines across the wastes, natural features such as rivers and streams or prominent watersheds often being used to divide larger tracts of waste between communities. The distribution of common land generated distinctive boundary patterns. Linear tracts of waste running along the edge of settled land were often divided into sections by roughly parallel boundaries between settlements, as in the Fens, the Lincolnshire heaths and marshes (Figure 8) or the North Downs in Surrey. Where a block of common land was surrounded by a ring of settlements, each claiming a segment of the waste, the boundaries sometimes converged on a point on the common. Particularly striking examples include Rymer Point (Norf.), where eleven parishes converged, the Dry Tree on Goonhilly Downs (Corn.), the meeting point of five parishes, and Six Hills on the Leicestershire–Nottinghamshire wolds, where eight parishes converged on the county boundary.[138] On Exmoor and

---

[134] See A. J. L. Winchester, 'Dividing lines in a moorland landscape: territorial boundaries in upland England', *Landscapes*, 1 (2) (2000), pp. 16–34; A. J. L. Winchester, *Discovering Parish Boundaries*, 2nd edn (Princes Risborough, 2000).

[135] Examples include Hamsterley Common (Dur.) (common to Hamsterley, Lynesack & Softley and South Bedburn), Fylingdales Moor (Yorks. N.R.) (common to Fylingdales and Hawsker-cum-Stainsacre), and the area of Dartmoor around Woodcock Hill (Devon) (common to Bridestowe and Sourton).

[136] For examples, see Wood, *Memory of the People*, p. 197 (Ashford, Derby., 1618); N. Whyte, *Inhabiting the Landscape: Place, Custom and Memory, 1500–1800* (Oxford, 2009), pp. 59–86, who maps recorded boundary perambulations in Norfolk, c.1550–1800 (p. 64); Winchester, *Parish Boundaries*, pp. 39–41.

[137] Smith, *Toons and Tenants*, pp. 43–4.

[138] Rackham, *History of the Countryside*, pp. 312, 356; H. S. A. Fox, 'The people of the Wolds in English settlement history', in M. Aston, D. Austin and C. Dyer (eds), *The Rural Settlements of Medieval England* (Oxford, 1989), pp. 87–9.

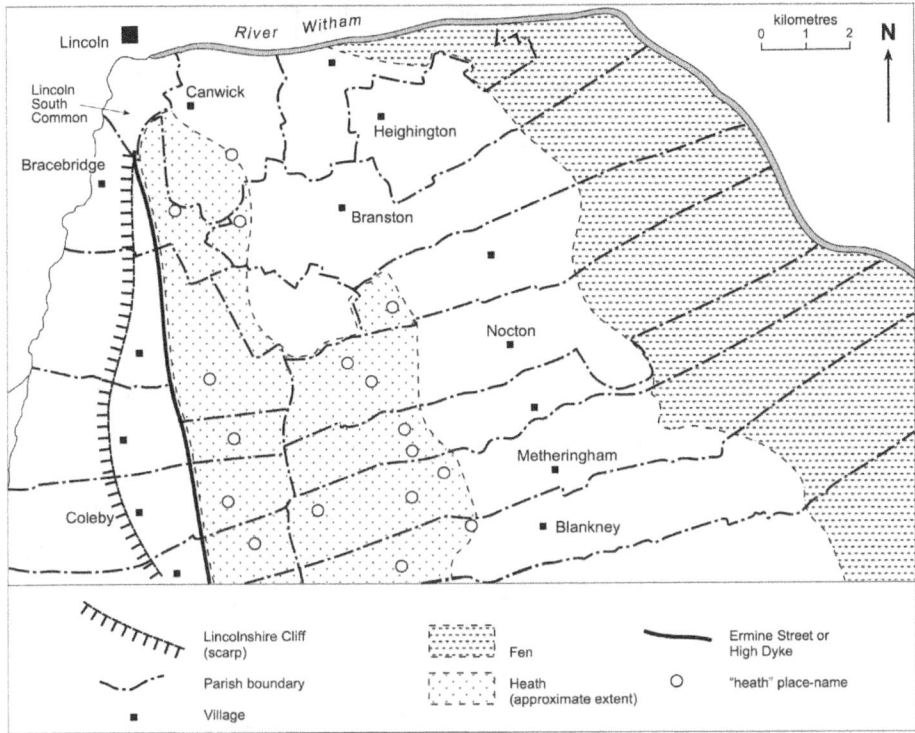

Figure 8. Parish boundaries and former common land, central Lincolnshire. The boundaries were drawn to give each parish a share of both heathland on the Lincolnshire Cliff ridge and wet fenland stretching to the River Witham.

Dartmoor, where the central core of moorland was royal forest, the division of the outer moors between settlements flanking the forests formed incomplete patterns of this type (Figure 9). On occasion, the agreement to fix a boundary line across the waste is documented but in most cases it is impossible to say whether boundaries were the result of being imposed from above (perhaps the implication of some of the most regular patterns) or negotiated between neighbouring communities.

How boundaries were marked on the ground also varied from place to place and over time. In some instances, a physical linear boundary was constructed to partition the wastes at a comparatively early date, such as the thirteenth-century dykes in the Fens or the banks and walls across Lakeland fells marking boundary lines between estates.[139] More often, 'mere' stones were set or pits dug, as in the Southern Uplands of Scotland in the early eighteenth century, when estate boundaries across the open hillsides were settled.[140] In the Highlands, where individual hamlets acquired exclusive use of parts of the waste, boundaries previously marked by cairns were formalised in some areas

---

[139] Darby, *Medieval Fenland*, pp. 75, 149; *Harvest*, pp. 29–30.

[140] M. Robson, *Dykes, Ditches and Disputes: A History of Boundary and Field Enclosures in the Borders* (privately printed, Isle of Lewis, 2004), pp. 35–9.

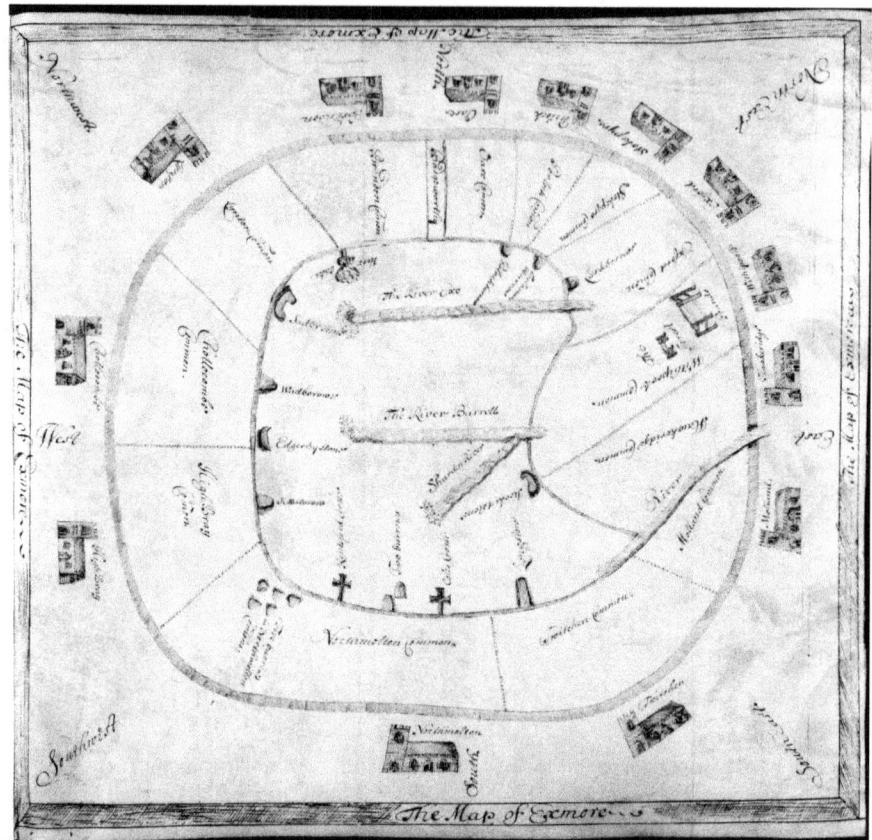

Figure 9. Plan of Exmoor, 1675. Stylised plan of Exmoor Forest, flanked by the commons belonging to the surrounding villages (represented by churches). Boundary markers across the open moorland, identifying the limits of the forest wastes, are shown prominently. They include boulders, crosses, a tree (the 'Hore Oake') and barrows ('burrowes'). The forest pounds for impounding stray livestock are shown on Withypool Common (TNA, MPB 1/54).

by physical walls or 'march dykes' in the later seventeenth and eighteenth centuries.[141] However, many boundaries across common land continued to take the form of sight lines across open country, running between intervisible boundary markers. Some markers were natural landmarks, like prominent boulders, rock outcrops and isolated trees, or pre-existing manmade features such as prehistoric barrows; others were deliberately placed as boundary markers, including stones, crosses, stakes, mounds and cairns (Figure 10).[142] They became points charged with meaning in an otherwise unmarked landscape, demarcating the limits of property rights over the waste.

---

[141] Dodgshon, *From Chiefs to Landlords*, p. 17.

[142] For examples of boundary markers across common land, see Whyte, *Inhabiting the Landscape*, pp. 66–74, 148–52 (re. Norfolk); Fox, *Dartmoor's Alluring Uplands*, pp. 174–9; Winchester, *Parish Boundaries*, pp. 46–54.

Figure 10. Boundary markers across open common land: Newby manor, near Ingleton, Yorkshire. (a, above) A natural boulder, perched on a limestone outcrop (at SD 734 780), marking the manorial boundary on Scales Moor. Recorded as 'Mossy Stone on Rock' in 1847 (TNA, IR30/43/234), and as 'the stone in the More' in 1754 (NYCRO, ZUC/1/3/1), it remains readily identifiable, despite being in a landscape with many rocks. (b, below) Boundary stone (at SD 728 723), where the manorial boundary runs as a sight line across the slopes of Ingleborough. Probably eighteenth-century in date, it is carved with the letters 'N' and 'I' for Newby and Ingleton.

These physical manifestations of boundaries created by the legal framework structured the use of common land, defining the resources available to each community. However, they were no more than a framework outlining the limits to property rights on the ground. The plurality of uses and users of a common inevitably engendered competition and even conflict over resources within its boundaries, so that systems of regulation were required. The next chapter turns to explore how local communities managed their commons in the later medieval and early modern centuries.

CHAPTER 3

MANAGING COMMUNAL RESOURCES

THE POTENTIALLY CONFLICTING INTERESTS of different users required effective regulatory systems to ensure that the exploitation of communal resources ran smoothly. Pressures on commons changed over time as demand for resources fluctuated in the face of population growth or decline, and economic and technological change. Consequently, patterns of use depended on local circumstances and could vary over the space of a few miles and over comparatively short periods of time. Regulating commons therefore needed to be tailored to local circumstance.

In the medieval and early modern periods, most common land was regulated through the institutions of the manor or estate to which it belonged, the rules they formulated creating a body of customary law, particular to the locality. Across Britain, the regulatory institutions were local seigniorial courts: the manor court (especially the court leet) in England and Wales; the barony court in Scotland; the 'swainmote' court in forest areas. Called by the lord and presided over by his steward, the court generally required the attendance of all tenants, from whom was drawn a jury who determined cases and formulated rules. Its principal role was to uphold the lord's rights and privileges and also to foster harmonious relations within the local community.[1]

Regulations made and policed by a court sought to achieve those two ends and were specific to the estate in question. In some places (especially in the Midland and northern counties of England), the rules and the sanctions which applied when they were broken were drawn together into 'pain lists' laying out the suites of byelaws which, together with more formal articles of enquiry, formed a checklist of matters to be looked into by the court (Figure 11).[2] Comparatively few such written statements of

---

[1] For manor courts, see M. Bailey, *The English Manor c.1200–c.1500* (Manchester, 2002), pp. 167–89; C. Harrison, 'Manor courts and the governance of Tudor England', in C. Brooks and M. Lobban (eds), *Communities and Courts in Britain 1150–1900* (London, 1997), pp. 43–59; C. W. Brooks, *Law, Politics and Society in Early Modern England* (Cambridge, 2008), pp. 241–77; B. Waddell, 'Governing England through the manor courts, 1550–1850', *The Historical Journal*, 55 (2) (2012), pp. 279–315; for barony courts, see W. C. Dickinson (ed.), *The Court Book of the Barony of Carnwath, 1523–1542* (Edinburgh, 1937), pp. xi–cxii. For their role in managing resources, see R. S. Dilley, 'The Cumberland court leet and the use of the common lands', *Trans CWAAS*, new ser. 67 (1967), pp. 125–51; *Harvest*, pp. 33–48 and *passim*.

[2] For published examples, see *Harvest*, pp. 152–66; R. Sharpe France, 'Two custumals of the manor of Cockerham, 1326 and 1483', *Transactions of the Lancashire & Cheshire Antiquarian*

byelaws survive, so many courts' deliberations presumably continued to be structured around oral memory of local custom. Taken together, pain lists, articles of enquiry and the decisions of the courts themselves can be used to reconstruct how regulations evolved across the years, particularly in the two centuries 1550–1750, from which most records survive. Even commons which fell outside manorial regulation were governed by comparable suites of byelaws. The mid-sixteenth-century 'Rewell and ordynaunce of Wallyngfen', the intercommoned wetland in the East Riding of Yorkshire, governed from 1425 to 1781 by an extra-manorial court, was closely modelled on manorial pains,[3] as were the fen byelaws laid down by the township communities of Spalding and Pinchbeck (Lincs.) in the fifteenth and sixteenth centuries.[4]

The courts appointed officers to supervise the exercise of common rights and to bring anyone in breach of the rules to court. Some appointed a small committee of 'bylawmen' to police the regulations; others charged officers with overseeing specific uses of common land: 'pinders' to supervise the common pastures, impounding any stock which was not there legally; 'moss reeves' or 'mosslookers' to manage peat- and turf-cutting rights, for example.[5] Offenders were presented at the court and, if deemed guilty, were usually subject to a financial penalty. Although the earliest statements of manorial rules tend to specify the offence but not to prescribe the sanction,[6] court orders and lists of pains from the sixteenth and seventeenth centuries almost invariably detail the penalty to be imposed 'for every default'.

However, a court's formal rules sometimes stood at arm's length from the day-to-day management of common land. There is ample evidence of less formal rule-making bodies, whose decisions were not always written down. Village or neighbourhood meetings, outside the formal structures of seigniorial courts, were found both in medieval lowland England and in the more pastoral communities of northern England and Scotland, where the term 'byrlaw' (from Old Norse *byjar-log*, a 'law community' or 'law district') survived to describe them.[7] Sometimes regulations made by such

---

Society 64 (1954), pp. 38–54; W. Cunningham (ed.), 'Common rights at Cottenham and Stretham in Cambridgeshire', *Camden Miscellany, Vol. XII* (London, 1910), pp. 173–287.

[3] Hull History Centre, U DDBA/10/2. I am grateful to David Crouch for allowing me to use his transcript of this document. See D. Crouch and B. McDonagh, 'Turf wars: conflict and cooperation in the management of Wallingfen (East Yorkshire), 1281–1781', *AgHR*, 64 (2016), pp. 133–56.

[4] H. E. Hallam, 'The fen bylaws of Spalding and Pinchbeck', *Lincolnshire Architectural and Archaeological Society*, 10 (1963), pp. 40–56.

[5] See *Harvest*, pp. 44–5.

[6] In medieval byelaws from southern English villages, penalties differentiated to fit each regulation occur only from *c*.1350 (W. O. Ault, *Open-Field Husbandry and the Village Community: A Study of Agrarian By-laws in Medieval England* (Philadelphia, 1965, *passim*) and medieval jury charges from northern England specify offences but not penalties: BL, Additional MS 40,010, ff. 185v.–186v.; *Harvest*, pp. 152–9; Durham University Library Archives & Special Collections, Chester Deanery Manorial Records, bundle 3/2.

[7] W. O. Ault, 'Village assemblies in medieval England', *Album Helen Maud Cam*, vol. I (Louvain, 1960), pp. 13–35; Ault, *Open-Field Husbandry*, pp. 40–54; *Harvest*, pp. 42–5; Dickinson, *Carnwath*, pp. cxiii–cxvi.

MANAGING COMMUNAL RESOURCES

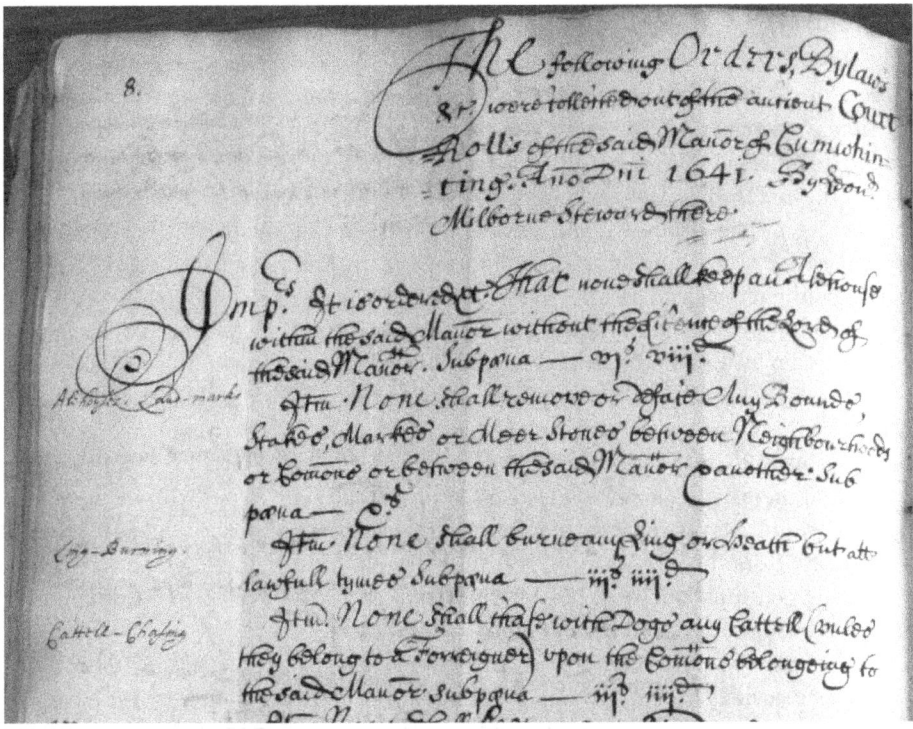

Figure 11. 'Pains' from Cumwhinton, near Carlisle, Cumberland. Part of a list of twenty-seven orders extracted from the court rolls in 1641. The third and fourth entries concern common land, forbidding heath-burning outside the legal times and outlawing the chasing of cattle on the common with dogs, unless they were 'foreign' cattle grazing illegally (CAS, D/AY/3/2).

bodies were copied into the court record, but references to agreements made by meetings outside the courts make it clear that an unwritten body of grassroots regulation also existed.

Byelaws articulated local custom. At one level they were grounded in the need to provide local responses to particular social, economic and environmental challenges, but they also contained a core of common custom, parts of which had a national – or even trans-national – distribution. Two regulations, in particular, are encountered so widely that they may be considered to have been almost universal. The first was a prohibition on putting diseased livestock, particularly scabbed horses, to graze on the common, in order to control infection. It was a widespread and probably ancient rule, found on the continent as well as in England.[8] The fifteenth-century jury charge from Fountains Abbey (Yorks.) stated that 'it is agans the lawe' (presumably meaning the local customary law) for a man to keep a scabbed horse other than on his own

---

[8] *Harvest*, p. 103; M. De Moor, L. Shaw-Taylor and P. S. Warde (eds), *The Management of Common Land in North-West Europe. c.1500–1850* (Turnhout, 2002), p. 133.

property.[9] Similar regulations recorded elsewhere in the fifteenth century[10] suggest that this customary rule was deeply embedded well before it was reinforced by a statute of 1540, which forbade putting infected horses on any common.[11]

Similarly ancient and ubiquitous was the requirement that pigs should be kept ringed, to prevent them from grubbing, and often 'bowed' or 'yoked' as well, to prevent them breaking through hedges. The byelaw was widespread across England,[12] a similar rule is recorded in Flanders,[13] and settlers transferred the rule to New England in the seventeenth century.[14] Again, custom informed statute, when an act of 1543 forbade putting unringed pigs into woodland.[15]

It is hardly surprising that different communities met the challenges of managing common land by formulating similar regulations. These were common-sense solutions to universal problems. How deep their roots lay is difficult to judge. Identical responses in communities far apart need not imply that they descended from a common rootstock but it seems likely that many were drawn from deep-seated agrarian custom, evolving orally long before being recorded in courts rolls and pain lists. Byelaws were also framed within the wider legal context, both of the common law and of statute, particularly from the mid-sixteenth century, when courts leet in England were given additional statutory duties, some of which related to the management of common resources, as noted above.[16]

The upsurge in the recording of pains in the century or so after 1570 must also be seen in a wider cultural context. It was almost certainly driven by the need for clarity in local law at a time of stress and litigation, when rising population generated social conflict and tension over access to resources.[17] A sharper articulation of the law of property was also advantageous to landowners as 'improvement' changed their perceptions, instilling a drive to realise the economic potential of their estates, which, in turn, heralded an attack on common land.[18]

---

[9] BL, Additional MS 40,010, f. 186.

[10] E.g. at Windermere (Westmld), undated, but pre-1477: *Harvest*, p. 156 (no. 1.27); Cockerham (Lancs.), 1326, 1483: Sharpe France, 'Two custumals', pp. 43, 48; Lartington (Yorks. N.R.), 1416: NYCRO, ZPS 1/2; and Wimbledon (Surrey), 1487: *Wimbledon Ct R.*, pp. 48–9.

[11] 'The Breeding of Horses' (32 Hen. VIII, c.13).

[12] *Harvest*, pp. 103–4; Ault, *Open-Field Husbandry*, *passim* (indexed p. 101).

[13] De Moor et al., *Management of Common Land*, p. 132.

[14] As at Sandwich, Connecticut, in 1638: F. Freeman, *The History of Cape Cod: The Annals of the Thirteen Towns of Barnstable County, Volume II* (Boston, 1862), p. 40.

[15] 35 Hen. VIII, c.17, sec. xvii.

[16] See F. J. C. Hearnshaw, *Leet Jurisdiction in England, Especially as Illustrated by the Records of the Court Leet of Southampton* (Southampton, 1908), pp. 122–30.

[17] R. W. Hoyle, 'Introduction', in *Custom, Improvement and the Landscape in Early Modern Britain* (Farnham, 2011), pp. 9–11; J. Healey 'The political culture of the English commons, c.1550–1650', *AgHR*, 60 (2) (2012), pp. 266–87.

[18] M. Leslie and T. Raylor (eds), *Culture and Cultivation in Early Modern England: Writing and the Land* (Leicester, 1992), pp. 35–57 (A. McRae on husbandry manuals); 64–8 (A. Low on enclosure). The scale of early modern enclosure is discussed below, pp. 132–4.

As the law concerning property became more acute, the workings of manor courts became more formalised. Among the numerous farming manuals and legal treatises published across the sixteenth and seventeenth centuries were court-keeping manuals, guiding estate stewards in the right ordering for holding courts baron and courts leet.[19] The power of the printed word would itself affect the deliberations of a court, tending to privilege the manual (and the influence of its owner, the steward) over local custom and oral tradition, and thus moving byelaw-making one step away from the grassroots. Other factors behind the upsurge in the recording of pains in the sixteenth and seventeenth centuries may have included a desire on the part of lords to maximise their revenue from courts (for which a clear statement of byelaws and penalties would be invaluable) and the spread of the vernacular and of literacy, a cultural shift which encouraged the recording of pains in English for the first time.[20]

In formulating rules regulating common rights, the courts aimed, first, to protect the lord's interests by defining more precisely the limits of what could be taken from the common and by whom, and, second, to foster 'good neighbourhood' in the exercise of common rights by laying down a framework of neighbourly conduct to minimise potential disputes. In practice, three main strategies were available to achieve those ends. Courts could restrict the use of a resource by specifying quantitative (but not necessarily numerical) limits; they could place spatial limitations on the exercise of a right by allocating sections of the common for particular purposes; and they could impose seasonal restrictions by enforcing closed seasons on the taking of particular resources. Running through their deliberations was a concern to limit the potential for conflict when different uses of the common cut across each other.

REGULATING GRAZING RIGHTS

Limiting Quantity

The courts' overarching concern was to prevent 'overcharging' of the common, by both excluding the livestock of those without a common right and ensuring that legitimate graziers observed the correct limits. Control of grazing numbers first required the common to be secured against illegal grazing by outsiders. Commons were therefore driven regularly to gather in all animals grazing there and any 'foreign' livestock were impounded in the manorial pinfold. Some manors in Cumbria, for example, appointed 'pounders' or 'grassmen' to drive the common once a month and impound all animals which did not belong to tenants of the manor.[21] Then, limits needed to be placed on those with a legal grazing right. Preventing their livestock from overcharging

---

[19] Those printed up to 1546 are listed in F. W. Maitland and W. P. Baildon, *The Court Baron* (London, 1891), pp. 3–4. Later manuals included J. Adames, *The Order of Keeping a Court Leet and Court Baron* (several editions from 1603); W. Sheppard, *The Court-Keepers Guide* (numerous editions from 1649).

[20] See Harrison, 'Manor courts and the governance of Tudor England'.

[21] C. E. Searle, 'Customary tenants and the enclosure of the Cumbrian commons', *Northern History*, 29 (1993), pp. 132–3. See also below, p. 219.

the common was achieved by one of the two legal principles introduced in Chapter 2, either common 'without number', which was nevertheless limited by the rule of levancy and couchancy, or a stinted right, which limited the commoner to a specified number of livestock.

The over-wintering rule inherent in levancy and couchancy prevented commoners from sub-letting their rights in exchange for a fee. Articles of enquiry of c.1400, probably from the east Midlands, required the court to ask 'if any commoner maintains any beasts in your common of strange men that be not commoners, taking profit unto himself in surcharge of your common'.[22] Similar rules against taking in the cattle of 'out men' are found in other fifteenth-century records.[23] Yet the practice persisted, being explicitly forbidden in both fenland and upland manors in the seventeenth century, and implicitly ruled out by reiterations of the principles of levancy and couchancy.[24] Agistment of this type was repeatedly cited as a factor in the overstocking of commons in Cumbria in the early eighteenth century.[25]

At the heart of the rule of 'levancy and couchancy' was a desire to ensure equitable access to the common. A right of common 'without number' implicitly presupposed that, if adhered to, there was no danger of the carrying capacity of the common being exceeded. It also assumed a simple farming model in which each holding possessed a flock or herd which was supported in winter solely by the produce of the farmland. These assumptions were already becoming anachronistic by the sixteenth and seventeenth centuries, in the face of increased trade, including droving and short-term purchases of livestock for fattening, and buying in hay for winter fodder.[26] However, manor courts with unstinted commons continued to reiterate the rule of levancy and couchancy into the eighteenth century, sometimes in the Lake District apparently in an attempt to forbid or at least limit the longstanding practice of wintering young sheep away on lowland pastures.[27]

Stinting, by contrast, assumed that some idea of the total number of livestock that should be allowed to graze on a common was known.[28] Once the carrying capacity had been calculated, the total stint could be apportioned between those with grazing rights. A rare glimpse of the process comes from Libberton (Lanarkshire) in 1542 when some of the older and better-informed commoners were ordered to 'say what the

---

[22] J. S Beckerman, 'The articles of presentment of a court leet and court baron, in English, c.1400', *Bulletin of Institute of Historical Research*, 47 (1974), p. 232 (English modernised).

[23] Hull History Centre, U DDBA/10/2 (Wallingfen, 1430); Sharpe France, 'Two custumals', p. 50.

[24] Cunningham, 'Common rights at Cottenham and Stretham', pp. 233, 278. For uplands see *Harvest*, pp. 93–8.

[25] Searle, 'Customary tenants and enclosure', pp. 140–4.

[26] *Harvest*, pp. 81–2.

[27] As at Eskdale between 1659 and 1778: *Contested Common Land*, p. 96; at Nether Wasdale: below, p. 218; and Derwentfells: *Harvest*, pp. 96–7; Searle, 'Customary tenants and enclosure', pp. 136–7.

[28] The following paragraphs draw on A. J. L. Winchester and E. A. Straughton, 'Stints and sustainability: managing stock levels on common land in England, c.1600–2006', *AgHR*, 58 (2010), pp. 30–48.

common may bear'. Thereafter each tenant was to put to the common only as many beasts as was thought fitting for his holding; overstinting ('ouresowmes') would be punished severely.[29]

Stints were usually expressed as 'gates' in northern England, 'leazes' in southern counties, and 'soums' in Scotland, each 'cattlegate' or 'cowleaze', for example, giving the right to graze one horned beast, a 'sheepgate' or 'sheep leaze' the right to graze a sheep.[30] More local terms included 'beast-goings' in Suffolk and 'shutes' in Somerset.[31] Equivalency formulae were used to determine the number of other livestock which could be grazed for each stint, five to ten sheep per cattlegate and two cattlegates per horse being typical ratios.[32] In early stinting arrangements the number of stints was generally determined by the fiscal rating of a holding in virgates or 'yardlands' (in southern England), bovates or 'oxgangs' (in northern counties), ploughgates (in southern Scotland) or merklands or davochs (further north).[33] Later stinting arrangements sometimes used the amount of rent or tax paid. The aim was to link a grazing right to the size or value of the holding, as was inherent in the rule of levancy and couchancy, but to express it in numerical terms.

Stinting could also help to ensure a match between stocking levels and the carrying capacity of a common, since the currency value of a stint could be adjusted to local conditions, by varying either the relationship between stints and fiscal assessment or the equivalency formulae for different species and types of livestock.[34] Stinting also coped better with the realities of early modern farming. A commoner could purchase animals to put on the common, as long as he kept within his numerical limit; his right was no longer governed by the rule of levancy and couchancy. Ultimately, stinting could sever the link between a grazing right and the land to which it was attached, striking at the heart of legal understandings of common right.

Many early stinted grazings took the form of separate communal cow pastures and ox pastures, which were not, strictly speaking, common land. Found widely across the Midlands and northern England, some had medieval roots; others were enclosed from

---

[29] Dickinson, *Carnwath*, p. 210.
[30] For 'gates' see *Harvest*, pp. 71–2, 83; the term was also used in the north Midland counties: *VCH Staffs.* VII, p. 19; W. E. Tate, *The Parish Chest: A Study of the Records of Parochial Administration in England*, 3rd edn (Chichester, [1969] 1983), p. 259 (Clayworth, Notts.). 'Leazes' as units of grazing are recorded widely in southern counties, e.g. *VCH Som.* III, pp. 5, 44–5, 171; *VCH Wilts.* IX, pp. 70, 146; *VCH Sussex* VI (pt I), pp. 83, 198, 208–9, 254, 263–4.
[31] P. M. Warner, 'Blything Hundred: a study in the development of settlement, AD 400–1400' (PhD thesis, University of Leicester, 1982), pp. 229–33; *VCH Som.* V, p. 105; X, p. 130.
[32] For examples, see *Harvest*, pp. 71–2; *Contested Common Land*, pp. 44, 99, 117; I. D. Whyte, *Agriculture and Society in Seventeenth-Century Scotland* (Edinburgh, 1979), p. 83; R. A. Dodgshon, *From Chiefs to Landlords: Social and Economic Change in the Western Highlands and Islands, c.1493–1820* (Edinburgh, 1998), p. 175; A. Bil, *The Shieling 1600–1840: The Case of the Central Scottish Highlands* (Edinburgh, 1990), p. 136.
[33] A. Ross, 'Scottish environmental history and the (mis)use of Soums', *AgHR*, 54 (2006), pp. 213–28; Bil, *The Shieling*, pp. 135–8; Dodgshon, *Chiefs to Landlords*, pp. 143–5, 167–9, 174–5.
[34] For examples from Perthshire, see Bil, *The Shieling*, pp. 135–7.

the waste in the two centuries c.1450 to c.1650.[35] Writing in 1523, Fitzherbert noted that many settlements had 'a commyn close taken in out of the commen or feldes ... for their oxen or kyen or other catell, in the whiche close every man is stynted and sette to a certayntie howe many beestes he shall have in the same'.[36] Some were 'commonable closes' in the open fields,[37] but many were sections of rough pasture, separated from the common waste and managed as a shared resource, providing grazing close to the farm for the milk cows and oxen which required intensive tending.[38] Although they formed an integral part of a community's communal rough grazings and were tantamount to common land, many did not fall within the strict legal definition of a common. When the lord retained no residual interest in the grazing (as was often the case), a stint became a sole profit rather than a profit in common. Moreover, stintholders often co-owned the pasture, so that ownership of the soil no longer lay with the lord of the manor.[39] By the sixteenth century – in the Pennines at least – rights in stinted pastures were becoming separate units of property, capable of being bought, sold or leased independently of holdings of land.[40]

On common land proper, stinting was often a response to grazing pressures with which the less transparent rule of levancy and couchancy had failed to cope. Joan Thirsk pointed out many years ago that unstinted systems survived longer in upland areas where the acreage of common land was much greater than in the lowlands.[41] In the constrained grazing regimes on the fields and meadows of open-field villages in Midland England, stints were being applied from the thirteenth century.[42] In these areas, where comparatively little common land survived, the stints limiting grazing rights on the fallow fields probably extended to common on the wastes as well, though this is rarely stated.[43]

Explicit references to stinted wastes are found by the fourteenth century. Overburdening of a common pasture at Wall with Pipehill (Staffs.) led to the imposition of a stint of 100 sheep, 6 oxen, 4 cows and 4 heifers for each virgate in 1370, while grazing rights on downs and heathland in Sussex were being measured in 'leazes' by

---

[35] *VCH Yorks. E.R.* VII, p. 154 (stinted pasture at Marton, 1322); *Harvest*, pp. 69–70.

[36] J. Fitzherbert, *The Boke of Surveyeng and Improume[n]tes* (London, 1523), f. iii^v.

[37] As in Worcestershire: B. K. Roberts, 'Field systems of the West Midlands', in A. R. H. Baker and R. A. Butlin (eds), *Studies of Field Systems in the British Isles* (Cambridge, 1973), p. 203.

[38] Baker and Butlin, *Studies of Field Systems*, pp. 135 (north-east); 203 (west Midlands); 248–9 (east Midlands); *Harvest*, pp. 68–73 (northern English uplands); R. T. Fieldhouse, 'Agriculture in Wensleydale from 1600 to the present day', *Northern History*, 16 (1980), pp. 172–3.

[39] *Gadsden*, § 1-47; B. Harris and G. Ryan, *An Outline of the Law Relating to Common Land* (London, 1967), §§ 1-50–1-53.

[40] For examples, see Winchester and Straughton, 'Stints and sustainability', p. 35n.

[41] J. Thirsk (ed.), *Agrarian History of England and Wales IV (1500–1640)* (Cambridge, 1967), pp. 12, 182–4.

[42] Winchester and Straughton, 'Stints and sustainability', p. 34.

[43] An exception was at Fisherwick (Staffs.) where Longdon court fixed the stint for sheep on the waste and the fallow fields in 1561: *VCH Staffs.* XIV, p. 249.

the fourteenth century.[44] Some wetland commons were stinted by the late Middle Ages, as were some upland commons, where stinting may have been a legacy of agistment on forest pastures.[45]

By the sixteenth and seventeenth centuries stinting was widespread on common land, particularly for sheep, and was found across a range of environments. On manors in the south-west Midlands, sheep were widely stinted by the later fifteenth and early sixteenth century, often at the rate of sixty sheep per yardland.[46] Downland in Wiltshire was often stinted for sheep,[47] as were both downland and heath at Studland on the Isle of Purbeck (Dorset) by the 1580s.[48] Halstock Down (Devon), a small common on the edge of Dartmoor, was stinted for cattle in the summer months in 1590.[49] At Wimbledon (Surrey) a scale of stints was laid down by the court in 1559, and further stinting was ordered in 1590 to resolve a dispute between the inhabitants of Putney and Barnes who intercommoned along the township boundary.[50] By the seventeenth century, stinting is recorded on fen and marsh in Cambridgeshire,[51] on the wet 'carrs' and moors in low-lying parts of the East Riding of Yorkshire,[52] and on heaths at Bladon (Oxon.) and in the environs of London, at Harefield, Acton and Chelsea.[53] These examples were part of a wider trend on lowland commons in the centuries 1550 to 1750. Janette Neeson concluded that 'almost all' Northamptonshire manors made stinting orders during the eighteenth century, for example.[54]

Clear evidence that overstocking prompted stinting to be introduced or modified is sometimes found. At Havering (Essex) the 'surcharged' state of the wastes led

---

[44] *VCH Staffs.* XIV, p. 292; *VCH Sussex* V (pt I), p. 153 (Eastergate, 1378–79); VI (pt I), pp. 263–4 (Wiston, 1357).

[45] Deep Carr common, Burton Pidsea was stinted by 1381: *VCH Yorks. E.R.* VII, p. 33; Outwell, in the Fens, by the fifteenth century: H. C. Darby, *The Medieval Fenland* (Newton Abbot, 1974), p. 70. Above, p. 40.

[46] C. Dyer, *Lords and Peasants in a Changing Society* (Cambridge, 1980), p. 325.

[47] Examples include Ogbourne Maizey (stinting recorded in sixteenth century): *VCH Wilts.* XII, p. 147; Upton Scudamore's rights on Norridge commons (recorded 1582): *VCH Wilts.* VIII, p. 85; Upavon (recorded 1609): *VCH Wilts.* X, p. 167; Chilmark (recorded 1631): *VCH Wilts.* XIII, p. 120; and Compton Bassett (recorded 1700): *VCH Wilts.* XVII, p. 157.

[48] M. Forrest (ed.), *Ralph Treswell's Survey of Sir Christopher Hatton's Lands in Purbeck 1585–6*, Dorset Record Society 19 (Dorchester, 2017), pp. 159–64.

[49] H. Fox, *Dartmoor's Alluring Uplands: Transhumance and Pastoral Management in the Middle Ages* (Exeter, 2012), p. 86.

[50] *Wimbledon Ct R.*, pp. 15–17, 26, 110–19, 156–8.

[51] For example, in the Cambridgeshire Fens at Fen Drayton (agreement 1680); Swavesey (suggestions of stinting 1620); and Willingham (stints recorded 1655): *VCH Cambs.* IX, pp. 296, 388, 406.

[52] For example, at Sutton by Hull and Atwick on the coast (*VCH Yorks. E.R.* I, p. 474; VII, p. 210) and further inland on the flatlands south-east of York at Riccall, Thorganby, Thornton and Wilberfoss (*VCH Yorks. E.R.* III, pp. 85, 117, 177, 194).

[53] *VCH Oxon.* XII, p. 25; *VCH Mddx* III, p. 248; VII, p. 23; XII, p. 148.

[54] J. M. Neeson, *Commoners: Common Right, Enclosure and Social Change in England, 1700–1820* (Cambridge, 1993), p. 113.

to the introduction of stinted grazing rights in 1566.[55] At Wimblington (Cambs.), the fen commons had become overstocked by 1669, when a detailed agreement introduced stinting arrangements; further south, at Comberton, it was said in 1672 that the traditional stint (three cattle per commonable messuage and three cattle and fifteen sheep per half yardland) had failed to prevent the common from becoming overburdened; the stint was therefore reduced.[56] In Norfolk, stinting was seen as the answer to achieve the 'better usage' of Banham Common in the agreement of 1630, establishing a scheme which was generous to cottagers.[57] The halving of stints 'on the hill' at Semley (Wilts.) in 1668 and on Bladon Heath (Oxon.) in the eighteenth century again suggests that overgrazing was a problem.[58]

Stinting was likewise seen as a solution to overgrazing on some large upland commons in northern England by the end of the eighteenth century. Grassroots efforts to impose stinting in the Lake District are recorded by manor courts at Nether Wasdale (Cumb.), where an abortive attempt to stint was made in 1769, and Coniston (Lancs.), where the court attempted to replace the rule of levancy and couchancy by limiting grazing rights to ten sheep (defined as one cattlegate) for every shilling of customary rent in 1796.[59] Likewise, graziers at Twisleton (Yorks. W.R.) proposed a scheme to stint Scales Moor in 1810 at the rate of one beastgate for every shilling of Land Tax paid.[60] None of these schemes stood the test of time, the court at Coniston reverting to the principles of levancy and couchancy in 1818; a revised and more formal stinting agreement being drawn up for Scales Moor in 1842. These cases suggest that stinting was seen as a way of imposing order on common land at a time when 'common without number' was no longer effective.

The benefits of stinting surfaced early in literature on improvement. Writing in 1523, Fitzherbert argued that all common pastures, including moors and heaths, should be stinted, 'for elles wolde the ryche men in the begynnynge of Somer bye shepe and other maner of catell and eate up the commens', thus oppressing the poor. In his mind, the absence of stinting led to a free-for-all.[61] Over a century later, Walter Blyth saw 'commoning without stint' as an impediment to agricultural advancement, as everyone would put as many cattle as they could on an unstinted common, 'and so Overstock the same'. However, if a common were stinted in relation to the 'Proportion of Land or Dwellings to which the Common [right] is due', those with insufficient livestock

---

[55] M. K. McIntosh, *A Community Transformed: The Manor and Liberty of Havering, 1500–1620* (Cambridge, 1991), pp. 127–8.
[56] *VCH Cambs*. IV, p. 113; V, p. 184.
[57] A. Wood, *The Memory of the People: Custom and Popular Senses of the Past in Early Modern England* (Cambridge, 2013), p. 326.
[58] *VCH Wilts*. XIII, p. 74; *VCH Oxon*. XII, p. 25.
[59] Below, p. 218; E. A. Straughton, *Common Grazing in the Northern English Uplands, 1800–1965* (Lampeter, 2008), pp. 149–52.
[60] *Contested Common Land*, pp. 116–17.
[61] Fitzherbert, *Boke of Surveyeng*, ff. iii^v–iiii.

to exercise their right could derive income from letting their stints to others.[62] Blyth thus identified the twin advantages of stinting as being to prevent overstocking and to enable pasture rights to be converted into marketable assets. In this, he was anticipating the arguments of later writers.[63]

As will be discussed in later chapters, stinting became an integral part of the move towards increased regulation of common land in the nineteenth century. It had so many advantages that the survival of common 'without number' is perhaps surprising. Yet the Royal Commission on Common Land estimated that around 46 per cent of common land in England and Wales remained unstinted grazing land in 1958.[64]

Heafs and Sheepwalks

Assigning separate grazing areas to individual commoners was widespread on upland commons, making use of the territorial 'hefting' instinct of sheep, whereby each flock had its own home or 'lairing place'. Recognising a flock's grazing ground as the exclusive preserve of a particular farm became a key tool in the day-to-day management of pasture rights on the hills. Individual sheep heafs were the norm on common land across the Lake District by the sixteenth century;[65] a presentment at Loweswater court in 1479 for 'wrongful *hefyng* in the mountains' suggesting that the practice was established by late medieval times.[66] In Eskdale, the allocation of grazing to individuals extended to the lower fells as well, sections of which were assigned to specific farms as cow pastures in 1587.[67] The wide-open hills of mid-Wales were divided by the nineteenth century into closely-defined 'sheepwalks' assigned to each farm (Figure 12),[68] and comparable arrangements were found in Orkney, where a 'cloggand' or 'clogang' (a term derived from Old Norse *klaufa-gangr*, 'place frequented by cloven-hoofed animals') was the part of a common restricted to the grazing animals of an individual or a small group of farms.[69]

It did not generally involve physical demarcation, though a dispute over grazing on the slopes of Sca Fell (Cumb.) in 1749 was resolved by placing a line of stones to mark the boundary between heafs.[70] Most boundaries were known but invisible, the heafs and sheepwalks fragmenting many upland commons in the minds of the commoners into a mosaic of areas which were, for grazing purposes, tantamount to private property.

---

[62] W. Blyth, *The English Improver Improved* (London, 1653 edn), unpaginated section [dedicatory epistle, 4th prejudice].
[63] See Winchester and Straughton, 'Stints and sustainability', pp. 45–8.
[64] *RCCL Rep.*, p. 22, para. 73.
[65] *Harvest*, pp. 109–13, 129–38. In contemporary records, 'heaf' is sometimes rendered 'heath'. For descriptions of heafs in the Lake District, see below, p. 220; A. J. L. Winchester, *The Language of the Landscape* (Dent, 2019), pp. 123–6.
[66] Cockermouth Castle muniments, box 299/6, Loweswater court, 24 September 1479.
[67] *Harvest*, pp. 110–11; *Contested Common Land*, pp. 94–6.
[68] *Contested Common Land*, pp. 94–7, 141–4.
[69] W. P. L. Thomson, *Orkney: Land and People* (Kirkwall, 2008), p. 248.
[70] CAS, DNT/10, articles of agreement, 1749.

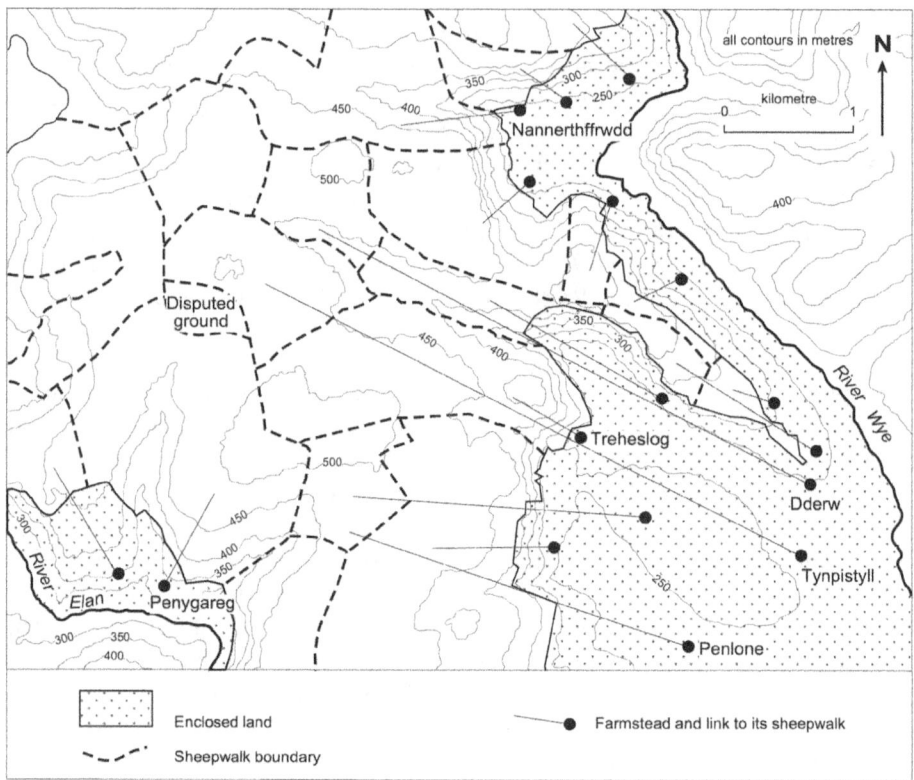

Figure 12. Sheepwalks, Cwmdeuddwr Common, Radnorshire. Source: Elan Valley Estate Office and Dderw Estate Office, plans.

Managing sheep heafs formed much of the courts' work in some Lake District manors, as they sought to resolve disputes and foster 'good neighbourhood' by confirming the boundaries between heafs, reiterating custom or tweaking the layout of heafs as circumstances required. In one instance, at New Hutton (Westmld) in 1723, the tenants agreed to allow a farmer whose heaf was insufficient for his stock of sheep to have extra grazing on the outer edge of the common, 'in order to prevent Incroachments'. This both suggests that only parts of the common were divided into heafs at that date and that heafing was seen as a means of securing the boundaries of a manor's wastes from neighbouring intruders.[71]

Although few lists, let alone maps, of heafs survive, these were deep-seated customary arrangements, giving each farm exclusive rights to a defined part of the common. If sheep strayed, no one was to 'hounde and beat' them from his heaf; nor to keep sheep anywhere other than on the heaf assigned to his farm; nor to drive his sheep through another man's heaf. No one was to bring his sheep down another farm's 'downfall' except in severe weather and then he was to 'carrie them back againe as the

---

[71] CAS, DLONS/L5/2/11/253.

snowe thawes and to followe it'.⁷² In Orkney, no one was to go through his neighbour's 'cloggand' with a sheep dog, except in the presence of reputable witnesses.⁷³

On the hills of Wales, the exclusive rights exercised by individual commoners on their sheepwalks were a form of virtual enclosure, which resulted in disputes over the legal status of sheepwalks in the nineteenth century. In mid-Wales, the section of common assigned to a farm was its *libert* (a term derived from the English 'liberty') but might embrace the grazing grounds of several separate flocks. Each of these subsections, equivalent to a heaf, was in Welsh termed *arhosfa* (literally 'staying place') or *cynefin* ('haunt'), mirroring the northern English term 'lairing place' and expressing the sense of belonging between a flock and its hillside.⁷⁴

The earliest explicit references to sheepwalks on the Welsh hill commons date from the mid-eighteenth century, though it was said of northern Cardiganshire in 1747 that the practice had existed 'time out of mind'.⁷⁵ An early indication that part of the waste might be deemed an integral part of a farm comes from Llanwrthwl (Brec.), where a deed of 1624 explicitly included 60 acres (24 ha) of waste or common as part of a holding.⁷⁶ There are suggestions that the division of commons into sheepwalks may have intensified in the eighteenth and nineteenth centuries. As reductions in sheep numbers since the 1990s have shown, a certain stocking level is required to maintain sheepwalk boundaries, implying that sheepwalks could only have been defined with the precision seen in the nineteenth century once sheep numbers had risen to a critical level. That may have been the context in the later eighteenth century, when landowners in north Wales were said to have converted wastes into private sheepwalks by requiring tenants to graze the common adjacent to their farms. The Crown agent claimed in 1835 that, having established sheepwalks, proprietors were claiming the wastes as their own property.⁷⁷

Some sheepwalks which belonged to groups of farms were later divided, as near Machynlleth (Montgom.), for example, where part of a sheepwalk common to four farms in 1763 had been divided into separate sheepwalks by 1840, and in Snowdonia, where shared sheepwalks in Penmachno (Caern.) were divided between farms in the early nineteenth century.⁷⁸ Sheepwalks came to be treated as private property, sold

---

72   See below, p. 219; and *Harvest*, pp. 109–13.
73   Thomson, *Orkney: Land and People*, p. 248.
74   I. Wmffre, 'Toponymy and land-use in the uplands of the Doethïe valley (Cardiganshire)', in H. James and P. Moore (eds), *Carmarthenshire and Beyond: Studies in History and Archaeology in Memory of Terry James*, Carmarthenshire Antiquarian Society Monograph Ser. 8 (2009), pp. 278–9.
75   Ibid., p. 278.
76   R. Silvester, 'The commons and the waste: use and misuse in mid-Wales', in I. D. Whyte and A. J. L. Winchester (eds), *Society, Landscape and Environment in Upland Britain* (Birmingham, 2004), p. 60.
77   D. W. Howell, *Land and People in Nineteenth-Century Wales* (London, 1977), p. 25.
78   E. Davies, 'Hafod, hafoty and lluest: their distribution, features and purpose', *Ceredigion*, 9 (1) (1980), pp. 15–16; F. Richardson, 'The enclosure of the commons and wastes in Nantconwy, North Wales, 1540–1900', *AgHR*, 65 (1) (2017), pp. 62, 66–7.

with the farm to which they were attached, and claimed as 'freehold mountain land', despite a test case in 1875 which decided that they were merely management units on the common.[79] It is tempting to relate the persistence of the idea that each farm had exclusive rights over a section of the common for its sheepwalk to the native Welsh conception of common land as *cytir*, that is joint land, in which each commoner possessed a share.

'Good Neighbourhood'

Communal grazing required commoners to act considerately and to submit to rules aimed at maintaining friendly relations. In the sixteenth century, Thomas Tusser complained of the damage caused by inconsiderate commoners: 'Some pester the commons with jades and with geese, with hog without ring and with sheep without fleece'.[80] Overgrazing with poor quality livestock, whether scrawny sheep or vicious, worthless horses ('jades'), or destruction of the grazing by geese, which poisoned pasture with their droppings, or unringed swine which churned up the soil, inevitably made for ill-feeling.[81] 'Good neighbourhood' was fostered by regulations addressing many aspects of livestock management.

Rules requiring animals to be marked to show ownership were widespread, particularly where wastes were extensive or where communities intercommoned. Township marks were required on some intercommoned wastes: in 1393 each township with stock grazing on the forest of Long Mynd (Shrops.) had its own mark by which to know their animals.[82] Village brands for cattle grazing in Whittlewood Forest (Northants) were semi-heraldic in character and included a bugle, stag's head, fleur-de-lis and cross, though Potterspury's brand was a mundane muck fork.[83] Around London, animals on Edmonton Marsh (Mddx) were to be marked with a 'parish brand' in 1561–62;[84] those on Putney Common (Surrey) in 1621 with 'the towne marke', probably a brand, as the physical 'marke' was to be kept by one of the tenants.[85] The parish cattle mark for Wanstead (Essex) took the form of a 'Q' surmounted by a cross.[86] At Sudbury (Suff.) the branding of cattle on the town's commons, recorded in 1644, had been replaced by 1725 by the use of wooden bobbins ('Tottles or Gruggs'), threaded onto their horns.[87]

---

[79] *Contested Common Land*, p. 144.

[80] T. Tusser, *Five Hundred Points of Good Husbandry*, introduced by G. Grigson (Oxford, 1984), p. 99.

[81] For regulations reflecting these issues, see *Harvest*, pp. 103–5.

[82] Shropshire Archives, 125/1.

[83] P. A. J. Pettit, *The Royal Forests of Northamptonshire: A Study in Their Economy 1558–1714*, Northants Record Society XXIII (1968), p. 153n.

[84] *VCH Mddx* V, p. 168.

[85] *Wimbledon Ct R.*, pp. 208–9.

[86] *VCH Essex* VI, p. 330.

[87] H. R. French, 'Urban agriculture, commons and commoners in the seventeenth and eighteenth centuries: the case of Sudbury, Suffolk', *AgHR*, 48 (2) (2000), p. 179.

MANAGING COMMUNAL RESOURCES

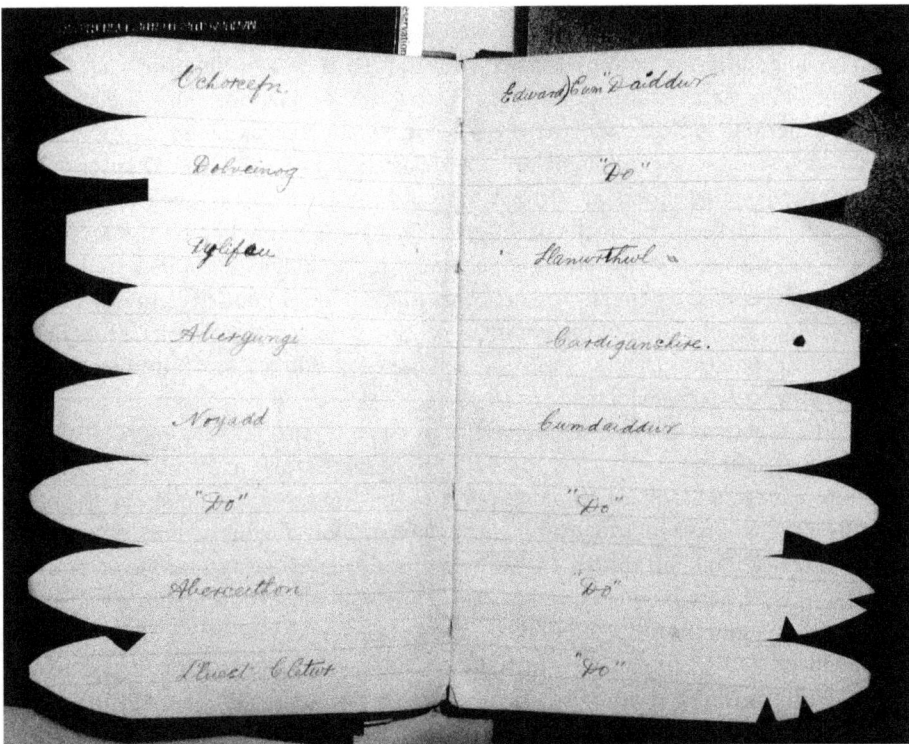

Figure 13. Sheep ear marks from mid-Wales. A shepherd's self-made, practical record, documenting the ear marks used to identify sheep on common land. The outer edges of each page are cut to represent the left and right ear marks of different farms. (Exercise book, inscribed 'John R Thickens, Dolchgenog, Cwmystwyth, 1922', in private collection.)

Where commons were large, each commoner often had their own mark. From the scattalds of the Northern Isles to the hill commons of northern England and Wales, sheep marks distinguished each individual's flock (Figure 13). In northern England the ear mark nicked into the ear and the 'smit' mark on the fleece were known as the 'house mark' and descended with the holding rather than with the individual, making them stable 'signatures' of some antiquity.[88] On the spacious pastures of the Lincolnshire Fens commoners likewise had individual marks. At Cottenham in 1639 all cattle and sheep put on the commons (except for milk cows) were to be branded with their owner's 'usuall brand' and each commoner was to bring a copy of his brand to the township officers who would enter them into a book.[89] Livestock marking appears to have been less common in open-field communities, perhaps because stock there were herded more closely, by village herdsmen.[90]

[88] *Harvest*, pp. 105–9; NYCRO, ZNK III/2/1 (North Loftus 1581).
[89] Cunningham, 'Common rights at Cottenham and Stretham', p. 232.
[90] No rules governing the marking of livestock are indexed in Ault, *Open-Field Husbandry*.

This highlights another regional difference in the management of grazing on common land: differing herding regimes. Beyond the general prohibition that no one was to 'bait or slate' (chase or harass) livestock on a common, more specific rules governed herding practices. 'Drift ways' were sometimes assigned to individuals, along which to drive their animals to upland pastures, as on the Lake District fells at Eskdale, the Pennine moors at Alston Moor and the Clee Hills in Shropshire.[91] Such routes sought to keep the flocks of different farms separate when on the move, and hence to ensure harmony between commoners. On commons without a tradition of heafs or sheepwalks, a general principle was that 'all mens goods are to goe quietlie horn by horne in all places of the common pasture';[92] in consequence, the practice of 'staffherding' or 'staff driving' (where a commoner wielding a staff turned away the stock of others) was forbidden.[93]

Herding practices differed between village communities and the more dispersed farms of pastoral areas. Writing in 1523, Fitzherbert drew a distinction between livestock management on 'commen mores or hethes' and that on common pastures in open-field areas. On the latter, 'catell gothe daylye before the herdeman', who tended the community's animals during the growing season, preventing them from straying into the fields.[94] Late medieval byelaws from England make it clear that members of the village community were required to place their flocks and herds under the care of the village herdsman and to contribute to his wages.[95] The practice continued in villages such as Netherwitton (Northumb.), where orders in 1666 and 1671 required 'common hirds' to watch the beasts and horses on the East Common and West Moor, respectively, across the summer months.[96] Equivalent rules were found in lowland Scotland, requiring the township's beasts to be put under the care of a common herd.[97] Town communities also appointed herds. The burgesses' cattle on the Town Moor at Newcastle upon Tyne were tended by the town's 'neateherd' and his four assistants, whose duties, as recorded in 1653, required them to proceed through the town each morning, blowing horns to warn the burgesses that it was time to bring out their cattle to be driven to the Moor.[98] On many upland commons, by contrast, herding was carried out by individual commoners or their servants by 1600. There is earlier

---

[91] *Harvest*, pp. 110–13; R. C. Purton (ed.), 'A Description of ye Clee, ye L'dships, Comoners and Strakers adjoined, made about 1612, 10 Jac.', *Transactions of the Shropshire Archaeological Society*, 2nd ser. 8 (1896), pp. 195–8; T. Rowley, *The Shropshire Landscape* (London, 1972), p. 52.

[92] As it was put at Ravenstonedale (Westmld) in 1588: CAS, WDCAT/19/1, 'Orders touching common wealth', no. 9.

[93] For herding regulations, see *Harvest*, pp. 114–16. Presentments for 'staffedryving' are found in Herefordshire: Glamorgan RO, CL Manorial Box 4, court roll 1562–91, mm. 7v., 11; HARC, AM 33/9/3 (Bishops Frome, 1622).

[94] Fitzherbert, *Boke of Surveyeng*, f. iii^v.

[95] Ault, *Open-Field Husbandry*, nos. 73, 133, 193.

[96] Northumberland Archives, ZTR XII/2.

[97] R. A. Dodgshon, *Land and Society in Early Scotland* (Oxford, 1981), p. 169.

[98] E. M. Halcrow, 'The Town Moor of Newcastle upon Tyne', *Archaeologia Aeliana*, 4th ser. 31 (1953), pp. 152–4.

evidence for the employment of communal herds by hamlet communities deep in the Pennines, but suggestions that such communal arrangements were fading away by the later sixteenth century.[99]

One specific aspect of the regulations governing shepherding concerned the control of rams in the autumn, to prevent them from running with the ewes until a specified date, in order to control the timing of lambing in spring. Associated regulations aimed to maintain the quality of the community's flocks by forbidding farmers from putting poor quality rams (termed 'riggalds') on the common.[100] The dates between which rams were excluded from the commons were determined by the intended lambing dates and thus varied across environments. An order from Wimbledon in 1562, which sought both to maintain the quality of rams and to achieve the required lambing date in February, excluded 'Riggel Rams' from the common between 1 August and Michaelmas (29 September).[101] At Shelve (Shrops.) rams were to be kept from the common between 29 August and St Luke's Day (18 October),[102] a date also found in northern England, which achieved lambing in mid-March. In the heart of the fell country in the north, by contrast, rams were allowed back onto the common up to a month later, to ensure an April lambing time.[103]

Safeguarding the common good also extended to control of vermin. Many of the birds and animals on which bounties were paid by the parish authorities from the sixteenth to the nineteenth centuries under the Tudor vermin acts would have been killed on common land in a drawn-out process of attrition which altered the fauna of commons. Wildcat, badger, martens (both polecats and pine martens), ravens, kites, buzzards, crows and a host of other wildlife were persecuted.[104] On upland grazing commons, where foxes posed a perennial danger to lambs, organised fox-hunting, at which participation was a community obligation, is recorded in the later seventeenth century.[105]

MANAGING FUEL AND OTHER RESOURCES

Access to domestic fuel supplies and building materials from common land made a major contribution to the local economy in many areas. The value of these rights varied from region to region, their absence from byelaws from open-field areas of Midland England leading Joan Thirsk to conclude that the importance of common land in those areas was largely restricted to grazing.[106] In the more pastoral areas of upland, forest

---

[99] See *Harvest*, p. 114.
[100] Ibid., pp. 57–8.
[101] *Wimbledon Ct R.*, pp. 124–5.
[102] Shropshire Archives, 1037/1/175.
[103] *Harvest*, pp. 57–8.
[104] See R. Lovegrove, *Silent Fields: The Long Decline of a Nation's Wildlife* (Oxford, 2007).
[105] Cockermouth Castle Muniments, box 120, Braithwaite & Coledale court verdicts, 30 May 1690, 16 April 1691; John Rylands Library, Manchester, English MS 1155, Thornthwaite manor court order, 9 October 1678 (quoted in Winchester, *Language of the Landscape*, pp. 226–7).
[106] J. Thirsk, 'Field systems of the East Midlands', in Baker and Butlin, *Studies of Field Systems*, p. 249.

and fen, the natural resources available from common land were more diverse, their value being reflected in numerous attempts to regulate their use. Commons continued to supply fuel to many communities until the spread of coal in the nineteenth century and oil in the twentieth.[107]

Peat and turf, the principal fuels in fenland and much of upland Britain until the twentieth century, were extracted under the common right of turbary in England and Wales and in Scotland under the right of 'feal and divot'. Firewood lay at the heart of common of estovers, while gorse (also cut under rights of estovers) was a significant fuel in lowland communities. Rights to these resources were guarded jealously. At Scalby (Yorks. N.R.) in the 1650s only those with common rights might take 'any Breckons, Whynns [i.e. gorse] or Turves from of the Comons or Moores belonging to the mannor' and they were not to sell the produce to outsiders.[108] As demand for domestic fuel was directly related to the number of households, an underlying theme in byelaws governing fuel gathering is the courts' response to population growth, particularly the expansion in the number of landless households from the sixteenth century. A range of strategies, again involving quantitative, spatial and seasonal restrictions, attempted to manage access to fuel resources, to ensure equitable access in a context of rising demand but also to limit the environmental damage caused by fuel gathering. Fuel and building materials overlapped (turf could be burnt but was also used for walls and roofs; bracken and heather were both fuels and thatching materials, for example), placing a double demand on some resources. These themes are illustrated in the regulations governing both turbary rights and rights to a variety of vegetation on commons.[109]

Turbary: Peat and Turf

The legal framework governing turbary rights stated that no person was to dig more peat or turf than was necessary for domestic use in a house within the manor; nor was peat or turf to be sold, given or taken outside the manor.[110] As it was put at Renwick (Cumb.) on the edge of the north Pennines, no one was to dig more than was 'neadfull for their owne fireing', as to do otherwise was 'a waist of the mosse'.[111] In 1542 the barony court at Carnwath (Lanarkshire) issued the draconian ruling that anyone who 'cast mair heldyng' ('elding' meaning fuel) than was needed to sustain their own hearth, in order to take it away and sell it, was to lose their land.[112] The specific context of turbary rights depended on the relationship between supply and demand. Peat deposits were extensive in lowland fens and mosses and on peat moorland in the

---

[107] P. Warde and T. Williamson, 'Fuel supply and agriculture in post-medieval England', *AgHR*, 62 (1) (2014), pp. 75–6.

[108] East Riding Archives and Local Studies, Beverley, DDX/24/27, Section Z [hereafter 'Scalby pains'], ff. 17v–18.

[109] For regulation of these resources in upland northern England, see *Harvest*, pp. 126–33.

[110] As expressed in an order from Clapham (Yorks. W.R.) in 1704: West Yorks. RO, WYL 524/179, m. 6v.

[111] Oxford, Queen's College Archive, 5A60.

[112] Dickinson, *Carnwath*, pp. 211–12.

hills but they were often under pressure elsewhere. In lowland Scotland, for example, peat was scarce by 1700 and tight restrictions were placed on its exploitation.[113]

As population growth put pressure on peat resources, the response of the courts was to restrict cutting and sometimes to distinguish between the rights of cottagers and landholders. Even in the Fens, turf-cutting rights could be stinted from an early date – at Waterbeach (Cambs.) a limit expressed as feet of turf per messuage was in place by the fourteenth century and was still followed in 1617.[114] Equitable access to turbary resources was sometimes pursued by allocating a section of the peat diggings to each commoner. On the wetland common of Wallingfen (Yorks. E.R.) the regulations drawn up in 1425 required each commoner to come to the fen at noon on St Helen's Eve (2 May) to take 'a resonable place ... for turfe gravyng'.[115] At Cottenham (Lincs.) in 1639 each commoner was allocated a 'Crofte or layer of turves to be digged', 4 poles long and 18 feet wide, to serve them for the following three years.[116] 'Peat pots' in the Lake District were exclusive to individual commoners: no one was to dig peat except in his own allocated place, nor to carry away peat dug on his neighbour's peat pot or allow others to dig peats in his own peat pots. As peat beds were worked out, new peat pots were assigned by officers of the manor court.[117] Comparable allocations for the purposes of taking fuel were found on the heaths and fens of Norfolk in the sixteenth century, where fuel 'doles' were assigned to individuals, even when the common remained a single unit for grazing purposes.[118]

Quantitative limits often distinguished between a more generous allowance for landed households and lower limits for the landless. In the Cambridgeshire Fens this was expressed in numbers of turves: at Wicken in the 1650s commonable tenements were limited to 4,000 turves each year from one area and 2,000 from another fen, while 'undersetles' (sub-tenants or lodgers) were restricted to one-quarter of those amounts.[119] In several manors the limits were expressed by volume. At Worlington Abergavenny (Suff.), where only commonable houses had turf-cutting rights, effectively excluding some cottagers, they were limited to three cartloads or two wagon loads in the 1770s.[120] In Yorkshire, cottagers were restricted to eight cartloads of peat each year at Calton (1544) and ten at Fylingdales (1682). At Guisborough (1708) farmers were limited to twenty-five loads of turf and ling (heather); cottagers to ten loads. At Harrington (Cumb.) in 1717 rights were limited by value: landed tenants could take 1s 0d (i.e. 12d) worth; cottagers 4d worth; at Loweswater (Cumb.) in 1677 by a combination of a time limit and a quantity: cottagers could dig peat for three days (three 'dayworks') and take 100 turves. Cottagers might be required to defer the start

---

[113] Whyte, *Agriculture and Society in Seventeenth-Century Scotland*, p. 83.
[114] *VCH Cambs.* IX, p. 251.
[115] Hull History Centre, U DDBA/10/2.
[116] Cunningham, 'Common rights at Cottenham and Stretham', p. 241.
[117] *Harvest*, pp. 129–31.
[118] N. Whyte, *Inhabiting the Landscape: Place, Custom and Memory, 1500–1800* (Oxford, 2009), p. 113.
[119] *VCH Cambs.* X, p. 564.
[120] L. Shaw-Taylor, 'The management of common land in the lowlands of southern England c.1500 to c.1850', in De Moor et al., *Management of Common Land*, p. 76.

Figure 14. William Stewart MacGeorge, 'A Galloway peat moss', 1888. Peat-digging brought people out to the turbary grounds in May. This painting illustrates both the hard toil winning peats entailed and the environmental damage it caused.

of peat-digging until several days after farming households or they might be restricted to digging only where 'convenient' to the farming families, keeping away from the 'peat pots' assigned to landed holdings. In a very direct response to population growth in a lead-mining area where, on the face of it, the supply of peat was plentiful, the court at Alston Moor, deep in the peat-blanketed north Pennines, laid out clear restrictions on cottagers' rights in 1679: they were not to dig peat on the common without leave of 'adjacent neighbours' and in any case were to exercise their rights only on outlying sections of the common at a distance of at least one mile from their cottages.[121]

Further control was achieved by seasonal restrictions. May was the month for peat-digging and an opening date was sometimes imposed, often in the first week of May.[122] At Scalby a terminal date of 31 May was set because the common was 'greatly abused by graveing many Turves towards Midsummer that rott on the Comon and are never lead away'.[123]

The environmental impact of turbary rights was multi-faceted. Accessing peat and turf sometimes involved burning off the vegetation. On the heather moorlands of the North York Moors, no one at Scalby was to dig on another man's 'burn' for the first

---

[121] *Harvest*, pp. 129–33; R. S. Dilley, 'Agricultural change and common land in Cumberland, 1700–1850' (PhD thesis, McMaster University, 1991), p. 317; NYCRO, ZCG III 1/1 (Fylingdales, 1682), ZFM 54 (Guisborough 1708). See also Dilley, 'Cumberland court leet', pp. 141–6.

[122] *Harvest*, pp. 128–9; digging could only take place between 10 May and 10 June (Guisborough, 1599: NYCRO, ZFM 54); between 4 May and 31 May (Scalby pains); from 4 May (Ingleby Greenhow: Kent Archives, U1886/M10/5).

[123] Scalby pains 1657.

three days (and was limited to the amount a man could dig on his own 'burn'); at Ingleby Greenhow two men were appointed to burn as much moor each spring as would be sufficient for the whole township's fuel needs.[124] 'Muirburn' was likewise a necessary prelude to turf-cutting at Killearn (Stirlingshire) in the later eighteenth century.[125] It may be that moor-burning was associated more generally with turbary rights in heather-clad areas.[126]

The extractive nature of turbary rights, involving digging and stripping, could lead to both environmental degradation and conflict with other uses of common land. Where turf was stripped too close to a road or track, the traffic of hooves, wheels and feet could reduce a wide swathe of the common to bare ground, so, to prevent this, byelaws forbade turf-cutting within a fixed distance of a track or too close to the head-dyke.[127] The deeper excavations of peat-digging prompted conscious attempts to limit environmental damage by seeking to preserve the vegetated sod on worked-out turbaries. A widespread requirement was to 'bed' the peat workings: those exercising turbary rights were to 'bedd, cover and levell again' the bottom of their peat diggings (Clapham (Yorks. W.R.), 1704); to 'cover all the pitts they make with greenswarth' (Burley in Wharfedale (Yorks. W.R.), 1634); to bed the peat pots with sods 'green side up' (Thornthwaite (Westmld), 1672). A later regulation from Thornthwaite elaborated that no peat was to be cut 'where no descent can be made for the water' and all peat cutters were to 'take care to make proper drains for the water and turn down the sod with the green side up for preserving the Herbage and preventing the loss of Cattle'.[128] A similar concern lay behind orders from the mosslands of the Lancashire Fylde. One from Treales in 1736 required those digging turves to leave 'halfe a yard above the clay' and to ensure that they did not 'dig theire moss so low' that there would not be 'suficient fall for the water'.[129]

The destructive potential of peat and turf digging is also illustrated in orders from north-east Scotland. On some commonties and peat mosses in Aberdeenshire, the presence of 'firr stoks' (ancient stumps and logs of Scots pine) embedded in the peat tempted some to extract them as firewood by digging down, 'abusing' the mosses by leaving dangerous holes and pits. At Skene in 1627 seven men admitted 'holling and selling of fir' and transgressing a former order controlling 'firholling'. At Leys in 1636

---

[124] Ibid.; Kent Archives, U1886/M10/5.
[125] A. Fenton, *The Shape of the Past 2: Essays in Scottish Ethnology* (Edinburgh, 1986), p. 108.
[126] For moor-burn more generally, see below pp. 75–6.
[127] For example, within 40 feet of any 'cartgayt' (Wallingfen, 1425: Hull History Centre, U DDBA/10/2); within 50 yards of a racecourse on the common (Hutton-in-the-Forest, 1637: CAS, DVAN 1/4/2/2); within 220 yards of the 'head hedges' (Dilley, 'Cumberland court leet', p. 142).
[128] West Yorks. RO, WYL 524/179; Leeds, Brotherton Library, YAS/MD 413/9–10 (pp. 5–6); John Rylands Library, Manchester, English MS 1155 (orders dated 1672, 1770). For similar regulations from the Highlands in the twentieth century, see below, p. 211.
[129] Lancs. RO, DDK/1536/1. A similar order had been made at Westby in 1584: Lancs. RO, DDCL/1138, Westby court, 14 May, 26 Eliz.

the barony court attempted to stop 'all holling of firr' in the commonty and forbade tenants from taking fir stumps to Aberdeen for sale.[130]

Peat and turf digging could do long-lasting damage to a common. At Urie (Kincardineshire) demand for fuel from the nearby town of Stonehaven exacerbated the problem by the early eighteenth century. Orders forbidding the selling of peat, turves and heather to the townspeople were made as early as 1604 but by 1730 the muirs and grasslands were said to be 'so cast up and destroyed that in a short time [they] would be quite wore out and rendred useless unless timously prevented'. Digging was forbidden in specified areas, the number of exclusion zones increasing across the decade. Rules akin to those from northern England were laid down: peat was to be dug 'without undermining the moss' and the 'underlair' was to be levelled. The sod was to be laid carefully on the bottom after digging 'that the same may grow green again'. By the 1740s the 'wasting' of the peat mosses was explicitly put down to population growth ('the late increase of houses') and attempts were made to limit new building.[131]

Managing the cut peat and turf also engaged the courts' attention. Where cattle grazed a turbary, damage to the stacked, drying peats by trampling was a perennial danger. On intercommoned low-lying moorland at Burton Agnes (Yorks. E.R.), a dispute in 1572 turned on whether cattle damaging cut peats could be distrained.[132] At Scarisbrick, on the mosses of south-west Lancashire in 1703, cattle and sheep were generally to be kept out of the turf-cutting areas between 1 May and 25 July, and the court reinforced the order ten years later by charging the moss reeves to ensure that no one allowed damage by trampling to occur.[133] Once they were dry, failure to remove peats from the common was both wasteful and damaging to the vegetation. At Guisborough (Yorks. N.R.) old turves were to be laid down before new ones were dug and any left on the moor after 20 August could be taken away by any inhabitant without penalty.[134] Equivalent orders were found elsewhere. One from Pinchbeck and Spalding (Lincs.) in 1591 stated that any dug turves ('Hassocks') left on the fen at Martinmas (11 November) could be removed by any commoner for his own use;[135] another from Urie in north-east Scotland in 1741, requiring peat and turves to be removed from the mosses and muirs by 1 September, allowed landowners to dispose of any that were left as they saw fit.[136]

---

[130] *Spalding Club Miscellany V* (1852), pp. 219, 225–6.

[131] D. G. Barron (ed.), *The Court Book of the Barony of Urie in Kincardineshire, 1604–1747* (Scottish History Society XII, Edinburgh, 1892), pp. 4, 33, 105, 131–3, 153–5, 158–9, 168–9.

[132] B. McDonagh, 'Landscape, territory and common rights in medieval East Yorkshire', *Landscape History*, 40 (2) (2019), p. 85.

[133] W. G. Hale and A. Coney, *Martin Mere: Lancashire's Lost Lake* (Liverpool, 2005), p. 117.

[134] NYCRO, ZFM 54.

[135] Hallam, 'Bylaws of Spalding and Pinchbeck', p. 53.

[136] Barron, *Court Book of Urie*, p. 165. Other dates included: 19 September (at Westward (Cumb.), 1803: Dilley, 'Cumberland court leet', p. 146); 1 November, later brought forward to 10 October (at Thornthwaite (Westmld), 1770, 1778: John Rylands Library, Manchester, English MS 1155); 11 November (Ingleby Greenhow (Yorks. N.R.), 1618: Kent Archives, U1886/M10/1).

Firewood

Access to wood and timber was central to common of estovers, though fuel economies varied greatly from region to region before the spread of coal, and firewood was not ubiquitous.[137] The traditional 'botes' (a term derived from OE *bōt*, 'repair, remedy') allowed tenants to take wood and timber from the landlord's estate for necessary purposes, the four main ones being repair of buildings ('housebote'), constructing implements ('ploughbote'), maintaining hedges ('haybote') and gathering firewood ('firebote').[138] Many of the trees providing for those rights grew on farmland or parks: it is striking that most manor court orders referring to wood and timber concern woodland and trees on private land. Most firewood came from dead wood, underwood and bushes that were unsuitable for other uses; on wooded commons, commoners were therefore limited to certain categories of wood in order to protect more valuable timber. At Minchinhampton (Glos.) the tenants could take 'firebote' from their common wood or 'custom wood' but not from the demesne woods on the common.[139] In the thirteenth century, firewood rights were restricted to dead wood in some areas, including Ashdown Forest and the Forest of Dean.[140] Where living trees could be taken, they were the less valuable species – birch and alder were specified for firewood in both Ashdown Forest (Sussex) and the private forest of Windermere (Westmld), for example.[141]

At the heart of harvesting a sustainable supply of firewood from common land lay a perennial truth, that grazing livestock would destroy saplings and prevent the regeneration of trees unless preventative measures were taken. Where woodland on a common was managed as coppice, grazing rights had to be restricted until the crop of fresh poles springing from the coppice stools was old enough to withstand browsing. Typically, that meant excluding grazing animals for the first seven or eight years after the coppice was cut, rotational coppicing allowing grazing to continue in the older stands of trees.[142] The length of the coppicing cycle varied. In Wychwood Forest (Oxon.), where a twenty-one-year cycle was common in the eighteenth century, coppices were enclosed for seven years and then thrown open to common grazing for the following fourteen years.[143] A longer cycle appears to be recorded at Hurstbourne Tarrant (Hants), where four of the twelve coppice blocks were closed at any one time

---

[137] Warde and Williamson, 'Fuel supply', pp. 62, 67–8.
[138] *Gadsden*, § 2-38.
[139] C. E. Watson, 'The Minchinhampton custumal and its place in the story of the manor', *Transactions of the Bristol & Gloucestershire Archaeological Society*, 54 (1932), esp. pp. 259, 361–2.
[140] *VCH Sussex* II, p. 314; C. E. Hart, *Royal Forest: A History of Dean's Woods as Producers of Timber* (Oxford, 1966), pp. 37, 94. Cf. Barnby (Notts.), cited above, p. 28.
[141] *Ashdown Forest*, p. 25; *Harvest*, p. 125.
[142] Coppices in Northamptonshire forests were opened to grazing after seven years in the sixteenth century (Pettit, *Royal Forests of Northamptonshire*, p. 153). At Longhope (Glos.) commoners were excluded for seven years by a custom recorded in 1660 (*VCH Glos*. XII, p. 238). Seven-year exclusions are also recorded in Oxfordshire (*VCH Oxon*. XIV, p. 179; XV, p. 59) and at Cawood (Yorks. W.R.) (B. Waddell, *Landscape and Society in the Vale of York, c.1500–1800*. Borthwick Paper 120 (York, 2011), p. 32).
[143] *VCH Oxon*. XV, p. 59.

for eight years, implying a twenty-four-year cycle.[144] Conversely, at Crawley (Oxon.) a seven-year exclusion of grazing stock recorded in the sixteenth century had been extended to all but the last two years of a twelve-year coppicing cycle by the 1840s.[145]

On open pastures, pollarding provided a method of securing a regular crop of poles from trees around which animals continued to graze.[146] In Norfolk, pollarding allowed wood production and grazing to co-exist and wooded commons to survive on the heavier clay lands of the south and centre of the county. By the late sixteenth century commoners were making use of woodland on the commons close to their houses, some of which had been deliberately planted. Such 'outruns' or 'plantings' were often managed as pollards into the nineteenth century.[147] At Wimbledon (Surrey), another common with pollards, the protective role of gorse in keeping livestock away from trees was recognised in an order from 1581 forbidding the cutting of 'furzes' within 2 feet of vulnerable young oak trees.[148]

Where firewood resources were under pressure, quantitative limits were sometimes imposed. At Eskrick (Yorks. W.R.) in 1753 wood cutting was allowed only for one month each spring and limited to three loads per house or two loads for a cottage.[149] At Wimbledon (Surrey), which shared in the more general shortage of firewood in the vicinity of London by the later sixteenth century, successive orders limiting wood-cutting rights suggest a persistent concern over wood supplies. The overwhelming impression is that demand for firewood was outstripping supply in the manor by the seventeenth century.[150]

Gorse ('Furze' or 'Whin')

Gorse (*Ulex* spp.), known as 'furze' in southern England and 'whin' further north, was a fuel resource of great importance in much of lowland England, particularly among the rural poor.[151] Burning hot and quickly, it was also favoured for commercial ovens and kilns, to the extent that the demands of bakers, maltsters and brickmakers added pressure to finite resources. Maintaining a supply of gorse could require careful management.

As with bracken and peat in the uplands, sections of furze were sometimes allocated to individuals. In Oxfordshire 'furze lots' belonging to individual holdings were to be

---

[144] L. E. Tavener, *The Common Lands of Hampshire* (Southampton, 1957), p. 50. Twenty-four-year cycles are also recorded in late eighteenth-century sources from Perthshire: T. C. Smout (ed.), *Scottish Woodland History* (Edinburgh, 1997), pp. 170–1.

[145] VCH Oxon. XIV, p. 179.

[146] See S. Petit and C. Watkins, 'Pollarding trees: changing attitudes to a traditional land management practice in Britain 1600–1900', *Rural History*, 14 (2) (2003), pp. 157–76.

[147] P. Dallas, 'Sustainable environments: common wood pastures in Norfolk', *Landscape History* 31 (1) (2010), pp. 23–36.

[148] *Wimbledon Ct R.*, pp. 146–7.

[149] Waddell, *Landscape and Society in Vale of York*, p. 32.

[150] See below, pp. 265–6. For context, see Warde and Williamson, 'Fuel supply', p. 63.

[151] Neeson, *Commoners*, pp. 159–60, 174–6; Shaw-Taylor, 'Management of common land', pp. 75–6; Warde and Williamson, 'Fuel supply'.

found on some heaths by the seventeenth century.[152] At Lower Heyford in the 1660s the manor court ordered all tenants to meet in mid-October to view the furze and to set it out by lots; anyone carrying furze from another's lot would incur a penalty.[153]

A customary quantitative limitation, found widely across England, stated that gorse could only be carried from common land in bundles or faggots borne on the back or head; carting it away on a wheeled vehicle was forbidden. Byelaws to this effect have been noted from Buckinghamshire, Norfolk, Northamptonshire, Oxfordshire, Surrey, Warwickshire and the East Riding of Yorkshire.[154] An order from Brancaster (Norf.) in 1569, forbidding those who had horse and cart from taking gorse from the common but permitting the poor to collect it in bundles on their heads, implies that those with holdings of land would have access to fuel on their own property; the landless were therefore given priority on the common.[155]

Ensuring a continuing supply of gorse sometimes required active intervention, to the extent of planting furze on the common, as occurred on the town common at Marlborough (Wilts.) in the later seventeenth century.[156] Seasonal restrictions might be imposed, as at Bushey (Herts.) in 1707, where cutting was forbidden across the growing season, from May Day to Michaelmas.[157] Periodic bans on taking gorse, found quite widely in the later sixteenth and seventeenth centuries, were presumably attempts at environmental management, aimed at allowing the gorse time to regenerate. Usually forbidding cutting for one to three (occasionally four) years, such time-limited restrictions again had a wide distribution.[158]

Heather

Ling (*Calluna vulgaris*) and other heathers (*Erica* spp.) were valuable both when young and tender, as food for sheep and grouse, and also as older, woody shrubs, for use as a fuel and as a thatching material. Heather's value in two incompatible forms led to inherent tensions which required community control in order to uphold the common good, especially where burning was practised on moorland to destroy old woody plants in order to encourage fresh new growth. As John Leland put it when describing

---

[152] For example, at Tackley, Brize Norton and Langford: *VCH Oxon.* XI, p. 201; XV, p. 229; XVII, p. 186.
[153] *VCH Oxon.* VI, p. 195.
[154] *Contested Common Land*, pp. 171–2; L. Rigby, *The History of Stoke Common* (Stoke Poges, 1975), p. 18; *Wimbledon Ct R.*, pp. 120–1, 190–1; K. Layton-Jones (ed.), *The Common Story: A History of Tooting Common* (Wandsworth, 2019), p. 76; McDonagh, 'Landscape, territory and common rights', p. 84; Thirsk, *Agrarian History of England and Wales IV*, p. 459; E. P. Thompson, 'Custom, law and common right', in his *Customs in Common* (Harmondsworth, 1993), p. 145; Neeson, *Commoners*, p. 175; Shaw-Taylor, 'Management of common land', p. 76; *VCH Oxon.* XII, p. 85.
[155] Norfolk RO, HARE 6338, 27 October 1569.
[156] *VCH Wilts.* XII, p. 207.
[157] Warde and Williamson, 'Fuel supply', p. 65.
[158] Examples have been noted in Norfolk (*Contested Common Land*, pp. 171–2); Oxfordshire (*VCH Oxon.* XII, pp. 225, 246); Gloucestershire (*VCH Glos.* VIII, p. 233); Surrey (*Wimbledon Ct R.*, pp. 176–7, 195–7; Layton-Jones, *Common Story*, p. 76); Cumberland (CAS, DVAN 1/4/2/2, no. 15); and Yorkshire N.R. (Scalby pains, 1672).

the moors of the northern Yorkshire Dales in the sixteenth century, burning aimed to improve the quality of the grazing for a few years 'ontil the ling overgrow hit' again.[159] As noted above, burning was also undertaken in connection with turbary rights, in order to gain access to the peat below.

Moor-burning was part of the life of communities in England and Scotland from the medieval period. Burning ling or fern to 'get better pasture' for livestock was recorded in Sherwood Forest (Notts.) in 1251 and in Ashdown Forest (Sussex) in 1273, where tenants could burn furze and broom 'if it be necessary for their common pasture', as long as they did not burn woodland. In 1338, fire from moor-burning on the margins of Exmoor (Som.) spread accidentally onto the heath of the royal forest.[160] The potential dangers of burning and the inherent conflict with other uses of heather surface repeatedly. An order from Fylingdales in the North York Moors forbidding the burning of 'Thatch linge' suggests that stands of heather suitable for thatching could be identified and were protected.[161] Restrictions on burning were required, particularly over the timing of fires. Statutory limits, forbidding burning from the end of March until harvest, were imposed in Scotland in 1424, replacing an earlier statute of 1401, which had prohibited burning except in March.[162] Concern for the impact of moor-burning on neighbouring lands lay behind the English legislation of 1609–10, which forbade the burning of 'Linge Heath Hather Furres Gorsse Turffe Ferne Whynnes Broome and the like' after the end of March, citing the destruction of wildfowl and 'mooregame' (grouse), the clouds of smoke which were said to cause storms, and the danger of wind-driven fires destroying crops and property.[163]

The English statute built on customary practice recorded in northern England in late medieval sources, as burning ling 'over the tyme of mydemarch' was said to be forbidden under common law in fifteenth-century Yorkshire.[164] In Co. Durham, the magistrates were prompted to take action 'in eschewyng of more bryne [i.e. 'moor burn'] which gretly hurtyth the hole contre' and the dates they laid down, forbidding the burning of moor between 16 March and 1 October, were 'accordyng to the lawe and custome of this realme of long tyme used'.[165]

---

[159] Quoted in *Harvest*, p. 136.
[160] O. Rackham, *The History of the Countryside* (London, 1986), pp. 296, 320; *VCH Sussex* II, p. 314.
[161] NYCRO, ZCG III 1/1, no. 33.
[162] Records of the Parliaments of Scotland to 1707 (https://www.rps.ac.uk), nos. 1401/2/15, 1424/22.
[163] 7 Jas. I, c.17.
[164] BL, Additional MS 40,010, f. 187.
[165] W. Greenwell (ed.), *Bishop Hatfield's Survey*, Surtees Society 32 (1857), p. xiii (undated memorandum, probably fifteenth-century). Local byelaws could be more specific, e.g. restricting burning to March (NYCRO, ZCG III 1/1 (Fylingdales); Scalby pains, f. 16); to before 10 March (Barron, *Court Book of Urie*, p. 69); forbidding it between 25 March and 29 September (Mashamshire, 1692: NYCRO, ZS*).

Bracken

Bracken (*Pteridium aquilinum*) was a highly valued resource, in demand until the nineteenth century for potentially competing uses and thus requiring careful management to avoid conflict.[166] The plant had three principal values in the early modern period.[167] Its dried fronds were traditionally spread as litter for livestock when kept indoors during the winter, replacing straw in pastoral communities with little arable land, both in the uplands and in lowland areas such as Ashdown Forest and the New Forest. It was again a substitute for straw as a thatching material, its hard, shiny stems being used for roofing in the Lake District, for example, until slate replaced thatch from the seventeenth century. These were 'necessary uses', to support the house and land to which the right was attached, but bracken was also exploited commercially, by burning it into potash for sale, increasing the demand for the plant and leading to potential clashes with domestic exploitation. Although not a 'necessary use' (unless for domestic consumption) – and thus, strictly speaking, not a valid application of common of estovers – the burning of bracken seems to have been accepted, particularly in the seventeenth and eighteenth centuries. It was widespread on Lake District commons and on Cannock Chase (Staffs.), where it was burnt 'in heaps for the sake of the ashes, which they ... rowle them up in balls and so sell them ... for washing and scouring, and send much up to London', in the 1690s.[168] These different uses were reflected in a host of byelaws, particularly in upland areas like the Lake District.

Manor court juries attempted to achieve sustainable exploitation by drawing on the full range of restrictive measures they were able to impose. Banks of bracken-covered hillside were divided into defined stands of the plant, known as bracken 'rooms', 'dales' or 'dalts', assigned to individual commoners and protected by the weight of the courts' authority. Offenders might be penalised for taking bracken assigned to another's holding. Quantitative restrictions were also found, usually expressed in terms of manpower, a frequent limit being one gatherer per holding.

Seasonal restrictions were the principal device to resolve potential conflict between competing uses and were found in both upland and lowland contexts. Cutting was allowed only from late August on some lowland commons.[169] Where bracken was a thatching material, as in the Lake District, how it was harvested led to an inherent

---

[166] The following discussion summarises A. J. L. Winchester, 'Village byelaws and the management of a contested common resource: bracken (*Pteridium aquilinum*) in highland Britain, 1500–1800', *Digital Library of the Commons*, http://hdl.handle.net/10535/1234. See also *Harvest*, pp. 133–6; R. S. Dilley, 'Common land in Cumbria, 1500–1800' (MPhil thesis, University of Cambridge, 1972), esp. pp. 159–60.

[167] See L. Rymer, 'The history and ethnobotany of bracken', *Botanical Journal of Linnean Society*, 73 (1976), pp. 151–76.

[168] C. Fiennes, *The Illustrated Journeys of Celia Fiennes 1685–c.1712*, ed. C. Morris (London, 1982), p. 147.

[169] 24 August at Bringsty (Heref.): see below, p. 247; 29 August at Lakenheath (Suff.): G. Crompton and J. Sheail, 'The historical ecology of Lakenheath Warren in Suffolk, England: a case study', *Biological Conservation*, 8 (1975), p. 308.

Figure 15. Harvesting bracken, Eskdale (Cumb.), probably in the 1920s. The wholesale mowing of bracken for animal bedding continued well into the twentieth century on many commons, including those in the Lake District, the New Forest and mid-Wales.

tension between uses: fronds for thatching needed to be harvested carefully by pulling the stems or by cutting with a sickle, whereas wholesale gathering for bedding or burning could be accomplished by mowing with a scythe. Several byelaws drew a distinction between the cutting, pulling or shearing of bracken fronds, which was allowed from a date in late August or mid-September, and the mowing of brackens, usually forbidden until around Michaelmas (29 September). Whatever dates were laid down, the intention was presumably to enable those who needed to select fronds for thatching to gather them before wholesale clearance of the dying bracken began.

Commercial exploitation of bracken by burning appears to have been accepted as a customary practice, despite the fact that it could not be justified as a 'necessary use'. Rules were devised to accommodate it. An idea of the intensity of competition for the resource can be gained from regulations such as those specifying that no one was to gather bracken before sunrise on the allotted 'bracken day' or imposing stricter limitations on cottagers than farmers. Cottagers were sometimes required to defer cutting bracken for one or more days after the named 'bracken day' or were assigned a lower manpower limit.[170] As with the rules governing the exploitation of other resources on common land, the underlying aim of these quite sophisticated management regimes was to preserve 'good neighbourhood' in the face of competing demands.

---

[170] As at Dalston (Cumb.) in 1687: Dilley, 'Common land in Cumbria', p. 160.

THE DECLINE OF MANORIAL REGULATION

On the surface, the wealth of byelaws contained in the records of seigniorial courts suggests that ordered regimes, tailored to local circumstance, ensured the disciplined use of common land in the early modern centuries. There is a temptation to view the strategies employed to ensure fair and neighbourly exploitation of resources in a somewhat rosy light. However, as the presentments for breaches of byelaws indicate, disorder was to some degree a feature of common land: indeed, the need for byelaws itself suggests that tensions and strained relations were perennially not far beneath the surface. As the examples cited in this chapter show, the courts were not always successful in responding effectively when demographic growth and agrarian change put increasing pressure on common grazings and fuel resources.

The records of byelaws, orders and presentments in manor and barony courts show that these institutions endured for several centuries, certainly from the late medieval period to the early eighteenth century; the volume of pain lists and orders in the century 1650–1750 demonstrates that many courts remained active then. Ultimately, however, most courts failed. It is generally agreed that many had lost their effectiveness by the nineteenth century, some having ceased to meet altogether or being held only sporadically.

Traditional local regulatory regimes comparable to those discussed in this chapter were found across western Europe in the early modern centuries.[171] Like their continental counterparts, the British seigniorial courts exhibited most of the design principles identified by Elinor Ostrom as being essential for sustainability in institutions for the collective governance of common pool resources (CPRs).[172] Those who had rights to take resources from the common were clearly identified; rules governing use were related to local conditions; those affected by the rules had a say in modifying them; adherence to the rules was monitored; the sanctions imposed on those breaking them were related to the seriousness and context of the offence; low-cost, local systems of conflict-resolution were in place to resolve disputes; and external authorities did not challenge the local institutions.[173] Why, then, did the manorial courts ultimately fail to provide effective regulation of common land in Britain?

In a later work, Ostrom identified a series of threats to CPR institutions, of which three seem particularly relevant to local seigniorial courts.[174] The courts' decline coincided with one of Ostrom's threats, 'rapid exogenous change', which in the British context included population growth, the enclosure movement and the wider drive for 'improvement'. 'Transmission failure' across the generations may also have played a part, eroding the collective memory of local custom and byelaws, while 'opportunistic

---

[171] See the regional case studies in De Moor *et al.*, *Management of Common Land*.

[172] E. Ostrom, *Governing the Commons: The Evolution of Institutions for Collective Action* (Cambridge, 1990), pp. 89–102.

[173] See De Moor *et al.*, *Management of Common Land*, pp. 52–3, 249–52. The question is explored in detail for commons in Flanders in T. De Moor, *The Dilemma of the Commoners: Understanding the Use of Common Pool Resources in Long-Term Perspective* (Cambridge, 2015).

[174] E. Ostrom, *Understanding Institutional Diversity* (Princeton, 2005).

behaviour' can also be seen in the persistence of overgrazing and in the depredations accompanying the exploitation of fuel and other resources in some areas.

These themes have been explored in the context of common land in the Chiltern Hills by Frances Kerner. Comparing commons which were enclosed with those which survived, she identified the longevity of individual manor courts as a critical factor in sustaining effective regulation. Continuity of lordship could be important. In particular, handing over the physical bundles of administrative records to future office holders and transmitting an understanding of the rationale behind the regulations were key to long-term stability. The physical records, often including written evidence of commoners' rights, embodied custom and communal memory, while the thinking behind them provided a solid foundation on which to build effective responses to challenges and changing circumstances. When that understanding had gone, stable regulation tended to be lost.[175]

Ashdown Forest (Sussex) provides an example of ineffectual manorial governance at a time when manorial lords sought to curtail customary rights in order to improve the common land for game. In the first decade of the nineteenth century the manor court attempted to restrict the cutting of litter (including bracken, heather and gorse) by imposing seasonal limits and to curtail turf-cutting by placing quantitative restrictions. A further attempt at active management was made in 1830, imposing tighter seasonal restrictions overseen by a committee. But these moves failed to prevent unchecked exploitation of the commons: by the 1870s 'everybody now takes what he wants'. Tensions between lord and commoners escalated, culminating in actions for trespass in a prolonged dispute between 1876 and 1882, which reached the high court.[176]

In the very different environment of Cumbria, studies have chronicled a decline in most manor courts from the early eighteenth century. The number of presentments fell by more than half between the 1680s and the 1720s and halved again by the 1760s, suggesting that many courts were no longer able to provide effective control, though some continued sporadically to make orders regulating common land well into the Victorian era or even beyond.[177] By the middle decades of the eighteenth century order appears to have broken down on many Cumbrian commons, leading to regular complaints of overgrazing which encouraged support for enclosure.[178] The courts' loss of effectiveness in managing common land coincided with a decline in other aspects of their role, including dispute resolution, which increasingly moved from the local arena to the formal legal system, and recording transfers of copyhold property, as enfranchisement converted customary tenures into freeholds.

Brodie Waddell's survey of manor court business in 113 manors, mainly in Yorkshire, across the three centuries from 1550 to 1850 painted a more positive picture. The types of business the courts transacted became increasingly restricted but their role

---

[175] F. Kerner, 'Enclosure and survival: common land in the Buckinghamshire Chilterns, c.1600–c.1900' (PhD thesis, University of Lancaster, 2016), pp. 264–71.
[176] *Ashdown Forest*, pp. 17–33 (quotation p. 138).
[177] Dilley, 'Cumberland court leet', p. 132; Dilley, 'Agricultural change and common land', pp. 546–7; Straughton, *Common Grazing in the Northern English Uplands*, pp. 124–34; below, p. 218.
[178] Searle, 'Customary tenants and enclosure'.

in managing communal resources and maintaining infrastructure (roads and paths, watercourses and drains, fences, etc.) continued. After 1750, as Waddell puts it, 'the long-term reorientation of manorial business was unmistakable', but management of common grazing and other uses of wastes remained relatively important.[179]

Further research is needed to explore the decline of manorial regulation of common rights. On current evidence, it seems that by 1800 many surviving manor courts had become hollow shells of an institution, shorn of many of their former functions but still occasionally attempting – perhaps with a hint of desperation – to regulate the use of common land on behalf of the community.[180] Their decay had often left an institutional vacuum by the nineteenth century, when increasingly diverse pressures came into play on common land – a theme which is taken up in Chapter 7.

---

[179] Waddell, 'Governing England through the manor courts', pp. 301–7.
[180] Straughton, *Common Grazing in the Northern English Uplands*, pp. 107–60; and see below, pp. 163–4, 218.

CHAPTER 4

COMMONS AS COMMUNAL SPACES

COMMONS WERE PEOPLED PLACES, frequented by individuals and groups as they drove and tended livestock, cut gorse and bracken or dug turf and peat, depending on the season. Some laboured alone: a boy tending his grandfather's cattle on Ashdown Forest in the early nineteenth century later commented, 'Terribly lonely work it was'.[1] However, encounters on common land were part of the fabric of society in medieval and early modern times, as the lives of those labouring there intersected with others passing through. A witness in a dispute over commons in Wensleydale (Yorks. N.R.) in 1579 recalled bargaining for butter and cheese with local womenfolk who were milking their cows and ewes as he crossed the common. Another remembered chatting (sitting 'one hour together') with commoners digging peat, when he was fetching his father's cattle home.[2] In the heathland environments of southern and eastern England, the windmills which stood on high points on many commons would, likewise, have been places for exchange of news and gossip, as the grain carts came and went. Voices and laughter were as much part of the soundscape of common land as the wind and the cries of birds. On a small Bedfordshire common one May evening in 1653, a lady encountered 'a great many young wenches', tending sheep and cows, who were sitting in the shade 'singing of ballads'.[3] Commons were part of the daily lives of young people and children, where work, play, merriment and courtship intertwined.

Commons thus played a part in medieval and early modern life in ways which extended far beyond the uses sanctioned by formal property rights: by no means all those who spent time on common land were exercising common rights. This chapter turns to explore one aspect of this: the use of commons as places for communal gatherings, large and small. Four reasons for going out onto common land to assemble with others stand out: to discharge obligations to those in authority, to trade, to engage in sport and to protest. From folk moots in the early medieval centuries, to cattle fairs and horse races in the later medieval and early modern periods, and evangelical preaching and political rallies in the eighteenth and early nineteenth centuries, men, women and children were drawn to gather on common land, especially, but by no means exclusively, on commons close to towns.

---

[1] *Ashdown Forest*, p. 223.
[2] TNA, E178/2627, depositions of John England and William Robinson, 30 September 1579.
[3] G. C. Moore Smith (ed.), *The Letters of Dorothy Osborne to Sir William Temple* (Oxford, 1959), p. 51.

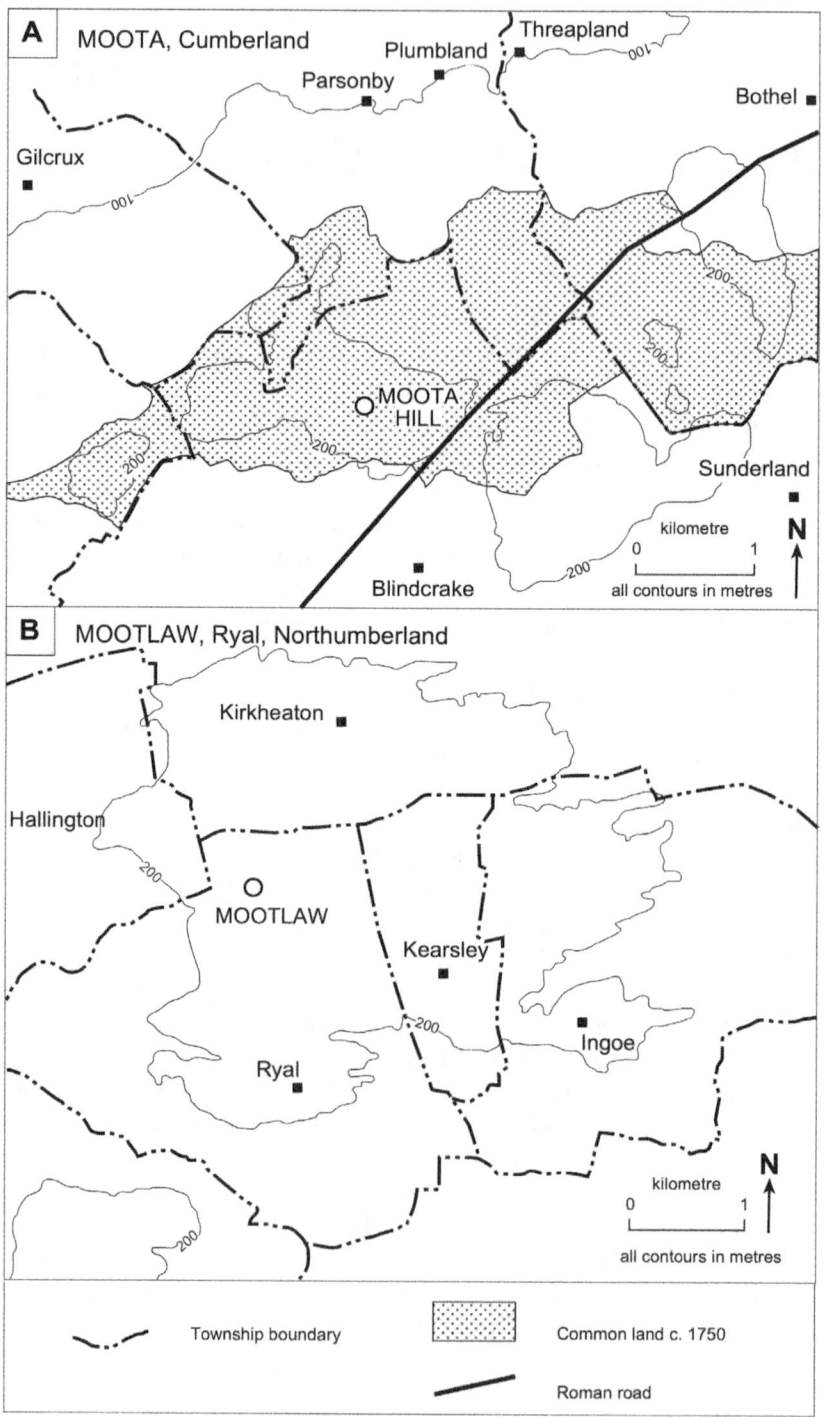

Figure 16. Early medieval meeting places on common land: Moota (Cumb.) and Mootlaw (Northumb.).

What bound these disparate activities together was the simple fact that commons were stretches of open, uncultivated ground, where there was space to assemble and, as shared space not wholly appropriated by individuals, they were perceived as places which 'belonged' to all. There was a high degree of overlap between these communal assemblies: fairs were often accompanied by sports of various kinds, and large gatherings of all types attracted a cast of extras, ranging from hawkers, itinerant musicians and players to preachers, pickpockets and thieves – all gravitated to common land when large numbers of people assembled there. Inevitably, the boundaries between different categories of gatherings on common land are somewhat artificial.

PUBLIC OBLIGATIONS

From early times, the open spaces of heath and moor were integral parts of systems of social control and national and local defence. Commons were meeting places associated with secular administration and the execution of justice; they were the location of look-out points and signalling stations to protect against invasion; and they were open spaces on which archery practice, military musters and training took place and, on occasion, the sites of battle.

Periodic public outdoor assemblies were a feature of the tribal societies of early medieval Britain, almost certainly predating the formal administrative system of hundreds and wapentakes in England, which crystallised in later Anglo-Saxon times. By the tenth century, the hundred was a fiscal and policing unit and its court, meeting every four weeks, dispensed justice. The meeting places of hundreds and wapentakes were often in remote, open locations in a 'no man's land' on the boundaries between communities – or perhaps, as Aliki Pantos has suggested, places felt to belong to everyone.[4] A memory of these early places of assembly is preserved in place-names containing the Old English *(ge)mōt* ('meeting, assembly'), often combined with *hlaw* (a tumulus or burial site), recording the use of prehistoric barrows as landmarks. Examples include several 'Mutlow(e)' place-names in Cambridgeshire, one of which, a Bronze Age barrow on Mutlow Hill in Great Wilbraham parish, may have been the assembly place for the three hundreds whose boundaries converged nearby.[5] Moot Low, again the name of a barrow, at Brassington (Derby.); Mootlaw, a hilltop at Matfen (Northumb.); and Moota (Cumb.), a windswept ridge with wide views across the Solway Firth, are comparable names (Figure 16).[6] Sometimes the modern form of a name obscures its origins. Nutshambles, near Epsom (Surrey) (*mot scaemol*, 'assembly bench'), is a linear earthwork at a high point where several roads converged, close to fields

---

[4] M. Gelling, *Signposts to the Past: Place-Names and the History of England* (London, 1978), pp. 210–14; A. Pantos, '"On the edge of things": the boundary location of Anglo-Saxon assembly sites', in D. Griffiths, A. Reynolds and S. Semple (eds), *Boundaries in Early Medieval Britain* (Oxford, 2003), pp. 38–49.

[5] *VCH Cambs.* VI, p. 125; X, pp. 98, 189. For almost identical names, recording meeting places for Whittlesford, Thriplow, and Armingford hundreds, see *VCH Cambs.* VI, p. 199; VIII, pp. 1, 152.

[6] HLE 1009015 (Brassington); 1015850 (Matfen); D. Whaley, *Dictionary of Lake District Place-Names* (Nottingham, 2006), p. 242.

called 'Copthorn' from which the hundred took its name; Nothing Hill, near Kingsclere (Hants) (*gemōt þing hyll*, 'meeting assembly hill'), a prominent hilltop, again where a hundred court was held.[7] Such assembly places brought even remote stretches of common land into the structures of medieval life, periodically drawing communities to high points, away from hearth and home to places which stood above and apart from the world of everyday life.

As the location of public assemblies, common land was also the place of judicial killings, hundredal execution sites often being separate from but close to the meeting place.[8] Hilltop places of execution from later in the medieval period are recorded in the numerous 'gallows hill' place-names, found from Shetland to Cornwall, with concentrations where criminal jurisdiction remained late in seigniorial hands, as was common in Scotland. Such names include not only Gallow(s) Hill but also Gallow Knowe and Gallow Law and, in Gaelic-speaking areas of Scotland, Cnoc na Croich ('hillock of the gallows'). In total, over 230 survive on the modern map, most of them in Scotland.[9] Gallows survived longest on urban commons: on the Knavesmire, common land on the edge of the city of York, the site of public executions until 1801; on Southampton Common, last used in 1785; and on Kennington Common, south of London, where Jacobite rebels were executed after the 1745 rising, for example.[10] In Scotland, the sites of execution were moved to town and city centres only in the final quarter of the eighteenth century.[11] Memories of medieval gallows on moorland just outside boroughs recur in the place-name 'Gallowgate', given to roads leading to execution sites on moorland outside Glasgow, Newcastle upon Tyne, and Richmond (Yorks. N.R.), for example.[12]

---

[7] A. Pantos, 'The location and form of Anglo-Saxon assembly places: some "moot" points', in A. Pantos and S. Semple (eds), *Assembly Places and Practices in Medieval Europe* (Dublin, 2004), pp. 158–9; S. Brookes, 'On the territorial organisation of early medieval Hampshire', in A. J. Langlands and R. Lavelle (eds), *The Land of the English Kin* (Leiden, 2020), p. 282.

[8] Pantos, 'Location and form of Anglo-Saxon assembly places', pp. 167–9.

[9] The Gazetteer of British Place-Names (www.gazetteer.org.uk) records 231 names which can be interpreted as 'hill or hillock with a gallows', of which 161 are in Scotland and 70 in England. Gallow(s)-/Galla- combined with the generic 'hill' are the most frequent (193 occurrences, of which 130 are in Scotland and 63 in England). Other generics are less frequent: 'knowe' (nine examples, all in Scotland); 'law' (six, of which four are in Scotland and two in Northumberland); 'moor'/'muir' (two, in Stirlingshire and Northumberland); 'down' (one in Berkshire); and 'ber'/'berry' (from OE *beorg*) (five occurrences, two in Dumfriesshire; three in Yorkshire W.R.). Gaelic *croich* ('gallows') occurs fifteen times, thirteen of which take the form Cnoc na Croich.

[10] *Town Commons*, pp. 62–3; *VCH Hants* III, p. 492n; F. H. W. Sheppard (ed.), *Survey of London, Vol. 26, Lambeth: Southern Area* (London County Council, 1956), p. 31.

[11] R. E. Bennett, *Capital Punishment and the Criminal Corpse in Scotland 1740–1834* (London, 2018), pp. 187–205.

[12] *Charters and Documents Relating to the City of Glasgow 1175–1649, Part 2*, Scottish Burgh Records Society 15 (Glasgow, 1894), no. XLVII; OS Six-Inch map, Northumberland 97 (1858), Yorkshire 39 (1854). At Cockermouth (Cumb.), Gallowbarrow ('gallows hill') lay on the moor south of the town: OS Six-Inch map, Cumberland 54 (1867).

Nicola Whyte's work on the relationship between commons and the 'deviant dead' in Norfolk stressed the longevity of sites associated with the grisly rituals of capital punishment. Gallows were often placed on manorial and parish boundaries in prominent places, where they would cut the skyline, visually reinforcing their function as expressions of power. Once established, medieval gallows sites were sometimes re-used in the eighteenth century for gibbets, when felons' corpses were hung in chains. It is striking that the eight gibbet sites marked on William Faden's map of Norfolk in 1797 were where boundaries had formerly run across open common or heath.[13] The chilling sight of a decaying body swinging in the wind from a gibbet on the common heath was not unusual across early modern Britain.[14] Through the rituals of the ultimate expression of justice and secular power, common land thus acquired an association with the rejection of those who deviated from society's norms.

* * *

As height was intrinsic to their location, beacons and look-out points, also manifestations of power and authority, were often situated on hilltop commons. The coastal guarding duties of unknown antiquity recorded in the services of *vigiliis marinas* in Cornwall and *vigilia maris* or 'seawake' in Cumberland would presumably have made use of vantage points on waste ground and there is some evidence for an organised system of beacons and observation posts on hills in southern England during the Viking Age.[15] Place-name elements recording look-out posts include OE *tōt* ('lookout'), as in the numerous occurrences of Toot Hill; OE *weard* ('watch'), as in the many Ward Hill and Wardlaw names in Scotland and northern England; Welsh *disgwylfa* ('place of observation'), in the hills of mid-Wales; and Gaelic *faire* ('watch, lookout'), as in Beinn na Faire, on the Kintyre peninsula, overlooking the sea.

A signalling system in England, in use until the mid-seventeenth century, established a network of fire beacons, arranged by hundred. They were most numerous where the external threat was most severe – along the south coast and close to the border with Scotland – and most of the hills carrying 'beacon' names probably record signalling fires in those centuries. In seventeenth-century Cumberland, for example, five of the county's eight beacons were on common land overlooking the Irish Sea and the

---

[13] N. Whyte, 'The deviant dead in the Norfolk landscape', *Landscapes*, 4 (1) (2003), pp. 24–39; N. Whyte, *Inhabiting the Landscape: Place, Custom and Memory* (Oxford, 2009), pp. 154–62.

[14] Other examples of gibbets on common land included Knockin Heath (Shrops.): R. Gough, *History of Myddle*, ed. David Hey (Harmondsworth, 1981), p. 122; Stanway Heath (Essex): *VCH Essex* X, p. 270; Finchley Heath (Mddx): *VCH Mddx* VI, p. 49; and Whitley Common (Warw.): *VCH Warw.* VIII, p. 198.

[15] J. Baker and S. Brookes, *Beyond the Burghal Hidage: Anglo-Saxon Civil Defence in the Viking Age* (Leiden, 2013), pp. 181–99. For the duty of *vigiliis marinas* in Cornwall, see ibid., p. 183; for *vigilia maris* in Cumberland, see A. J. L. Winchester, 'Early estate structures in Cumbria and Lancashire', *Medieval Settlement Research*, 23 (2008), pp. 14–21.

Solway Plain or on high points further inland.[16] That at Moota Hill suggests re-use of an earlier assembly point, as also occurred at Matfen (Northumb.), where the platform of a medieval beacon survives on the hilltop at Mootlaw (Figure 16).[17]

Manning fire beacons and keeping watch in times of danger were duties borne by local communities, reinforcing the association of common land with state power.[18] At Shute Hill in east Devon, for example, the parish churchwardens' accounts record payment for making a beacon in 1562–63 and a further payment for building a 'beacon house' there in 1567–68, for the watch man.[19] Occasionally, the physical remains of medieval and early modern beacons survive on commons, either as the mound on which the beacon would be built or as a built structure.[20]

Defence of the realm in the early modern period also involved military musters on common land, again organised in England on the basis of the hundred or wapentake.[21] In Norfolk and Dorset in the 1620s the militia from groups of three or four hundreds assembled together on named commons, the Norfolk hundreds of Blofield, East and West Flegg and South Walsham mustering on Lingwood Heath, near Acle, for example; the Dorset trainbands of Dorchester, Bridport and Sherborne divisions gathering on Modbury downs.[22]

At times of crisis during the seventeenth and eighteenth centuries, commons could see large shows of force, like the 10,000 Royalist troops mustered on Aldbourne Chase (Wilts.) in 1644, or the defending forces mustering on the town commons at Roodee and Bullingdon Green, during the sieges of Chester and Oxford, respectively.[23] Commons around London saw especially large military gatherings. General Monck's army assembled on Finchley Common at the Restoration in 1660 and there were encampments of 5,000 soldiers there during the Jacobite rebellion of 1745 and 'several regiments' during the Gordon riots in 1780.[24] Hounslow Heath was increasingly used for military camps during the seventeenth century, notably by James II, who established a camp there to bear down on the capital; musters continued to be held on the Heath

---

[16] On Muncaster Fell, Moota Hill, Sandale Fell, Beacon Hill (near Ivegill) and Penrith Fell (now Beacon Hill): T. Denton, *A Perambulation of Cumberland 1687–1688*, ed. A. J. L. Winchester with M. Wane, Surtees Society 207 (Woodbridge, 2003), p. 58. The other three beacons were on the coast at St Bees Head and Workington and on the tower of Carlisle Castle.

[17] Moota: Denton, *Perambulation*, p. 58; Matfen: HLE 1015850.

[18] For the system of beacons in the sixteenth century, see L. Boynton, *The Elizabethan Militia, 1558–1638* (London, 1967), pp. 132–9.

[19] HLE 1020312.

[20] For example, beacon mounds survive at Beacon Hill, Morden (Dorset) and Fire Beacon Hill, Dittisham (Devon): HLE 1016280, 1019949; remains of structures at Bircham Common (Norf.), Melbury Hill (Dorset), Culmstock Beacon (Devon) and the Armada Beacon on Alderley Edge (Ches.): HLE 1020825, 1016893, 1308946, 1019850.

[21] See Boynton, *Elizabethan Militia*, pp. 13–30.

[22] W. Rye, *State Papers Relating to Musters, Beacons, Ship Money &c in Norfolk* (Norwich, 1907), pp. 77–8, 129; *William Whiteway of Dorchester His Diary 1618 to 1635*, Dorset Record Society 12 (Dorchester, 1991), p. 99.

[23] *VCH Wilts*. XII, p. 72; *VCH Ches*. V (pt ii), p. 300; *VCH Oxon*. V, p. 79.

[24] *VCH Mddx* VI, p. 49.

throughout the eighteenth century.²⁵ Military encampments took place on commons close to other garrison towns as well, as at Colchester (Essex), where several regiments spent the summer months of 1741 on Lexden Heath before departing for Flanders.²⁶

Where tensions spilt over into armed conflict and civil war, many of the skirmishes and more organised confrontations took place on common land, as the names of generations of battlefields attest. They stretch from Blore Heath (Staffs.), where Yorkist and Lancastrian forces met in 1459; to the Civil War battlefields in Yorkshire at Adwalton Moor (1643), Marston Moor (1644) and Rowton Heath (1645); Sedgemoor on the wetlands of the Somerset Levels, where the Duke of Monmouth's rebellion was crushed in 1685; and Sheriffmuir, near Dunblane, a high plateau on the Ochil Hills where Jacobite and Hanoverian forces met in 1715. In the last episode of civil war in Britain, the retreating Jacobite army in 1745–46 fought a skirmish at Clifton Moor (Westmld) and a more substantial engagement at Falkirk Muir before their final defeat at Culloden Moor in April 1746. The litany of 'moor', 'muir' and 'heath' battlefield names is a reminder that commons provided the open space needed for battle – the ability to keep the enemy in sight; the space for cavalry charges and volleys of missiles, manoeuvres to outflank the enemy and, if need be, clear room for retreat.

The gallows and beacon sites, muster grounds and battlefields were on the same land on which, at other times, flocks and herds of livestock grazed and turf and furze were cut. As theatres where the rituals of state power and authority were played out, they represent another – and significant – dimension to the place of common land in medieval and early modern society.

TRADE

Common land also played an important economic role in enabling the flow of trade, both by carrying routeways along which goods were transported and as the location of the fairs which formed the nodal points in medieval and early modern systems of exchange. Long-distance routes traversed commons, especially across high ground like the ridgeways along the downs of southern England and the major Pennine crossings of the north, while the convergence of routes made many commons the location of crossroads, large and small. As a result, common land was often a place of movement, passed through by pedlars and packhorse trains, riders on horseback or carts trundling to market. That flow of people and goods brought attendant dangers. Fairs saw money change hands and some of those traversing commons on packhorse routes and drove roads might be carrying substantial sums. Where a road left habitations and stretched out across a common, a traveller's risk of danger increased, as is testified by stories of robbery and murder at lonely places on routes across moor and heath.²⁷ Merchants

---

²⁵ *VCH Mddx* III, pp. 95–6.
²⁶ *Ipswich Journal*, 6 June 1741, p. 3; 10 October 1741, p. 3; 24 October 1741, p. 3.
²⁷ E.g. those associated with Dead Man Hill (Nidderdale), the fair at Boss Moor and Hollow Mill Cross on the Yorkshire/Westmorland boundary: A. Raistrick, *Old Yorkshire Dales* (Newton Abbot, 1967), pp. 111–13. For robberies of drovers in northern England in the 1680s, see

carrying large sums might be easy prey – men like John of London and William of Norfolk, robbed and killed on the down at Michinhampton (Glos.) in 1371, the former carrying the then vast sum of £40.[28] Highway robbery, though punishable by death, was an omnipresent threat on common land in the seventeenth and eighteenth centuries, as the locations of robberies by the highwaymen of myth and legend make clear. Perhaps the most notorious were the routes crossing commons on the approaches to London: Bagshot Heath, Hampstead Heath, Finchley Common and, most infamous of all, Hounslow Heath.[29]

During the seventeenth and eighteenth centuries one element of the traffic crossing common land became increasingly important. This was the movement of herds of livestock to the meat markets of London, a flow which linked the Highlands and Islands of Scotland and the mountains of Wales to the capital. The pioneering work of A. R. B. Haldane in Scotland and K. J. Bonser in England identified a network of drove roads streaming south from the Highlands and east from Wales to converge on London. Although it is by no means clear how strong their evidence base was, the maps of drove routes they identified vividly portray the relentless flow of cattle and their drivers towards the great markets of south-east England, at Barnet fair and Smithfield itself, and at the great fair at St Faith's (Norfolk), to which numerous Scottish herds were driven for fattening.[30]

Across the Highlands, hundreds of cattle, in droves around a mile in length, made their way across the open moors and hills, heading south to converge on the major livestock fair at Crieff (replaced by Falkirk from the 1770s). In the more enclosed landscapes of lowland Scotland and England, drove routes ran along green roads and trackways as well as over common land, generally keeping to higher ground. When turnpike roads became widespread in the eighteenth century, the drovers would sometimes prefer to take a longer route across commons in order to avoid paying tolls. On the dip slope of the Chiltern Hills, strips of common land running parallel to enclosed tracks formed a series of routes taking Welsh cattle towards London.[31]

Where drove routes ran across common land, a significant legal question arose: did drovers have the right to graze their herds on a common while resting there? They were not livestock belonging to the local community, nor did their owners usually possess land in the locality to which a common grazing right was attached. The drove

---

A. Macfarlane, *The Justice and the Mare's Ale: Law and Disorder in Seventeenth-Century England* (Oxford, 1981), pp. 136–40.

[28] *Calendar of Patent Rolls 1370–74*, p. 378.

[29] *VCH Mddx* III, p. 96; VI, p. 49. See also the litany of robberies admitted by the condemned before execution, available at Old Bailey Online (https://www.oldbaileyonline.org/): examples from between 1679 and 1732 include OA16791219, OA16910501, OA17130925, OA17200413, OA17220718, OA17321009, among many others.

[30] A. R. B. Haldane, *The Drove Roads of Scotland* (Edinburgh, 1952); K. J. Bonser, *The Drovers. Who They Were and How They Went: An Epic of the English Countryside* (London, 1970).

[31] R. E. Lowdon, 'To travel by older ways: a historical-cultural geography of droving in Scotland' (PhD thesis, University of Glasgow, 2014), esp. ch. 5; Bonser, *The Drovers*, esp. pp. 148–201; F. Kerner, 'Enclosure and survival: common land in the Buckinghamshire Chilterns c.1600–c.1900' (PhD thesis, University of Lancaster, 2016), p. 74.

roads were punctuated by 'stances', stopping places where the cattle were rested overnight. Across the Highlands, these were open grassy patches or sheltered hollows on the moors and hillsides, which were recognised through repeated use and often visible in the landscape as they grew green from the nutrients deposited by the cattle. More often, stances were enclosed fields beside the drove road, sometimes close to an inn, for which a small payment was made, which could provide a significant and regular source of income for landowners en route.[32]

Where stances were located on commons in Scotland, they were viewed as a customary privilege of long standing, until improvement from the mid-eighteenth century placed them under threat and landowners began to demand payment for their use. As late as 1846, the closure of a stance at Inveroran, deep in the Grampian Mountains near Bridge of Orchy (Argyll), resulted in a court case when the drovers claimed that the stance was part and parcel of the drove road and that they had a prescriptive right to rest their herds there.[33]

The drove routes were also punctuated by fairs where cattle were traded on for the next stage in their long road to market, and horses were also bought and sold. The great livestock fairs associated with the drove routes out of Scotland were, of necessity, held on areas of common land where large numbers of animals could be driven and shown for sale. The main cattle fair (or 'tryst') in Scotland was held in October at Crieff (Perthshire), where the Highland drove routes converged and around 30,000 black cattle were sold each year in the 1720s. As a result of the increasing cost of pasturage, the fair at Crieff lost out from the 1770s to that at Falkirk, which was held at first on open muirland at Reddingrigg, just south of the town, until that commonty was divided c.1772, and it moved after 1785 to Stenhousemuir, north of the town.[34]

Further fairs punctuated the droving routes in northern England, including those on the common at Stagshaw Bank (Northumb.), north of Corbridge on the drove route south from Carter Bar; Brough Hill (Westmld), beside the major Stainmore–Bowes route through the Pennines; and Middleham Moor (Yorks. N.R.), close to the market town on the edge of the Yorkshire Dales.[35] Each can be linked back to a medieval grant of a fair but their heyday was in the droving era of the long eighteenth century. More local Yorkshire fairs, on stretches of common land which swarmed periodically with cattle brought down by Scottish drovers, included those at the remote inns at

---

[32] For a well-documented example, see P. Roebuck, 'Cattle-droving through Cumbria after the Union: the stances on the Musgrave estates, 1707–12', *Trans CWAAS*, 3rd ser. 12 (2012), pp. 143–58, and follow-up note in 3rd ser. 13 (2013), pp. 256–9.

[33] Lowdon, 'To travel by older ways', pp. 182–3, 196–202. The Court of Session upheld the claim but the ruling was overturned by the House of Lords in 1848.

[34] Ibid., pp. 216–21.

[35] Bonser, *The Drovers*, pp. 132–5, 142. Brough Hill: M. E. Gowling, *The Story of Brough-under-Stainmore* (Stainmore, 2011), pp. 88–90.

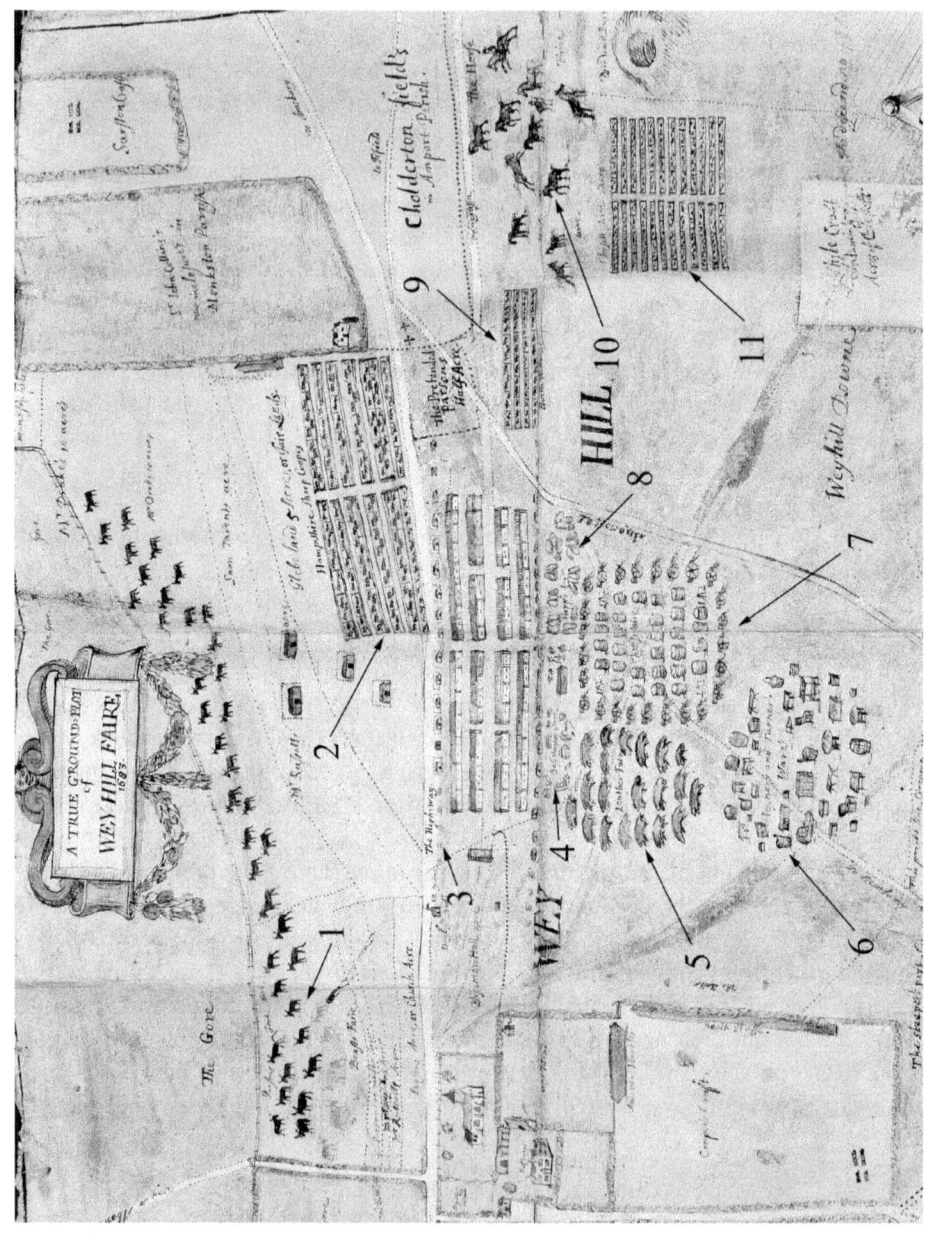

Figure 17. 'Ground Plot of Wey Hill Faire', 1683 (detail). This remarkable pictorial plan shows the range of livestock and products traded at one of the largest fairs in southern England, on open ground near Andover (Hants). In the centre, beside the highway, are rows of booths; surrounding them are: 1. 'Beaste Faire'; 2. 'Hampshire Sheep Coopes'; 3. 'yarne faire'; 4. 'Basketmen's Ware'; 5. 'Leather Fair'; 6. 'Joyner's and Turner's Wares'; 7. 'Cheesefaire'; 8. 'Hopp's fair'; 9. 'North Wilt[shire sheep]'; 10. 'The Horse Faire'; and 11. 'Dorsett-shire Sheep' (Oxford: Queen's College Archive 3V165).

Gearstones, on bleak moorland in the heart of the Pennines close to Ribblehead, and on Boss Moor, a common between Malham and Grassington.[36]

As well as the drovers' fairs, there were numerous other livestock fairs, many of them held on commons. As the nodes of regional and national trading networks, markets and fairs were frequently held in the same locations. Typically, the grant of a weekly market to a medieval borough or market town also included one or more fairs annually, so that many fairs were held on commons close to towns. They included large fairs of regional importance, such as those on the Town Moor at Newcastle upon Tyne (the Lammas fair, in August, first recorded in 1318, and the Cow Hill fair, in October, granted in 1490), and the Michaelmas fair for hops and cheese on Magdalen Hill Down, just outside Winchester, where horses bred on the Somerset Levels were also traded. Numerous fairs were held at smaller market towns, like Penrith's cattle and sheep fairs, held on Penrith Fell overlooking the town.[37] Not all had medieval roots. Potential income from tolls encouraged landowners to establish fairs on commons they owned as the economy grew in the eighteenth century. Appleby's famous horse fair in Westmorland had its origins in a new cattle fair established on common land outside the town at Gallows Hill in 1775, for example, while the re-writing of the rural landscape of lowland Scotland in the decades around 1800 brought new livestock fairs, like that founded in 1805 by the Duke of Gordon on the Muir of Rhynie, outside his new planned village of Rhynie (Aberdeenshire).[38]

Some long-established fairs on rural commons were of regional significance to the early modern economy. Three well-documented examples demonstrate their wide hinterlands and the range of goods traded. The downland fairs of the West Country included the White Down (or St Wyte's) fair at Cricket St Thomas (Som.), a two-day fair established in 1361 on common land beside the Chard–Crewkerne road, which served a hinterland stretching across south Somerset, east Devon and western Dorset. Described in 1633 as a 'great fair in Whitsuntide week', its mid-seventeenth-century toll books suggest that the main trade was in cattle, sheep and leather, and that cattle were brought from as far afield as Glamorgan to be sold.[39] One of the largest livestock fairs in the south in the early modern period was Weyhill Fair (Hants), held on open

---

[36] Bonser, *The Drovers*, pp. 139, 164–5; Raistrick, *Old Yorkshire Dales*, pp. 110, 112. An aristocratic visitor's (less than complimentary) description of the fair at Gearstones in 1792 is recorded in J. Byng, *The Torrington Diaries: Tours through England and Wales between the Years 1781 and 1794* (London, 1934), III, p. 58.

[37] E. M. Halcrow, 'The Town Moor of Newcastle upon Tyne', *Archaeologia Aeliana*, 4th ser. 31 (1953), pp. 155–6; C. Fiennes, *The Illustrated Journeys of Celia Fiennes, 1685–c.1712*, ed. C. Morris (London, 1982), p. 66; P. Edwards, *The Horse Trade of Tudor and Stuart England* (Cambridge, 1988), pp. 32, 91; Denton, *Perambulation*, p. 318.

[38] A. Connell, *Appleby Gypsy Horse Fair: Mythology, Origins, Evolution and Evaluation*, CWAAS Extra Ser. XLIV (Kendal, 2015), pp. 20–4; R. Perren, 'From couper to farmers' cooperatives: livestock fairs and markets in north-east Scotland from 1800 to 1900', *AgHR*, 65 (2) (2017), pp. 216–17.

[39] *VCH Som.* IV, p. 138; J. H. Hamer, 'Trading at Saint White Down Fair, 1637–1649', *Proceedings of the Somersetshire Archaeological & Natural History Society*, 112 (1968), pp. 61–70.

land just west of Andover.[40] By the 1680s, it was drawing sheep from Hampshire, Dorset and Wiltshire, as well as cattle and horses, and also had sections for the sale of products as diverse as cheese, leather, basketry, yarn, joinery and hops (see Figure 17).

In the north, Rosley Hill Fair (Cumb.), held every fortnight between Whitsun and Martinmas (11 November) on rising ground on the common at Westward, a few miles south-east of Wigton, served a similar function, drawing on the Scottish droving trade but also serving as a regional fair for the Solway area. It was described in 1688 as 'the best fair for Irish & Scotch horses, and for cattle & sheep, in all the north' and was also noted for its trade in linen cloth.[41] A century later it was recorded that cattle spread over the common to the west of the main fairground and horses to the east and that, as well as linen, there were stalls selling a host of other goods: gingerbread, haberdashery, 'hats, caps and cloaks', 'brooms, baskets, beehives' and pottery ('bright *Borslem-ware*').[42] Even a remote common like this could be a focal point, periodically drawing large gatherings of people and livestock from wide hinterlands as the wheels of trade turned.

Fairs were rarely only trading events; they were also social gatherings, accompanied by an increasingly varied array of activities. The fair encountered by Celia Fiennes on Beggar's Hill, a common 'full of bushes and furze and heath', at Rye (Sussex) on St Bartholomew's Day (24 August) 1697 may have been 'the saddest faire I ever saw, ragged tatter'd booths and people', but she thought it noteworthy for its 'musick and dancing'.[43] The livestock fair on White Down (Som.) also possessed a social dimension, if an altogether wealthier one, by the later eighteenth century. One of the fair days was a 'Carriage-day', when gentry from a broad hinterland 'disported themselves, feasting and dancing on the green sward', with 'Wrestling, cudgel-playing and single-stick' and, by the 1840s, horse racing and a foot race.[44] Bush Fair, a large cattle fair on Mark Hill Common at Latton (Essex), was also a pleasure fair and had even acquired a permanent 'tea booth' before 1778.[45]

A large fair drew a 'mixed multitude', as it was put at Falkirk in the 1830s.[46] A description of Kelton Hill Fair, near Castle Douglas, one of the oldest and largest fairs in southern Scotland, in 1792 paints a vivid picture of the transformation of an open common into a vibrant and noisy crush at fair time:

---

[40] *VCH Hants* IV, pp. 396–8.
[41] Denton, *Perambulation*, p. 181.
[42] 'Description of Roslay-Hill Fair', in E. Clark, *Miscellaneous Poems* (Whitehaven, 1779), pp. 43–4. See also J. D. Marshall, *Old Lakeland: Some Cumbrian Social History* (Newton Abbot, 1971), pp. 93–5; Edwards, *Horse Trade*, pp. 29, 67.
[43] Fiennes, *Journeys*, p. 129.
[44] R. W. Greenfield, 'Meriet of Mariet and of Hestercombe', *Proceedings of the Somersetshire Archaeological & Natural History Society*, 28 (1882), pp. 144–5; Hamer, 'Trading at Saint White Down Fair', pp. 69–70.
[45] *VCH Essex* VIII, pp. 188, 192.
[46] Quoted in Lowdon, 'To travel by older ways', p. 222.

From Ireland, from England, and from the most distant parts of North Britain, horse-dealers, cattle-dealers, sellers of sweetmeats and of spiritous liquors, gypsies, pickpockets, and smugglers are accustomed to resort to this fair ... Through the whole fair day, one busy, tumultuous scene is here exhibited of bustling backwards and forwards, bargaining, wooing, carousing, quarrelling, amidst horses, cattle, carriages, mountebanks, the stalls of chapmen, and the tents of the sellers of liquors, and of cold victuals.[47]

It is not surprising that the phrase 'a Kelton Hill Fair' was used in Galloway to mean 'a rumpus, a noisy uproar'.[48] As fair days drew to a close, dancing, heavy drinking and brawling (the 'crowns crack'd, and bleeding noses ... oaths and uproar' recalled at Rosley Hill Fair in the 1770s) would have been a familiar feature of many a fairground.[49]

Fairs thus possessed a social, recreational side which would eventually eclipse the original trading function of those that survived. Edward Thomas's evocation of a fair on a Hampshire heath gives a vivid impression of the two faces of fairs by the nineteenth century. At its core was the funfair, 'a double row, a grove, of tents and booths, roundabouts, caravans, traps and tethered ponies'. Behind the stalls, on the open heath, was the business end of the fair. Livestock were being traded: 'groups of cart-mares with huge pedestalled feet ... or of men bending forward over long ash sticks and talking in low tones'; there were bulls, 'silent and quiet', with bowed heads, and 'Droves of bullocks [being] driven through the furze'.[50]

SPORT AND RECREATION

Space for recreation and amusement has been one of the assets of common land for many centuries, especially where commons lay close to towns and villages. Much of the recreational use was informal, commons being a ubiquitous part of the landscape of play for the young. Generations of children romped on village greens and on common land close to settlements; teenagers roamed further afield; while courting couples sought more remote spots in woodland, heath or moor.

Occasionally, records of village gatherings on a local common survive to provide a glimpse of communal activity. At Temple Sowerby (Westmld), for example, the village moor came alive each St James's Day (25 July) in the later seventeenth century, as the venue for the community's sports. There were 'races for great horse & little; men & boyes & women; with pitching, throwing of the ham, shooting with the bow, bowling, leaping, dancing and such like active exercises'.[51]

---

[47] R. Heron, *Observations made in a Journey through the Western Counties of Scotland in the Autumn of MDCCXCII* (Perth, 1793), vol. II, pp. 129–30.
[48] *Dictionaries of the Scots Language* (https://www.dsl.ac.uk), s.v. 'Kelton Hill Fair'.
[49] Clark, 'Roslay-Hill Fair', p. 45.
[50] E. Thomas, *The South Country* (repr. Toller Fratrum, 2009), pp. 227, 230.
[51] CAS, DCHA/11/4/2, p. 462. I am grateful to Jane Platt for sharing her transcript of Thomas Machell's description in advance of publication.

As well as the plethora of amusements associated with fairs, some sports became fixtures on common land, the infrastructure needed for them adding new features to the landscape. Archery, which made the transition from military obligation to sport as bows were replaced by guns, was practised on common land in some places. The archery butts, which parish and town authorities were obliged by statute to provide, might be built on common land, as at Bristol, where they were constructed annually on the marsh in the mid-sixteenth century.[52] Courses laid out for golf and horse racing (discussed below) were widespread by 1800, while the commons fringing London were home to sport in many guises. There were bowling greens on Hampstead Heath and Putney Heath by the later seventeenth century, for example,[53] and shuttlecock tournaments between gentlemen of the western and northern counties on Finchley Common in 1766.[54] Cricket was played on commons in south-eastern England from the sixteenth century, one of the earliest references to the game coming from Guildford (Surrey) around 1550, when schoolboys were playing 'creckett' on a patch of common land at other times used for bear-baiting.[55]

One of the most widespread and enduring sports to take place on commons was horse racing. Its roots lay deep, since horse races, along with fairs and other sports, seem to have accompanied the tribal and public assemblies of the early medieval period, forming part of the glue binding pre-Conquest society together.[56] Racing in the Scandinavian era may be recorded in the 'Hesket(h)' place-names in northern England, and in Wickham Skeith (Suff.) and The Skaith (Embleton, Northumb.), if the interpretation of Old Norse *skeið* as 'racecourse' is correct. They occur in locations where racing on broad stretches of waste land is certainly plausible: in Inglewood Forest, by the marshes fringing the Ribble estuary, and on the edge of the North York Moors, for example.[57] Racing accompanied the buying and selling of horses at fairs and, no doubt, took place widely in informal contests of horsemanship.[58] It comes into focus as a feature of life on common land when it became more organised from the sixteenth century, with horses running to win trophies.

Some of the earliest documented racecourses were on commons close to towns and originated as 'town plate' meetings, where a prize, often a silver bell, was offered by

---

[52] S. J. Gunn, 'Archery practice in early Tudor England', *Past & Present*, 209 (2010), p. 55.

[53] Hampstead Heath, 1679: London Metropolitan Archives: City of London, E/MW/H/7, f. 6 (translation at www.camdenhistorysociety.org/hampstead-court-rolls); Putney Heath, 1696: *VCH Surrey* IV, p. 81.

[54] *VCH Mddx* VI, p. 49.

[55] Surrey History Centre, BR/OC/1/2, f. 40.

[56] Pantos, 'Location and form of Anglo-Saxon assembly places', p. 166.

[57] M. Atkin, 'Viking racecourses? The distribution of *Skeið* place-name elements in northern England', *Journal of English Place-Name Society*, 10 (1978), pp. 26–39; D. Whaley, 'The other millennium: English place-naming after the Norman Conquest', *Journal of English Place-Name Society*, 46 (2014), pp. 26–7. However, G. Fellows-Jensen (*Scandinavian Settlement Names in the North West* (Copenhagen, 1985), p. 133) suggested that *skeið* might signify grazing land along a boundary.

[58] For example, racing is recorded as having taken place in post-medieval centuries at horse fairs at All Cannings (*VCH Wilts.* X, p. 29) and Cricket St Thomas (*VCH Som.* IV, p. 138).

the urban authorities.⁵⁹ Early references record racing at Leith (in 1504), on the forest of Galtres outside York (1530s) and regular races held each Shrove Tuesday from 1540 on Roodee, the common beside the River Dee, just outside the city walls at Chester.⁶⁰ Many more were recorded by the early seventeenth century. Examples include the races on Kingmoor, outside Carlisle, where the prizes were silver-gilt 'horse and nage bells' dating from the mid-sixteenth century,⁶¹ on Killingworth Moor (Northumb.), first recorded in 1632 when the corporation of Newcastle upon Tyne paid £20 for two silver pots to be run for there,⁶² and on Coddington Moor, near Newark (Notts.), where a cup was endowed in 1620 and rules were drawn up in 1624.⁶³ Races are recorded at sixteen royal burghs in Scotland by 1670, most of them held on the beach, on common links or on riverside meadows.⁶⁴

Urban race meetings boomed across the late seventeenth and earlier eighteenth centuries, reflecting the increasing leisure and wealth of urban elites.⁶⁵ As a result, racecourses became fixtures in the landscape of many urban commons. Kersal Moor, near Manchester, where racing was recorded in 1687, developed into Manchester's first racecourse by the 1750s; there were courses on Doncaster Town Moor, the West Common at Lincoln, the Town Moor at Newcastle upon Tyne (replacing the town's earlier racecourse on Killingworth Moor), the Knavesmire at York (replacing a course on meadowland beside the Ouse on Clifton and Rawcliffe Ings in 1731), and, near smaller towns, at Mile End Heath at Colchester (Essex), Westwood Common at Beverley (Yorks. E.R.), Bromyard Downs (Heref.) and even Lyndhurst (Hants) (Figure 18).⁶⁶

Royal and aristocratic patronage played a prominent role in some of the most famous courses in the seventeenth and eighteenth centuries. The aristocracy had been drawn to Newmarket Heath in Suffolk in the reign of James I, and Charles II's patronage led to a new round course being laid out in 1666, establishing Newmarket as a centre of racing for the elite.⁶⁷ Royal patronage also lay behind the renown of the racecourse at Hambleton, on the scarp of the North York Moors. Racing was established there by 1612 but it was the gift of gold cups a century later by Queen Anne and George I which secured its place as 'the Newmarket of the North' until racing was transferred to York

---

[59] See R. W. Tomlinson, 'A geography of flat-racing in Great Britain', *Geography*, 71 (3) (1986), pp. 228–39; M. Huggins, *Horse Racing and British Society in the Long Eighteenth Century* (Woodbridge, 2018).

[60] J. Burnett, 'The sites and landscapes of horse racing in Scotland before 1860', *Sports Historian*, 18 (1) (1998), p. 56; Huggins, *Horse Racing and British Society*, p. 26; *VCH Ches*. V (pt ii), pp. 255–7.

[61] *VCH Cumb*. II, p. 441.

[62] Tyne & Wear HER 7761.

[63] C. Brown, *A History of Newark-on-Trent* (Newark, 1907), II, p. 44.

[64] Burnett, 'Sites and landscapes of horse racing', pp. 62–3, 68–9.

[65] Huggins, *Horse Racing and British Society*, pp. 7–9, 28.

[66] *VCH Lancs*. IV, p. 217 & n; *Town Commons*, pp. 71–2; Halcrow, 'Town Moor', pp. 154–5; Tyne & Wear HER 4022; J. Rice, *History of the British Turf* (London, 1879), p. 26; *VCH Essex* IX, p. 403; *VCH Yorks. E.R*. VI, p. 206; for Bromyard, see below p. 249.

[67] D. Oldrey, T. Cox and R. Nash, *The Heath and the Horse: A History of Racing and Art on Newmarket Heath* (London, 2016), pp. 17–37, 210–11, 320–1.

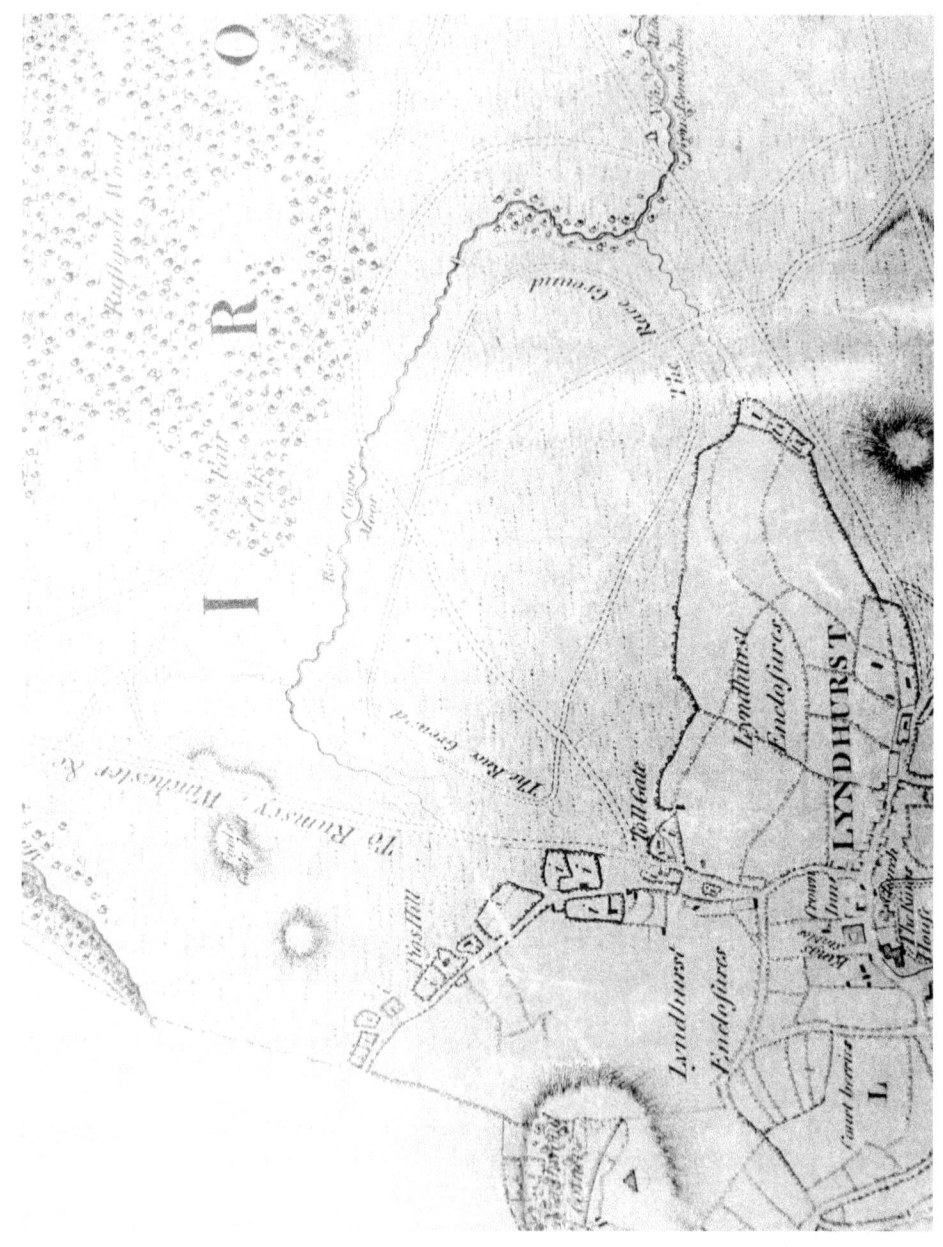

Figure 18. Racecourse on the common at Lyndhurst (Hants). Source: A. and W. Driver, *A Plan of His Majesty's Forest, called the New Forest ...*, 2nd edn, 1814.

and then Richmond in the 1770s. Daniel Defoe noted that the 'very great races' at Hambleton, held annually, encouraged horse breeding among local gentlemen.[68]

Racing at Ascot Heath, on the sprawling Berkshire heathlands, began under royal patronage in 1711 and became so firmly established that its continuing existence was secured under the terms of the Windsor Forest enclosure act of 1813.[69] On Epsom Downs a tradition of racing along the common to Banstead Downs reached back at least to the early seventeenth century. The racecourse was thus long-established when the Earl of Derby founded the two famous races there, the Oaks (in 1779) and the Derby (in 1780).[70]

Early racecourses were by no means solely an urban phenomenon. Even Cumbria, remote from royal patronage and urban racegoers, possessed numerous racecourses on its spacious commons. At least a dozen 'horse courses' were noted on common land in Cumberland in 1688. Some were on coastal dunes – the 'sandy plain' at Drigg had been made a racecourse by Sir William Pennington, lord of the manor, comparatively recently – but most were inland. One, stretching four miles across several contiguous commons on rising ground on the northern edge of the Lake District, ended on the top of Moota Hill (the ancient assembly place and beacon site, mentioned earlier), 'the ascent of which hill being so great a climbe that they call that part of the hill Trotter [as] few horses can gallop up to the top thereof but are forced to trot'.[71] Courses were also widespread on the moors in the Eden Valley. It was noted in the later seventeenth century that the commons around Appleby were generally not 'ruff & stony' but 'plane & champion ground' and that 'there is scarce one that has not an horse course upon it'.[72] The racecourse on Langwathby Moor, east of Penrith, already famous in Elizabeth's reign, was founded, according to tradition, by a local squire and 'brave Horsman', who persuaded other local gentry to contribute to a £20 plate which was run for yearly on Midsummer day, attracting both English and Scottish aristocracy.[73]

Early courses normally ran straight across a common, involving little modification of the surface. Posts marked the start and finish and sometimes distances between. Newark races met 'at the staffe at Coddington Moore' in 1624, for example.[74] Straight runs gradually gave way to circular courses: there was a 'round course' at Newmarket by 1665 and the old course along the Downs from Banstead to Epsom was replaced by a new 'orbicular' course by 1711. These tended to involve more alteration of the face

---

[68] Bonser, *The Drovers*, pp. 180–1; D. Defoe, *A Tour through the Whole Island of Great Britain*, ed. P. Rogers (Harmondsworth, 1971), p. 524.
[69] *VCH Berks*. II, pp. 305–6.
[70] *VCH Surrey* III, pp. 253 & n, 272.
[71] Denton, *Perambulation*, pp. 83, 154, 165, 196, 337. Other courses are mentioned on pp. 125, 157, 182, 258, 284, 304, 316, 319.
[72] CAS, DCHA/11/4/2, p. 462.
[73] *VCH Cumb*. II, p. 440; E. Sandford, *A Cursory Relation of all the Antiquities and Familyes in Cumberland, circa 1675*, ed. R. S. Ferguson, CWAAS Tract Ser. IV (1890), p. 43.
[74] Brown, *Newark-on-Trent*, II, p. 44.

of a common: marker posts, levelling and draining, and cords to separate riders and spectators became more frequent across the eighteenth century.[75]

Many smaller rural courses faded away from the middle decades of the eighteenth century, sometimes suppressed by complaints about the depravity and morally corrupting behaviour associated with racing. Legislation in 1740, which sought to rein in 'the excessive increase of horse races', banned races where the prizes were of less than £50 in value, favouring the urban courses. It had an immediate impact, the number of places with meetings in the British racing calendars dropping by two-thirds (from 122 in 1735 to 46 in 1742), though numbers rose again from the 1760s. The presence of improved turnpike roads boosted courses close to them as the more remote courses (including the famous course at Hambleton) declined, while the rising tide of enclosure reduced the extent and number of commons on which racing could take place.[76]

Another sport closely associated with common land was golf. In eastern Scotland, it was an established practice on some commons by the sixteenth century, especially on the sandy links along the coast.[77] When Pilmuir links at St Andrews were leased in 1553 as a rabbit warren, the protected rights of the burgh's inhabitants famously included 'playing at golf, football, shooting at game and all manner of other pastimes'. Commercial use of the common heralded recurrent 'rabbit wars', particularly in the twenty years following the sale of the links (which later became St Andrews Old Course) to a rabbit farmer in 1797. During the legal battle which followed, the right to play golf and to destroy the rabbits was confirmed.[78] The first formal golf club was formed at Leith in 1744 and societies proliferated in Scotland across the later eighteenth century. Few English commons saw golf until after 1860, exceptions being the club at Blackheath (Kent), probably founded in 1766, and Kersal Moor, near Manchester, where a course was laid out in 1818.[79]

DISSENT

The open spaces afforded by moorland and heath were also natural places for groups to congregate in order to protest or to organise and express dissent, both political and religious. Such gatherings may be thought of as grassroots commandeering of common land, subverting its use for official public assemblies. From those participating in the rebellions of late medieval and Tudor times to the Chartists of the 1830s and 1840s, and from religious dissenters of the sixteenth century to the Primitive Methodists

---

[75] Huggins, *Horse Racing and British Society*, pp. 33, 194–8.
[76] Ibid., pp. 14–15, 29, 141–3.
[77] R. Browning, *A History of Golf: The Royal and Ancient Game* (London, 1955, repr. 1990), pp. 30–1.
[78] N. Reid, 'Five centuries of dispute: the common lands of St Andrews', *Scottish Archives*, 21 (2015), pp. 30–43; A. C. Loux, 'The Great Rabbit Massacre: a "comedy of the commons"? Custom, community and rights of public access to the Links of St Andrews', *Liverpool Law Review*, 22 (2000), pp. 123–55.
[79] Browning, *History of Golf*, pp. 35–44, 90. For the use of common land for golf courses from the 1860s, see below, pp. 202–3.

of the early nineteenth, those taking a stand against authority, whether secular or religious, have been drawn to common land.

The role of commons as gathering grounds for insurgents came into focus during the Peasants' Revolt of June 1381, when the massed rebels from Kent famously camped on Blackheath before their entry into London, and Blackheath featured again after the failure of the revolt, when it became the mustering place for loyal troops assembling to put down the rebellion.[80] The insurgents of the Pilgrimage of Grace who gathered in force across northern England in 1536 were well organised and summoned their supporters to meet locality by locality, often on common land. They mimicked the military musters of the state, calling the inhabitants of each wapentake (or ward in the four northernmost counties) to meet at recognised muster points, suitably armed. In south-east Yorkshire, the men of East Osgoldcross (or 'Marshland') wapentake were summoned to Hook Moor; those of the wapentake between the Ouse and Derwent to Skipwith Moor; those of Harthill wapentake to Kexby Moor, for example. Further west, there were musters on moorland at Monubent, near Bolton-by-Bowland, and on Clitheroe Moor (Lancs.). In Westmorland, the men of the East Ward were ordered to gather on Sandford Moor, near Appleby, the accustomed mustering ground for service on the Scottish border. In Cumberland, the beacon on Moota Hill was the gathering place for Allerdale ward and the honour of Cockermouth. Commons on the edges of territories were chosen as convenient places for meetings between different groups of insurgents: Endmoor (Westmld) provided a midway point for the host gathered at Dent to meet 500 townsmen from Kendal, while Sandale Hill (Cumb.), on the belt of common land along the northern edge of the Lake District fells, fulfilled a similar role when the men of Leath ward met a delegation from Carlisle.[81]

Little more than a decade later, common land was again the location of many of the episodes of riot and rebellion in southern England in the 'commotion time' of 1549. It was also central to the rebels' concerns, as enclosure and other abuses of common land were key grievances. The roots of the rebellion included an enclosure riot on Northaw Common, near Potter's Bar (Herts.), in May 1548 and the destruction of enclosures on Bristol Common by a band of young men a year later. The culmination of the unrest was Kett's Rebellion, an organised insurgency in East Anglia across the summer of 1549, in which the basket of grievances included enclosure, overstocking of commons and abuse of fold-course rights over common land by landowners. The rebels set up camps on heathland, most notably on Mousehold Heath, just outside Norwich, where several thousand of Robert Kett's followers 'inkennelled' themselves in July 1549, until the rebellion was crushed six weeks later.[82]

Andy Wood has pointed out continuities in the sites of insurrection from the fourteenth century to the sixteenth, suggesting that 'a deep social memory of popular

---

[80] R. B. Dobson, *The Peasants' Revolt of 1381*, 2nd edn (London, 1983), pp. 129–31, 307, 323.
[81] M. Bush, *The Pilgrimage of Grace: A Study of the Rebel Armies of October 1536* (Manchester, 1996), pp. 82–8, 225, 252–3, 298, 350–2.
[82] D. MacCulloch, 'Kett's rebellion in context', *Past & Present*, 84 (1979), pp. 36–59; A. Wood, *The 1549 Rebellions and the Making of Early Modern England* (Cambridge, 2007), pp. 41, 49, 55–69.

rebellion endured'.[83] In part this was a product of rebel appropriation of the spatial structures of local society, as when insurgents gathered on the muster grounds customarily used by the militia in each hundred or wapentake. The repeated siting of rebel camps on particular commons is striking: Norfolk rebels had gathered on Mousehold Heath during the Peasants' Revolt of 1381,[84] and there had been encampments on Blackheath (Kent), a vantage point overlooking London, in 1381, 1450 and 1497.[85]

The power of memory of place is also hinted at in an abortive rising in Oxfordshire in 1596, protesting against the enclosure of arable land for sheep which was blamed for inducing the dearth of the mid-1590s. A rebel gathering was planned on Enslow Hill, near Bletchingdon, but only 'some ten persons with pikes and swords' turned up. The choice of Enslow Hill was significant: its place as a gathering ground was deep-seated, as it was one of the ancient meeting places for Ploughley hundred and there was a tradition that it had been the site of an earlier rising, possibly in 1549. Although the intended rising failed to materialise, another layer of association with the struggle between authority and rebellion was added when two of the would-be rebels were executed as traitors on Enslow Hill.[86] Common land could thus accrue layers of associational memory, linking it in the eyes of the local community to tumultuous episodes in the local past.

During the following century, the activities of the Diggers concerned common land itself. Their direct action in the revolutionary months following the execution of Charles I in 1649 challenged the established order of property rights – the ownership of common land was central to their agenda. Gerard Winstanley and his comparatively small bands of followers took spades and other implements onto a handful of commons in order to dig and manure them and sow grain. Their aim was to assert a communist ideal, that all land, including common land, was 'a common treasury for every man', and to show that common land, which 'hath brought forth nothing but heath, mosse [and] furseys [furze]', could be made fruitful for the common good. No one should claim land as their own; rather, the common people would 'labour together, and eat bread together upon the Commons, Mountains, and Hills'. The initial digging on St George's Hill at Cobham (Surrey) spawned further Digger communities on commons in Buckinghamshire, Essex and Northamptonshire but, meeting fierce resistance, the movement had fizzled out by the spring of 1650.[87]

---

[83] Wood, *1549 Rebellions*, pp. 9–10.

[84] H. Eiden, 'Joint action against "bad" lordship: the Peasants' Revolt in Essex and Norfolk', *History*, 83 (269) (1998), pp. 19–20.

[85] Dobson, *Peasants' Revolt*, pp. 129–31; I. M. W. Harvey, *Jack Cade's Rebellion of 1450* (Oxford, 1991), pp. 81–2; I. Arthurson, 'The rising of 1497: a revolt of the peasantry?', in J. Rosenthal and C. Richmond (eds), *People, Politics and Community in the Late Middle Ages* (Gloucester, 1987), pp. 5–8.

[86] J. Walter, 'A "rising of the people"? The Oxfordshire rising of 1596', *Past & Present*, 107 (1985), pp. 90–143; Wood, *1549 Rebellions*, p. 244; *VCH Oxon.* VI, pp. 2, 64, 157.

[87] V. Di Palma, *Wasteland: A History* (London, 2014), pp. 12–16, provides a useful summary, including the extracts from Winstanley's writings, quoted above. For a fuller account, see C.

Figure 19. Chartist meeting at Basin Stones, Todmorden, in 1842, by Alfred Walter Bayes. An evocation by a local artist of one of the open-air meetings on moorland near the Chartist hotbed of Todmorden.

Later political protests on common land sometimes gravitated to commons where echoes of earlier protests would have continued to resonate. Mousehold Heath saw successive gatherings. Striking wool-combers camped there during a major strike in 1752, for example, and the Chartists held a rally on the Heath in 1848.[88] Katrina Navickas has explored the recurrent use of certain moors around the industrial towns of the south Pennines for political meetings across the early nineteenth century, from the republican cells of United Englishmen, who undertook nocturnal military drilling on moorland in the years around 1800, through gatherings of strikers and food rioters, to the great Chartist assemblies of the 1830s and 1840s.[89] Where commons drew repeated gatherings, the places themselves became symbols of protest as they gained layers of association with successive political assemblies. Hartshead Moor, near Cleckheaton (Yorks. W.R.), saw gatherings of the United Englishmen in 1801, Luddites in 1811–12, an anti-New Poor Law protest in 1838, Chartist meetings in 1838–39 and a

---

    Hill, *The World Turned Upside Down: Radical Ideas during the English Revolution* (Harmondsworth, 1975), pp. 107–50.

[88] N. MacMaster, 'The battle for Mousehold Heath 1857–1884: "popular politics" and the Victorian public park', *Past & Present*, 127 (1) (1990), p. 137n.

[89] K. Navickas, 'Moors, fields and popular protest in South Lancashire and the West Riding of Yorkshire, 1800–1848', *Northern History*, 46 (1) (2009), pp. 93–111; K. Navickas, *Protest and the Politics of Space and Place, 1789–1848* (Manchester, 2016), pp. 224–47, on which the following paragraphs are based.

celebration of the French Revolution in 1848. Strikers gathered on Kersal Moor, on the fringes of Manchester, in 1808, 1818 and 1831 and Chartists in 1838–39. On Skircoat Moor, just outside Halifax, a radical meeting calling for Parliamentary reform was held in the wake of the Peterloo Massacre in 1819 and this political heritage was revitalised in a series of Chartist gatherings there between 1839 and 1848. The Chartists, who borrowed the idea of open-air camp meetings from the Primitive Methodists, regularly held meetings on common land in the 1840s, sometimes on prominent Pennine hill tops, like Stoodley Pike, near Todmorden, and Blackstone Edge (cf. Figure 19), but also on lowland commons such as that held by the River Wear at Bishop Auckland (Dur.) in June 1840, and the great gathering in 1848 on Kennington Common (Surrey), which had been the site of several Radical meetings since the 1790s.[90]

The Pennine moorland itself formed part of the theatre of political protest. As Navickas puts it, gatherings on moorland commons allowed protesters to 'stand apart and above from the magistrates, manufacturers and other inhabitants anxiously observing from the town below'.[91] The landscape of the moors converted a meeting into a spectacle, height and visibility from a distance being used both to draw support and to intimidate those in authority. Straggling lines of protesters or more organised processions converging on a meeting point exhibited the full strength of the protest. The visibility of groups on open ground could taunt the authorities from a distance but the space and broken terrain of the common meant that crowds could melt away if they approached.

The association between common land and political dissent fuelled the conception of commons as wild, dangerous places. A satirical pamphlet, published in 1794 at the height of the anti-Jacobin emergency, when calling for reform was equated with sedition, centred on the supposed discovery of an imaginary Jacobin tract on Wimbledon Common. The pamphlet claimed that copies of the tract were circulating 'upon the wilds and woalds of our most uncultivated counties', clearly linking radical politics to places characterised by the open spaces of common land.[92]

* * *

Commons also hosted religious assemblies, providing the space to accommodate a crowd or, in other circumstances, the distance from settlement to protect gatherings which the authorities would wish to suppress. In an era when religion and politics were so closely intertwined, an element of religious protest was inherent in some of the sixteenth-century rebellions mentioned above, the Pilgrimage of Grace being the

---

[90] R. P. Hastings, *Chartism in the North Riding of Yorkshire and South Durham 1838–1848*, Borthwick Paper 105 (York, 2004), p. 18; K. Navickas, 'Kennington Common, protest and public space', in *Kennington 1848: Another Look* (Friends of Kennington Park, 2019), pp. 35–6; M. Gorman, *Saving the People's Forest: Open Spaces, Enclosure and Popular Protest in Mid-Victorian London* (Hatfield, 2021), p. 38.

[91] Navickas, 'Moors, fields and popular protest', p. 93.

[92] Anon., *Some Account of a very Seditious Book, lately found upon Wimbledon Common* (London, 1794), pp. 1–3.

COMMONS AS COMMUNAL SPACES

Figure 20. 'Fox's Pulpit', Pardshaw Crag, Cumberland, where Quakers met in the open air during the summer months from the 1650s until they built a meeting house in 1672.

obvious example. More specifically religious dissent also spilled out onto common land in the early days of the Reformation, as when George Wishart, the Scottish Protestant martyr, preached on the edge of moorland at Mauchline (Ayr), in 1545, having been debarred from the kirk, or at Colchester (Essex) in 1554, when an Anabaptist preacher gathered more than twenty protesters on Mile End Heath, just outside the town, in opposition to papacy.[93]

Forests and pastoral areas with large commons were noted as fertile ground for radical religious groups during the decades of religious turmoil in the seventeenth century.[94] Commons themselves became meeting places for separatists, especially during the early days of Quakerism. Having made his way through the Yorkshire Dales, bedding down overnight on bracken on a common, George Fox preached to a gathering of the separatists on Firbank Fell (Westmld) in June 1652, using the event to make his point that the open common was no less holy ground than a church building.[95] The Quaker groups established in the area continued to hold open-air meetings on hillsides in nearby Dentdale (Yorks. W.R.) later in the 1650s.[96]

---

[93] M. Sanderson, *Ayrshire and the Reformation: People and Change, 1490–1600* (East Linton, 1997), p. 67; *VCH Essex* IX, p. 123.
[94] Hill, *World Turned Upside Down*, pp. 46–7.
[95] J. L. Nickalls (ed.), *The Journal of George Fox* (London, 1975), pp. 104, 109.
[96] D. Boulton, *Early Friends in Dent: The English Revolution in a Dales Community* (Sedbergh, 1986), p. 35.

When the MP for Cumberland complained in 1656 that Quakers met 'in multitudes and upon moors', he was probably thinking of the settled Quaker groups in the vicinity of Cockermouth, which met on common land, during the summer months at least, at Settraw near the village of Sunderland, on Broughton Moor and at Pardshaw Crag (Figure 20), a limestone outcrop on the common near Dean, where meetings continued for a couple of decades until a meeting house was built in 1672.[97] Tellingly, it was said that meeting on those 'high-crags or clinty rocks' enabled the Pardshaw Quakers to 'readily espye any who came to disturb their conventicles; and so they were wont to disperse before they were caught'.[98] Elsewhere, Langrigg Common, north of Carlisle, saw a large meeting during a later Quaker mission in 1673; a small, isolated Quaker group met for worship on a hill common in mid-Wales in all weathers in the 1650s; and both Baptists and Quakers met on the common at Salford Furze, on the ridgeway near Chipping Norton (Oxon.), in the seventeenth century, according to a tradition recalled in 1904.[99]

Open-air 'field conventicles' were also a feature of dissenting Presbyterian congregations during the Covenanting times in seventeenth-century Scotland. Public outdoor preaching, often on moors and hills in the summer months, spread across much of southern Scotland from 1662, drawing large numbers. By 1676, Lilliesleaf Moor in Teviotdale (Roxburghshire) was known as 'a com[m]on and ordinary place and randevouze of these seditious, rebellious and disorderly meettings'. A conventicle on the Hill of Beath, near Dunfermline (Fife), in June 1670 was said to have been attended by around 1,000 people, many of whom had spent the Saturday night out on the hill.[100] The harsh suppression suffered by the Covenanter preachers enhanced the fame of places of open-air preaching on remote hillsides. On some, monuments were erected in the nineteenth century, such as the pillar topped by a communion cup, standing in a hollow on Skeoch Hill in Galloway, beside four rows of flat 'communion stones' on which the worshippers were said to have sat during services in the summer of 1678 (Figure 21), or the inscribed 'Preaching Stone' on the Keir Hills in Nithsdale, a few miles to the north, where James Renwick (executed 1688), the last Covenanter martyr, preached in the mid-1680s.[101]

Open-air meetings continued to be a feature of Scottish dissent in the early eighteenth century. A dissident minister, John Hepburn (d.1723), of Urr in Galloway, was noted for his field preaching, in one case drawing 7,000 people 'all sitting in rows on

---

[97] J. T. Rutt, *The Diary of Thomas Burton Esquire ... from 1656 to 1659, Vol. I* (London, 1828), p. 170; N. Penney (ed.), *The First Publishers of Truth* (London, 1907), pp. 37, 41, 43, 46.

[98] Denton, *Perambulation*, p. 116.

[99] Penney, *First Publishers*, p. 67. There had also been small meetings on commons near Carlisle in 1653: ibid., p. 68. W. C. Braithwaite, *The Beginnings of Quakerism*, 2nd edn (York, 1955), p. 487; R. C. Allen, *Quaker Communities in Early Modern Wales* (Cardiff, 2007), p. 30; *Oxfordshire Weekly News*, 20 July 1904, p. 5 (letter to the editor from C. W. Hannis).

[100] N. McIntyre, 'Saints and subverters: the later Covenanters in Scotland, c.1648–1682' (PhD thesis, University of Strathclyde, 2016), pp. 118–29.

[101] Canmore (National Record of Historic Environment, Scotland: https://canmore.org.uk/), ID 65006; ID 65294.

Figure 21. Covenanter monument and communion stones, Skeoch Hill, Kirkpatrick Irongray, Kirkcudbrightshire. The monument was erected in 1870.

the steep side of a green hill' near Drumlanrig, a gathering which saw his congregation, many of whom were poor, walk fifteen miles to hear him.[102] The radical Covenanter sect, the Cameronians, renewed their covenants at a meeting on Auchensaugh Hill, in the heart of the Southern Uplands, near Douglas (Lanarkshire), in a three-day meeting said to be 1,000 strong, in 1712.[103] In the years around 1740 a secession congregation met on Craigmailing Hill, south of Linlithgow (West Lothian), for a few years (1738–42) until they had built a church.[104] In one instance, religious dissent and agrarian protest merged, when, in April 1724, it was a 'mountain preacher' who encouraged the Galloway Levellers in their direct anti-enclosure protests, by inveighing against new enclosures which, he said, involved 'making Commonty Property'. The following morning, the protesters, fired up by 'that ancient Levelling Tenet', set about throwing down enclosure walls in the vicinity.[105]

The Evangelical Revival also saw large gatherings on common land, especially near towns, where it was the space commons provided as open-air auditoria, rather than

[102] Defoe, *Tour*, p. 594.
[103] A. Livingston, 'The Galloway Levellers: a study of their origins, events and consequences of their actions' (MPhil thesis, University of Glasgow, 2009), p. 44.
[104] Canmore, ID 47987.
[105] J. W. Leopold, 'The Galloway Levellers' revolt of 1724', in A. Charlesworth (ed.), *Rural Change and Conflicts since 1500* (Hull, 1983), p. 18.

their seclusion, which drew the crowds. In the summer of 1739, George Whitefield, the Methodist, preached on Blackheath (after the local vicar had been forbidden from allowing him to preach in his church); on Hackney Marsh on a race day; and on Kennington Common on several occasions. One of his audiences on Kennington Common was estimated to have consisted of more than 30,000 who came on foot, 'besides many horsemen, and about eighty coaches'. It was said that Whitefield's voice could carry nearly a mile and that the hymn-singing could be heard two miles away.[106]

Such 'field preaching' was revived in the early nineteenth century by the Primitive Methodists, for whom open-air camp meetings were a distinguishing feature. Two of the initial camp meetings which formed the springboard for Primitive Methodism in 1807 were held on commons in the Staffordshire moorlands to the north of Stoke-on-Trent. After an initial meeting in a field at Mow Cop, the Primitives' leader, Hugh Bourne, held a second, much larger meeting on the common on the summit of the Mow, which lasted for three days, attracting enthusiastic worshippers from a distance and involving the setting up of lines of tents and other fixtures on the common.[107]

Open-air meetings became part of the wider world of nonconformist evangelism in the nineteenth century, both revivalist 'tent meetings' and fund-raising 'tea meetings' sometimes taking place on commons. The Baptists of Stroud (Glos.) proposed holding a 'monster tea meeting' on the nearby Rodborough Common in 1867, taking their inspiration from 'immense' outdoor tea meetings which had been held in Wales.[108] Six years later, in the summer of 1873, the Gloucestershire Gospel Tent was pitched for a week on the same common.[109]

* * *

As the location of such a multiplicity of communal gatherings from the medieval period onwards, commons remained public spaces, notwithstanding the private property rights which governed their economic exploitation. However, the association between commons and public assemblies was far from uniform, as communal gatherings tended to occur at specific locations, often sanctioned by long use. Folk moots, military musters, fairs and sports – even protests and preaching – drew people to particular places; other stretches of common land remained the preserve of the grazing flocks or of widows gathering fuel. The experience of common land in the lives of medieval and early modern people was thus full of contrasts: some commons were on some occasions peopled places, teeming with life; at other times a common could be a lonely – even fearful – place, distant from the comforts of hearth and home and sometimes associated with death. Despite containing tangible symbols of power (such as beacons

---

[106] J. P. Gledstone, *George Whitefield, M.A.: Field Preacher* (New York, 1901), pp. 92–4, 100, 106; *Town Commons*, p. 73.

[107] *Christian Messenger*, 1901/361, at https://www.myprimitivemethodists.org.uk/content/subjects-2/primitive-methodist-history/the_second_mow_cop_camp_meeting. For Primitive Methodist meetings on Cockfield Fell and Bringsty Common, see below, pp. 225, 247–9.

[108] *Stroud Journal*, 2 November 1867, p. 5.

[109] *Stroud News & Gloucestershire Advertiser*, 6 June 1873, p. 4.

and gibbets), commons were spaces less closely monitored by those in authority, making them ambivalent places, to be avoided by some but attracting others who sought the comparative freedom they offered, away from habitations and prying eyes.

As 'waste' on or beyond the margins of civilisation, common land possessed something of the aura of wilderness and, hence, had a tendency to garner fear and superstition: setting out onto a lonely common as dusk fell would not have been for the faint-hearted. Quarries, pits and pools could present physical danger, but natural and manmade landmarks alike were often clothed with a supernatural aura, perpetuated by local folklore.[110] Echoes of the dark side of common land abounded, in the sites of gallows and gibbets and haunted prehistoric burial mounds; or in folk memories of robberies, murders and suicides, sometimes pinned to the land by place-names referring to death.[111] Commons thus accumulated associations, becoming places of communal memory, which added further dimensions to their meaning, beyond their role as an agrarian resource.

---

[110] For examples from Herefordshire, see J. Moir, '"A World unto Themselves"? Squatter settlement in Herefordshire, 1780–1880' (PhD thesis, University of Leicester, 1990), pp. 7–10.
[111] Such as Deadman Hill (SU 20 17) in the New Forest, Deadman's Corner (SX 70 70) on Dartmoor, or the two occurrences of Deadman's Gill (NY 82 18 and NY 90 11) on the wilds of Stainmore in the Pennines.

CHAPTER 5

LIVING ON THE EDGE: COMMONS AND THE POOR

TO QUOTE ANOTHER OF Alan Everitt's memorable phrases, commons were places of 'homely things and humble people'.[1] An association between common land and the poorest members of the community had become well established by the seventeenth century, to the extent that commons and poverty were seen as going hand-in-hand. In 1651, Samuel Hartlib, the champion of enclosure, asked rhetorically why 'there are fewest poore where there are fewest *Commons*'. Commons, he said, engendered idleness, training up the poor 'for the Gallowes or beggary', rather than for useful service.[2] To those in authority, common land was synonymous with people on the margins of mainstream society – not only the parish poor but also squatters living on the commons and itinerant groups. Commons were often viewed as hotbeds of lawlessness and immorality, 'edgy' places on the edges of parishes, where clandestine or illegal activities took place.

In the debates over enclosure in the late eighteenth and early nineteenth century, the relationship between commons and the poor loomed large on both sides of the argument. Both agreed that access to the resources of common land was a key feature of the lives of the poor. To advocates of enclosure, such dependence bred idleness and poverty, so the commons should be enclosed; to opponents, it was wrong that enclosure should deprive the poor of the support they obtained from common land. Enclosure could thus be seen as an attack on the livelihood of the poor, a view succinctly expressed in the much-quoted anonymous ditty from the period, which critiqued enclosure in class terms:

> The fault is great in Man or Woman
> Who steals a Goose from off a Common
> But what can plead that Man's excuse
> Who steals a Common from a Goose.[3]

---

[1] A. Everitt, 'Common land', in J. Thirsk (ed.), *The English Rural Landscape* (Oxford, 2000), p. 231.
[2] S. Hartlib, *Samuel Hartlib, his Legacie or an Enlargement of the Discourse of Husbandry used in Brabant and Flaunders* ... (London, 1651), p. 54.
[3] For the provenance of this ditty, see J. Boyle, 'The second enclosure movement and the construction of the public domain', *Law and Contemporary Problems*, 66 (1–2) (2003), pp. 33n–34n. Variants of the stanza abound, lines 1 and 3 often being quoted as 'The law locks up the man or woman ... But leaves the greater villain loose ...'. The version quoted here is

Striking at the heart of the issue, by exposing 'the artificial and controversial nature of property rights',[4] its choice of the cottager's humble goose as the victim of enclosure confirms the conflation of common land with the interests of the poor in the eyes of contemporaries.

The historical consensus on the effects of enclosure on the poor veered between extremes across the twentieth century. The view proposed by the Hammonds in *The Village Labourer* in 1911 saw enclosure as 'fatal' to small farmers, cottagers and squatters, as the resources of common land were more valuable to them than any small allotments they might receive on enclosure. The contrary position put forward by J. D. Chambers and others in the middle decades of the century argued that enclosure created employment and was beneficial to the poor. Thanks to the work of Keith Snell, Janette Neeson, Steve Hindle and others, the pendulum has now swung back to recognise the value of common land to the poor and the loss that enclosure represented.[5]

MAKING A LIVING FROM COMMON LAND

For the poor, the key resources provided by common land were grazing for a few animals and fuel for the fire. The belief that access to the common pastures allowed poor families to keep a cow is embedded deeply in popular conceptions of the rural past. It certainly featured strongly in contemporary comment during the era of enclosure: once a common had gone, the poor had to sell their cows, bringing to an end a tradition of cottagers owning their own livestock. As the value of a cow in all its produce might equate to a substantial proportion of the wage of a farm labourer, the loss of access to common land represented a body blow to those poor families who had livestock.[6] Such a simplistic view masked a more complex reality and begs several questions. How does it square with the evidence, summarised in Chapter 2, that

---

that published in 1819 by Edward Birch, who claimed to have found it on a handbill posted in Plaistow (Essex), opposing the enclosure of Epping Forest: *The Gentleman's Mathematical Companion*, vol. 4, no. xxii (1819), p. 556.

[4] Boyle, 'Second enclosure movement', p. 34.

[5] The earlier literature is reviewed in K. D. M. Snell, *Annals of the Labouring Poor: Social Change and Agrarian England, 1660–1900* (Cambridge, 1985), pp. 138–44. Snell's important chapter on the effects of enclosure (pp. 138–227) reset the dial after the dominance of the Chambers view. Other key studies include J. M. Neeson, *Commoners: Common Right, Enclosure and Social Change in England, 1700–1820* (Cambridge, 1993), pp. 158–82; D. Woodward, 'Straw, bracken and the Wicklow whale: the exploitation of natural resources in England since 1500', *Past & Present*, 159 (1998), pp. 43–76; S. Hindle, *On the Parish? The Micro-Politics of Poor Relief in Rural England c.1550–1750* (Oxford, 2004), pp. 27–48; A. Wood, *The Memory of the People: Custom and Popular Senses of the Past in Early Modern England* (Cambridge, 2013), pp. 156–62. The following paragraphs draw on these works.

[6] For the keeping of livestock by the poor, see Snell, *Annals of the Labouring* Poor, pp. 174–8. Estimates of the value of a cow vary. Arthur Young, writing in 1801, estimated it at 5s 0d to 6s 0d per week, which would be approaching the weekly wage of a labourer (ibid., p. 177); others have suggested that it might represent 40 per cent of a labourer's annual wage: Hindle, *On the Parish?*, p. 30.

only some cottagers possessed formal grazing rights through holding commonable cottages? Were other cottagers excluded from grazing or did custom allow them to graze livestock? A study of cow-keeping, based on comments made around 1800 in lowland England from Oxfordshire to Norfolk, has suggested that only in a minority of parishes was cow-keeping ubiquitous among labourers, the overall picture being that no more than a significant minority of the landless kept cows.[7] If replicated elsewhere, perhaps the importance of grazing on common land to the economy of the poor has been overstated, even if, in the absence of a cow, the common might provide scratchings for poultry or perhaps a goat or a donkey.

Nevertheless, common land yielded other vital resources to the poorest as they strove to make ends meet. Most important was fuel, in the form of sticks, furze, turf and peat, heather and, in places, even dried cow dung. Again, the pecuniary value of fuel ought not to be under-estimated; it might have been as much as one-fifth of a labourer's annual wage in the later eighteenth century.[8] At Stoke Poges (Bucks.) it was said in 1806 that it cost a poor household 16s a year to cut turf from the common for fuel, whereas the cost of purchasing coal would have been six times as much (£4 16s 3d).[9] Diets could be supplemented with nuts, wild fruit and herbs; cottage roofs repaired with sods and thatched with reeds, bracken or heather. Common land attracted 'improvisers and people of infinite resource',[10] using raw materials from which basic goods, such as mats, baskets and besoms, could be made to generate a modicum of income. Much of that use was seasonal and based on informal custom rather than formal common right. The legal niceties of the distinction between old-established 'commonable cottages' and more recent cottages without rights were probably largely irrelevant to the day-to-day use of many commons. Customary use by the poor was often challenged but was nevertheless a fact of early modern life.

Some commons offered employment. In 1601, for example, it was said that the poor of Cawston (Norf.) made the greatest part of their living by 'graving flags [sods] and cutting lyng' on the common for other inhabitants.[11] Where mineral resources were exploited, the demand for manual labour in quarries, coal and lead mines or in lime, clay or gravel pits provided employment for the poor. In the sixteenth and seventeenth centuries, contemporaries were clear that commons attracted those with little, like the 'multitude of poore people belonging to the said forest [of Feckenham (Worcs.)] which live in and by the said comon'.[12] Living on the resources of common land was a reality to many, so that, when enclosure took place, the impact on the poor of the loss of the commons struck deep into popular consciousness and became a theme which has echoed down English history ever since, even if the enduring image of the cottager's cow has been overstated.

---

[7] L. Shaw-Taylor, 'Labourers, cows, common rights and Parliamentary enclosure: the evidence of contemporary comment, c.1760–1810', *Past & Present*, 171 (2001), pp. 113–22.
[8] Hindle, *On the Parish?*, p. 30.
[9] L. Rigby, *The History of Stoke Common: A Poor's Fuel Allotment Charity* (Stoke Poges, 1975), p. 7.
[10] *Ashdown Forest*, pp. 37–8.
[11] N. Whyte, *Inhabiting the Landscape: Place, Custom and Memory, 1500–1800* (Oxford, 2009), p. 111.
[12] Comment dated 1631, quoted by Wood, *Memory of the People*, p. 157.

GYPSIES AND OTHER TRAVELLERS

Common land also came to be associated with groups of itinerants on the margins of society. Vagrants – the masterless men and women of the road who featured prominently in debates about the poor in the later sixteenth and early seventeenth century – would have been seen crossing commons as they made their way from town to town. They passed through, rather than making commons their homes, as begging and seeking employment took them to settled places, sleeping in barns and under hedges.[13] By the later eighteenth century, however, encampments of bands of itinerants had become a feature of many commons, as gypsies, potters and tinkers stayed on common land for a time before moving on.

When gypsies were first recorded in Britain in the early sixteenth century they were first and foremost entertainers, specialising in fortune-telling and dancing, who travelled from town to town, plying their trade at fairs. Despite draconian Tudor legislation between 1530 and 1554, which attempted to banish them, they stayed and by the early seventeenth century the distinction between gypsies and vagrants had begun to blur. The travellers of the seventeenth and eighteenth centuries encompassed a wide spectrum of people on the margins of society – pedlars, hawkers, tinkers, runaways, Irish and Scots – as well as the descendants of the Tudor 'Egyptians', who seem to have travelled in larger groups than most others.[14] To settled communities, travellers were outsiders, a breed apart surrounded by clouds of suspicion and fear and subjected to enduring prejudice as 'idle, dirty, [and] deceitful'.[15]

Some gypsy groups in sixteenth-century England travelled long distances, presumably following fairs. Gypsies at Dorchester Assizes in 1559 had travelled out of Scotland via Carlisle, for example. By the 1590s large groups of 'idle persons', some described as gypsies, included over one hundred souls passing through Nottinghamshire in 1591 on their way to Gainsborough Fair; even larger groups were recorded in Yorkshire and south-western counties in 1596. A seasonal pattern of travel which continued to structure the lives of some southern English gypsy groups into the nineteenth century seems to be recorded by the early seventeenth century. In 1616 a group apprehended in Hampshire travelled across the summer months, presumably from fair to fair, but spent the winter in a more settled existence in London.[16]

To what extent the travelling entertainers of the sixteenth century stopped on common land, as opposed to simply passing through it, is unclear, though gypsy encampments were said to be held regularly near Blackheath, on the south-eastern approach to London, and at 'Devil's Arse a Peak' (Peak Cavern), the cave on the common just outside Castleton (Derby.) which was one of the 'wonders' of the Peak District.[17] By the eighteenth and nineteenth centuries, the association between gypsies and common

---

[13] A. L. Beier, *Masterless Men: The Vagrancy Problem in England, 1560–1640* (London, 1985), esp. pp. 69–85.
[14] Ibid., pp. 59–62.
[15] D. Cressy, 'Trouble with gypsies in early modern England', *Historical Journal*, 59 (2016), p. 58.
[16] Ibid., pp. 55, 63–6, 67.
[17] Beier, *Masterless Men*, p. 59.

land had become stronger. In lowland England the gypsy economy increasingly drew on the resources of commons, both for raw materials and for seasonal employment. As makers of baskets, besoms, brooms, beehives, clothes-pegs, door mats and meat skewers, they could harvest their raw materials (poles, withies, sticks, heather and rushes) from common land. In the Chilterns, the clay pits, sand pits and brick kilns on commons provided employment in late autumn and spring.[18] More generally, commons became temporary homes to gypsy groups across south-eastern England as they travelled to take up seasonal farm work, especially at harvest time. Not all common land lent itself to encampments: travellers needed shelter, firm footing for tents, a water supply, and stopping places which were well-placed for paid work or for markets for the gypsies' goods.[19] Favoured commons became points on a circuit, visited at intervals. Gilbert White wrote in 1775 that the two gypsy clans which passed through Selborne in eastern Hampshire came round two or three times each year.[20]

In the northern counties of England 'potter' had become a synonym for 'gypsy' by the early nineteenth century, as bands of itinerant pot-sellers traded Staffordshire earthenware across the region. They were numerous in Cumbria, an 'alien and visible minority' who wintered on patches of waste close to market towns, travelling out to sell their wares across the summer months.[21] They were a regular sight on village commons, spreading their wares on the ground, 'while the village maids and matrons gathered round, to become purchasers', as Thomas Wilkinson of Yanwath, near Penrith, noted in 1812. He also claimed that one of the most frequent arguments put forward in favour of enclosure in Cumbria was that 'by inclosing the Common we should get quit of the Potters'.[22]

COTTAGES AND COTTAGERS

In the centuries between c.1550 and c.1850 many commons in England and Wales once more became a frontier of colonisation, providing space where cottages could be built to house an expanding rural population. The preamble to the Act of Settlement and Removal (1662) noted that the mobile poor would settle in parishes which had the best resources, including those with 'the largest commons or wastes to build cottages and the more woods for them to burn and destroy'.[23] Squatter cottages sprang up on roadside wastes, on the sides of greens and small patches of common, on heaths and forest margins and on larger tracts of common land. They were particularly numerous in south-eastern counties of England, in the New Forest and the Forest of Dean, in

---

[18] D. Mayall, *Gypsy-Travellers in Nineteenth-Century Society* (Cambridge, 1988), pp. 31, 54–60; A.-M. Ford, 'On common ground', in *Our Common Heritage: A Collection of Six Essays about the Social History of Chiltern Commons* (Chilterns Conservation Board, 2015), p. 72.

[19] A point made in relation to the New Forest by Mayall, *Gypsy-Travellers*, p. 29.

[20] G. White, *The Natural History and Antiquities of Selborne*, Folio Society edn (London, 1994), p. 178.

[21] J. D. Marshall, *Old Lakeland* (Newton Abbot, 1971), pp. 119–23.

[22] T. Wilkinson, *Thoughts on Inclosing Yanwath Moor and Round Table* (Penrith, 1812), pp. 30–1.

[23] Act of Settlement & Removal, 13 & 14 Chas. II, c.12, preamble.

industrialising areas in the Midlands, along the length of the Welsh Marches and in Wales itself. No fewer than ninety-six settlements of at least ten dwellings had grown up on commons in Herefordshire by the early nineteenth century.[24] In Scotland, by contrast, where squatters would have infringed the rights of the proprietors of a commonty, the landowners' absolute rights suppressed cottage-building, except where explicit permission had been granted.[25]

Where the chronology of cottage-building on a common can be reconstructed, its roots often reached back to the later sixteenth and early seventeenth century, but numbers exploded after c.1750. On the Gloucestershire side of Gorsley Common in the hills west of Newent four cottages had been built before 1624 but the number increased to eighteen by 1775 and to more than thirty by 1838, for example (Figure 22).[26] At Woodgreen (Hants), on the north-western edge of the New Forest, where a handful of cottages were built from the 1660s, the 1740s and 1750s saw the construction of more than half of the forty cottages there by the 1790s, and the number of families living on the common doubled again between 1801 and 1841.[27] That cottage-building on common land continued well into Victoria's reign is made clear by the Inclosure Commission, whose reasons for consenting to the enclosure of Westhope Hill (Heref.) and common land at Llangwm (Denb.) in 1863 included the statement that 'it will put an end to the system of squatting, which is rapidly swallowing up the common'.[28]

Early cottage-building was in theory constrained by the 1589 act requiring that all cottages should have four acres (1.6 ha) of land, though this was deemed not to apply to labourers' cottages within one mile of quarries or other mineral workings.[29] But the act did not stem the flow, particularly in Wales and the western counties of

---

[24] Local and regional studies include J. P. Bowen, 'Cottage and squatter settlement and encroachment on common waste in the 16th and 17th centuries: some evidence from Shropshire', *Local Population Studies*, 93 (2014), pp. 11–32; C. Griffin, 'Enclosure from below? The politics of squatting and encroachment in the post-Restoration New Forest', *Historical Research*, 91 (252) (2018), pp. 274–95; N. Herbert, 'The squatter and rural settlement in the Georgian Age: Woolridge Common, Hartpury', *Transactions of the Bristol & Gloucestershire Archaeological Society*, 133 (2015), pp. 175–206; J. Moir, '"A World unto Themselves"? Squatter settlement in Herefordshire, 1780–1880' (PhD thesis, University of Leicester, 1990); R. Silvester, 'Landscapes of the poor: encroachment in Wales in the post-medieval centuries', in P. S. Barnwell and M. Palmer (eds), *Post-Medieval Landscapes* (Macclesfield, 2007), pp. 55–67.

[25] I. D. Whyte, 'Population mobility in early modern Scotland', in R. A. Houston and I. D. Whyte (eds), *Scottish Society, 1500–1800* (Cambridge, 1989), pp. 39–40; R. Houston, 'Custom in context: medieval and early modern Scotland and England', *Past & Present*, 211 (2011), pp. 54–5.

[26] *VCH Glos.* XII, pp. 37, 179; R. Suggett, *Houses and History in the March of Wales: Radnorshire 1400–1800* (Aberystwyth, 2005), p. 256.

[27] D. Moody, 'Godshillwood and Woodgreen: a squatter settlement on the edge of the New Forest, 1600–1840', *Proceedings of the Hampshire Field Club Archaeological Society*, 71 (2016), pp. 131–3, 137.

[28] *Special report of Inclosure Commissioners, 1863*, case nos. 8, 10.

[29] D. Tankard, 'The regulation of cottage building in seventeenth-century Sussex', *AgHR*, 59 (1) (2011), pp. 19–35; C. Hill, *The World Turned Upside Down* (Harmondsworth, 1975), p. 43.

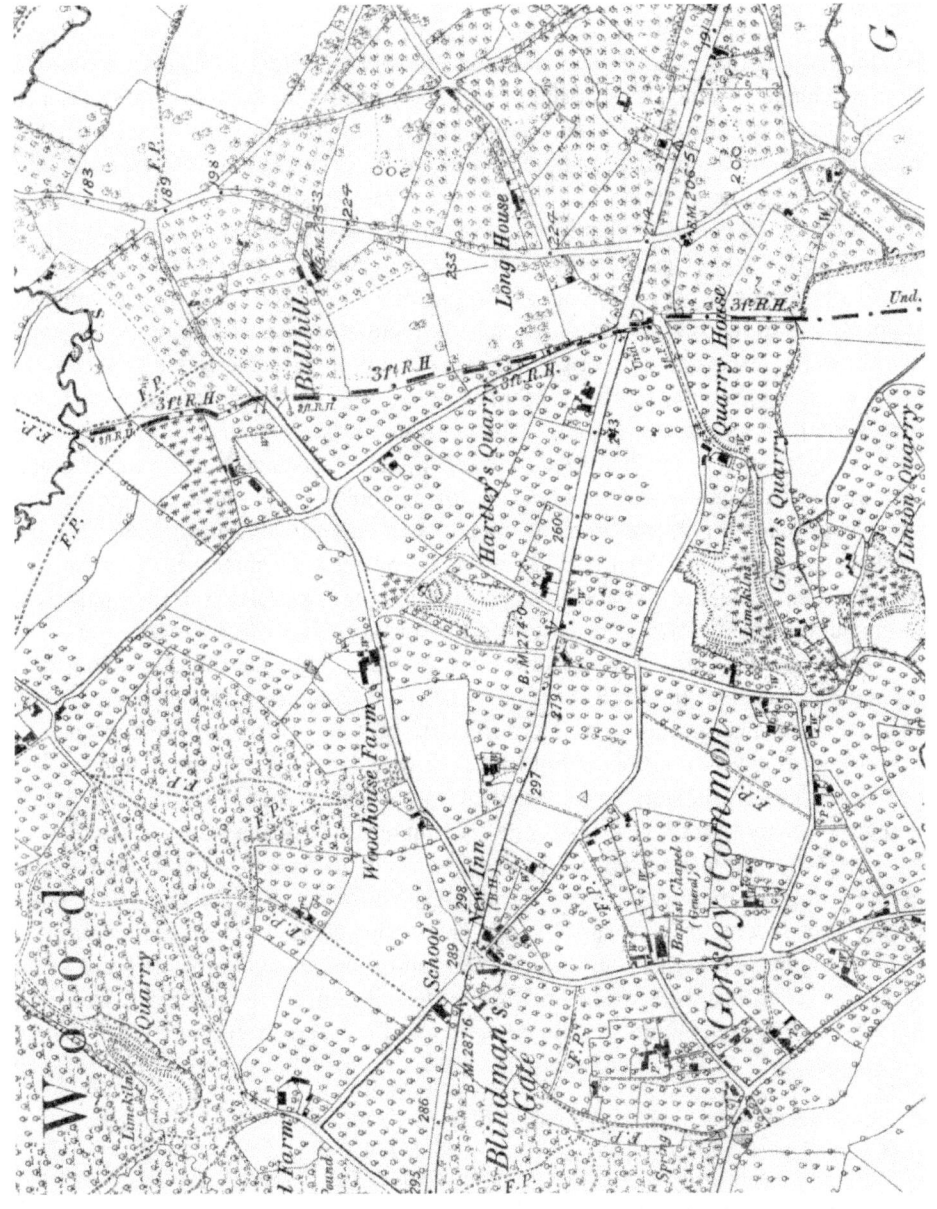

Figure 22. Gorsley Common, straddling the Herefordshire/Gloucestershire boundary near Newent. Cottage settlement from the seventeenth century resulted in the almost complete enclosure of the common as small paddocks and orchards (OS Six-Inch map: Herefordshire 47SE, surveyed 1883–87).

England where the tradition of the 'one-night house' (in Welsh, *tŷ unnos*) was strong. Folklore stated that, if a cottage could be erected overnight so that smoke issued from its chimney by daybreak, it should be allowed to stand. Contemporary evidence of the custom in operation is rare, though generalised claims were widespread.[30] For example, William Gilpin, vicar of Boldre, on the edge of the New Forest, from 1777 to 1804, claimed to have known a cottage built 'during the course of a moonlight night', with 'a fire kindled, and the family in possession' by morning.[31] A rudimentary house thus erected would develop in time into a more permanent structure, set in a small enclosure serving as a garden and potato patch.[32] More often, the cottage builders probably had to rely on the tacit agreement, or blind eye, of the owner of the common and those possessing common rights. Cottages built on roadside waste impinged far less on existing property rights than those built on a common proper, where squatters would compete for grazing and fuel rights with existing commoners.

If occupation went unchallenged for twenty years, a cottager's claim would stand in law, so lords of the manor amerced cottage-builders in the manor court and sometimes made a point of breaking cottage hedges and walking or riding through gardens and paddocks which encroached on the waste. In some cases, as at Gorsley (Glos.), for example, the aim of disturbing the cottagers' occupation of their plots was to encourage squatters to take leases. As a result of such pressure, rents were often paid.[33] However, in some areas landowners amerced cottagers at the manor court but did not demand rent. In the New Forest, the Crown Commissioners reported in 1789 that the numerous cottage encroachments there were held 'without paying any rent or acknowledgement to the Crown' but that they were generally presented at the forest courts, which, presumably largely ineffectually, ordered them to be pulled down, fining the perpetrators.[34] At Whixall and Prees in northern Shropshire, squatters were amerced 6d in the manor court, in effect licensing their cottage; later, leases were granted, the rents paid by cottagers forming a substantial part of the manorial income by the later seventeenth century.[35] Lords might thus connive at cottage-building on their commons. They and the farming community with common rights were often willing to countenance cottage-building, especially on commons which were not heavily used by commoners, as the inhabitants of cottages could be a ready source

---

[30] Mentions of the tradition are gathered in C. Ward, *Cotters and Squatters* (Nottingham, 2002). See also Moir, '"A World unto Themselves"?', pp. 162–6.

[31] W. Gilpin, *Remarks on Forest Scenery and other Woodland Views ... illustrated by the scenes of New-Forest in Hampshire, Vol. II* (London, 1794), p. 40.

[32] Silvester, 'Landscapes of the poor', p. 57; Suggett, *Houses and History*, pp. 256–9. Nicholas Herbert ('The squatter and rural settlement', pp. 178–9) has noted the lack of contemporary evidence for 'one-night houses'.

[33] Herbert, 'The squatter and rural settlement', pp. 176–7, 183; Moir, '"A World unto Themselves"?', pp. 142–53.

[34] S. Crocker, *Squatters and Social Crime: Encroachments in the New Forest in the Eighteenth Century*, Hampshire Papers, 2nd ser. 6 (Hampshire Field Club & Archaeological Society, 2018), p. 15.

[35] Bowen, 'Cottage and squatter settlement', pp. 14, 17–18. Similar evidence comes from Lilleshall, where poor cottagers were amerced but paid no rent: ibid., pp. 30–2.

of agricultural labour.[36] Conversely, where a single lord could impose control over a common, cottage-building could be prevented. The impact of contrasting degrees of manorial control at local level can sometimes be seen in the distribution of cottages, as on commons in the Stiperstones (Shrops.), where the absence of cottages on the eastern flanks of the hill in Gatten, where the landowner's grip was strong, contrasts with their proliferation in the mining district around Pennerley.[37]

Squatter settlements were closely tied to availability of employment. At local level, in the Kentish Weald for example, common-edge cottages were more numerous in parishes where employment in the textile industry was available.[38] Industrialising areas correlated with particularly large concentrations. In Derbyshire, where lead miners were allowed to occupy cottages on the wastes while they were actively engaged in mining, there were seventy-six cottages in the Youlgreave area and thirty on the wastes at Wirksworth by around 1650. At West Bromwich in the Staffordshire Black Country, opportunities for industrial employment encouraged cottage-building on the edges of the heaths – there were ninety-nine cottages on the wastes there by 1723.[39] In the Forest of Dean and in the Shropshire coalfield, where the mines, quarries and ironworks provided increasing employment in the eighteenth and early nineteenth centuries, cottage-building on the wastes mushroomed after 1750, the number of cottages in the Forest of Dean increasing more than six-fold, from 134 in 1752 to 879 by 1812.[40] In the township of Great Dawley in the Shropshire coalfield, where eleven cottages had been recorded by 1572, the number trebled from fifty-six by 1753 to over 150 by 1812.[41]

The fuel and grazing resources available on common land played a part in attracting settlement, especially on heathland and wooded commons which offered greater scope for scraping a living than did more open land.[42] Squatters rarely possessed formal common rights but merely holding a cottage and a small plot emboldened some to claim rights, as recorded in Savernake Forest (Wilts.) in 1580.[43] Not surprisingly, the presence of squatters could result in tension with other users of a common. The various impacts of cottagers on existing property rights are illustrated in evidence from Shropshire in the seventeenth century. In one of the riots which broke out at Broseley between 1605 and 1607, where workers in the coal pits had been allowed

---

[36] A theme explored in Moir, '"A World unto Themselves"?', *passim*.

[37] D. Pannett, 'Commons of the Stiperstones mining district', *Transactions of the Shropshire Archaeological & Historical Society*, 95 (2020), pp. 61–82.

[38] J. Thirsk, *Agrarian History of England and Wales, Vol. V, part I* (Cambridge, 1984), p. 312.

[39] Ibid., pp. 135, 145.

[40] *VCH Glos.* V, pp. 301–3, cited by Herbert, 'The squatter and rural settlement'.

[41] *VCH Shrops.* XI, p. 107.

[42] In Shropshire, for example, more cottages were built on the heaths and partly wooded commons of the north of the county than elsewhere: J. P. Bowen, '"The struggle for the commons": commons, custom and cottages in Shropshire during the sixteenth and seventeenth centuries', in J. P. Bowen and A. T. Brown (eds), *Custom and Commercialisation in English Rural Society: Revisiting Tawney and Postan* (Hatfield, 2016), pp. 115–16.

[43] Wilts. & Swindon History Centre, 1300/87. I am grateful to Graham Bathe for this reference.

to build cottages on the wastes, the colliers were attacked by freeholders and other tenants who claimed that their common rights were being reduced.[44] Elsewhere in the county, cottagers' animals made them unwelcome neighbours: in the forest of Treflach in Oswestry lordship it was said in 1602 that squatters were 'noysome neighbours' as their goats destroyed the underwood, while in 1650 the dogs kept by cottagers on the fringes of the Weald Moors were attacking and killing livestock on the commons.[45]

Many cottages sat in small plots of ground encroached from the common, typically containing around 0.5–0.75 of an acre (0.2–0.3 ha), which provided garden produce and fruit, sometimes for sale.[46] In Herefordshire it was said in 1657 that 'servants' (probably to be interpreted as landless young men) would, on marriage, lease a plot of land 'and thereon they build a Cottage, & plant an Orchard, which is all the wealth they have for themselves, and their Posterity'.[47] Many Herefordshire cottages and their orchard plots formed productive islands in a sea of furzy waste. Orchards were also a feature of cottage settlement on the edge of the New Forest by the middle of the eighteenth century.[48]

However, most cottagers relied on income from other sources. In the later eighteenth century, some in the New Forest made a living by cutting furze and supplying the local brick-kilns; others worked on farms and in a local shipyard and ropewalk.[49] In Ashdown Forest (Sussex) cutting cartloads of litter for neighbouring farmers provided seasonal employment for cottagers and labourers in autumn and winter in the nineteenth century.[50] In nineteenth-century censuses, many cottagers were recorded as farm workers or industrial labourers; some were craftsmen.[51] Although many inhabitants of common land may have been poor and uneducated, there is evidence of modest wealth among some cottager families of long standing, and even, on Woodgreen Common (Hants) in the early nineteenth century, of 'cottage speculators', who built cottages to let.[52] The cottagers on the commons thus provided a source of labour and their independence, built on access to the resources of the commons, could prevent them from becoming a charge on the poor rate.

---

[44] M. D. G. Wanklyn, 'Rural riots in 17th-century Shropshire', in A. Charlesworth (ed.), *Rural Social Change and Conflicts since 1500* (Hull, 1983), pp. 11–12.

[45] W. J. Slack (ed.), *The Lordship of Oswestry, 1393–1607* (Shrewsbury, 1951), p. 60; Bowen, 'Cottage and squatter settlement', p. 16.

[46] For examples, see Moody, 'Godshillwood and Woodgreen'; Herbert, 'The squatter and rural settlement'.

[47] J. Beale, *Herefordshire Orchards, a pattern for all England. Written in an epistolary address to Samuel Hartlib Esq.* (London, 1657), p. 32.

[48] Moody, 'Godshillwood and Woodgreen', pp. 132–3.

[49] Crocker, *Squatters and Social Crime*, pp. 9, 14; Griffin, 'Enclosure from below?', p. 290.

[50] *Ashdown Forest*, passim.

[51] For Herefordshire, see Moir, '"A World unto Themselves"?'.

[52] Moody, 'Godshillwood and Woodgreen', pp. 138–40. See also Herbert, 'The squatter and rural settlement', p. 198.

Squatters were adept at exploiting the border spaces between jurisdictions, both on the edges of parishes and on the boundaries between counties.[53] The attraction of Woolridge Common (Glos.) stemmed from an anomaly in its manorial status, having been separated at the Dissolution from the manor whose tenants exercised common rights there.[54] Beaulieu Rails (Hants) lay along the margin between Beaulieu manor and the New Forest wastes, again exploiting a jurisdictional boundary, while Nomansland, on the northern edge of the New Forest, was but one example of settlement on supposedly ownerless wastes.[55] Extra-parochial status, a feature of forest commons in the Forest of Dean and the New Forest, distanced those who dwelt there from the religious and secular authority of the local parish church. Woodgreen, for example, became a recipient of pregnant unmarried women, brought there to give birth, so that their illegitimate children (whose place of settlement would be the parish of their birth) could be deemed to be the responsibility of no parish.[56] Such marginality placed some squatter settlements outside the institutional structures of early modern society, enhancing the sense that these were places on the edge.

The new landscapes created by cottage-building took a variety of forms, from a scatter of cottages along the common edge to larger, haphazard clusters which gelled over time to become new villages. At one end of the spectrum were the commons where cottages were comparatively few in number, like Myddle Wood Common (Shrops.), for example, where there appear to have been around nine cottages by 1700.[57] Where cottages were more numerous, some formed beads of encroachment around the edges of a common. In the *cantref* of Maelienydd (near Llanbister, Radnorshire), where a survey of 1734 listed over 400 encroachments onto common land, including 154 cottages without land attached, the landscape of squatter settlement survives in an irregular fringe of houses set in small fields around the margins of the common.[58] The names given to cottages in mid-Wales were often in English and tended to be ironic ('Grand Porch', 'The Castle') or humorous ('Morning Surprise', for a 'one-night house').[59] Likewise, the squatter cottages of the New Forest were almost wholly restricted to the edges of the commons, most forming fringes around the edges of private estates. Only a few stood as isolated islands in the heart of the Forest. Concentrations included those around the enclaves of enclosure at Burley and Brockenhurst and the almost continuous string of cottages set in small plots at Beaulieu Rails (East Boldre) along

---

[53] J. Broad, 'Boundary settlements and overlapping jurisdictions: marginal communities and Little Londons', in R. W. Hoyle (ed.), *Histories of People and Landscape* (Hatfield, 2021), pp. 182–4.
[54] Herbert, 'The squatter and rural settlement', pp. 180–4.
[55] Griffin, 'Enclosure from below?', pp. 285–7. Others included the No Man's Heaths on the Leicestershire/Warwickshire boundary and near Malpas (Ches.): Broad, 'Boundary settlements', pp. 176–8, 185.
[56] Moody, 'Godshillwood and Woodgreen', p. 136.
[57] R. Gough, *History of Myddle*, ed. D. Hey (Harmondsworth, 1981), pp. 63, 247–8.
[58] Silvester, 'Landscapes of the poor', esp. pp. 58–64.
[59] Suggett, *Houses and History*, p. 258.

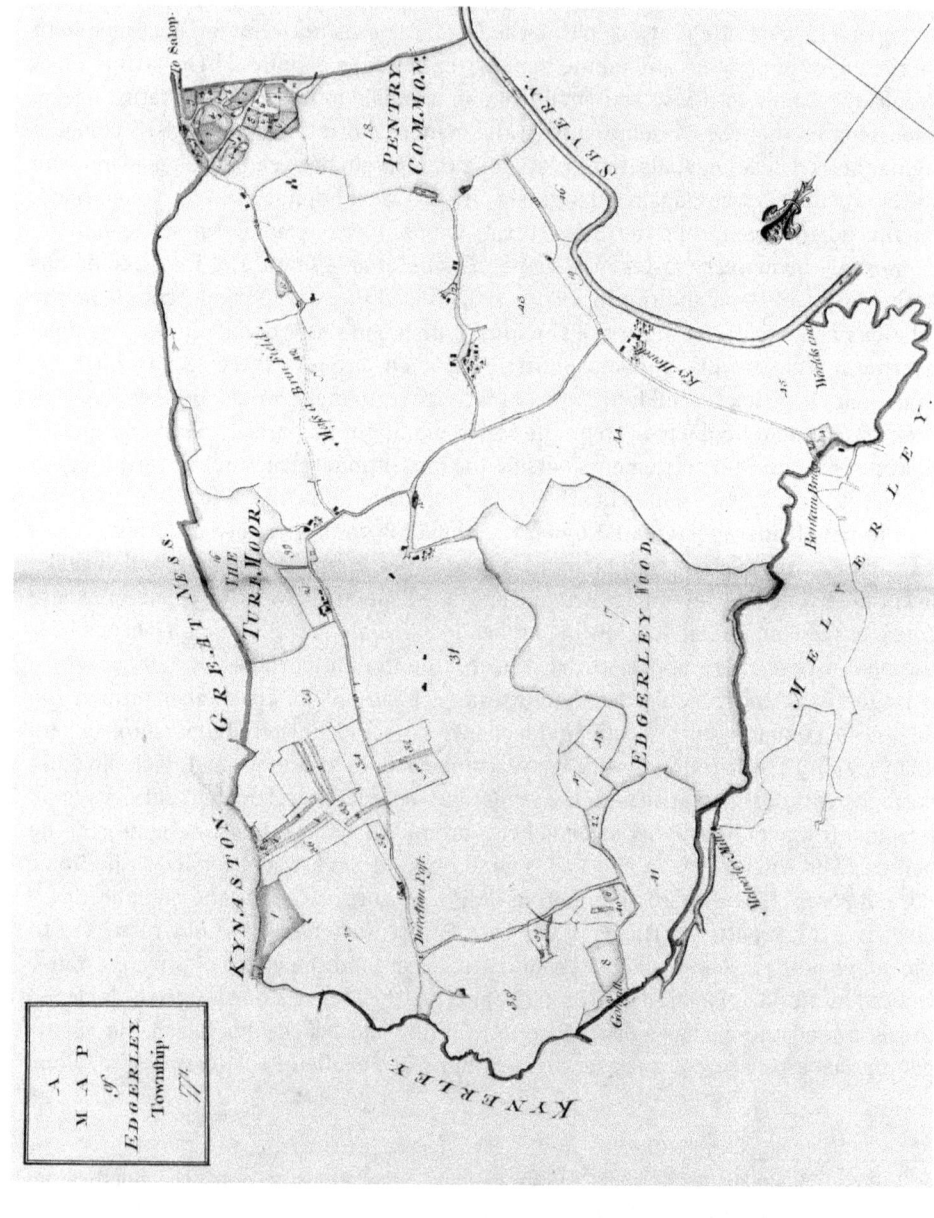

Figure 23. Edgerley township, Shropshire, in 1771, showing the cluster of cottages close to the parish boundary at the northern end of Pentre Common. The township's other common land, the Turf Moor (for turbary) and Edgerley Wood, were devoid of cottages (Shropshire Archives, 6001/2482).

the eastern edge of Beaulieu Heath, a four-mile strip of encroachments which had developed before 1789.[60]

Other cottage settlements took the form of unplanned clusters of dwellings which could swallow up much of a common. David Moody's description of Woodgreen (Hants) as 'a dispersed colony of sinuous lanes and curvilinear plots, typical of the organic growth of squatter settlement' could equally apply to many other cottage settlements on common land.[61] Gorsley Common (Glos.) (Figure 22) was criss-crossed by lanes running through a patchwork of small enclosures containing a sprawl of cottages covering most of the common.[62] Such densities of cottage-building were typical of industrialising regions. In the seventeenth century, Richard Baxter described the cottages of the nailers, scythe-smiths and iron-workers of the populous Black Country commons around Dudley as being 'like a continued village'.[63] In mid-Wales, new villages such as Kingswood (Montgom.) and Fawyddog (Brec.) originated as clusters of squatter cottages on common land.[64] By the mid-nineteenth century, larger cottage settlements had acquired buildings characteristic of established village communities: public houses, places of worship (generally Dissenting, often Primitive Methodist, chapels) and shops – shopkeepers or provision dealers were recorded in almost one-third of commons settlements in Herefordshire, for example.[65]

In some parishes the new concentration of cottages on a common supplanted an earlier settlement to become the core of the community. Hartpury (Glos.) is a case in point. There, the parish church and manor house stood beside the River Leadon on the west side of the parish, while the modern village of Hartpury, on the eastern edge of the parish along the Gloucester–Ledbury road, originated in a string of cottages on Woolridge Common.[66] Even more dramatic was the transformation of the scatter of cottages on roadsides and patches of heath at Great Dawley in the Shropshire coalfield. The cottages which had sprung up along the Wellington–Bridgnorth road at Dawley Green since the sixteenth century had coalesced by the early nineteenth century to form the commercial centre of the town of Dawley.[67]

* * *

The cottagers' independence fed into contemporaries' perceptions of cottage communities. They were seen as outsiders, often condemned *en masse* as morally corrupt.[68] Noted for their resourcefulness, their independence also generated fear and disapproval. Some of the language used of commons dwellers was extreme. An

---

[60] TNA, F17/169, reproduced in Crocker, *Squatters and Social Crime*, p. 13; also pp. 15–19.
[61] Moody, 'Godshillwood and Woodgreen', p. 133.
[62] VCH Glos. XII, p. 37; OS Six-Inch map, Herefordshire 47SE (1887; surveyed 1883–87).
[63] Cited by Hill, *World Turned Upside Down*, p. 44.
[64] Silvester, 'Landscapes of the poor', pp. 62–4.
[65] Moir, '"A World unto Themselves"?', p. 131.
[66] Herbert, 'The squatter and rural settlement', pp. 188–92, 205.
[67] VCH Shrops. XI, pp. 107–9.
[68] See Moir, '"A World unto Themselves"?', pp. 4–6

inhabitant of Broseley (Shrops.), railing against the colliers living in cottages on the wastes there in the early seventeenth century, called them 'lewd and bad persons … thieves … horrible swearers, common drunkards … whoremongers'. Recent migrants, they were 'the dregs of many countries' and 'not worthy to live in the commonwealth'.[69] Immigrant squatters in the Forest of Dean c.1630 were viewed in the same light, while, more broadly, the authorities saw common-edge cottages as the 'breeders, nurseries and receptacles of thieves, rogues and beggars'.[70] That view was elaborated by John Norden in 1618:

> Where great and spacious wastes, mountaines, woods, forests and heaths are … many … cottages are set up, the people given to little or no kinde of labour, living very hardly with oaten bread, sowre whay and goates milke, dwelling far from any church or chappell, and are as ignorant of God or of any civill course of life as the very savages amongst the infidels.[71]

These seventeenth-century tropes of idleness and immorality persisted. New Forest cottagers were said in 1748 to 'live by pilfering and cheating out of the forest'; William Gilpin later described them as 'an indolent race, poor and wretched in the extreme', also accusing them of depending on 'the precarious supply of forest pilfer'.[72] The Shropshire cottagers who were subject only to amercement and paid no rent were 'idle' and generally 'more chargeable to the parish' than others; those on the Lilleshall estate were the poorest and, in many instances, 'profligate' people.[73] Before it was enclosed in 1799, Heveningham Common (Norf.), it was said, had been 'the source of all sorts of immorality, poaching, smuggling, &c &c'.[74] More generally, the authors of the Board of Agriculture reports in the decades either side of 1800 concurred: cottagers on commons were 'idle, useless, and disorderly'.[75]

Proponents of enclosure argued that it would cure these perceived ills by forcing the poor to take up 'honest' employment, thus converting 'immoral' cottagers into respectable ones. John Clark, arguing for the enclosure of commons in Breconshire in 1794, claimed that common land was '*hurtful to society*, by holding forth a temptation to idleness, that *fell* parent to vice and immorality'.[76] Such thinking can also be read as reflecting the landowning class's fear of the cottagers' independence. John Bishton's

---

[69] Wanklyn, 'Rural riots', p. 11.

[70] B. Sharp, 'Common rights, charities and the disorderly poor', in G. Eley and W. Hunt (eds), *Reviving the English Revolution* (New York, 1988), pp. 127–8 and p. 118, citing *Proceedings in Parliament*, 1610.

[71] J. Norden, *The Surveiors Dialogue* (London, 1618), pp. 111, 114.

[72] Moody, 'Godshillwood and Woodgreen', p. 140; Griffin, 'Enclosure from below?', p. 285; Gilpin, *Remarks on Forest Scenery*, II, p. 41.

[73] J. Plymley, *General View of the Agriculture of Shropshire* (London, 1803), p. 113; Bowen, 'Cottage and squatter settlement', pp. 30–3, citing James Losh, writing of the Lilleshall estate, 1820.

[74] Quoted in Wood, *Memory of the People*, p. 343.

[75] As it was put by C. Vancouver, *General View of the Agriculture of Hampshire and the Isle of Wight* (London, 1813), p. 505.

[76] J. Clark, 'On commons in Brecknock', *Annals of Agriculture*, XXII (1794), p. 633.

trenchant views on the evils of cottages on common land in Shropshire in 1794 included the telling comment that a cottage and a small patch enclosed from the common, while of little economic value, 'operates on their minds as a sort of independence'.[77] Indeed, Keith Snell has argued that 'much contemporary opposition to open fields and commons stemmed ... from opposition to the perceived independence and self-reliant resourcefulness which they conferred'.[78]

COMMONS AND PARISH POOR RELIEF

By no means all cottages built on common land in the early modern centuries were 'squatter' cottages. The Poor Law statutes brought common land into the basket of resources available to parish authorities for the support of the poor, the acts of 1598 and 1601 empowering parishes to build dwelling houses for the poor on common wastes, as long as the lord of the manor agreed.[79] Across the seventeenth and eighteenth centuries, pauper cottages, belonging to the parish, came to be built widely on commons across lowland England, fostering the belief that common land could (indeed, should) be seen as a resource for the benefit of the whole community. As early as 1625 seven cottages had been built for the poor on the wastes of the Norfolk villages of Geldeston, Stockton and Gillingham, for example.[80] The number of such cottages varied widely. Two built by Cottisford parish (Oxon.) on heathland close to the county boundary formed the core of a squatter settlement, Juniper Hill, which continued to grow into the nineteenth century.[81] Those on a patch of common at Seer Green in Farnham Royal parish (Bucks.), built by 1753, took the form of a neat row of four houses set on the waste without land attached to them.[82] In Herefordshire, by contrast, parish cottages became numerous. There were twenty on the wastes at Woolhope by 1649 and one common, Bleathwood Common in Little Hereford parish, was made over to the overseers of the poor in 1748 explicitly for building houses for the poor.[83]

More generally, common land was seen by parish authorities as an endowment which could be drawn on to support the poor and, hence, to keep the poor rate down. From her study of Norfolk, Sara Birtles concluded that more than one-third of all parishes in the county made use of their commons to relieve the poor, whether directly or indirectly. Sometimes sections of the common were enclosed to generate funds for poor relief, thus reducing the sums needing to be raised through the rates. Even without such direct appropriation of common land, parish authorities might

---

[77] J. Bishton, *General View of the Agriculture of the County of Salop* (Brentford, 1794), p. 24.
[78] Snell, *Annals of the Labouring Poor*, p. 173.
[79] Hindle, *On the Parish?*, p. 302.
[80] Whyte, *Inhabiting the Landscape*, p. 84.
[81] Broad, 'Boundary settlements', p. 184; *VCH Oxon.* VI, pp. 105, 113.
[82] F. Kerner, 'Enclosure and survival: common land in the Buckinghamshire Chilterns c.1600–c.1900' (PhD thesis, University of Lancaster, 2016), pp. 79–80.
[83] Moir, '"A World unto Themselves"?', pp. 155, 157. For parish houses on Bringsty Common, see below, p. 247.

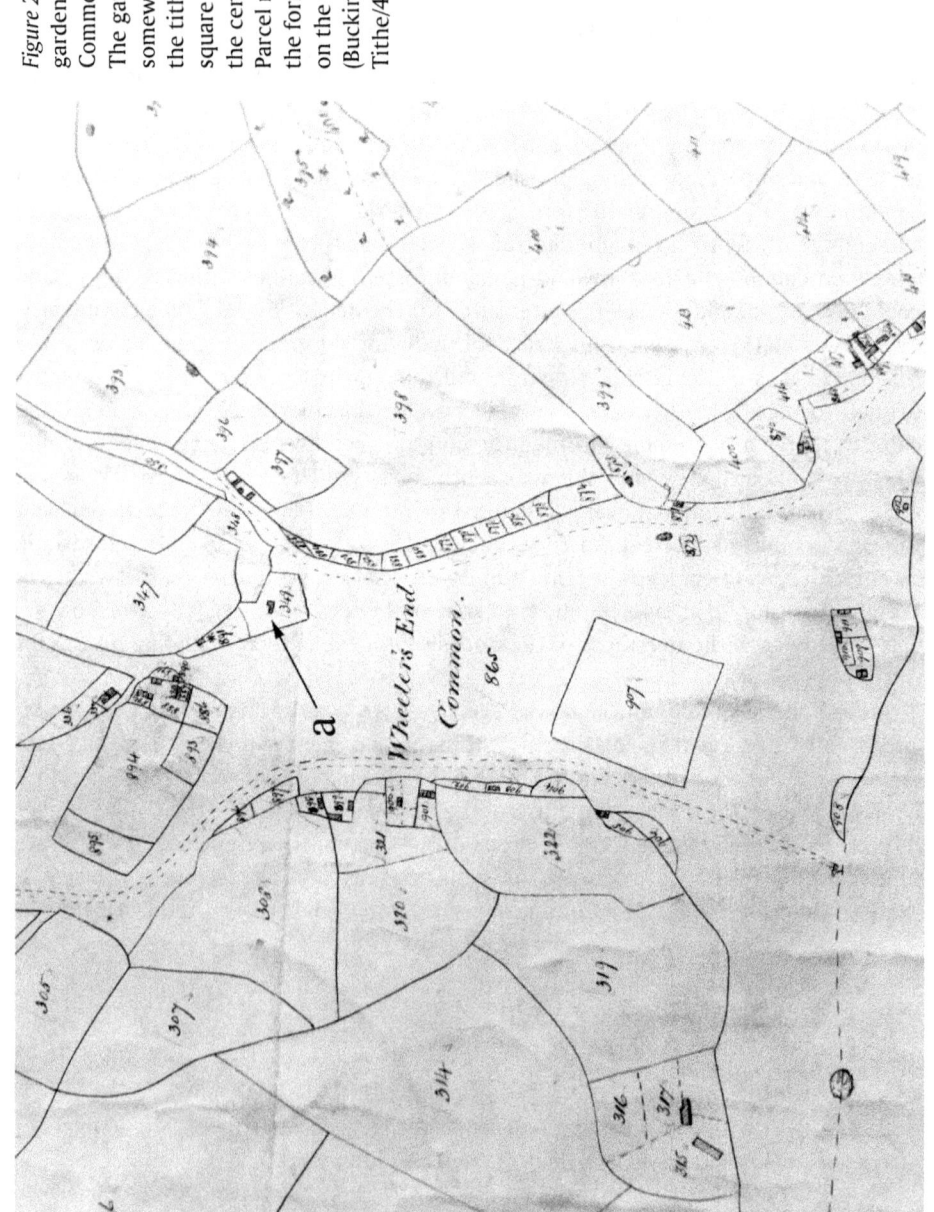

Figure 24. Botany Bay gardens, Wheeler End Common, West Wycombe. The gardens are represented, somewhat schematically, on the tithe plan of 1849 by the square enclosure (no. 907) in the centre of the common. Parcel no. 349 (labelled 'a') was the former parish workhouse, on the edge of the common (Buckinghamshire Archives, Tithe/420).

endorse customary use by the poor, licensing them to take resources (particularly fuel) from common land even if they did not have a formal right to do so. As a result, on enclosure, the parish poor as a group were sometimes compensated for loss of access to those resources.[84] As Birtles suggested, the rights of the poor over common land were not simply the product of custom; they derived in part from provisions associated with the Old Poor Law.[85]

As well as cottages for the poor, commons gained further simple structures in the eighteenth and early nineteenth centuries as a result of the growing acceptance that common land was an appropriate location for community buildings. The parish schools built on common land in the eighteenth century are one example.[86] In Cumbria, at least ten charity schools were built on moorland, sometimes in mutually (in)convenient locations on a common midway between settlements.[87] Almshouses were often built on a patch of the common given to the parish by the lord of the manor.[88] Those near Lythe Hill at Haslemere (Surrey), built in 1676 by James Gresham, the lessee of the town's market tolls, to house the 'decayed inhabitants of the borough', gave the common its modern name of Almshouse Common.[89] Most almshouses were on lowland commons close to settlement, but the Shireburn Almshouses near Stonyhurst (Lancs.), dating from soon after 1707, were built on the open common at the east end of Longridge Fell, 250m above sea level and remote from other houses.[90]

As the scale of accommodation for the poor grew in size, poor houses and parish workhouses were sometimes located on commons.[91] Gilbert's Act (Relief of the Poor Act 1782) enabled parishes to combine to provide for the poor, and at least one Gilbert Union workhouse – that at Bridge (Kent) for the Petham Union – was built on common

[84] Below, pp. 146–52.
[85] S. Birtles, 'Common land, poor relief and enclosure: the use of manorial resources in fulfilling parish obligations 1601–1834', *Past & Present*, 165 (1999), pp. 74–106. See also J. Broad, 'Housing the rural poor in southern England, 1650–1850', *AgHR*, 48 (2) (2000), pp. 151–70.
[86] In Norfolk, for example: Birtles, 'Common land, poor relief and enclosure', p. 90.
[87] At Great Orton, Croglin and Mockerkin, for example. For these and other schoolrooms on common land in Cumbria, see J. Platt (ed.), *The Diocese of Carlisle, 1814–1855: Chancellor Walter Fletcher's 'Diocesan Book', with additional material from Bishop Percy's parish notebooks*, Surtees Society 219 and CWAAS Record Ser. XXII (Woodbridge, 2015), pp. 81, 89, 102, 309 (n. 251), 323 (n. 338), 357, 362; W. Head, 'Mockerkin Endowed School', *Lorton & Derwent Fells Local History Society Newsletter*, 31 (2004), pp. 7–8; S. Jefferson, *The History and Antiquities of Allerdale Ward above Derwent in the County of Cumberland* (Carlisle, 1842), pp. 76, 207–8.
[88] Examples include those at Teddington (built 1738) and Twickenham (built 1704): *VCH Mddx* III, pp. 82, 155; and at Kelvedon Hatch (eighteenth century): *VCH Essex* IV, p. 72.
[89] *VCH Surrey* III, p. 49.
[90] C. Hartwell and N. Pevsner, *Lancashire: North* (London, 2009), pp. 349–50. The almshouses were physically removed and rebuilt at Hurst Green in 1947.
[91] Examples include those on Greenacres Moor in Oldham (Lancs.) (1731); on Nether Common, Belper (Derby.) (1732); on Tooting Bec Common (Surrey) (1790); and on wastes at Foulsham (Norf.) (1782) and Norton-in-the-Moors (Staffs.) (1798): www.workhouses.org.uk; K. Layton-Jones (ed.), *The Common Story: A History of Tooting Common* (Wandsworth, 2019), p. 11.

land.[92] Gilbert's Act also included the provision that parish authorities could enclose up to 10 acres (4 ha) of common land for the benefit of the poor, which resulted in the creation of common gardens like Botany Bay gardens on Wheeler End Common at West Wycombe (Bucks.), established by the parish authorities in 1789 (Figure 24).[93] Similar gardens for the parish poor on Westwood Common at Laxton (Notts.) had gone within living memory when they were mentioned fleetingly in 1830.[94]

In these various ways, local authorities, backed by statute, were putting into practice the idea that common land should benefit the whole community, particularly the poor. Pauper cottages, common gardens and workhouses were the product of a shift in conceptions of the 'ownership' of common land, which increasingly saw commons as a communal resource to be used for the public good, notwithstanding the private property rights which governed their agrarian use. Furthermore, drawing common land into the formal structures of poor relief helped to 'tame' the commons, reducing their use by marginal groups eking out a living on their own terms.

---

[92] Relief of the Poor Act 1782 (22 Geo. III, c.83); for Bridge workhouse, see http://www.workhouses.org.uk/Bridge/.

[93] 22 Geo. III, c.83, sec. xxvii; Kerner, 'Enclosure and survival', pp. 170, 173–4.

[94] J. V. Beckett, *A History of Laxton: England's Last Open-Field Village* (Oxford, 1989), p. 159.

CHAPTER 6

THE AGE OF 'IMPROVEMENT': PRIVATISATION AND THE RECONFIGURATION OF COMMON LAND

MUCH OF THE LITERATURE on the history of common land has focused on its demise through enclosure in the eighteenth and nineteenth centuries, dwelling on the causes and consequences of its loss – the drivers behind enclosure, the process and its impact. In England, common rights were extinguished over more than 6.8 million acres (2.75 million ha) of land, 21 per cent of the total land surface, as a result of Parliamentary enclosure (largely in the century between c.1760 and c.1860), converting almost all open fields and much manorial waste into private property no longer used communally.[1] The same process took place in Wales and, within a different legal framework, the period saw the loss of most common grazings across large parts of Scotland.[2] The impact of enclosure – on the landscape, the agrarian economy and the livelihoods of the rural poor – has been the subject of much literature, a dominant theme being the negative impact on the poor, as customary uses of common land were swept away.[3] This chapter takes a rather different approach, focusing not only on the loss of common land but also on

---

[1] M. Turner, *English Parliamentary Enclosure: Its Historical Geography and Economic History* (Folkestone, 1980), pp. 178–81. On the basis of a sample of enclosure awards, John Chapman suggested that this figure may be an under-estimate by perhaps 500,000 acres (200,000 ha): J. Chapman, 'The extent and nature of Parliamentary enclosure', *AgHR*, 35 (1987), p. 28.

[2] Regional studies of enclosure include J. Chapman and S. Seeliger, *Enclosure, Environment and Landscape in Southern England* (Stroud, 2001); I. Whyte, *Transforming Fell and Valley: Landscape and Parliamentary Enclosure in North West England* (Lancaster, 2003); I. Whyte, '"Wild, barren and frightful": Parliamentary enclosure in an upland county: Westmorland, 1767–1890', *Rural History*, 14 (1) (2003), pp. 21–38; R. O'Donnell, *Assembling Enclosure: Transformations in the Rural Landscape of Post-Medieval North-East England* (Hatfield, 2015); F. Richardson, 'The enclosure of the commons and wastes in Nantconwy, North Wales, 1540–1900', *AgHR*, 65 (1) (2017), pp. 49–73; and J. R. Barrett, *The Making of a Scottish Landscape: Moray's Regular Revolution* (Fonthill, 2015).

[3] Among the most influential works have been K. D. M. Snell, *Annals of the Labouring Poor: Social Change and Agrarian England, 1660–1900* (Cambridge, 1985); and J. M. Neeson, *Commoners: Common Right, Enclosure and Social Change in England, 1700–1820* (Cambridge, 1993).

how some commons came to be reconfigured as a result of enclosure. Paradoxically, improvement and Parliamentary enclosure did not always result in complete 'privatisation', as the process perpetuated communal use of some areas of common land under redefined regimes.

From the seventeenth century, 'improvement' came to dominate agricultural discourse, becoming an all-pervading imperative which had dramatic consequences for commons. Improvement represented a shift of paradigm, changing perceptions of the value of common land and culminating in its widespread loss. Commons were viewed as 'wasted' land, crying out to be 'reclaimed' and improved, as part of a wider change in attitudes to land, when profit and securing private property rights became dominant motives.

The idea of improvement can be traced back to the sixteenth century.[4] At its heart lay a desire to increase income from land, one aspect of which involved changes in land use, including reclamation of marsh, enclosure of open fields, and changed management of woods and meadows.[5] In his *Boke of Surveyeng and Improume[n]tes* (1523), Fitzherbert saw enclosure of common pastures, as well as arable land and meadows, as a prerequisite to increasing the value of a township. It would involve each tenant – including cottagers – being assigned a fair portion of the common pasture, with the result that 'the ryche man [would not] overpresse the poore man with his catell' and that graziers would save on the wages of shepherd, herdsman and swineherd.[6] Under Edward VI, the 'Statute of Improvement' reiterated the provisions of the medieval statutes of Merton and Westminster II, reminding lords of their rights of approvement which allowed them to enclose manorial waste.[7]

By the 1640s, improvement had become what has been termed 'a national mission'.[8] Moreover, the interchangeability of the terms 'common' and 'waste' reflected (and reinforced) the view that common land was somehow 'wasted', with the connotation that it was 'not being used properly'.[9] Contemporaries knew, of course, that commons were far from being unused, but the idea of rightful use introduced a moral dimension: the 'wasted' condition of common land required remedy. In the minds of early modern improvers, the desire to reclaim common land went hand-in-hand with the prospect of rectifying the social and moral deficiencies associated with it (idleness, godlessness, immorality). As Buchanan Sharp put it, 'Just as enclosure provided an opportunity to

---

[4] For a wide-ranging discussion, see P. Slack, *The Invention of Improvement: Information and Material Progress in Seventeenth-Century England* (Oxford, 2015), esp. pp. 4–8.

[5] The role of the Crown in driving 'improvement' in the sixteenth century is discussed in J. Thirsk, 'The Crown as projector on its own estates, from Elizabeth I to Charles I', in R. W. Hoyle (ed.), *The Estates of the English Crown, 1558–1640* (Cambridge, 1992), pp. 297–352.

[6] J. Fitzherbert, *The Boke of Surveyeng and Improume[n]tes* (London, 1523), f. liiii–liiii^v.

[7] Improvement of Commons Act 1549 (3 & 4 Edward VI, c.3).

[8] P. Warde, 'The idea of improvement, c.1520–1700', in R. W. Hoyle (ed.), *Custom, Improvement and the Landscape in Early Modern England* (Farnham, 2011), p. 137.

[9] V. Di Palma, *Wasteland: A History* (London, 2014), pp. 22–4.

uproot the briars and turn the waste to fruitful and productive tillage, so the poor would be uprooted and improved.'[10]

By virtue of its self-evidently unimproved state, common land thus became a central target for improvers. The flurry of writing on improved husbandry among Samuel Hartlib's circle in the early 1650s included Sylvanus Taylor's *Common Good, or the Improvement of Commons, Forrests, and Chases by Inclosure* (1652) and the quasi-anonymous E. G.'s *Waste Lands Improvement* (1653). Forests, 'fenny grounds' and wastes were, in E. G.'s view, wild and vacant land which remained in that state 'like a deformed chaos', much to the nation's 'discredit and disprofit'. They should be enclosed, manured and converted to tillage.[11] The improvers of that time tended to view commons simply as empty spaces, capable of being divided to create new farms, with little appreciation of the limits to cultivation often imposed by the physical character of the land.[12] By the 1730s, the 'national mission' of improvement had reached Scotland, where, as John Barrett has put it, farming 'was elevated into a virtuous pursuit for visionary gentlemen'.[13] More than one author of early essays on improved husbandry in the northern kingdom announced himself as 'a lover of his country'.[14]

Improvement was thus a notion which came snapping at the heels of traditional uses of common land from the seventeenth century. Across the middle and later decades of the eighteenth century, and across Britain, it was put into practice by applying a rational, practical and increasingly scientific approach to farming. The agricultural 'revolution' which gathered pace across the century had many facets: new crops and crop rotations; improved machinery and livestock; more intensive use of the land – as well as the land reform of which enclosure of common land was a central plank. By the height of the wave of Parliamentary enclosure during the Napoleonic wars, the improvement rhetoric could be deafening. In a speech in Parliament in 1801, Sir John Sinclair, first president of the Board of Agriculture, famously saw wasteland enclosure as a military campaign: 'let us not be satisfied with the liberation of Egypt or the subjugation of Malta, but let us subdue Finchley Common; let us conquer Hounslow Heath; let us compel Epping Forest to submit to the yoke of improvement'.[15]

---

[10] B. Sharp, 'Common rights, charities and the disorderly poor', in G. Eley and W. Hunt (eds), *Reviving the English Revolution: Reflections and Elaborations on the Work of Christopher Hill* (New York, 1988), p. 130.

[11] E. G., 'Waste Land's Improvement', dated October 1653 (BL, Thomas Tract, E715 (18)), printed in J. Thirsk and J. P. Cooper (eds), *Seventeenth-Century Economic Documents* (Oxford, 1972), pp. 135–40. The improvement literature of the 1650s is discussed by Sharp, 'Common rights, charities and the disorderly poor', pp. 113–17; Di Palma, *Wasteland*, pp. 57–9.

[12] R. W. Hoyle, 'Introduction: Custom, Improvement and Anti-improvement', in *Custom, Improvement and the Landscape*, p. 24.

[13] Barrett, *Making of a Scottish Landscape*, pp. 63–5 (quotation p. 65).

[14] W. Mackintosh, *An Essay on Ways and Means for Inclosing, Fallowing, Planting &c.* (Edinburgh, 1729); J. Dalrymple, *An Essay on the Husbandry of Scotland with a Proposal for the Improvement Thereof, by a lover of his country* (Edinburgh, 1732).

[15] J. Sinclair, *Memoirs of the Life and Works of ... Sir John Sinclair, Bart* (Edinburgh, 1837), vol. II, p. 111.

ENCLOSURE OF COMMON WASTE, 1600–1900

Though the peak years of enclosure and the loss of common land fell in the later eighteenth and nineteenth centuries, the extent of enclosure in the seventeenth century is now recognised as having been substantial. It has been suggested that as much land in England was enclosed in the seventeenth century as in the eighteenth and nineteenth centuries put together.[16] Much of this was enclosure of open fields but inroads were made into common waste as well. It is not surprising that the enclosure of waste often loomed large in seventeenth-century disputes over custom.

In the early seventeenth century, Crown initiatives played a major role in wasteland enclosure. On its extensive estates and areas subject to forest law, relinquishing Crown rights and enclosing former wastes could be interpreted as fostering the public good, through granting tenancies to the landless, civilising the 'wild' people dwelling on commons, and improving the nation's food supply by expanding arable production. However, from the mid-1620s, private gain came to predominate, as improvement was used by the Crown as a means of raising capital by granting away newly enclosed land. Abolishing forest law and replacing common rights by grants of land to be held in severalty had the result of 'making unsaleable assets saleable'. Protest and violence accompanied many of the Crown's attempts to improve its estates, both by disafforestation and by wetland drainage, since both involved expropriation of rights and disruption to the local economy.[17]

Among the best-known projects to improve waste lands during the seventeenth century were the concerted attempts to drain wetland commons, many promoted by the Crown.[18] The most ambitious (but not the earliest) drainage schemes were in the Fens. First proposed in the late sixteenth century, large-scale, capital-intensive drainage took place in two main phases, the first under the direction of the Dutch engineer Cornelius Vermuyden in the 1630s; the second led by the 1st Duke of Bedford in the 1650s. Both involved major engineering works, of which the largest were the Seventy Foot Drain (or Old Bedford River) of the 1630s and the Hundred Foot Drain (or New Bedford River) of the 1650s, which ran for twenty miles to re-route the Great Ouse. Both phases also removed substantial blocks of former common land in the form of allotments made to the 'adventurers' or 'undertakers' who financed the works – those from the second phase totalled 95,000 acres (38,450 ha).[19]

Vermuyden's earlier contract to drain the levels in Hatfield Chase and around the Isle of Axholme (Lincs.) from 1626 had sparked rioting and sustained resistance because of the loss of commons it entailed: at Epworth the commoners lost more than half of

---

[16] M. Overton, *Agricultural Revolution in England: The Transformation of the Agrarian Economy 1500–1850* (Cambridge, 1996), p. 148.

[17] R. Hoyle, 'Disafforestation and drainage: the Crown as entrepreneur?', in Hoyle, *Estates of the English Crown*, pp. 354, 388.

[18] For an overview, see C. Taylor, 'Fenlands', in J. Thirsk (ed.), *The English Rural Landscape* (Oxford, 2000), pp. 167–87, especially pp. 179–85.

[19] T. Williamson, *England's Landscape: East Anglia* (London, 2006), pp. 202–6, provides a useful summary.

their commons, a reduction from 13,400 acres (5,420 ha) to 5,960 acres (2,410 ha) of the wetland pastures which were central to the area's pastoral economy. Furthermore, drainage disrupted the winter flooding of the Isle's fenland, which brought a 'thick, fatt water', rich in silt, to replenish the fertility of the pastures. Other grievances included the loss of the common right of piscary, which allowed the inhabitants to set nets to trap fish in the fens on Wednesdays and Saturdays.[20]

Drainage was also attempted in the Somerset Levels during the 1620s and 1630s. Although moves to drain King's Sedgemoor, in which Vermuyden was also involved, met stiff resistance and came to little, smaller areas of wetland in the valley of the Brue were successfully reclaimed. As elsewhere, the loss of former common land to the Crown and its agents reduced the extent of the pastures available to commoners.[21] More localised schemes of wetland reclamation in the seventeenth century included the embankment and drainage of coastal marshes in north-west Norfolk and attempts to drain the wetlands around Martin Mere in south-west Lancashire.[22]

Reclaiming wetland was only one aspect of wasteland enclosure in the seventeenth century, the cumulative effect of which was to diminish considerably the extent of common land across lowland England. Disafforestation of Crown forests was one factor, commons in forests as far apart as Bernwood (Bucks.), Leicester, Morfe (Shrops.), Needwood (Staffs.) and Knaresborough (Yorks. W.R.) being surveyed and divided in the 1610s and 1620s.[23] The former royal forest of Ashdown (Sussex) was divided in 1693, the commoners' use being restricted thereafter to less than half of the 14,000-acre (5,666-ha) forest.[24] Commons were also disappearing outside forest areas. Perhaps 40,000 acres (16,200 ha) of lowland wastes in Lancashire were enclosed across the early modern period, representing around one-quarter of the waste which had existed there in 1500.[25] In Co. Durham seventeen lowland moors, probably totalling well in excess of 7,000 acres (2,800 ha), mainly in the north-eastern and central parts of the county, were divided during a surge in enclosure between 1630 and 1680, which saw many of the county's open fields also being enclosed.[26]

---

[20] J. Thirsk, 'The Isle of Axholme before Vermuyden', *AgHR*, 1 (1) (1953), pp. 16–28; L. E. Harris, *Vermuyden and the Fens: A Study of Sir Cornelius Vermuyden and the Great Level* (London, 1953); K. Lindley, *Fenland Riots and the English Revolution* (London, 1982), pp. 26–32, 72–9. For Epworth, see below, p. 229.

[21] M. Williams, *The Draining of the Somerset Levels* (Cambridge, 1970), pp. 86–110; Hoyle, 'Disafforestation and drainage', pp. 376–81.

[22] E. Griffiths, 'Draining the coastal marshes of north-west Norfolk: the contribution of the le Stranges of Hunstanton, 1605–1724', *AgHR*, 63 (2015), pp. 221–42; *Contested Common Land*, pp. 166–7; J. Virgoe, 'Thomas Fleetwood and the draining of Martin Mere', *Transactions of the Historic Society of Lancashire and Cheshire*, 152 (2003), pp. 27–47. See also J. Thirsk (ed.), *The Agrarian History of England and Wales, Vol. IV, 1500–1640* (Cambridge, 1967), pp. 184–5.

[23] Hoyle, 'Disafforestation and drainage', pp. 363–75.

[24] *Ashdown Forest*, p. 22.

[25] B. Shannon, 'Approvement and improvement in the lowland wastes of early modern Lancashire', in Hoyle, *Custom, Improvement and the Landscape*, p. 201.

[26] R. I. Hodgson, 'The progress of enclosure in County Durham, 1550–1870', in H. S. A. Fox and R. A. Butlin (eds), *Change in the Countryside: Essays on Rural England 1500–1900* (London, 1979),

Commons were also enclosed in upland areas. In Bowland (Yorks. W.R.) the lower slopes of the hill commons belonging to villages in the Ribble and Hodder valleys were enclosed between 1587 and the early 1620s. In all, nearly 10,400 acres (around 4,190 ha) were taken in and around Slaidburn and on the southern slopes of Easington Fell, much of it prompted by a Crown initiative to increase revenue from entry fines and new rents.[27] Upland enclosures later in the century included the flanks of Longridge Fell (Lancs.) and moorland at Castleton, in the Derbyshire Peak District.[28]

A step change in the scale of wasteland enclosure took place from the mid-eighteenth century. In England and Wales the process which enabled vast acreages of common land to be converted into private property and, in many cases, reclaimed and improved, was enclosure by act of Parliament, whereby commissioners were appointed to survey a common and assign shares to those with a legal interest in it, both the owner of the soil and those possessing common rights. The plots thus allocated became private property, no longer subject to common rights, and the former common was physically divided into sections by new field boundaries around the allotments. This means of unscrambling the multiple legal interests over common land was achieved through private acts of Parliament applying to individual commons until the process was simplified by the Inclosure Act 1845, which established a permanent body of enclosure commissioners.[29]

A majority of the common land which survived in England and Wales in 1700 was swept away across the eighteenth and nineteenth centuries, much of it as a result of Parliamentary enclosure. Precision is impossible but estimates derived from the acts and awards which concerned only wasteland enclosure (totalling around 2,000 cases) suggest that 2.1 million acres (850,117 ha) or possibly as much as 2.3 million acres (930,810 ha) were enclosed,[30] figures which will under-estimate the full extent of wasteland enclosure, as they exclude awards relating to open fields which also enclosed some waste. Even on these low estimates, it appears that at least 60 per cent of the common wastes which survived until 1700 had gone by 1900.

Most wasteland enclosure acts dated from the first half of the nineteenth century: 60 per cent of them fell between 1790 and 1820 and the process continued well into

---

pp. 84–9. The acreages for moorland enclosure are derived from data given in R. I. Hodgson, 'Coalmining, population and enclosure in the Seasale colliery districts of Durham (northern Durham), 1551–1810: a study in historical geography' (PhD thesis, Durham University, 1990), pp. 276–87.

[27] J. Porter, 'Waste land reclamation in the sixteenth and seventeenth centuries: the case of south-eastern Bowland, 1550–1630', *Transactions of the Historic Society of Lancashire & Cheshire*, 127 (1978), pp. 1–23.

[28] Lancs. RO, DDK/1532/14; B. Frazer, 'Common recollections: resisting enclosure "by agreement" in seventeenth-century England', *International Journal of Historical Archaeology*, 3 (2) (1999), pp. 89–92.

[29] For the process of Parliamentary enclosure, see Michael Turner's introduction to W. E. Tate, *A Domesday of English Enclosure Acts and Awards* (Reading, 1978), pp. 23–38.

[30] M. Williams, 'The enclosure and reclamation of waste land in England and Wales in the eighteenth and nineteenth centuries', *Trans IBG*, 51 (1970), p. 63; W. E. Tate, *The English Village Community and the Enclosure Movements* (London, 1967), p. 88.

the middle decades of the century. Not surprisingly, the greatest acreages were found in counties with large areas of upland terrain in northern England and Wales, but large areas of wetland commons, in Lincolnshire and in the Somerset Levels, for example, were also enclosed across the century 1760 to 1860.[31] By one estimate, 'perhaps a million acres' (c.400,000 ha) of upland commons in northern England were enclosed by act of Parliament.[32] In Co. Durham, for example, despite the enclosure of some lowland wastes in the seventeenth century, over 17 per cent of the county's land area was enclosed between 1750 and 1870, almost all of it moorland or fell on the north Pennines.[33] The counties with the highest proportions of their land surface affected by Parliamentary enclosure of wastes were Cumberland (where it accounted for 23.7 per cent of the county area), Radnorshire and Co. Durham (17.7 per cent each) and Westmorland (16 per cent).[34] In Wales as a whole, where Parliamentary enclosure overwhelmingly concerned wastes, it affected 10 per cent of the land surface.[35]

Wasteland enclosure continued after the surge in the years around the Napoleonic wars, reaching a second peak in the middle decades of the nineteenth century, during what F. M. L. Thompson called the 'second agricultural revolution'. The enclosure process was streamlined by the Inclosure Act 1845, which coincided with developments which increased the scope for reclamation of common land. Field under-drainage, which mushroomed with the availability of cheap tile drains in the 1840s, allowed improvement of land which would previously have been difficult to reclaim, while the introduction of external fertilisers and feed stuffs (notably oilseed cake, valued for enriching the dung of livestock to which it was fed) boosted fertility.[36] Common waste accounted for over 90 per cent of enclosures after 1850, and more than 500 enclosure awards, affecting 334,910 acres (135,536 ha) of waste, were made after 1845.[37]

Even without recourse to Parliamentary enclosure, a transformation of common wastes could still occur. Informal, piecemeal enclosure and more formal enclosure by agreement (without recourse to an act of Parliament) were widespread in some areas, including southern counties of England.[38] On the hill commons in Nantconwy, north Wales, the traditional exclusive use of parts of a common by individual farms enabled landowners to treat much of the waste as private land, claiming ownership of

---

[31] Williams, *Draining of Somerset Levels*, pp. 123–68; D. B. Grigg, *The Agricultural Revolution in South Lincolnshire* (Cambridge, 1966), pp. 28, 50–3.

[32] I. Whyte, 'Taming the fells: Parliamentary enclosure and the landscape in northern England', *Landscapes*, 6 (1) (2005), p. 48.

[33] Hodgson, 'Progress of enclosure in Co. Durham', p. 89.

[34] Williams, 'Enclosure and reclamation of waste land', p. 64.

[35] J. Chapman, 'Parliamentary enclosure in Wales: comparisons and contrasts', *Welsh History Review*, 21 (4) (2003), p. 762.

[36] See A. D. M. Phillips, *The Underdraining of Farmland in England during the Nineteenth Century* (Cambridge, 1989); F. M. L. Thompson, 'The second agricultural revolution, 1815–1880', *Economic History Review*, new ser. 21 (1968), pp. 62–77.

[37] Williams, 'Enclosure and reclamation of waste land', p. 63; Overton, *Agricultural Revolution*, p. 151; Chapman, 'Extent and nature of Parliamentary enclosure', p. 31.

[38] Chapman and Seeliger, *Enclosure, Environment and Landscape*.

sheepwalks, allocating them to their tenants' farms and, in places, building boundary walls between them. Much of the common land in the area had, in effect, become private property by the mid-nineteenth century, despite there being only a single Parliamentary enclosure award.[39]

In Scotland, the legal framework to common land resulted in different legal processes of enclosure. As commonties were jointly owned, separating the shares of individual proprietors was a necessary prerequisite to enclosure. The Commonty Act 1695 provided the legal mechanism for achieving this, enabling any proprietor to instigate division by raising a summons at the Court of Session, which was empowered to appoint commissioners to oversee the division locally. Around 500,000 acres (200,000 ha) of commonty were divided under the terms of the act over the following two centuries. The 1695 act was prompted by a desire to prevent 'the discords that arise about Commonties', rather than by a direct drive towards reclamation and improvement.[40] Initially, take up of the powers granted by the act was limited but the number of commonties divided rose steeply as the improvement movement spread during the middle decades of the eighteenth century, reaching a peak in the 1770s. It continued at a steady rate until the 1880s, many of the later divisions applying to scattalds in Shetland.[41]

Once divided, a commonty could be enclosed and improved by its owners without further recourse to law: the rights of servitude enjoyed by a proprietor's tenants were not protected as were common rights in England and Wales, so former commonties could be incorporated into the wholesale improvement of a landed estate.[42] Whereas wasteland enclosure in England and Wales often took the form of new rectilinear fields on the former common which abutted against older, less geometrical field boundaries on farmland, in Scotland all categories of traditional land use – ploughland, meadows and commonty – were often reorganised in what John Barrett has called Scotland's 'regular revolution', a wholesale re-writing of the rural landscape of much of Scotland.[43]

Across Britain, landscapes of improvement were characterised by straight lines: ruler-straight occupation roads with wide verges, giving access to new rectangular enclosures; unwavering 'rhynes' (drainage ditches) slicing the Somerset Levels; dry stone walls running directly up fellsides and across moors; a grid of hedge banks parcelling the land into blocks (Figure 25). These were landscapes created on drawing boards and transferred, often within the space of months rather than years, to the

---

[39] Richardson, 'Enclosure of commons and wastes in Nantconwy', pp. 62–7.

[40] I. H. Adams, 'The legal geography of Scotland's common lands', *Revue de l'Institut de Sociologie*, 2 (1973), pp. 291–6; R. A. Dodgshon, *Land and Society in Early Scotland* (Oxford, 1981), pp. 194–5; I. D. Whyte, *Agriculture and Society in Seventeenth-Century Scotland* (Edinburgh, 1979), pp. 213–14.

[41] R. Gibson, *The Scottish Countryside: Its Changing Face, 1700–2000* (Edinburgh, 2007), p. 31, citing data from I. H. Adams, *Directory of Former Scottish Commonties*, Scottish Record Society, new ser. 2 (Edinburgh, 1971).

[42] R. Houston, 'Custom in context: medieval and early modern Scotland and England', *Past & Present*, 211 (2011), pp. 55, 58, 75.

[43] Barrett, *Making of a Scottish Landscape*, pp. 9–10 and *passim*.

Figure 25. Oxenhope Moor (Yorks. W.R.): a landscape of Parliamentary enclosure. The contrast between the rectangular improved fields in Oxenhope, enclosed under an act of 1771 (award 1777), and the heather-clad, unenclosed common of Haworth Moor on the left, is accentuated under a light covering of snow. For Oxenhope enclosure award, see S. Wood, *Haworth, Oxenhope and Stanbury from Old Maps* (Stroud, 2014).

land.[44] Reclamation followed. Most of the newly enclosed commons across lowland Britain were converted into more productive farmland through a labour-intensive drive to clear scrub, pare and burn, plough and harrow, remove stones and lay field drains. Some became and remained productive arable land; some improved grassland. Most of the semi-natural vegetation of lowland commons disappeared, banished to the margins in unused corners and roadside verges. John Clare's bitterly nostalgic verse evokes vividly the transformation of lowland commons through enclosure. The dappled world of marsh, pasture and wood became a closed-off, 'naked' landscape of ploughland and fallow, as trees and bushes were cleared, streams diverted, footpaths stopped and lanes railed in by fences. The freedom to wander, the flowers and birdsong he recalled from pre-enclosure days were lost: 'Inclosure came & all your glories fell', he wrote.[45]

---

[44] For descriptions of the new landscapes of Parliamentary enclosure of wastes, see, for example, Whyte, 'Taming the fells', pp. 52–4; Whyte, *Transforming Fell and Valley*, pp. 63–87; Williams, *Draining of Somerset Levels*, pp. 187–96.

[45] J. Clare, 'The Village Minstrel' (published 1821), lines 1048–1118 (quotation: line 1105), in E. Robinson and D. Powell (eds), *The Early Poems of John Clare 1804–1822, Volume II* (Oxford, 1989), pp. 168–70.

Scope for reclamation was more limited in the uplands, but lower hills and the margins of fell and moorland were similarly tamed, often as improved grassland. Beyond the limit of improvement in England and Wales, the transformation of property rights was not accompanied by land use change: common land became private property but the rough, unimproved face of mountain and moorland remained. However, afforestation of newly enclosed land was sometimes mooted as an appropriate means of making barren land productive. In 1794 it was suggested that the 'steep and rocky sides of mountains' in Breconshire should be enclosed and planted, particularly with oak, for example.[46] In lowland England, parts of the Greensand heathlands of the Bagshot area of Surrey were deemed in 1844 to be 'only fit for plantations' and were planted with conifers, mainly Scots pine and larch.[47] Afforestation was more widespread in Scotland, particularly from the 1760s. Coniferous plantations of larch and pine and plantings of a variety of deciduous species (oak, ash, beech, sycamore) transformed large areas of the lowland landscape, 'clothing muirs and heathland with a profitable cash crop'.[48]

RE-MAKING COMMON LAND THROUGH ENCLOSURE

Parliamentary enclosure in England and Wales was essentially a local process, and the 'regular revolution' in Scotland took place estate by estate. Enclosure commissioners and estate managers had to grapple with challenges posed by local circumstances, whether these lay in the nature of the land being enclosed or the benefits members of local communities derived from the common. In places, one outcome of enclosure was a continuation of communal use on parts of the land which had been enclosed, patterns of rights and use often having been re-configured in the process.

Land set aside for continuing communal use fell under several headings. One category, found widely in enclosure awards across England, was the public stone quarries and sand, gravel, chalk and clay pits assigned at enclosure to enable local people to take mineral resources for necessary use. The immediate need was for materials to make access roads and to build enclosure walls (in upland areas), but material from these public quarries and pits might also be taken for the maintenance of buildings. They were numerous but mostly small, typically covering a couple of acres; some were short-lived but others continued to be recognised as common resources in the 1950s.[49]

Other types of communal use survived where parts of a common were deemed to be unimprovable and the benefits of enclosure marginal at best, as when the value of the land allotted at enclosure was outweighed by the cost of fencing it. As a result, some enclosures covered only part of the waste, leaving unimprovable areas unenclosed. One of the largest areas of hill common which was subject to an enclosure act but

---

[46] J. Clark, 'On commons in Brecknock', *Annals of Agriculture*, XXII (1794), p. 637.
[47] A. G. Parton, 'Parliamentary enclosure in nineteenth-century Surrey: some perspectives on the evaluation of land potential', *AgHR*, 33 (1985), pp. 51–8.
[48] Barrett, *Making of a Scottish Landscape*, pp. 153–5 (quotation p. 155).
[49] See the lists in Hoskins & Stamp, pp. 247–350.

remained undivided was in Fforest Fawr, the 'Great Forest of Brecknock', in the Brecon Beacons. The act of 1815 divided almost 40,000 acres (15,900 ha) of mountain grazings between the Crown and the commoners. The commoners' share (17,106 acres; 6,923 ha) consisted of two large blocks on the west and east ends of the forest, centred on the mountain ridges of Fan Hir and Fan Fawr, respectively. The cost of enclosing and dividing these tracts of hill was prohibitive to the commoners, so the enclosure act was amended to enable the commissioners to make an award which left the commoners' allotments undivided. The removal of a block of common in the middle of the forest as the Crown's share disrupted grazing arrangements and, in 1821, a meeting of the commoners resolved to stint their parts.[50]

Comparable outcomes arose from enclosure elsewhere. Five of the twenty-three Parliamentary enclosure awards from the North York Moors excluded the higher moors from their provisions, leaving common rights unaffected, for example, while at Dufton (Westmld) the high and bleak moorland south of Cross Fell remained as common, while the lower slopes of the Pennine scarp were enclosed.[51]

Even where enclosure applied to the whole of a common, unimprovable parts sometimes remained open as shared grazing grounds. In the North York Moors more than one-third of the area enclosed by act of Parliament was 'permissive' enclosure, whereby those allocated sections of the high moors were not obliged to fence their allotments. The Pickering award of 1785 acknowledged that parts of the moor would remain open after enclosure and laid down regulations for the management of the unfenced portion.[52] On the fells in north-west England similar permissive arrangements left the highest parts of Casterton Fell (Westmld) and Broughton High Moor in Furness (Lancs.) unenclosed.[53] The attempt to enclose moorland at Wolsingham (Dur.) in 1765 was only partly successful, as more than half of the acreage laid out in allotments was not taken up by those to whom it had been allotted and remained open moor,[54] while the enclosure walls and carriage road specified in the enclosure award for Mynydd Cribe in Snowdonia in 1830 failed to be built and the mountainous common stayed undivided.[55]

Another aspect of incomplete enclosure was where one common right – usually common of pasture – was extinguished but other rights, notably common of turbary, continued to be exercised. In the early enclosure of the wastes around Castleton in the Peak District in 1691, almost all the moorland was divided, but a block of 70 acres (28 ha) at the furthest extremity of the township was to be left 'for digging & delveing turffes', perpetuating common of turbary over a limited area, after common pasture rights had gone.[56]

---

[50] J. Lloyd, *The Great Forest of Brecknock* (London, 1905), pp. 65–84; W. Rees, *The Great Forest of Brecknock: A Facet of Breconshire History* (Brecon, 1966), pp. 19–22.
[51] J. Chapman, 'Parliamentary enclosure in the uplands: the case of the North York Moors', *AgHR*, 24 (1976), p. 10; Whyte, *Transforming Fell and Valley*, p. 27.
[52] Chapman, 'Parliamentary enclosure in the uplands', pp. 7–10.
[53] Whyte, *Transforming Fell and Valley*, p. 27.
[54] Hodgson, 'Coalmining, population and enclosure', p. 226.
[55] Richardson, 'Enclosure of commons and wastes in Nantconwy', p. 67.
[56] Frazer, 'Common recollections: resisting enclosure', pp. 90, 93.

Figure 26. Commonty at Wilton, near Hawick, 1764. Plan drawn on the division of the commonty, showing the three peat mosses (labelled a, b, and c) which, with their surrounding 'spread grounds', were to remain in common (NRS, RHP 181).

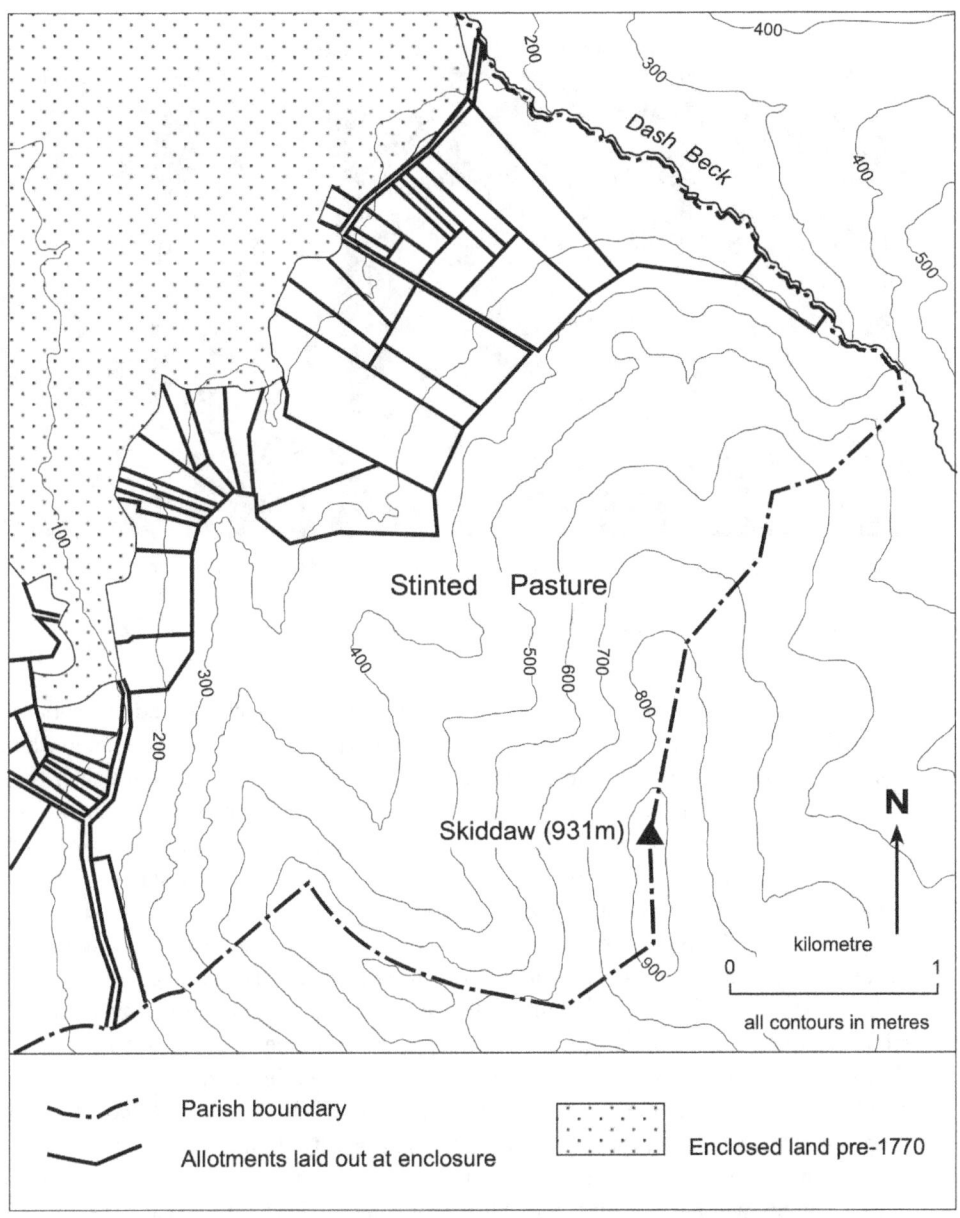

Figure 27. Partial enclosure: Bassenthwaite Common, Cumberland. Allotments were laid out by the enclosure award of 1771 on the lower slopes; the higher fellsides were to remain unenclosed as a stinted pasture. Source: CAS, Q/RE/1/92.

Figure 28. Bassenthwaite Common: improved land and stinted pasture. Plough ridges record cultivation of one of the enclosure allotments. The higher ground in the distance remains unenclosed as part of the stinted pasture created by the award of 1771.

A distinction between grazing and peat-cutting rights was also found in Scotland, where the Commonties Act 1695 provided for common peat mosses to be excluded when commonties were divided, because of the difficulty of dividing them equitably; they thus continued as communal resources.[57] When the commonty in Wilton, near Hawick (Roxburghshire), was divided in 1764, for example, three hollows in the broken hilly ground on the commonty's outer edges were assigned to the parishioners as common mosses. The area allocated for each included not only the peat moss itself but also a rim of 'spread ground' around the margin, where cut peats could be dried, creating islands of continuing communal use, surrounded by private property (Figure 26).[58]

Likewise, at Tatham (Lancs.), when the moorland commons were converted into stinted pastures in 1858 (a process discussed below), the redefinition of pasture rights did not impinge on the commoners' rights to cut rushes and turves. Even more striking were five Parliamentary enclosure awards from the North York Moors which perpetuated multiple rights over newly enclosed private allotments. In these cases, those with turbary rights could continue to come into the new enclosures to cut peat or turf.[59] In Snowdonia, the virtual enclosure of common land into private sheepwalks

---

[57] Division of Commonties Act (Scotland) 1695.
[58] NRS, RHP 181.
[59] E. A. Straughton, *Common Grazing in the Northern English Uplands, 1800–1965* (Lampeter, 2008), p. 197; Chapman, 'Parliamentary enclosure in the uplands', p. 6.

sometimes only concerned grazing; in some places, poor cottagers continued to exercise turbary rights on sheepwalks in the nineteenth century.[60]

Conversion to Stinted Pastures

In establishing new property rights over former common land, some enclosure awards perpetuated common grazing by creating stinted pastures. Legally, the land had been enclosed, in that ownership was vested in those to whom stinted grazing rights were allocated, so that the graziers owned the former common in undivided shares. In strictly legal terms the grazing rights had ceased to be common rights but, in practice, enclosure allowed communal use to continue.[61]

Establishing the full extent of stinted pastures created by Parliamentary enclosure would require a thorough investigation of all individual enclosure acts and awards, but evidence of the process comes from widely differing types of commons across the decades of enclosure. In Cumberland, ten instances have been noted, spanning the period 1770 to 1866.[62] Examples are found elsewhere in northern England and several stinted pastures were established at enclosure in the very different environment of East Anglia.[63]

In most cases, the act and award applied to the whole of a common but set aside part of it to be stinted and used communally. On the fringes of the Lake District fells, for example, the enclosure of Bassenthwaite Common (1771) allocated 1,819 acres (736 ha) on the lower slopes as allotments to individuals and 1,582 acres (640 ha) on the higher fells as a stinted pasture (Figures 27 and 28). At Watermillock (1835) the majority of the common (3,596 acres; 1,455 ha) was allotted, the remainder (883 acres; 357 ha) becoming a stinted pasture; on Bootle Fell (1866) only 431 acres (174 ha) was laid out in allotments, the greater part of the common (681 acres; 276 ha) remained as shared grazing, henceforth stinted. The primary factor determining which sections were divided into allotments and which reconfigured as a stinted pasture was the prospect of reclamation and improvement; those parts where the costs of physical enclosure would outweigh the potential increase in productivity or value remained shared rough grazing. It was the higher fells in the examples cited above, bare limestone pavements at Hutton Roof (Westmld), and the 'poor peaty moors' on the northern edge of the Bowland Fells at Caton and Claughton (Lancs.) which remained open as stinted pastures.[64]

Unsurprisingly, new stinted pastures were rarer in lowland England, reflecting the improvable character of most commons. At Kirkby-on-Bain (Lincs.) in 1796, for example, part of the common pasture covering the western half of the parish was divided but 'the worst part of the Moor' was left unenclosed and allocated as a stinted pasture, on

---

[60] Richardson, 'Enclosure of commons and wastes in Nantconwy', p. 72.
[61] *Gadsden*, § 1-25; Straughton, *Common Grazing*, pp. 193–204.
[62] Straughton, *Common Grazing*, p. 194, abstracting data from R. S. Dilley, 'The enclosure awards of Cumberland: a statistical list', *Trans CWAAS*, new ser. 100 (2000), pp. 225–39.
[63] S. Birtles, '"A green space beyond self-interest": the evolution of common land in Norfolk, c.750–2003' (PhD thesis, University of East Anglia, 2003), pp. 194–6, 306.
[64] Whyte, *Transforming Fell and Valley*, p. 27; Tate, *Domesday*, p. 150.

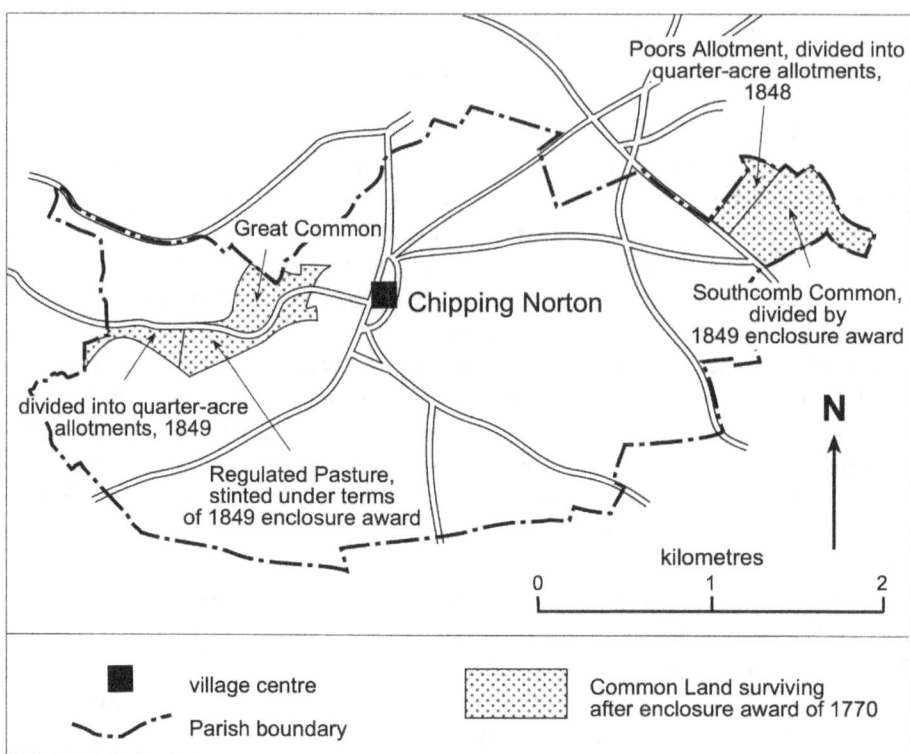

Figure 29. Chipping Norton, Oxfordshire: enclosure of common land since 1770 (after J. Grantham, *The Regulated Pasture*, 1997).

which the commoners were awarded cattlegates and the right to dig turves for their own use.[65] In Norfolk, a total of fifteen stinted pastures resulted from enclosure, of which six were charity pastures, vested in parish trustees, the original intention being to encourage the poor towards self-sufficiency by keeping livestock. Stints on most of the others (which were concentrated in north-west Norfolk) were limited to holders of 'ancient messuages', in two instances to specific properties adjacent to the patch of common in question.[66]

Stinting was again seen as a solution on coastal commons, where the costs of reclaiming salt marsh were prohibitively high. At Thornham on the north Norfolk coast, the enclosure act (1794) divided the marshes into two parts, one allocated to the lord of the manor, the other to remain common and to be used as a stinted pasture, managed by three 'Common Reeves' elected at an annual meeting of the stintholders.[67] It was likewise the salt marshes, 'which ... being subject to be overflowed by the Sea cannot conveniently be sub-divided by hedges or Fences', which were made stinted

---

[65] E. and R. C. Russell, *Old and New Landscapes in the Horncastle Area* (Lincoln, 1985), pp. 62–4.
[66] Birtles, '"A green space beyond self-interest"', pp. 194–6.
[67] *Contested Common Land*, pp. 168, 173–4.

pastures when the extensive commons at Holme Cultram (Cumb.) in the Solway lowlands were enclosed under an act of 1806.[68]

The process of stinting a common at enclosure was facilitated by the Inclosure Act 1845 which provided a framework of legal and management structures for newly regulated pastures. Later enclosures which led to stinting included 3,370 acres (1,364 ha) of Pennine moorland at Airton, near Malham (Yorks. W.R.) in 1854 and over 2,000 acres (800 ha) at Burn Fell and Lythe Moor in Tatham (Lancs.) on the Bowland Fells in 1858, but also the smaller, quarry-scarred lowland common at Cockfield (Dur.), regulated by stinting in 1868.[69]

More complex histories of enclosure sometimes involved the stinting of parts of a former common, as illustrated by three very different instances from lowland England. At Hurstbourne Tarrant (Hants) a new common was created by the enclosure award of 1820. The commons in the parish had covered twelve pieces of coppice woodland in which commoners had grazing rights when the trees were old enough, together with an open area known as the 'Grubbed Grounds', which had been cleared of woodland before 1771. The award of 1820 extinguished common rights in most of the coppiced woodlands and set out an area of 200 acres (80 ha) (the 'Grubbed Grounds' and part of the coppices) as a new 'perpetual common' for the use of the commoners, subject to 'a more intensive Right of Common', achieved by stinting.[70]

A similar process of partial enclosure occurred at Chipping Norton (Oxon.), where a two-stage process left a vestige of the former common pastures unenclosed (Figure 29). The open fields were enclosed in 1770, leaving three areas in communal occupation: the Great Common (124 acres; 50 ha); a piece containing 74 acres (30 ha) which was allotted to the 'owners and occupiers of messuages'; and a 20-acre (8-ha) plot awarded to the poor of the town. These were enclosed by a second award in 1849, part of the Great Common being divided into quarter-acre plots, the remaining 75 acres (30 ha) being converted into a stinted pasture with eighty-five stints, regulated under the framework laid down by the 1845 General Enclosure Act.[71]

At Edmonton (Mddx), enclosure created a short-lived stinted pasture. When Enfield Chase was enclosed in 1777 the parish was allocated an allotment of 1,231 acres (498 ha) in lieu of its unstinted grazing rights. Its use was overseen by surveyors responsible to the parish vestry and stinted grazing rights were introduced: two horned beasts and a horse for householders of over £10 rental value; one horned beast for householders of less than £10 per year. A little over twenty years later, the new stinted pasture was itself enclosed, when the Edmonton enclosure award of 1804 divided it and the parish's other commons into private property.[72]

---

[68] Quoted in CCD, Cumbria: Skinburness & Calvo Marshes (CL 26), 262/U/586.
[69] Airton: Tate, *Domesday*, pp. 109, 151, 318; Tatham: Straughton, *Common Grazing*, p. 197; Cockfield: below, pp. 226–8.
[70] L. E. Tavener, *The Common Lands of Hampshire* (Southampton, 1957), pp. 49–51.
[71] J. Grantham, *The Regulated Pasture (a History of Common Land in Chipping Norton)* (printed privately, 1997), esp. pp. 12, 23–33.
[72] *VCH Mddx* V, p. 168.

New Commons for the Poor

In lowland England, enclosure often set aside part of a common for the benefit of the poor. These 'poor's lands' fell into two categories: some were plots for communal use by the poor; others allotments which were administered, usually by the parish authorities, to generate income for poor relief. Across time there was a tendency for allotments in the first category to be let to generate funds, removing them from communal use. Most of those providing for continued communal use were fuel allotments, sections of the common allocated to the poor in lieu of their right to take peat or furze from the common, though some gave poorer households continued access to grazing. They were the result of both a growing acceptance that it was fitting for common land to be used to support poorer households (as discussed in Chapter 5) and also the impracticality of laying out numerous very small allotments in compensation for the limited common rights of landless individuals. The scale of the practice is illustrated by Sara Birtles' calculation that, of 420 enclosure acts in Norfolk between 1720 and 1834, over half (56 per cent) made explicit provision for poorer households.[73] The memory of such allotments survived in the names of numerous patches of land recorded by the Royal Commission on Common Land in the 1950s – the 'Poor Lots', 'Poor's Pieces', 'Poor's Patches', 'Poor's Fens' and 'Poor's Heaths' found across lowland England.[74]

The practice of granting allotments to the poor can be traced back to the early seventeenth century. In several Crown forests, pasture closes were allocated to the poor in lieu of their grazing rights and vested in trustees who managed them to generate income which was applied to poor relief.[75] In some instances, the land allotted continued to be exploited as a communal resource. At Brill and Oakley in Bernwood Forest (Bucks.), a 'Poor Folks' Pasture', on less fertile ground fairly remote from the villages, was allocated at enclosure in 1632 and was at first used communally as an agistment ground by the poor, under the supervision of a field keeper. In the 1680s, however, the grazing rights of the poor were stopped and the close was let in its entirety to a farmer, the income being applied as cash doles to the parishes' poor.[76]

At Slaidburn (Yorks. W.R.), where enclosure of large areas of waste in 1619 saw a 60-acre (24-ha) allotment allocated 'for the relief of the poor', a combination of rental income and direct communal exploitation was recorded by the 1740s. The close was

---

[73] S. Birtles, 'Common land, poor relief and enclosure: the use of manorial resources in fulfilling parish obligations 1601–1834', *Past & Present*, 165 (1999), p. 100. For poor allotments more generally, see S. Pinches, 'From common right to cold charity: enclosure and poor allotments in the eighteenth and nineteenth centuries', in A. Borsay and P. Shapely (eds), *Medicine, Charity and Mutual Aid* (Aldershot, 2007), pp. 35–53; H. Inui, 'The creation and administration of post-enclosure poor lands in English parishes, c.1630–1840', *AgHR*, 69 (2) (2021), pp. 192–212.

[74] Listed in the gazetteer of common land in England in Hoskins & Stamp, pp. 247–350. The survival of poor's allotments is discussed in D. R. Denman, R. A. Roberts and H. J. F. Smith, *Commons and Village Greens* (London, 1967), pp. 168–77.

[75] Hoyle, 'Disafforestation and drainage', p. 370; Sharp, 'Common rights, charities', pp. 128–33.

[76] J. Broad, 'The smallholder and cottager after Disafforestation – a legacy of poverty?', in J. Broad and R. W. Hoyle (eds), *Bernwood: The Life and Afterlife of a Forest* (Preston, 1997), pp. 90–100.

let but 'poor housekeepers' of Slaidburn township who were not in receipt of relief from the poor rates had a right to graze milk cows in the close for the summer season, on payment of 10s to the lessee of the close, again an arrangement akin to agistment. The poor householders also had the right to dig and dry turf on the allotment for fuel.[77] The mix of interests in the poor close made for tensions, which led to long-running disputes over its management and application of the charitable income across the later eighteenth and early nineteenth century. These included an episode in 1784 when poor householders took direct action, planting potatoes and sowing corn on parts of the close and laying out the rest for both meadow and grazing. After the ensuing legal action was settled at the end of 1785, the agistment of poor householders' cattle seems to have ceased.[78] In both these cases, the direct use of such pasture closes as communal grazing grounds for the poor was replaced over time by letting the grazing and applying the rental income in charitable payments to the poor.

Equivalent grazing allotments were made under Parliamentary enclosure in the eighteenth century. In several parishes in north-west Norfolk, substantial sections of common were allocated to poorer members of the community for grazing and fuel gathering. At Ashill, near Swaffham, three separate allotments were laid out at enclosure in 1786, one for fuel, one for geese and one for cattle and horses. Vested in trustees, their use was restricted to poorer households until 1859, when the trustees attempted, unsuccessfully, to enclose the allotments, bring them into cultivation and apply the rental income for the benefit of the poor.[79] At Snettisham, a large section of the common (584 acres; 236 ha) was reserved as a stinted pasture for the inhabitants of commonable cottages when the open fields were enclosed in 1766. It lasted until 1800, when it, in turn, was divided.[80] At Brancaster, when the open fields and heath were enclosed by an act in 1756, the award in effect created Barrow Common (88 acres, 36 ha) by throwing together two sections of 'heath and furzy ground' as a common specifically for the use of the poor, who were awarded stinted grazing and the right to cut gorse for fuel and were thenceforth excluded from the remainder of the former heath.[81]

During the height of Parliamentary enclosure, allocating a piece of the common specifically as a source of fuel for the poor became widespread. In Midland counties these allotments were often 'furze grounds', land explicitly set aside to grow gorse. In a Parliamentary report in 1795, Sir John Sinclair encouraged the practice, albeit hedging it around with caveats. He claimed that 'any portion of ground, however inconsiderable, planted with furze or quick growing wood, and dedicated to that purpose solely, would, under proper regulation, be as productive of fuel, as ten times

---

[77] R. W. Hoyle and C. J. Spencer, 'The Slaidburn poor pasture: changing configurations of popular politics in the eighteenth- and early nineteenth-century village', *Social History*, 31 (2) (2006), pp. 187–8.
[78] Ibid., pp. 193–5.
[79] Birtles, '"A green space beyond self-interest"', pp. 202–3.
[80] Birtles, 'Common land, poor relief and enclosure', pp. 95–6.
[81] *Contested Common Land*, pp. 163–74.

the space where no order or regularity is observed'.[82] At Kenilworth (Warw.), enclosed in 1757, a total of 40 acres (16 ha) of the common was allocated to remain 'common and unenclosed' for the poor to exercise 'a free and constant right to get furze go[r]ss or fern'.[83] Similar provisions were made in 1795 at Ettington (Warw.), where 4 acres (1.6 ha) 'of furze or heath ground' was allotted to the parish authorities 'to appropriate the same to the raising furze or other fuel for the use of necessitous, industrious and honest poor inhabitants', and in Gloucestershire, where 13 acres (5 ha) of Calmsden Downs was set aside for growing furze and five one-acre plots at Aston Subedge were to be planted with furze by the poor on a five-year rotation.[84] Yet Sinclair's advice was by no means always followed. Of the thirty-seven fuel allotments in Berkshire, many of them on the sands and gravels of heathland in the south-east of the county, only a few were used to grow furze; some were left as woodland and scrub for the poor to take kindling and turves, but most were let to generate income.[85]

Stoke Poges (Bucks.) provides an example of a fuel allotment which continued to be used communally for its intended purpose. Enclosure had been resisted because of the importance of the heath as a source of fuel (largely turf) for poorer inhabitants. In 1809 on the eve of the enclosure act, it was said that around ninety poor families each cut about 4,000 turves annually. The common was in a 'very mutilated state', having been 'cut all to pieces', and it was estimated that an acre of the turf ground would yield no more than 1,000 turves each year. On that basis, those seeking to ensure that the poor continued to have access to fuel sought to have 360 acres (146 ha) of the heath allocated as a fuel allotment. In the end, the act assigned 200 acres (80 ha), vested in the lord of the manor, the vicar, the churchwardens and overseers of the poor. The trustees drew up regulations in 1814, limiting each poor household to 2,000 turves annually, to be cut between 1 May and 29 September. They appointed inspectors to examine every cartload (for which those cutting turf were to pay a fee of 3d). Turf-cutting seems to have continued for much of the nineteenth century, though parishioners were increasingly tempted by the conifers which were encroaching on the common, which the trustees expressly excluded from the fuel rights.[86]

Where peat was the principal fuel, compensating the poor for their loss of turbary rights posed particular challenges. If too small an area were to be allocated as a common turbary it would soon be stripped of fuel, but leaving a sustainable area for long-term peat-digging could remove a large section of the common from enclosure (Figure 30). Three of the twenty-three enclosure awards from the North York Moors allocated areas as common turbaries, one of 2 acres (0.8 ha) at Easington being so small that it can hardly have been viable; another, by contrast, covering 250 acres (101

---

[82] G. Whittington, 'The common lands of Berkshire', *Transactions & Papers (IBG)*, 35 (1964), p. 131, quoting the Select Committee on the Cultivation and Improvement of the Waste, Uninclosed and Unproductive Lands of the Kingdom.
[83] Pinches, 'From common rights to cold charity', p. 43.
[84] *VCH Warw.* V, p. 83; *VCH Glos.* VII, p. 162; Inui, 'Post-enclosure poor lands', p. 205.
[85] Whittington, 'Common lands of Berkshire', pp. 133, 139.
[86] L. Rigby, *The History of Stoke Common: A Poor's Fuel Allotment Charity* (Stoke Poges, 1975), pp. 15–24, 27, 30–5.

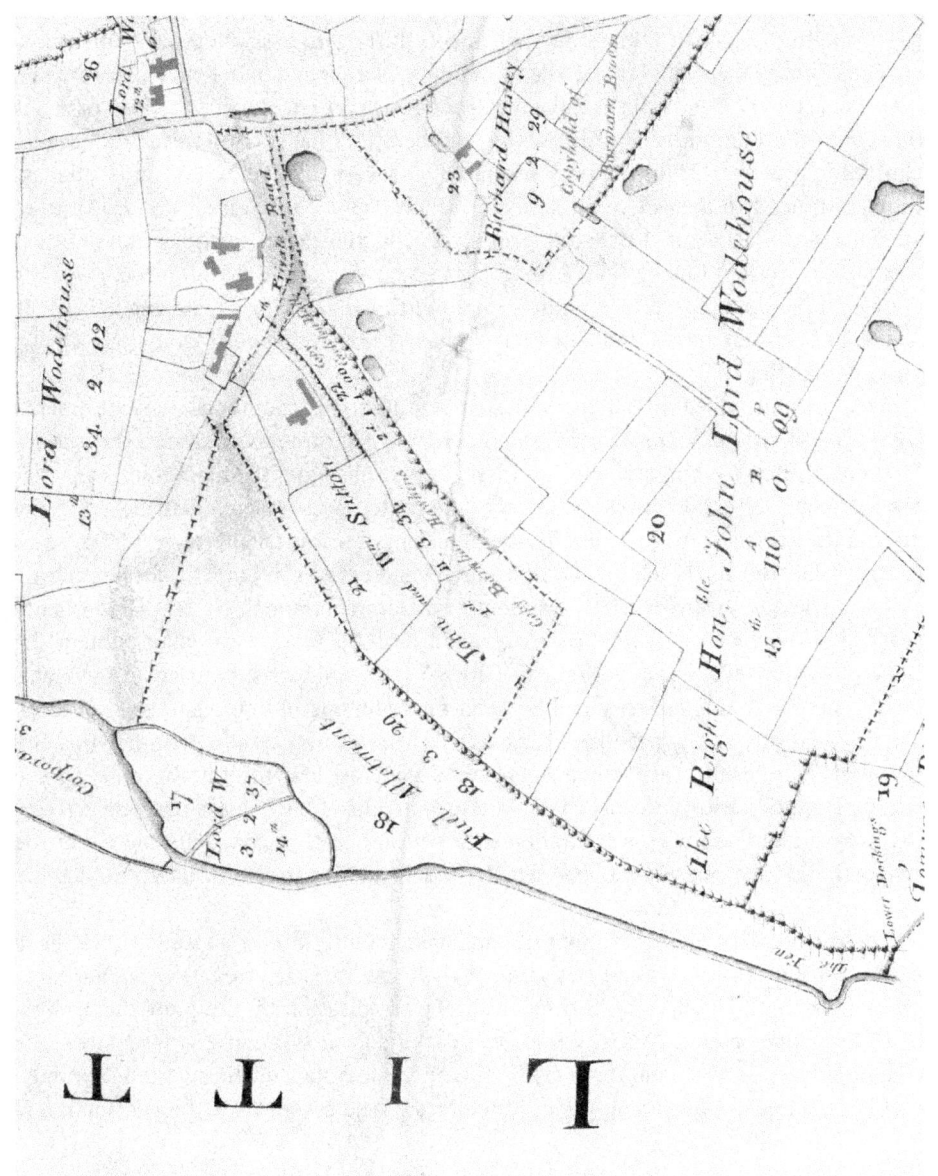

Figure 30. Barnham Broom, Norfolk, enclosure plan, 1812, showing the fuel allotment on Barnham Broom Fen, allocated to the poor (Norfolk Record Office, C/Sca2/15).

ha) of the High Moor at Ebberston.[87] In Lincolnshire, generous allotments of turbary grounds for all inhabitants of the Isle of Axholme were made under the enclosure and drainage act of 1795, which set aside a total of 400 acres (162 ha) for the four parishes there.[88] In the Cambridgeshire Fens, the 15.5-acre (6.2-ha) section of fen at Wicken, allotted to provide turf for the poor when the fens were divided in the 1660s, appears to have sufficed to answer their needs for around 150 years. A limit of 4,000 turves annually was placed on the 'Poor's ground' in the eighteenth century but the peat was almost worked out by the 1830s.[89] Less successful was a 20-acre (8-ha) turbary at Catcott (Som.), granted to the poor on the enclosure of King's Sedgemoor in 1799, where 'persons not authorised' dug fuel, so that by 1825 it had been 'much abused [by] improper cutting'.[90]

Even without the finite limits inherent in turbaries, communal fuel allotments were sometimes quite short-lived. The 20-acre (8-ha) allotment granted to the poor of Chipping Norton (Oxon.) at enclosure in 1770 was subsequently divided into quarter-acre plots in 1848, to be let at 5s 0d each, the rental income being distributed to the poor of the parish.[91] At Wavendon Heath (Bucks.) a substantial allotment of 150 acres (61 ha), allocated to the churchwardens and overseers of the poor for fuel gathering by the enclosure award of 1791, was removed from communal use less than twenty years later, when an agreement was reached in 1809 vesting the allotment in the Duke of Bedford for an annual rent of £300 which would then be used to buy coals for the poor.[92] A similar story can be seen on commons in many parts of southern and Midland England, where land allocated for the growing and cutting of furze in the later eighteenth century had been let to generate income for the poor by the mid-nineteenth century.[93] In Norfolk, the proportion of allotments used directly by the poor plummeted across the nineteenth century, with a concomitant rise in the proportion let to generate income, which grew from 55 per cent of allotment land in 1833 to 92 per cent by 1896.[94]

These examples suggest an almost inbuilt instability in fuel allotments, as those in authority in a parish sought to control their use in order to generate charitable income, rather than allowing continued direct exploitation by the poor themselves. In at least one instance, at Great Bedwyn (Wilts.), an enclosure act required the commissioners to allot land for growing furze for the poor but the award determined that it would be 'more advantageous' if the lord of the manor took the allotment and

---

[87] Chapman, 'Parliamentary enclosure in the uplands', p. 6.
[88] See below, pp. 229–33.
[89] *VCH Cambs*. X, p. 575.
[90] *VCH Som*. VIII, p. 30; Inui, 'Post-enclosure poor lands', p. 210.
[91] Grantham, *Regulated Pasture*, p. 14.
[92] Tate, *Domesday*, p. 69.
[93] Examples have been noted in Warwickshire (Ettington: *VCH Warw*. V, p. 83); Northamptonshire (Piddington: *VCH Northants* IV, p. 279); Oxfordshire (Wigginton and Brize Norton: *VCH Oxon*. IX, p. 170; XV, p. 216); Gloucestershire (Notgrove: *VCH Glos*. IX, p. 155); and Wiltshire (Swallowcliffe: *VCH Wilts*. XIII, p. 185).
[94] Birtles, '"A green space beyond self-interest"', pp. 202, 205.

paid an annual sum to the parish authorities to purchase fuel for the poor.[95] Tensions were exacerbated where the process of enclosure had established complex use rights over the allotment, as in the long-running disputes over the Slaidburn poor pasture, cited above. Other examples of conflict resulting from multiple interests in poor's allotments come from Norfolk. At Whitwell, near Reepham, the landowners asked the enclosure commissioners to allot a piece of heathland to the poor, with the intention that it should be let and the income used for a fuel charity. In their award of 1804, however, the commissioners decided instead that the Low Common should remain open for the poor to exercise their turbary rights. Twenty years later, the landowners reconfigured the use of the Low Common by giving up their own common rights over it while at the same time appointing a committee to superintend its use. The poor were no longer to cut turves themselves and the committee was to control grazing. At Snettisham, in the far north-west corner of the county, intermixed rights led to a grumbling dispute. At enclosure in 1766 a 90-acre (36-ha) allotment was set aside for the poorer householders to cut fuel each summer but the inhabitants of the parish were also given the right to take clay and sand from the allotment. When it was found that there was no sand on the allotment, the lord of the manor granted some of his own land for that purpose, taking 17 acres (7 ha) of the fuel allotment in exchange, which he planted with trees. In 1844 some of the poor felled trees in order to reach the fuel underneath, to which they claimed a right. Ten years later, communal use of the allotment was ended by a further enclosure award in 1854.[96] The General Enclosure Act of 1845, which was used to enclose some communally-used allotments made by previous enclosure awards, including both stinted pastures and fuel allotments, probably hastened the end of direct use of fuel allotments by the poor.

In general, the allocation of fuel allotments at enclosure had waned by the middle decades of the nineteenth century.[97] Doubts were expressed in the 1830s over the efficacy of awarding fuel rights to the poor, as the allotments had become over-used or exhausted, and coal, rather than sticks and turf, was becoming more widespread as a fuel. Moreover, the New Poor Law of 1834 had the effect of removing local, parochial responsibility for the poor. That was the context of the Inclosure Act 1845, which contained no provision for the award of fuel allotments, its concern for community resources focusing on recreation grounds and garden allotments.[98] The Commons Act 1876 reinforced the trend by empowering the Charity Commission to allow fuel allotments to be converted into recreation grounds or 'field gardens'.[99] In this, the acts reflected the changing conceptions of the value of common land which were gathering pace in the middle decades of the nineteenth century and form the starting point for the following chapter.

---

[95] Wilts. & Swindon Archives, EA 68. I am grateful to Graham Bathe for this reference.
[96] Birtles, '"A green space beyond self-interest", pp. 198–200.
[97] An exception occurred at Merrow Downs (Surrey), regulated in 1904 under the Commons Act 1876, when a section of the common was allocated to provide fuel and litter for the labouring poor: Eversley, p. 257.
[98] Birtles, 'Common land, poor relief and enclosure', pp. 103–5.
[99] Commons Act 1876, c.56, sec. 19.

* * *

Where shared use of part or all of a common was a product of Parliamentary enclosure, it generally entailed a change in the legal basis of rights and sometimes of the management of the communal resource. Those using an area allocated as a newly designated stinted pasture or a fuel allotment had generally lost any rights they had on the rest of the enclosed common. Fuel allotments were generally just that – other rights had been extinguished by enclosure. Moreover, the creation of stinted pastures at enclosure represented a commodification of common rights, as stints tended to become marketable commodities which could be traded separately from the land to which the former unstinted right had previously been attached. There was also an underlying dynamic. Where a stinted pasture was subsequently divided under the terms of a further enclosure award, or where fuel allotments proved to be temporary, being let to an individual to generate income for the poor, the process of reconfiguring rights to enable continuing communal use proved to be a halfway house on a journey from common right to private property.

CHAPTER 7

THE COMMONS REINVENTED

> Ye commons left free in the rude rags of nature,
> Ye brown heaths be-cloathed in furze as ye be,
> My wild eye in rapture adores every feature,
> Ye are dear as this heart in my bosom to me.[1]

JOHN CLARE'S HYMN TO the loss of his beloved heathlands of Northamptonshire, published in 1821, anticipated a fundamental change in perceptions of common land which took place across the nineteenth century. Clare was voicing nostalgia for a countryside rapidly being lost. His appreciation of land clothed 'in the rude rags of nature' was to become central to the value placed on commons by modern society. From the 1860s, common land came to be valued for recreation, public access and natural beauty, and later for its ecological character. No longer were commons a reservoir of untamed land waiting to be reclaimed and improved; now those which survived became a precious remnant to be conserved for the benefit of the nation at large. Paradoxically, however, that wider interest led to further loss of common land, as it came to be seen as an appropriate location for public buildings and, at times of crisis in the twentieth century, as a resource which could be drawn upon in the service of national defence. The new perceptions were part of a deep change in conceptions of land. If a wider public interest were accepted, it followed that limits would be placed on the freedom of action of those with property rights. How the common land which had survived the era of enclosure was used – indeed, how it *should* be used – became matters of public debate.

The shift of discourse from 'reclamation' to 'conservation' is conventionally placed in the 1860s, with the foundation of the Commons Preservation Society in 1865, but its roots can be traced back to the earlier decades of the century. It sprang from two very different sources – landscape aesthetics and public health. The idea that the public at large had a valid interest in natural beauty was being expressed in relation to the Lake District by the first years of the nineteenth century. After visiting the Lakes in 1802, Richard Warner declared that places deemed to be beautiful were 'the common property of the people', and Wordsworth later famously described the Lake District

---

[1] 'Song', from *The Village Minstrel and Other Poems* (London, 1821), vol. I, pp. 105–7 (reprinted in E. Robinson and D. Powell (eds), *The Early Poems of John Clare 1804–1822, Volume II* (Oxford, 1989), pp. 100–1).

as 'a sort of national property, in which every man has a right and interest who has an eye to perceive and a heart to enjoy'.[2] The public health dimension can be traced back to the House of Commons Select Committee set up in 1833 to consider how open spaces near larger towns might be secured to provide 'Public walks and Places of Exercise calculated to promote the health and comfort of the inhabitants'. Kennington Common and Hackney Downs, commons in the vicinity of London, were named as potential sites.[3]

Nothing concrete came of the Select Committee's work, and debate moved to the proposals contained in the bill which became the Inclosure Act 1845. Streamlining further enclosure encountered some opposition: it would, in the view of opponents like the radical MP Joseph Hume, 'take away from poor men ... the advantages which they now possessed in the enjoyment of air and exercise on these commons'. In the end, the 1845 act included two provisions to assuage the objectors: first, separate Parliamentary scrutiny would be required for any proposal to enclose commons within fifteen miles of London and within shorter distances of other major towns; second, the Inclosure Commissioners were empowered to set aside allotments 'for exercise and recreation for the inhabitants of the neighbourhood'.[4]

With the rapid expansion of the metropolitan built-up area in the mid-Victorian decades, the potential economic value of commons near London rocketed. Owners of common land were tempted to seek enclosure or (as formal enclosure became increasingly difficult as the pressure for preservation grew) to attempt to enclose parts as building plots by exercising their rights of approvement. Even without enclosure, owners of wastes in the metropolitan area could gain income from sales of gravel or clay or even by stripping turf and topsoil from their commons. Opposition grew: by the 1860s, preserving access to open spaces for London's working classes had become entwined with campaigns for electoral reform. A simmering anger underlay the mass demonstrations called to protect the capital's open spaces in the 1860s and 1870s, boiling over on occasion into direct action when fences were thrown down.[5]

The Commons Preservation Society (CPS), ancestor of the Open Spaces Society, was founded in 1865 on the back of discussions in a House of Commons Select Committee set up in 1864 to consider open spaces in the vicinity of London in the context of a bill put forward by Earl Spencer to enclose Wimbledon Common.[6] The Committee's report recommended that no further enclosures of common land should be allowed in the metropolitan area, that the public's rights over commons should be recognised, and that better management of commons should be instituted to regulate perceived

---

[2] P. Readman, *Storied Ground: Landscape and the Shaping of English National Identity* (Cambridge, 2018), p. 105.
[3] A. Howkins, 'The commons, enclosure and radical histories', in D. Feldman and J. Lawrence (eds), *Structures and Transformations in Modern British History* (Cambridge, 2011), p. 123.
[4] Ibid., pp. 124–8.
[5] See M. Gorman, *Saving the People's Forest: Open Spaces, Enclosure and Popular Protest in Mid-Victorian London* (Hatfield, 2021)
[6] For which, see below, p. 269.

nuisances. In the following decades the new Society played an influential role in battles to preserve some of the major commons in the London area.[7]

Led by a small but highly influential group of public figures, with a strong Radical Liberal element, the CPS made full use of legal processes to challenge both enclosure and destructive exploitation of commons, backing lawsuits and undertaking archival research in order to establish commoners' rights. The aim was not to restore what were sometimes viewed as vestigial anachronisms of past agrarian use but to inch towards demonstrating a wider public interest over common land.[8] Direct action was sometimes taken, most famously at Berkhamsted (Herts.) in 1866, when the CPS brought 120 navvies by train from London to demolish iron fences erected by the owner of the common, who had blocked access and enclosed over 400 acres (162 ha). The CPS played an active part in most of the battles to protect commons in the vicinity of London, its early campaigns forming an impressive roll-call of success. The long-running battle over Hampstead Heath was resolved when it was purchased by the Metropolitan Board of Works in 1868 to prevent enclosure. The campaigns over Wimbledon Common and Putney Heath (1865–70) and Wandsworth Common (1870–71) both resulted in the commons being transferred to boards of conservators on payment of annuities to the lord of the manor, Earl Spencer, in recompense for his loss of income from gravel extraction. Determined legal proceedings prevented further enclosure of Plumstead (1866–71) and Tooting Graveney (1868–71) commons; and the Society's backing of the Banstead Commons Protection Society, founded in 1876 in the face of aggressive attempts to enclose and build on parts of Banstead Heath and Downs, followed by protracted litigation between 1877 and 1889, secured the future of those commons.[9] The Society's lobbying rode on the tide of public sentiment in what Mark Gorman has termed 'a symbiotic relationship with an increasingly assertive metropolitan popular opinion'. When an anonymous voice in a crowd protesting against enclosures on Epping Forest in 1871 shouted 'They are our own', it caught the mood that London's open spaces were claimed by the people.[10]

As a result of the debates and battles over commons in the London area, the tide began to run strongly against enclosure. Legislation provided a statutory framework for retaining common land as public open space and for better regulation of its use. The Metropolitan Commons Act 1866 authorised the appointment of boards of conservators to regulate commons within a fifteen-mile radius of the capital, while the Commons Act 1876 was of more general significance, requiring the wider public benefit to be taken into account in all cases where enclosure was proposed. In effect, the age of enclosure was over. Common land was now seen as a 'common possession

---

[7] For the early history of CPS, see Eversley, *passim*; B. Cowell, 'The Commons Preservation Society and the campaign for Berkhamsted Common, 1866–70', *Rural History*, 13 (2) (2002), pp. 145–61; M. J. D. Roberts, 'Gladstonian Liberalism and environment protection', *English Historical Review*, 128 (2013), pp. 292–322.

[8] Roberts, 'Gladstonian Liberalism', pp. 312–13, 320.

[9] The legal battles over these commons are spelt out in Eversley, pp. 34–72, 130–45 and, for Berkhamsted, in Cowell, 'Commons Preservation Society'.

[10] Gorman, *Saving the People's Forest*, pp. 143, 149.

for the whole country'.[11] Indeed, commons carried a particular significance. In the context of the battles to protect common land in the New Forest in the 1870s, Paul Readman has noted that commons were symbolic of 'the people's rightful inheritance in the soil of their country'.[12]

From its early days, the CPS sought to preserve commons not only as open spaces for public recreation but also as havens of nature in its 'primeval' state to nourish the nation's soul.[13] The campaign for national protection of natural beauty, which gathered momentum across the later decades of Victoria's reign, culminated in the foundation of the National Trust in 1895. The role of the CPS, and in particular of its solicitor, Robert Hunter, in promoting the Trust ensured that acquiring common land was on the Trust's agenda from the beginning. When its powers and responsibilities were confirmed under the National Trust Act 1907, they explicitly included a duty to keep any common land it acquired 'unenclosed and unbuilt on as open spaces for the recreation and enjoyment of the public' and to prevent any attempts to encroach on or enclose it.[14] From an early date, the National Trust also sought to obtain an interest on commons by purchasing properties which had common rights attached to them: by 1944 it could claim common rights on sixteen Lake District properties by virtue of purchases made since 1902.[15] Across the twentieth century, the Trust became one of the largest owners of commons in England and Wales, now holding 119,600 acres (48,400 ha) of common land,[16] while the National Trust for Scotland (founded in 1931) became owner of common grazings and scattalds on its properties in crofting areas, such as the Balmacara estate near Kyle of Lochalsh and the islands of Yell and Fair Isle in Shetland.

Despite an increasing acceptance across the later nineteenth century that common land should provide public recreation, full public access was yet to come. In law there was no automatic right to wander freely over common land and owners and those grazing livestock or exercising other rights might be resistant. When a proposal to regulate Great Langdale Common (Westmld) was discussed in 1895, the desire to provide free access to the popular Lakeland fell tops clashed with the commoners' rights. A general right to wander over the fells would, claimed the lord of the manor's agent, 'be sacrificing the existing rights of the Commoners to the imaginary rights of the public' to create 'an entirely antagonistic right which in effect would be subversive to the rights of the Commoners'.[17] Such hostility shows that the wider public interest in common land was not universally accepted and that it could create tension with private property rights. The Law of Property Act 1925 took a first step in formalising

---

[11] P. Readman, 'Preserving the English landscape, 1870–1914', *Cultural & Social History*, 5 (2008), p. 209.
[12] Readman, *Storied Ground*, p. 183.
[13] Roberts, 'Gladstonian Liberalism', pp. 315–19.
[14] 7 Edward VII, c.136, sec. 29.
[15] B. L. Thompson, *The Lake District and The National Trust* (Kendal, 1946), pp. 72–3, 218.
[16] Acreage figure courtesy of Sharolyn Parnham, The National Trust, 2021.
[17] TNA, MAF/25/63, W. Little to Board of Agriculture, 10 August 1895, quoted in E. A. Straughton, *Common Grazing in the Northern English Uplands, 1800–1965* (Lampeter, 2008), p. 223.

public access to commons generally, by confirming access to metropolitan commons and commons in all urban districts. That provision, paradoxically, conferred a right of access to fells in the heart of the Lake District, including Great Langdale, which lay within the boundary of Ambleside Urban District. The act also contained provisions for landowners to make deeds of declaration, granting the public a legal right of access to rural commons. By the 1950s, access had been granted under those provisions to c.118,500 acres (c.48,000 ha) of common land, including almost all Crown wastes in Wales (76,680 acres; 31,030 ha) and Lancashire.[18] Wider public access on commons was not formally achieved until the Countryside and Rights of Way (CROW) Act 2000 in England and Wales and the Land Reform (Scotland) Act 2003.

Access to common land became part of a wider debate about the most appropriate use of land, as concepts of national planning became paramount during the middle decades of the twentieth century. Attention turned to the most fitting use of commons for the nation's benefit, and that extended well beyond recreation. In their preface to *The Common Lands of England and Wales* (1963), the editors of the New Naturalist series highlighted the value of common land as 'a precious reservoir of wild life' and urged that 'we can no longer afford to neglect this national asset'.[19] In the inter-war campaign for national parks and the wider drive for protection of the countryside, the themes of access, preservation of beauty and nature conservation began to coalesce. Although commons were requisitioned both for military use and to boost agricultural production during the Second World War (see below), post-war planning legislation, culminating in the National Parks and Access to the Countryside Act 1949, placed access and conservation high on the agenda. Most of the major areas of common land in the uplands of England and Wales were put under the protective umbrella of national parks in the 1950s: the Lake District, Snowdonia and Dartmoor in 1951; the North York Moors and Yorkshire Dales in 1952 and 1954 respectively; the Preseli Hills (as part of the Pembrokeshire Coast National Park) in 1952; and the Brecon Beacons in 1957. Belatedly, the New Forest, the largest concentration of common land in lowland England, was added to the list in 2005. Almost half (48 per cent) of all common land in England and 40 per cent of common land in Wales lies within national parks and a further 30 per cent is in Areas of Outstanding Natural Beauty in England. When other areas designated for landscape or ecological protection, such as Sites of Special Scientific Interest (SSSIs), are included, the proportion of common land in England protected by environmental designations rises to 88 per cent of the total acreage.[20] In Scotland, almost 16 per

---

[18] Law of Property Act 1925, sec. 193; *RCCL Rep.*, paras 85, 93 (pp. 31, 34) and p. 104n; Hoskins & Stamp, p. 227; J. W. Aitchison and E. J. Hughes, 'The common lands of Wales', *Trans IBG*, 13 (1) (1988), p. 106.

[19] Hoskins & Stamp, p. xiii.

[20] Pastoral Commoning Partnership, *Trends in Pastoral Commoning* (Carlisle, 2009), p. 27 (table 3.2); Aitchison and Hughes, 'Common lands of Wales', p. 106, who also note that 126 commons in Wales lay in AONBs but do not give the acreage.

cent of the total area of common grazings lies in SSSIs and more than one-fifth in Special Protection Areas for birds.[21]

In the debates from the 1930s one persistent concern was the perceived neglect of common land. The collapse of traditional management mechanisms, uncertainties over ownership and common rights (and even whether or not a piece of ground was common land), and the increasing and conflicting pressures on commons all led to calls for the appointment of a commission to grapple with what was seen as a national problem. A Royal Commission on Common Land was eventually established in 1955, after wartime emergency powers had lapsed. Its remit covered the whole of England and Wales and reflected the national planning ethos of the period. It was asked

> to recommend what changes, if any, are desirable in the law relating to common land in order to promote the benefit of those holding manorial and common rights, the enjoyment of the public, or, where at present little or no use is made of such land, its use for some other desirable purpose.[22]

The Commission's 137-page report in 1958 dispensed with the requirement to consider other desirable uses in fewer than eight pages. It envisaged four potential uses of common land – cultivation, afforestation, as water gathering grounds and military training areas – but concluded that 'the four alternatives are not always easy to reconcile with one another or with the uses by the public and the holders of private rights'. The Commissioners' report focused on the need for clarity over the extent of common land and the rights over it, public access, and management schemes to regulate its use. They recommended formal registration of commons in England and Wales; a change in the law to allow the public access to all common land as of right; and the establishment of management schemes under the auspices of the proposed Commons Registration Authorities.[23] In the event, it took almost half a century for the Commission's recommendations to be adopted. Registration of land and rights was accomplished fairly swiftly under the Commons Registration Act 1965 but the other recommendations gathered dust, despite being revisited and fleshed out by the Common Land Forum, set up by the Countryside Commission in 1983.[24] Public access to common land was eventually included in the Countryside and Rights of Way Act 2000, and new formal management schemes were facilitated by the Commons Act 2006.[25]

Common land has thus been reinvented since the mid-nineteenth century, as the commons which survived the age of enclosure gained new roles in modern society and culture. At one level, this reinvention was expressed in a re-writing of the legal

---

[21] G. Jones, *Trends in Common Grazings* (European Forum for Nature Conservation & Pastoralism, 2011), p. 34.
[22] *RCCL Rep.*, p. iii.
[23] Ibid., pp. 78–86, 88–94, 103–9 (quotation p. 79).
[24] Countryside Commission, *Common Land: The Report of the Common Land Forum* (Cheltenham, 1986).
[25] Countryside and Rights of Way Act 2000 (*Gadsden*, §§ 9-16 to 9-25); Commons Act 2006, part 2 (*Gadsden*, §§ 12-03 to 12-23 and pp. 676–83). See also *Contested Common Land*, pp. 72–83.

framework of property rights in common land. At grassroots level, effective systems of regulation appropriate to changing circumstances were required and a second theme concerns the attempts to fill the void in the management of commons left by the decline of seigniorial courts. Property rights and management systems were principally concerned with the traditional uses of common land; a third dimension of change involves the new uses to which common land was put in the national interest.

REFORMING THE LEGAL BASIS OF COMMON LAND

The legal framework of common land in both Scotland and England and Wales has been re-written by statute since the mid-nineteenth century. The contexts of reform north and south of the border were very different, the new legal basis in Scotland being a product of economic and social upheaval in the aftermath of the Highland Clearances; that in England and Wales resulting from the growing perception of common land as a public resource, outlined above. Although different in their aims, the new laws re-made the statutory definitions of common land and the rights over it under both legal systems.

The particular status of crofters' common grazings in the north-west Highlands, the Western Isles and Shetland stems from the Crofters Act 1886.[26] The Highland Clearances had disrupted patterns of use on the hill grazings in the nineteenth century, by bringing large tracts under the control of commercial sheep farms and removing smallholders to crofting settlements along the coasts.[27] Agitation for improved rights and security for crofters – including resentment over the loss of common grazings – grew, boiling over in the 'Crofters' War' of the 1880s. Direct action by crofters in the 'Battle of the Braes' on Skye in 1882 centred on attempts by three crofting townships to reclaim grazing rights on Ben Lee, which had been part of their common pastures until it was leased to a sheep farmer in 1865. It initiated several years of unrest and brought the crofters' grievances to national attention, resulting in the setting up of the Napier Commission, which paved the way for the legislation of 1886.[28]

The Crofters Act recognised crofting as a distinct form of tenure, giving crofters some security and establishing a Crofters Commission. In response to the grievances over the loss of common grazings available to crofting townships, the act provided for the enlargement of crofting holdings, empowering the Commission to assign additional

---

[26] Crofters Holdings (Scotland) Act 1886: 49 & 50 Victoria, c.29, Part V. For a summary of successive statutes relating to crofting, see D. J. MacCuish, 'Crofting legislation since 1886', *Scottish Geographical Magazine*, 103 (2) (1987), pp. 90–4. A few areas of common grazings (7,884 ha or 2 per cent of the total) survive outside the crofting counties, the largest being on Lochtayside and the Isle of Arran: G. Jones, *Trends in Common Grazings* (European Forum for Nature Conservation & Pastoralism, 2011), p. 18.

[27] The standard surveys are J. Hunter, *The Making of the Crofting Community* (Edinburgh, 1976); and T. M. Devine, *Clanship to Crofters' War: The Social Transformation of the Scottish Highlands* (Manchester, 1994).

[28] Hunter, *Making of Crofting Community*, pp. 131–64 (the 'Battle of the Braes' is chronicled on pp. 133–6); Devine, *Clanship to Crofters' War*, pp. 218–35.

areas of common grazing to townships and to regulate access to communal resources, including peat, heather for thatching and seaweed for manure. By making a share in the common grazing an integral part of each croft, the new legal framework replaced rights of servitude with a form of property right which was protected by legislation.

The Crofters Act provided the necessary legal basis on which to build statutory regulation of common grazings. Although it gave each holding in a crofting township a defined proportion of the pasture rights on the common grazings, it provided no mechanism for determining how many animals an individual could turn out. It was said in 1888 that the legislation had removed the authority of landlords to ensure equitable use of the common grazings and Sir Kenneth Mackenzie of Gairloch, a member of the Napier Commission, urged the establishment of crofters' meetings with the power to make byelaws and fix limits on the numbers of cattle and sheep individual crofters should be entitled to graze.[29]

Such meetings were duly provided for by further legislation in 1891, which empowered crofters sharing a common grazing to appoint a committee charged with regulating grazing and other matters 'affecting the fair exercise of their joint rights'.[30] As a result, many common grazings came to be managed by a grazing committee,[31] the regulations focusing squarely on farming matters: stocking rates (specifying the soum of each croft), herding, control of bulls and rams, and peat-digging.[32] In contrast to the statutory management bodies in England, discussed below, public access to common land was not their concern.

* * *

In England and Wales, the Commons Registration Act 1965 (hereafter 'CRA'), which effectively re-wrote the legal basis of common land, was one of the most consequential outcomes of Parliamentary deliberations over commons in the twentieth century. The CRA required statutory registers to be created and maintained by county councils, to record the extent of all common land, its ownership, the rights exercisable over it and the persons claiming those rights. Provisional registrations had to be made by 31 July 1970: any land that had not been registered by then was deemed not to be common land and any rights which had not been registered could no longer be exercised. Specially appointed Commons Commissioners considered objections and ruled in cases of dispute (of which there were many);[33] if no objections were made, a

---

[29] Reported in *Inverness Courier*, 31 July 1888, p. 4.

[30] Crofters Common Grazings Regulation Act 1891 (54 & 55 Victoria, c.41), sec. 1.

[31] In 2003 there were still 200 unregulated common grazings in Scotland: G. C. Parsons, 'North West Scotland and Western Norway: a comparative study of factors which can impact on small-scale agriculture within similar peripheral communities' (PhD thesis, University of Aberdeen, 2011), pp. 91–2.

[32] For examples, see below, pp. 210–13; J. R. Coull, 'Crofters' common grazings in Scotland', *AgHR*, 16 (2) (1968), pp. 146–51.

[33] In Wales, 46 per cent of commons registered were subject to objections: Aitchison and Hughes, 'Common lands of Wales', p. 97. For an extreme example of the complexity and

provisional registration became final.[34] Where the owner of a common was unknown, the Commons Commissioner was required to vest ownership in the local authority, usually the parish council.[35] In effect, the slate was wiped clean and only common land and rights registered under the CRA were thereafter recognised in law.

In England, a total of 7,039 individual commons were registered under the CRA, the majority of them very small pieces of land: 4,958 (70.5 per cent) of them contained under 5 acres (2 ha). In Wales, 1,636 individual commons were registered. Common land was more concentrated there, over half of all common land in the principality lying in twelve groups of contiguous hill commons. Few common rights tended to be registered on the smaller patches of common, whereas they were numerous on larger commons. Pasture rights predominated, while rights of estovers were registered on 22 per cent of Welsh commons and 10 per cent of English, and turbary rights on 12 per cent in Wales and 8 per cent in England.[36]

Many criticisms have been levelled against the CRA and the limitations of the registers it created. Held in county council offices, in typescript volumes with numerous scorings out and manuscript amendments, the registers rapidly became outdated as the act made no provision for them to be kept up-to-date. Furthermore, by attempting to shoehorn the richness of regional tradition into a standardised, nationwide register, the CRA created problems. Most striking was the requirement that grazing rights were to be quantified. The unspoken assumption was that all commons were stinted, giving each commoner a right to graze a certain number of stock; yet rights on almost half of commons were governed by the rule of levancy and couchancy and were 'pasture without number', even though limited by the over-wintering rule. It is generally agreed that the CRA led to widespread excessive registration of grazing rights.[37] Moreover, once a set number had been entered on the register, flexibility had gone and with it the ability to vary stocking levels in response to changing environmental or market conditions. By registering rights as fixed numbers, the newly articulated property regime turned grazing rights into a saleable commodity, which could be severed from the land to which they had been attached, a process which persisted until further severance was forbidden under the Commons Act 2006.[38]

Other areas in which the CRA failed to capture the reality of grazing rights included its inability to take account of the exclusive use of sections of a common by individual commoners which was inherent in the systems of sheep heafs in northern England and sheepwalks in Wales. In Wales, this sometimes resulted in the

---

contention sometimes facing commons commissioners, see CCD, Hereford & Worcester: Garway Hill Common (CL 4), 15/D/56–66.

[34] *Gadsden*, §§ 3-01–3-97. For a summary, see *Contested Common Land*, pp. 10–11, 54–6.

[35] *Gadsden*, § 5-22.

[36] J. Aitchison et al., *The Common Lands of England: A Biological Survey* (Aberystwyth, 2000), pp. 16–18; Aitchison and Hughes, 'Common lands of Wales', pp. 98, 100–1.

[37] This and other deficiencies were highlighted in Countryside Commission, *Common Land*, esp. appendix C, pp. 33–75. See also *Contested Common Land*, pp. 54–8.

[38] *Contested Common Land*, pp. 56–7, 195–6. The legality of severance had been confirmed in 2000 by the Bettison v. Langton case: *Gadsden*, § 2-18.

registration of individual sheepwalks as separate small commons over which only a single commoner claimed rights. The act allowed for different categories of livestock to be registered and for the registration of rights for part of the year only, but once entered on the register these became rigid and inflexible. A commoner who had registered a right to graze only sheep, for example, could not legally graze cattle or horses instead.

Informal patterns of customary use which were difficult to reconcile with formal common rights also became an issue at registration. On the Sugar Loaf Mountain Common near Abergavenny (Mon.), some commoners initially registered rights to take a range of products, including moss, leaf mould, 'whimberries' (bilberries) and other wild fruit, mistletoe, pea sticks and bean poles. However, these explicit claims were rejected by the Commons Commissioner, on the grounds that they fell under a general right of estovers.[39] Comparable claims were nevertheless registered elsewhere and, where unchallenged, became formalised in law. This was the case with the so-called 'samphire rights' on coastal commons in north Norfolk. Large numbers of individuals from local families registered identical suites of rights on the coastal marshes, typically expressed as the right to take 'samphire, sea lavender, seaweed, shellfish, bait, wildfowl and game, fish, sand and shingle, and estovers'. Around 300 such registrations were made at Brancaster and 117 at Thornham, for example.[40] In that area, the provisions of the CRA for registrations to become final if not challenged enabled traditional, customary uses such as these, which were generally deemed to be of uncertain legality, to be given full legal status under the CRA.

What is more, the new legal basis of common land in England and Wales after 1970 came at a time when commons were increasingly being designated as conservation areas, such as SSSIs. That process, with further environmental legislation and successive agri-environmental schemes from the later twentieth century, resulted in the legal framework surrounding the use of common land becoming increasingly multi-layered and, in some instances, containing inherent conflicts. The designation of many commons as SSSIs could cut across property rights, for example, by preventing the exercise of common rights of turbary or estovers, as these (involving digging peat, stripping turf or cutting vegetation) were often deemed to be 'operations likely to damage' the scientific interest of the site.[41]

MANAGING COMMONS IN THE POST-MANORIAL WORLD

By Victoria's reign it was generally agreed that effective management had broken down on many English commons. Few manor courts continued to regulate the use of common land successfully and only rarely had alternative management mechanisms been devised. Overstocking and illegal grazing were rife and the exploitation of other

---

[39] CCD, Gwent: Sugar Loaf Mountain Common (CL 4), 273/D/127–33, pp. 27–38.
[40] *Contested Common Land*, pp. 170–1, 175–7; *Gadsden*, § 2-42.
[41] See *Contested Common Land*, pp. 62–5.

resources went largely uncontrolled.⁴² The neglect of commons which had survived enclosure was a core part of the perceived problem of common land which, as seen above, occupied minds until the later twentieth century. In Scotland, by contrast, the decades following the crofting legislation of 1891 saw formal rules, based on templates overseen by the Crofters Commission, providing for close regulation of the common grazings,⁴³ in stark contrast to the absence of regulation on many English and Welsh commons by the early years of the twentieth century.

Manorial Regulation: Survival and Evolution
Where manor courts continued to regulate grazings on common land, they tended to evolve into the commoners' meetings which became a feature of many commons in the late nineteenth and twentieth centuries. The trend can be seen in Cumbria, where few courts continued to meet, let alone be active, after 1850. At Sedbergh (Yorks. W.R.), where the court continued to make orders into the early twentieth century, court sittings were infrequent and irregular. Those commoners present at each meeting formed the jury, as they sought to 'uphold [the] frail institution, rather than abandon it', as Eleanor Straughton put it – though the court did not survive beyond the 1920s.⁴⁴ The courts leet at Rodborough and Minchinhampton (Glos.) on the Cotswold scarp had delegated day-to-day management to committees of commoners by the mid-nineteenth century, so that traditional manorial regulation elided into a modern commoners' association. As at Sedbergh, the court became a vehicle for the interests of the commoners. The 1881 meeting of the Rodborough court leet was called at the instigation of a committee 'for preserving the rights of the Common of Rodborough', and in 1904 it was urged that courts should be held from time to time 'so that people might see that the commoners had their rights and meant to maintain them'.⁴⁵ The committee overlapped closely with the manor court jury and appears to have been the embodiment of continuity. Eleven of the thirteen members of the Rodborough commons committee appointed in 1881 had also served on the court jury that year and, when the secretary retired in 1932, it was noted that he had served on the committee for fifty-four years, having been appointed in 1878.⁴⁶ When Minchinhampton Common was conveyed to the National Trust in 1913, the role of the court leet was abolished and regulation of the common was vested in the commons committee, which was the forerunner of the modern management

---

42 A. Howkins, 'The use and abuse of the English commons, 1845–1914', *History Workshop Journal*, 78 (2014), pp. 119–20. Uncontrolled exploitation of Ashdown Forest in the later Victorian period is described in B. Short, 'Conservation, class and custom: lifespace and conflict in a nineteenth-century forest environment', *Rural History*, 10 (2) (1999), p. 134. For comments on upland commons, see F. W. Garnett, *Westmorland Agriculture, 1800–1900* (Kendal, 1912), pp. 16–18.
43 For the example of Assynt, Sutherland, see below, pp. 210–13.
44 Straughton, *Common Grazing*, pp. 124–34, 153–60.
45 *Stroud News & Gloucestershire Advertiser*, 20 May 1904, p. 7.
46 *Stroud Journal*, 11 June 1881, p. 4; *Gloucester Citizen*, 14 May 1932, p. 1.

committee.[47] A comparable evolution from court to commoners' association had occurred elsewhere by the 1950s.[48]

Some surviving courts possessed a strong social dimension. At Rodborough, for example, the highlight of the year was the annual Marking Day in May, when cattle and horses to be turned out on the commons (totalling around 600 in the 1930s) were branded on their hooves, and members of the commons committee were entertained to lunch at the Bear Inn on the edge of the common.[49] The court of the ancient borough of Stockbridge (Hants), which had been held regularly until 1880, became self-consciously archaic when it was revived by a new lord of the manor in 1922. Its main regulatory function was deciding the date for the opening of grazing on the Common Marsh and a hayward was appointed each year to oversee the common pastures. The court's annual meetings were ceremonial events, complete with regalia (seventeenth-century mace, seal and hayward's staff, all restored to pristine condition) and an address by the lord of the manor on matters of general interest in Stockbridge.[50]

The list of functioning manorial courts in England and Wales, drawn up for the Administration of Justice Act 1977, included only eighteen which continued to manage common lands. Half were concerned with upland grazing commons. Five of these were in northern England (at Bowes in the Pennines; and at Danby, Fyling, Spaunton and Whitby Laithe in the North York Moors); two (Mynachlog-ddu and the court of the barony of Cemaes) in the Preseli Hills of south-west Wales; and two (Dunstone and Spitchwick) managed commons at Widecombe in the Moor, on the eastern edge of Dartmoor.[51] These were exceptions; on most commons, manor courts had ceased to provide effective regulation of common rights by the later nineteenth century.

Statutory Management Mechanisms

New regulatory bodies were devised by the statutory regimes developed in the later nineteenth century to govern some commons. They were spearheaded by the Inclosure Act 1845, which required stinted pastures regulated under its provisions to be managed by one or more 'field reeves', a title borrowed from the language of open-field farming and applied somewhat incongruously to the regulation of pastures on moor and marsh.[52] More formal committees arose out of the Metropolitan Commons Act 1866, which made it possible for common land within the Metropolitan Police District to be regulated by 'boards of conservators', whose powers enabled them to improve the commons as public spaces and to manage their use. Twenty-seven

---

[47] CCD, Gloucestershire: Minchinhampton (CL 58), 213/D/115–126.
[48] E.g. Powick (Worcs.), Dorney and Boveney (Bucks.), Martin Down and Tidpit Common (Hants): Hoskins & Stamp, pp. 127, 249–50, 283.
[49] *Gloucester Citizen*, 14 May 1949, p. 4.
[50] L. E. Tavener, *The Common Lands of Hampshire* (Southampton, 1957), pp. 70–2; R. Hill, 'The manor of Stockbridge', *Proceedings of the Hampshire Field Club Archaeological Society*, 32 (1976), pp. 93–101.
[51] Administration of Justice Act 1977, c.38, Schedule 4, part iii.
[52] Inclosure Act 1845, secs 117–18. Field reeves continue to manage Cockfield Fell (see below, pp. 223–8) and Burgh Marsh (Cumb.), for example.

commons, totalling more than 4,100 acres (1,660 ha), were regulated under the act between 1869 and 1909, while a further c.7,000 acres (c.2,800 ha) were protected under the separate acts for Wimbledon Common and Putney Heath (1871), Wandsworth Common (1871) and Epping Forest (1878).[53]

Over the following few decades, the broad principles laid out in the Metropolitan Commons Act were applied to the management of common land elsewhere in England, severing the link between common land, the manor and farming and recognising the wider public interest.[54] Most wide-ranging was the Commons Act 1876, which rolled out the regulatory structure of boards of conservators to commons across the country.[55] It allowed individual commons to be opened to public access and placed under the control of conservators who had the power, subject to approval by the Home Office, to make and enforce byelaws to prevent 'nuisances' and 'for keeping order on the common'. The conservators' role was to oversee improvements to the common (by draining, manuring, planting trees and adding 'beauty') and also to regulate grazing by imposing stinting schedules. Over the forty years between 1879 and 1919, a total of thirty-six commons, totalling over 41,000 acres (16,600 ha), were regulated under the act. The list ranged across different environments and included both lowland commons – such as those on the Lizard peninsula (Corn.), Ashdown Forest (Sussex), Cleeve Hill (Glos.), and Skipwith in the Vale of York – and wide Pennine moors at Abbotside in Wensleydale (Yorks. N.R.), East Stainmore and Crosby Garrett (Westmld).[56] Legal wrangles ensued on some grazing commons when conservators drafted byelaws specifically to regulate grazing rights. In several instances, the Home Office proved reluctant to confirm such byelaws, seeing them as outside the central purposes of the 1876 act, which they interpreted as being to regulate public access and the nuisances it might cause. Regulation thus exposed a tension between the interests of commoners and the wider civic interest in access and recreation.

The comparatively small number of commons regulated under the act reflected, in part, the processes by which its powers could be accessed. Unlike the Metropolitan Commons Act, the 1876 act could not be imposed on a common: it required consent from the lord of the manor and two-thirds of those with common rights. Then, proposals for regulation had to be approved by the Land Commission (after 1889 the Board of Agriculture), which needed to be convinced that regulation would 'benefit the neighbourhood', through ensuring access for public recreation. Some applications were refused, that from Great Langdale on the grounds that, as noted above, the commoners were reluctant to allow wholesale public access.

A number of private acts established equivalent systems of management on specific groups of commons, to ensure their preservation for public enjoyment. The circumstances of these commons and the contests between competing interests

---

[53] Eversley, pp. 65, 70, 73, 332.
[54] Straughton, *Common Grazing*, p. 55.
[55] The following paragraphs draw on Straughton, *Common Grazing*, pp. 58–62, 204–37, which provides a detailed discussion of the 1876 act.
[56] *Gadsden*, § 1-12, pp. 859–60; Eversley, pp. 333–5; Howkins, 'Use and abuse of English commons', p. 110.

varied but, in each case, the legislation sought to foster traditional uses by protecting the rights of commoners but also to safeguard public access. The New Forest Act 1877 preserved the existing open spaces in the Forest by preventing the Crown from making new enclosures for timber production and it revived the Verderers' Court to represent the commoners and regulate common rights. By protecting the commons from enclosure and future planting it also sought to preserve the scenic beauty valued by the wider public.[57] The following year, the Epping Forest Act disafforested the area and appointed the Corporation of the City of London as conservators, with responsibility both to protect existing common rights and to preserve the common for public recreation.[58]

Similar aims lay behind other local statutory schemes. On the Malvern Hills, where a preservation committee had been established in 1876 to address threats to 'their present beauty', including encroachment by squatters and the 'defacements of the hills by cutting turf', the Malvern Hills Act 1884 established a body of conservators to preserve and regulate common rights and to ensure recreational access for the public at large. The conservators' business in the first few years included dealing with illegal fern cutting, gypsy encampments, encroachments, unringed swine and the impact of a new road on grazing rights.[59] The Nettlebed and District Commons (Preservation) Act 1906 sought a workable balance between a similar mix of interests on a group of commons in the Oxfordshire Chilterns, establishing a board of conservators, representing the lord of the manor and local authorities, to regulate clay digging and tree cutting, and confirming a public right of recreation across the commons.[60]

In the absence of manorial regulation, local authorities gained an increasing role in managing common land across the nineteenth and twentieth centuries. Even before local government reform in the 1890s, the scaffolding of parochial administration sometimes provided a structure for deliberating matters affecting common land, as parishes stepped into the void left by the seigniorial courts. Examples of parish vestries grappling with common land are found from the 1790s to the 1840s.[61] The establishment of civil parish councils in 1894 created formal bodies which could be used to raise questions concerning the management of local commons, as occurred in Cumbria, where several parish councils took the first steps in exploring the possibility

---

[57] Readman, *Storied Ground*, pp. 164, 184–5.

[58] For the legal battles to secure the future of Epping Forest, see Gorman, *Saving the People's Forest*, pp. 73–109; Eversley, pp. 73–110; Hoskins & Stamp, pp. 161–5.

[59] P. Hurle, *The Forest and Chase of Malvern* (Chichester, 2007), pp. 125–9.

[60] Eversley, pp. 254–6. Seeking to balance common rights and public access also saw commons at Great Torrington (Devon) vested in a body of conservators in 1889: Eversley, pp. 271–2; Local Act 52 & 53 Vict., c. clxvii.

[61] Examples include Beeston (Notts.), 1795: W. E. Tate, *The Parish Chest: A Study of the Records of Parochial Administration in England*, 3rd edn (Chichester, [1969] 1983), p. 262; Monken Hadley (Mddx), 1799: *VCH Mddx* V, p. 265; Yate (Glos.): R. Wallis, *Yate* (VCH, 2015), p. 63; King's Stanley (Glos.): *VCH Glos.* X, p. 251; Whitchurch (Heref.), 1807: J. Moir '"A World unto Themselves"? Squatter settlement in Herefordshire, 1780–1880' (PhD thesis, University of Leicester, 1990), pp. 278–9; and Llanllechid (Caern.): below, pp. 239–40.

of regulation or acted as a channel of communication between commoners and manorial authorities.[62] Where ownership was uncertain, parish councils sometimes assumed ownership of small patches of common, even before the provisions contained in the CRA. In the Kentish Weald, for example, Lamberhurst parish council was said in 1975 to have acted for many years 'as if it were the owner' of a small common close to the parish boundary, and to have received payment from people using it.[63]

Local authorities gained a more formal role under the Commons Act 1899, which gave district councils powers to manage and improve common land and village greens. The powers were rapidly taken up – forty-four commons of at least 10 acres (4 ha) were regulated under the act in the first decade of its passing and a total of 258 schemes (which included village and town greens) were in place by 1955. Numerous new schemes continued to be established under the act in the second half of the twentieth century (no fewer than 227 between 1955 and 1985), usually on commons where rights were no longer exercised or where ownership was unknown.[64]

In England and Wales, the processes of statutory regulation brought into the open the cross-currents of interest in common land, as conceptions of its value changed. By the close of the nineteenth century, a wider public interest was fully accepted, those with formal property rights in a common no longer being the only interested parties. As Eleanor Straughton has put it, the notion was gaining ground 'that a common was not safe in the hands of commoners – that a common might sometimes need to be saved from rather than for the commoner'.[65] There were also cross-cutting tensions among those making economic use of a common. Boards of conservators tended to take a legalistic view of use rights on a common, privileging formal common rights over customary usages. By the 1890s, both the New Forest and Ashdown Forest had associations of those who claimed ill-defined use rights and felt themselves 'put upon' by the 'real' commoners who regulated use of the commons through the conservators. Part of the tension was to do with 'tone', a mismatch between what middle-class visitors wished to experience on common land and the messy reality of informal, working-class use – untidy buildings, the behaviour of geese and donkeys, and the destruction of vegetation by cutting turf, bracken and heather.[66]

Informal Management: Commoners' Associations and Meetings

Despite the survival of a few manor courts and the work of boards of conservators and local authorities, only a minority of commons in England and Wales were regulated by formal bodies. On some commons, the void was filled by informal management bodies, especially where grazing continued. These ranged from ad hoc meetings to more formalised commoners' committees or associations, though they lacked the

---

[62] Straughton, *Common Grazing*, pp. 166–9.
[63] CCD, Kent: Free Heath (CL 30), 19/U/73.
[64] Eversley, pp. 336–8; *Gadsden*, §§1-12, 8-39–8-43; C. Short and M. Winter, 'The problem of common land: towards stakeholder governance', *Journal of Environmental Planning and Management*, 42 (5) (1999), p. 618.
[65] Straughton, *Common Grazing*, p. 68.
[66] Howkins, 'Commons, enclosure and radical histories', pp. 133–5; *Ashdown Forest*, p. 43.

statutory powers of the grazing committees in Scotland. Some are recorded in the nineteenth century but they became more numerous in the mid- and later twentieth century, in response to the need for a communal voice in dealings with government agencies. By no means all such meetings left formal documentation which has been deposited in record offices, making it difficult to gain a clear picture of their number and distribution.

Commoners' meetings were usually prompted by local circumstances. The process of Parliamentary enclosure had fostered collective action among commoners in order to protect their interests.[67] In the unusual circumstances of the enclosure of Fforest Fawr in the lordship of Brecon, where the sections allocated to the commoners remained communal grazings, a highly organised commoners' committee agreed to act together to defend their rights in 1813 and steered the direction of the enclosure in the years around 1820, continuing to battle to protect their rights across the nineteenth century.[68]

The sense that commoners could pursue joint endeavour broadened to issues other than enclosure. In Ashdown Forest, where the commoners included wealthy landowners, an association was established in 1830 which appointed a committee of four commoners and a nominee of the lord of the manor to control litter cutting and impound livestock found grazing illegally.[69] In a different context, the need for a communal voice to negotiate compensation when railways were built across common land prompted some meetings of commoners, as at Biggleswade (Beds.) in 1847 and Thatcham (Berks.) in 1851, for example.[70] When the commoners on Stretton Common on the Long Mynd (Shrops.) came to an agreement with the lord of the manor in 1869 to establish a committee, its purpose was to address illegal grazing and encroachments.[71] The commoners' meeting at Rushmere Heath (Suff.), founded in 1881, sought to protect the commoners' rights from a grasping landlord, while that established at Bridestowe (Devon) from 1893 was prompted by negotiations with the War Office over military use of the common.[72]

Regulating the day-to-day use of a common, as opposed to protecting commoners' rights, formed the focus of some early informal bodies in northern England. Committees of graziers were formed at Crosby Garrett (Westmld) in 1830, with a view to converting the common into a regulated, stinted pasture, and at Burgh-by-Sands (Cumb.) in 1838, to manage grazing on the Solway marshes (the latter, a decade

[67] As in the concerted, sometimes violent, opposition to enclosure: J. M. Neeson, *Commoners: Common Right, Enclosure and Social Change in England, 1700–1820* (Cambridge, 1993), pp. 263–81, 321–2.

[68] J. Lloyd, *The Great Forest of Brecknock* (London, 1905), pp. 39–43, 84; W. Rees, *The Great Forest of Brecknock: A Facet of Breconshire History* (Brecon, 1966), pp. 15–28.

[69] *Ashdown Forest*, pp. 150, 156, 258.

[70] Biggleswade: Bedfordshire Archives, RR 12/6; Thatcham: Berks. RO, D/EX 1466/2/11.

[71] Shropshire Archives, 1709/2/box 203, minutes of meeting of copyholders and tenant farmers, 21 May 1868, and draft agreement for protection of Stretton Commons, June 1869.

[72] http://rushmerecommonerstrustees.onesuffolk.net/history/; Devon Archives, 2750A/PV1 (I am grateful to Jan Wood for this reference).

THE COMMONS REINVENTED 169

before the enclosure award established a formal stintholders' meeting).[73] Informal grassroots bodies managing upland commons in the late nineteenth century included the meeting of stintholders on Scales Moor near Ingleton (Yorks. W.R.), which was meeting annually by 1884 to appoint a shepherd and agree a closed season, and the 'Inch Stick' or 'Notch Stick' meeting at Great Langdale (Westmld), held annually in the 1890s to decide the number of sheep to be put to the common.[74]

Committees were established throughout the twentieth century, the context of their foundation again reflecting local circumstances: the priorities on grazing commons were different from those on 'amenity' commons.[75] Commoners' meetings on the former were often supported by the landowner, as on commons near Ingleton (Yorks. W.R.), where the Ingleborough Estate's interest in grouse shooting encouraged strong management regimes from the 1920s, through its commoners' meetings, which appointed shepherds, regulated stock numbers and set dates for gatherings.[76] In the Lake District similar bodies included a stintholders' meeting at Borrowdale, held under the auspices of the lord of the manor from 1952, and a commoners' committee at Eskdale, established in 1945 at the suggestion of the parish council, with the consent of the lord of the manor.[77]

By contrast, the driving force behind the foundation of the Gower Commons Association in 1949, an umbrella body to represent the interests of graziers on all the commons on the Gower peninsula, was concern about the potential loss of common land for housing as the nearby Swansea conurbation grew.[78] On lowland commons where grazing had ceased, the context was different again. At Horsell (Surrey) the issues were preservation and the removal of nuisances. When the state of the common was raised with the parish council in 1904, it was asked rhetorically whether it should be 'left as now ... to be the sport of incendiaries, the Common receptacle of all kinds of refuse ... and a camping ground for Gypsies' or 'preserved and protected'. Six years later, in 1910, the lord of the manor established a committee to address these problems.[79]

In the mid-1950s, the members of the Royal Commission on Common Land encountered effective management bodies on some commons but concluded that 'for every common ... where the commoners have been successful in creating some form of organisation, however sketchy, there were perhaps two or more where they have failed or never tried'.[80] New commoners' committees were created in the 1960s in an attempt (not always successful) to ensure equity in the registration of rights under

---

[73] Straughton, *Common Grazing*, p. 146; *Contested Common Land*, p. 39.
[74] *Contested Common Land*, pp. 119–20; Straughton, *Common Grazing*, p. 170.
[75] As pointed out in Countryside Commission, *Common Land*, pp. 13–14.
[76] *Contested Common Land*, pp. 119–21.
[77] Straughton, *Common Grazing*, pp. 171–2, 174–83.
[78] S. Brackenbury and G. Jones, *Gower Commons: Successional Health Check* (2018), p. 11.
[79] https://www.horsellcommon.org.uk/about/a-brief-history-of-the-common/; *West Sussex Gazette*, 10 March 1910, p. 5.
[80] *RCCL Rep.*, pp. 52, 58–9 (quotation p. 58).

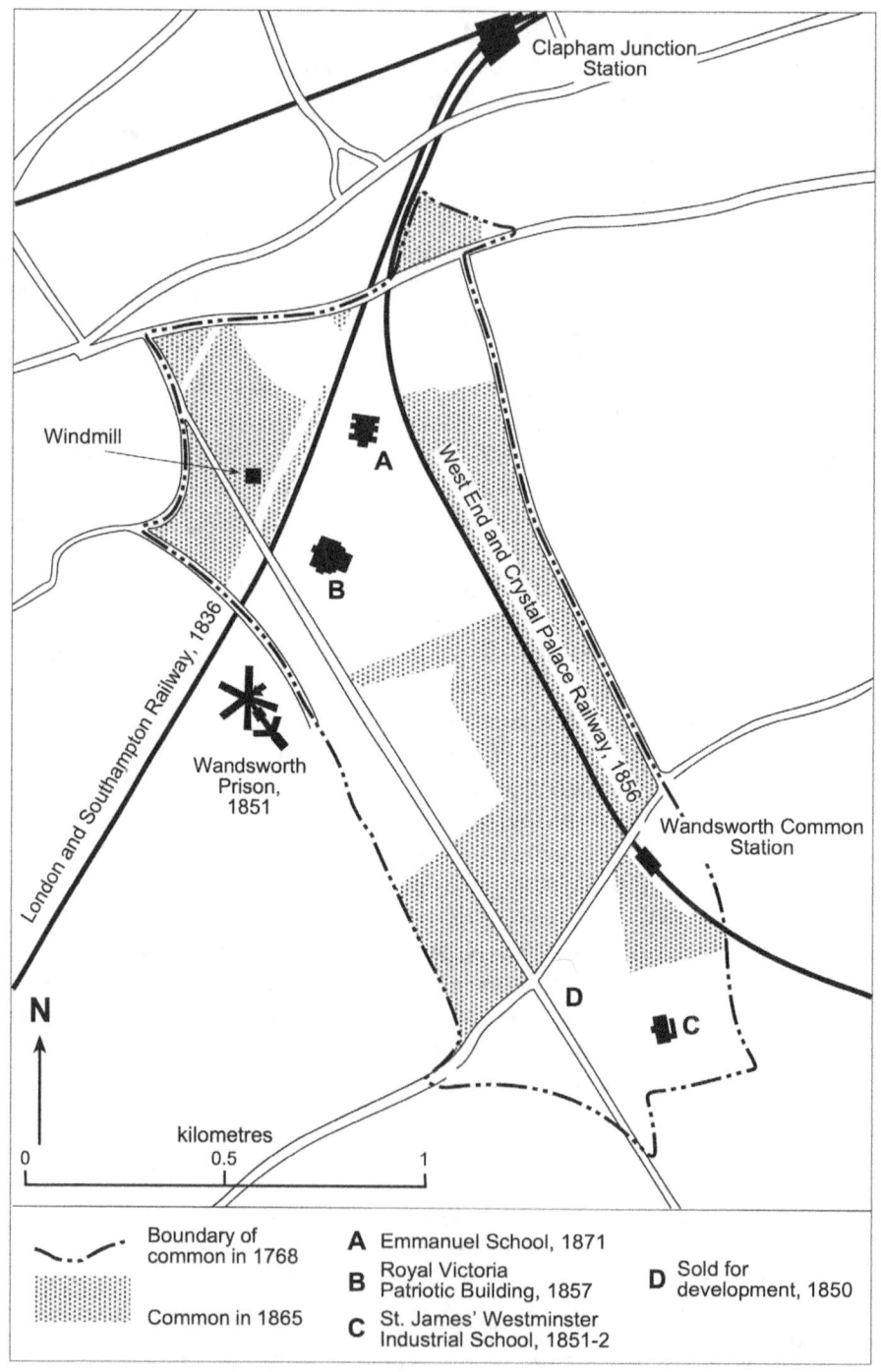

Figure 31. Wandsworth Common: land lost between 1768 and 1865. Sources: J. Rocque, *A Topographical Map of the County of Surrey* (1768); OS Six-Inch map, Surrey 7, surveyed 1865.

the CRA process.[81] In one important instance, a new statutory body was created to manage a major area of upland grazing commons. This was the Dartmoor Commoners' Council, established under the Dartmoor Commons Act 1985, to manage grazing rights on the Moor and promote good standards of animal husbandry, in the context of enhancing both the beauty of the commons and their use as a place of public recreation. The Council was to consist of twenty-six members, of whom twenty were graziers elected at commoners' meetings on the four sides of Dartmoor; the remainder were representatives of the National Park Authority and landowners and one was to be a veterinary surgeon.[82]

By the early twenty-first century many grazing commons possessed some form of management body, whether statutory (a board of conservators in England; a grazing committee in crofting areas) or informal.[83] One survey of commons in England and Wales in 2005 recorded only eight manor courts which continued to manage common land; thirty-one boards of conservators; and a total of eighty-four informally constituted commoners' associations. In addition, over thirty local authorities owned and managed common land.[84]

COMMON LAND AND NATIONAL ENDEAVOUR

Both the drive to ensure public access from the mid-nineteenth century, and the measures to secure environmental protection across the twentieth, were expressions of a wider perception of common land as a national resource. The view that commons could be used to answer public needs and to further national endeavour saw public bodies appropriate large tracts for civilian and military use, often removing control from the local sphere and taking commons away from their traditional roles as agrarian resource and community space.

Public Buildings and Infrastructure

The deep-rooted idea that common land was a fitting location for communal buildings, especially those for the benefit of the poor, was embedded in legislation in the 1840s and 1850s which aimed to facilitate gifts of up to one acre of common land for schools and 'literary and scientific institutions' such as reading rooms. It removed legal uncertainty by stating that commoners' rights over land given for such purposes would thereby be extinguished, thus perpetuating the practice of modest encroachments

---

[81] For example, at Ewyas Harold (Heref.): P. Parkes, 'A pasture in common: a twentieth-century environmental history of Ewyas Harold Common (Herefordshire)', *Rural History*, 16 (1) (2005), p. 121; and Eskdale (Cumb.): *Contested Common Land*, pp. 100–1.

[82] *Gadsden*, §§ 8-64–8.66.

[83] All of the eighteen commons sampled for a survey of grazing commons in 2007 had some form of management association: Pastoral Commoning Partnership, *Trends in Pastoral Commoning*, p. 155.

[84] Land Use Consultants, *Agricultural Management of Common Land in England and Wales* (DEFRA, 2005), appendix 1.2–1.5.

onto common land for community use.⁸⁵ However, the scale of public institutions built on common land changed across the nineteenth century. Commons offered ample and inexpensive open space for large building projects and, sometimes, a desirable remoteness. A broad array of public buildings was placed on common land in Victorian times, ranging from the comparatively small (not only schools and reading rooms but also isolation hospitals, for example)⁸⁶ to institutions on a grand scale.

Perhaps the most famous institution set in the wilds of a vast common was Dartmoor Prison at Princetown in Dartmoor Forest, an island in the forest wastes, where a new small town developed around the prison buildings within their circular perimeter wall, built as a prisoner of war camp during the Napoleonic wars and re-opened as a penal establishment in 1850.⁸⁷ More numerous were the institutions built on commons and heathland within easy reach of London in the mid-Victorian period. Wandsworth Common (Figure 31) was reduced significantly in size by piecemeal enclosure between 1794 and 1866. On its edges were the Surrey County Lunatic Asylum (1838–41) and Wandsworth Prison (1849–51).⁸⁸ In the 1850s several more sections were hived off to accommodate large institutions. They included a 20-acre (8-ha) section acquired in 1850 by St James's parish, Westminster, for the St James Industrial Schools which opened in 1852; and a 60-acre (24-ha) plot for the imposing Royal Victoria Patriotic Asylum, built 1857–59 as a home and school for the orphaned daughters of soldiers who died in the Crimean War. Thus reduced, defaced by gravel-digging and bisected by railway lines, the common's character had changed dramatically by 1870.⁸⁹

A concentration of public institutions sprang up on heathland along the Surrey–Berkshire–Hampshire boundary, open spaces seen as suitable for what Alan Crosby has wryly termed 'institutions for the secluded accommodation of society's undesirables – the dead, criminals, the insane, and public schoolboys'.⁹⁰ The new town of Woking (Surrey) originated in the purchase of 2,268 acres (918 ha) of Woking Common by the London Necropolis and National Mausoleum Company in 1854, the location being chosen for its low agricultural value as barren heath, its sandy soils being ideal for burials, and for its good communications, as both railway and canal ran across the common. Having obtained a local Act of Parliament to extinguish common rights over the heath,⁹¹ the company enclosed 400 acres (162 ha) for the Brookwood Necropolis, planned to be a landscaped setting of shrub and woodland on the open

---

[85] School Sites Act 1841, c.38, sec. II; Literary and Scientific Institutions Act 1854, c.112, sec. I.
[86] E.g. hospitals on Town Moor at Newcastle upon Tyne (opened 1882: Tyne & Wear HER 5896); Lincoln West Common (by 1886: OS Six-Inch map, Lincolnshire 70NW, 1887 edn); Sodbury Common (c.1900: VCH Glos. XIV (forthcoming), Old Sodbury); and Newbiggin Moor (OS Six-Inch map, Northumberland new ser. 61SE, 1924 edn).
[87] HLE, no. 1326422; H. Fox, Dartmoor's Alluring Uplands: Transhumance and Pastoral Management in the Middle Ages (Exeter, 2012), p. 20.
[88] Lunatic Asylum: HLE, no. 1001601.
[89] Eversley, pp. 70–2; Gorman, Saving the People's Forest, pp. 120–4.
[90] A. G. Crosby, 'A disappearing landscape: the heathlands of the Berkshire, Hampshire and Surrey borders', AgHR, 66 (2) (2018), p. 191.
[91] Woking Commoners Act 1854: Private Act 17 & 18 Vict., c.9.

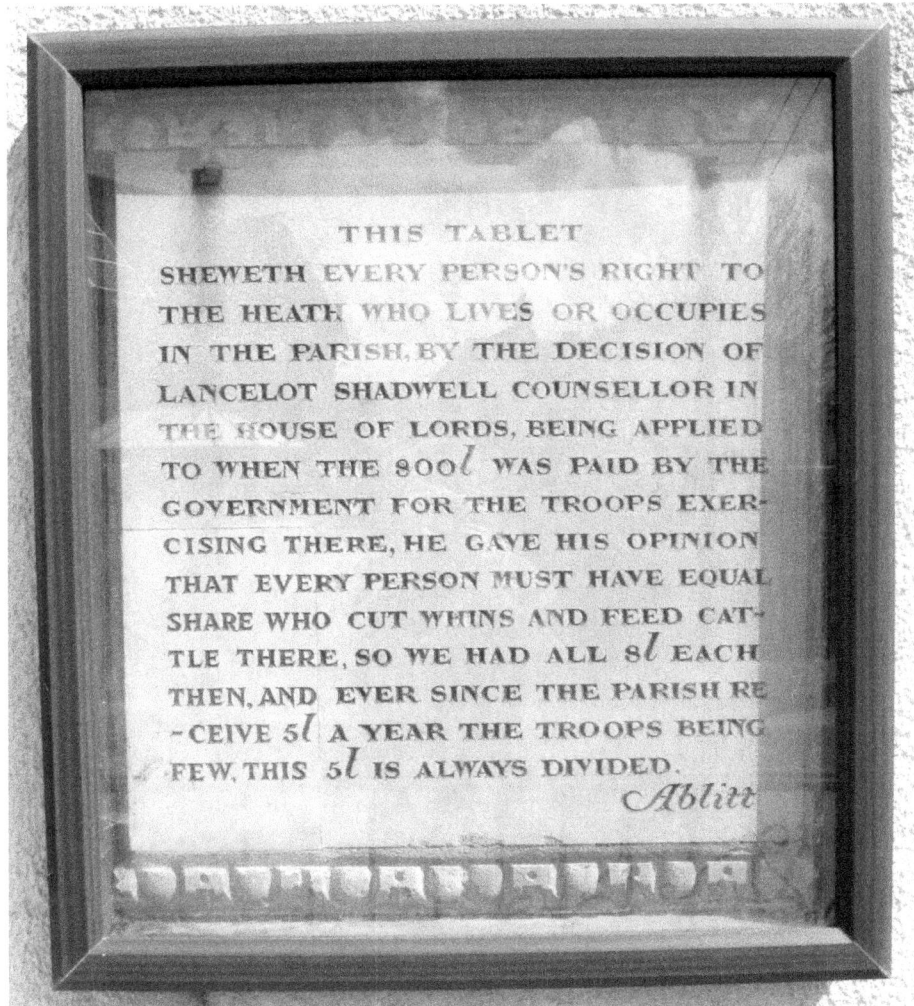

Figure 32. Tablet at Baptist Chapel, Rushmere Heath, Suffolk, originally placed outside his cottage in 1861 by Nathaniel Ablitt, 'an aged gentleman of somewhat eccentric habits and notions' (*Suffolk Chronicle*, 28 January 1865, p. 5), recording the substantial sum paid for the use of Rushmere Heath by the Ipswich and Woodbridge garrisons during the Napoleonic wars. The parish purchased £500 stock with the money in 1813; the arrangement ceased in 1817 (Suffolk Archives, FB97/D/1/4, p. 2). The inscription not only records the enduring military use of the heath but also the claim by the commoners (as opposed to the lord of the manor) to the compensation paid by the army.

Figure 33. Samuel Henry Alken, 'Farriers of the 17th Regiment of (Light) Dragoons (Lancers) shoeing a horse from a mobile forge, Chobham Camp, 1853'. The success of the camp on Chobham Common, Surrey, in 1853 resulted in large-scale purchase of heathland in the area by the War Department, converting the commons into a military training ground.

heath, to receive London's dead. The following year the company obtained a further act to enable it to sell its unwanted areas of heathland (the majority of its original purchase). As well as building plots for the expanding town of Woking, parts were sold for the Woking Convict Prisons (1858) and Brookwood Lunatic Asylum (1860). Other institutions on the nearby Berkshire heaths in Sandhurst parish included Wellington College (1853), a school originally for the orphaned children of army officers, and Broadmoor Criminal Lunatic Asylum (1863–64).[92] Large areas of former common land were thus lost.

The water supply schemes of the later nineteenth century represented another claim on common land for the public good. When they sought absolute control over upland commons within the catchment of a reservoir, strong passions were aroused by the threatened loss of both scenic beauty and public access. Manchester Corporation's strategy at Thirlmere in the Lake District from the 1870s was to purchase the manorial rights, as well as buying each individual property in the valley, in order not only to acquire the farmland (which was subsequently flooded or afforested) but also to secure ownership of common rights. By so doing, the Corporation succeeded in extinguishing common rights and thus converting the common into absolute freehold. The opposition provoked by the Thirlmere scheme is well-known and Manchester's powers were curtailed by legislation which required the Corporation to allow access to the fells.[93]

Birmingham Corporation's compulsory purchase of the Elan and Claerwen valleys in mid-Wales in the 1890s again converted common land into freehold by purchase of both rights in the soil and common rights over 40,446 acres (16,368 ha) of common hill grazings. By obtaining outright control, the Corporation was able to determine the grazing regime on the hills, which remained communal pastures (but not, legally, common land) on which each farm had its own defined sheepwalk.[94]

Defence of the Realm

Public institutions and water undertakings can be thought of as the civilian counterparts to the military use of common land, which expanded dramatically from the later nineteenth century, especially during and after the two world wars. The demands placed on commons across the twentieth century by national defence changed their face and resulted in a further loss of common land in England. Large areas were requisitioned for military purposes during the Second World War, some remaining under military control for decades afterwards.

The military impact on common land in the nineteenth century extended to both urban and rural commons. Woolwich Common was taken over in the third quarter of the eighteenth century, as a training ground and as accommodation for troops, and was purchased by the military authorities under the terms of an Act of Parliament in

---

[92] Crosby, 'A disappearing landscape', pp. 189–91.
[93] H. Ritvo, *The Dawn of Green: Manchester, Thirlmere and Modern Environmentalism* (London, 2009), esp. pp. 71–9, 130–1.
[94] *Contested Common Land*, pp. 137–48. Acreage figures from Hoskins & Stamp, p. 233n.

Figure 34. Second World War radar station, Barrow Common, Brancaster, Norfolk. One of a chain of low frequency radar stations providing coastal defence against enemy aircraft. Built in 1940, it closed in 1944.

1803, by which the common rights were extinguished.[95] Other early barracks were built on town commons at Colchester (in 1794) and on the Town Moor at Newcastle upon Tyne (built 1830).[96]

More ubiquitous was the use of common land for military training. Rushmere Heath, close to the garrison town of Ipswich, saw frequent, large-scale training and military reviews during the Napoleonic wars and continuing military use across the nineteenth century, for which compensation was paid to the commoners (see Figure 32).[97] Part of the common had been cleared as a drill ground by the 1870s.[98] The Surrey heaths were transformed by military activity. Practice fortifications had been built on Bagshot Heath when military exercises were held there in the 1790s but the militarisation of the heaths expanded from the 1850s, when permanent training grounds replaced summer camps. One large camp on Chobham Common in 1853 (see Figure 33) attracted the authorities to that area and from 1854 the War Department began to purchase tracts of common around what became the garrison town of Aldershot. As a result, common

---

[95] Eversley, pp. 224–5.
[96] *Town Commons*, pp. 54–5.
[97] Military reviews there were recorded in the press from 1803, e.g. *Morning Post*, 29 August 1803, p. 3; 19 August 1814, p. 3; *Suffolk Chronicle*, 14 September 1811, p. 4.
[98] Recorded as the 'soldiers' parade ground' in 1874 (*Ipswich Journal*, 5 September 1874, p. 5), it is shown on OS Six-Inch map, Suffolk 76SW, surveyed 1880.

rights over 8,200 acres (3,318 ha) of heathland were extinguished between 1854 and 1890, much of it on the Chobham Ridges, south of Bagshot. They included Pirbright Common (3,070 acres; 1,242 ha) bought by the War Office in 1875, and Bisley Common (3,000 acres; 1,214 ha), to which the National Rifle Association's ranges on Wimbledon Common were transferred in 1890.[99]

Rifle ranges became numerous, particularly on town commons, from the mid-nineteenth century. The formation of a volunteer corps in each county after 1858 was a key factor, as county authorities sought to provide ranges. On Lincoln's South Common, where target practice probably began in the mid-eighteenth century, the common was used by the local volunteers by the 1850s and contained three ranges by 1886.[100] When the National Rifle Association was founded in 1859, it chose Wimbledon Common as the site for its ranges and annual competition. The move to Bisley was prompted by the increasing recreational use of Wimbledon Common and the incompatibility of target practice with busy public space. Resentment at restrictions on public access and the danger of stray bullets played a part in the decision to leave.[101] Across the later nineteenth century, ranges appeared on many commons.[102] The short-lived Ranges Act 1891 explicitly permitted the War Office to acquire common land for rifle ranges but Parliamentary approval was subsequently required for every such purchase after the passing of the Military Lands Act 1892. The furore over the Ranges Act centred on a proposal to build ranges on 800 acres (324 ha) of common land in the New Forest, illustrating the increasing sensitivities surrounding what were deemed acceptable uses of common land by the end of the century.[103] Even military use which did not involve the construction of rifle ranges did not always sit easily with other uses and could provoke resistance. The decision of Queen's College, Oxford, the owner of Plumstead Common (Kent), to allow the War Office to use it as an exercise ground in the 1870s was one of the grievances which lay behind the riots there in 1876–77.[104]

Military training and ranges also spread to upland moors. An artillery camp at Halstock Down, near Okehampton, in the summer of 1875 initiated the use of Dartmoor – 10,000 acres (4,000 ha) of the high moorland was leased from the Duchy of Cornwall for military training in 1895.[105] Large areas of moorland in northern England were also acquired for military use but many of these (including the vast training areas at Otterburn (Northumb.) and Bellerby Moor (Yorks. N.R.)) were freehold land or previously enclosed commons, rather than common land.

---

[99] Crosby, 'A disappearing landscape', pp. 186–8; Hoskins & Stamp, p. 148.
[100] *Town Commons*, pp. 47–8.
[101] Below, pp. 270–1; https://longrangerifles.wordpress.com/reference/bisley/.
[102] E.g. Cockfield Fell (Dur.) and Bromyard Downs (Heref.): see below, pp. 224, 249–50.
[103] See Readman, *Storied Ground*, pp. 183–4; Eversley, pp. 167–9.
[104] R. Allen, 'The battle for the commons: politics and populism in mid-Victorian Kentish London', *Social History*, 22 (21) (1997), p. 65.
[105] Anon., 'The armed forces on Dartmoor: a brief history', https://assets.publishing.service.gov.uk/government/uploads/system/uploads/attachment_data/file/33309/armed_forces_ondartmoor_brief_history.pdf.

Figure 35. 'The Squatters', *Punch*, 7 February 1945. The man from the Ministry is dictating to his secretary, 'Referring to your recent enquiry, no decision has been reached as to why we are here, or what we are doing, or when we shall go away'. The Requisitioned Land and War Works Bill, then before Parliament, proposed that the government could retain requisitioned land, provoking strong opposition from those concerned to preserve common land and access to it.

The use of lowland commons as training grounds intensified in the run-up to and during the First World War. Military occupation could involve the construction of buildings and earthworks, such as the gun emplacement, ammunition sheds, huts and searchlight built on Stoke Common (Bucks.).[106] Tangible evidence from the period survives on several commons, notably in the remains of practice trenches. At Clyne Common, near Swansea, a network of zig-zag and crenellated trenches is thought to pre-date the Great War and to relate to training recorded on the common in 1907 and

---

[106] L. Rigby, *The History of Stoke Common: A Poor's Fuel Allotment Charity* (Stoke Poges, 1975), p. 37.

1909.[107] First World War practice trenches have been identified on urban commons at South Common, Lincoln, and Walmgate Stray, York,[108] and on rural commons such as White Moor, near Lyndhurst in the New Forest, and Frensham Common (Surrey).[109] Parts of an extended system, originally stretching to around 12 kilometres, survive on Berkhamsted Common in the Chilterns, dug by the Inns of Court Officers' Training Corps, which was based there from 1914 to 1919. The placing of a war memorial on the common, commemorating officers who had trained there, ensured that the episode became firmly fixed as part of the common's history.[110]

The First World War also saw the beginnings of the use of common land for airfields. As open expanses of level, well-drained land close to the European mainland, drier commons and heathlands in southern and eastern England were especially attractive. Early military landing strips from the First World War included those laid on the West Common at Lincoln and on Westwood Common, Beverley (Yorks. E.R.), the latter to guard against the threat from German Zeppelin airships.[111] As aerial warfare developed further after the war, commons were appropriated for more permanent airfields, as at Martlesham Heath (Suff.), where the commoners leased part of the common to the Air Council for 999 years for an Air Force Aerodrome in 1925.[112]

The Second World War saw a further extension of military use, though commons accounted for only part of the 750,000 acres (300,000 ha) of England and Wales requisitioned and occupied by the three armed forces.[113] Lowland commons housed a wide range of military facilities, from small sites such as radar stations (Figure 34), to storage depots, army training camps, prisoner of war camps and airfields. Some were short-lived, the common being returned after the war ended, but a decade after the Second World War, between 80,000 and 90,000 acres (over 30,000 ha) of common land was still used by the military. W. G. Hoskins disparagingly commented that, when commons were released, the military 'generally left behind an intolerable mess which the meagre compensation never fully sufficed to clear up'.[114]

---

[107] Historic Environment Record for Wales (https://coflein.gov.uk), National Primary Record No. 421565.

[108] *Town Commons*, p. 48.

[109] http://www.newforestexplorersguide.co.uk/heritage/lyndhurst/white-moor-military-connections.html; interviews with Ruth Deadman (Churt) and Hilda Rollinson (Frensham), 1997, for Surrey Heathland Project (summaries courtesy of Jackie Lake, Surrey County Council, 2013).

[110] N. Groves, 'From Berkhamsted to battlefield: WW1 training trenches on Berkhamsted Common', in Chilterns Conservation Board, *Our Common Heritage: A Collection of Six Essays about the Social History of Chiltern Commons* (2015), pp. 84–98.

[111] *Town Commons*, pp. 50–1.

[112] Suffolk RO (Ipswich branch), FC 37/A3/1.

[113] W. Foot, 'The impact of the military on the agricultural landscape of England and Wales in the Second World War', in B. Short, C. Watkins and J. Martin (eds), *The Front Line of Freedom: British Farming in the Second World War* (Exeter, 2006), p. 132.

[114] Hoskins & Stamp, p. 83. For examples, see Rigby, *Stoke Common*, p. 38; *Contested Common Land*, p. 173.

On some commons requisitioning resulted in a permanent change of use. Yateley Common, one of the largest commons in Hampshire, was the site of an RAF station established in 1942, which became Blackbushe Airport and was transferred to civilian use in 1946. Attempts to extinguish common rights over part of the airport site rumbled on in the courts, eventually failing on appeal in 2021.[115] Lakenheath Warren, covering a large part of the Suffolk Brecklands, had been used as a bombing range during the First World War and was brought back into military use in 1940, initially as a decoy airfield (with false lights, runways and aircraft) to draw fire from RAF Mildenhall. In 1941 around half of the common became an RAF airfield, which was handed over to the United States Air Force in 1948. A similar sequence occurred at Greenham and Crookham Commons (Berks.), opened as an airfield for RAF flight training in 1942, used by the United States Army Air Force from 1943, and then made over formally to the Americans during the Cold War in 1951. The re-fitting of the site as a base for Cruise missiles in 1982–83 resulted in Greenham Common becoming a flashpoint for anti-nuclear weapons protests, with a women's peace camp on the common outside the perimeter fence. The military base closed in 1992, after which restoration of the heathland – and of common rights – began.[116]

Concurrently, a huge expansion of military use took place on upland commons. Almost the whole of Dartmoor was requisitioned during the Second World War; a large block of Mynydd Epynt in the Brecon Beacons was acquired by the War Office in 1940; while in the north Pennines, much of Warcop Fell (Westmld) was requisitioned as a tank gunnery range in 1942. In each of these cases, tracts of common land remain in the hands of the Ministry of Defence. At Epynt the War Office claimed to have extinguished common rights on purchase; at Warcop, the Ministry bought out graziers' rights in 2003 and de-registered the common in 2018.[117]

Common land also contributed to the war effort by providing land which could be ploughed up in the drive for increased agricultural production, a process which radically altered the face of some lowland commons during the Second World War.[118] Some 21,000 acres (c.8,500 ha) of common land was requisitioned for agricultural use, in some cases heralding permanent change, as the Agriculture Act 1947 empowered the Ministry of Agriculture to purchase requisitioned land in order to maintain efficient agricultural output. The power was used on commons across lowland England. In Devon, Dorset and Hampshire reclaimed hill and downland commons were subject to compulsory purchase; in Cambridgeshire and Suffolk drained wetlands, both fen and marsh, were likewise retained.[119] In 1954 around 10,000 acres (4,050 ha) of common land was still under requisition by the state (see Figure 35).[120]

When requisitioned commons were released and returned to their owners, some reverted to being common grazings; others remained in an improved state, often

---

[115] England & Wales Court of Appeal (Civil Division), Decision, [2021] EWCA Civ. 398.
[116] See D. Fairhall, *Common Ground: The Story of Greenham* (London, 2006).
[117] Hoskins & Stamp, p. 234; *Financial Times*, 6 December 2018.
[118] For the example of Bromyard Downs, see below, pp. 251–2.
[119] Hoskins & Stamp, pp. 84, 255, 264–7, 268, 319; Tavener, *Common Lands of Hampshire*, p. 51.
[120] *Hansard*, House of Commons, 14 May 1954, col. 1656.

under cultivation, and effectively ceased to be common land. The fate of requisitioned land lay with the owner and the commoners at the end of the war and depended on whether agreement on future use could be reached. Some commons rapidly reverted to scrub or to rough grazing.[121] In Radnorshire, bracken and gorse spread on common land which had proved productive during the war, when commoners failed to reach unanimous agreement on more productive future use after it was returned. Active choice also led to permanent change of use, as at Hatherleigh Moor (Devon), which was laid down to permanent grass before being returned as it was of greater value to the commoners as pasture than as ploughland. As owner of the soil, it often fell to the lord of the manor to devise a scheme for future management and some owners came to arrangements with the commoners to enable requisitioned commons to continue as private farmland.[122] Examples included 100 acres (40 ha) of Lilley Hoo Common (Herts.), where the lord of the manor took over the land with the agreement of the commoners, and Westwood Common at Laxton (Notts.), where the lord bought out the commoners' rights and incorporated the common into his farms. Its value as cropland prevailed over its value as common grazing.[123]

After the requisitioning of commons during the Second World War, it is perhaps not surprising that common land continued to be viewed as spare ground which could be used for other government initiatives in the 1950s. Most notorious was the case of Winfrith Heath (Dorset), a large part of which was acquired for a nuclear research station (which government policy dictated should be sited away from built-up areas); the common rights over it were extinguished by Act of Parliament in 1957. Coinciding with the deliberations of the Royal Commission on Common Land, the land grab provoked strong passion within the commons preservation lobby, not least because Winfrith Heath was part of the inspiration for 'Egdon Heath' in Thomas Hardy's *The Return of the Native*. When the bill was debated in the House of Commons, the Labour MP Arthur Blenkinsop expressed concern that people should continue to be able to enjoy open spaces 'and not be faced always with chimneys of some vast new project wherever there is wild country in the British Isles'.[124]

* * *

As conceptions of the value of common land have changed since the mid-nineteenth century, the legal framework, the management structures and the use of commons have also changed. Increasingly, national needs have trumped private rights, reflected in the increasing number of commons owned or controlled by public bodies rather than private landlords. Commons have become places of public recreation, while the range of resources exploited by common right has shrunk, so that few rights other than

---

[121] For examples, see Hoskins & Stamp, pp. 264, 274, 313.
[122] D. R. Denman, R. A. Roberts and H. J. F. Smith, *Commons and Village Greens* (London, 1967), pp. 50, 90, 100–1.
[123] Hoskins & Stamp, p. 288; J. V. Beckett, *A History of Laxton: England's Last Open-Field Village* (Oxford, 1989), p. 40.
[124] *Hansard*, 30 May 1957 (vol. 571, cols 621–84), at col. 644. See also Hoskins & Stamp, p. 83.

grazing are now exercised. The management of common land increasingly focuses on environmental conservation, both aesthetic and ecological. As a result, the face of common land – upland and lowland, rural and urban – has changed markedly since the nineteenth century. The impact of these changes on the landscape and vegetation of commons forms the subject of the next chapter.

CHAPTER 8

THE CHANGING FACE OF COMMON LAND SINCE 1860

COMMON LAND IS ONLY 'half-wild' – hardly anywhere in Britain is ecology untouched by mankind. Typical landscapes of common land, such as moorlands and heaths, are the product of interactions between natural and human forces; they are potentially unstable and subject to change in response to variations in either. This chapter offers an overview of how the face of common land has changed since the mid-nineteenth century, looking at the relationship between evolving patterns of use and the ecological character of those commons which survived the age of enclosure. Key factors include changes in grazing pressure, the cessation of some traditional uses, notably the gathering of fuel, and, increasingly, the role of government agencies in steering management practices for conservation ends. In broad terms, economic and technological change across the twentieth century led to a divergence between actively used upland commons and abandoned lowland commons. Upland commons generally experienced an intensification of use, whether increased grazing pressure or active management as grouse moors, whereas grazing and fuel gathering ceased on many, but not all, lowland commons. Meanwhile, common land near towns tended to be brought into the service of modern urban populations, and 'municipalised' into recreational parkland. These three distinct trajectories of change since the 1860s are examined in turn.

One theme which recurs is the increasing role played by the state in pursuing conservation objectives, resulting in the active manipulation of the ecology of common land, both upland and lowland, from the later twentieth century. Central to this has been the language of 'favourable' and 'unfavourable' condition used to judge the ecological state of Sites of Special Scientific Interest (SSSIs).[1] Since 57 per cent of common land in England is in SSSIs, the impact of such thinking has been significant. Owners and occupiers of SSSIs are required to seek consent from state conservation bodies (now Natural England, Natural Resources Wales and NatureScot) for activities which might damage the ecology (such as peat-digging), and consent can be refused. Financial incentives have been introduced in the form of management

---

[1] Assessments are based on detailed surveys of vegetation in relation to a set of targets which must be met for 'favourable condition' to be recorded. See 'Common Standards Monitoring Guidance for designated Nature Conservation Sites': https://jncc.gov.uk/our-work/common-standards-monitoring-guidance.

agreements fostering the aims of nature conservation. Even where common land is not notified as SSSI, a succession of agri-environment agreements since the 1990s, whereby state funding is used to direct land use (often by paying farmers to reduce stocking levels), has had a major impact on the exercise of common rights. These developments represent a shift in control over commons from the holders of property rights (the owner of the soil and the commoners) to the state.[2]

UPLAND COMMONS: GRAZING AND GROUSE

Hill and Mountain

Since the nineteenth century, the dominant drivers of environmental change on common land in mountainous terrain have been fluctuations in grazing intensity. This has not only involved large swings in the absolute numbers of livestock on commons but also changes in the balance between cattle and sheep. Cattle grazing on commons declined, often ceasing altogether, so that many commons became almost exclusively sheep country. State policy has driven wide swings in livestock numbers since the mid-twentieth century, first by providing incentives to increase numbers, and then by encouraging a reduction in stocking levels in the interests of conservation. Data from hill farming areas show a dramatic pattern of change in the intensity of sheep grazing since 1950. In Cumbria, for example, the sheep population remained steady, at around 1.2 million, from 1900 until the later 1950s, but then more than doubled over the forty years from 1955, reaching over 2.6 million by 1995, the increase driven by headage payments (subsidies based on the number of animals kept), especially after 1976.[3] Sheep numbers in the Lake District National Park rose by more than a quarter in the decade after 1983, after subsidies were boosted by the EEC Annual Sheep Premium from 1981.[4] A very similar pattern is seen in data from the Elan Valley Estate (Radnorshire), in the heart of the hills of mid-Wales, where sheep numbers remained broadly stable across the first half of the twentieth century, before rising from the 1950s. The rise accelerated from the 1970s, stocking levels having nearly doubled by the late 1980s.[5]

By the 1990s, the tide was beginning to turn against sheep. Overgrazing on upland commons, exacerbated by the heavy footfall of hill walkers in tourist areas, came to be recognised as a problem. Close cropping of the fragile sward on steep, thin-soiled slopes could quickly tip over into erosion and, where grazing levels were high, the selective browsing of sheep led to a loss of biodiversity. Tastier plants declined, to be

---

[2] *Contested Common Land*, pp. 62–8.
[3] Natural England Lake District Team, *Grazing Regimes for Nature Recovery: Experience from 25 Years of Agri-Environment Agreements in the Lake District's High Fells* (Kendal, 2020), pp. 19–20. Headage payments were introduced under the hill sheep subsidies from the 1940s and replaced by the Hill Livestock Compensatory Allowance in 1976.
[4] M. Edwards, 'Sheep Farming on the Lake District Fells: adapting to change' (TS report, revised 2017), p. 11.
[5] J. P. Bowen and J. Martin, 'The "Big Freeze" of 1962–3: the loss of livestock, the issue of fodder supply and the problem of the commons in two upland hill farming regions of England and Wales', *AgHR*, 64 (2) (2016), p. 239.

replaced by a few unappealing and resistant species, notably matt grass (*Nardus stricta*), heath rush (*Juncus squarrosus*) and, on wetter ground, purple moor-grass (*Molinia caerulea*) and cotton grass (*Eriphorum vaginatum*).[6] From the late 1990s, a combination of agri-environment schemes and a reduction in the number of graziers exercising their common rights has reduced the numbers of sheep on upland commons. In Cumbria as a whole, for example, the number of sheep fell by a quarter from 2.6 million in 1995 to 1.9 million by 2010.

On many commons, agri-environment schemes were introduced at a time when grazing levels were already falling. As a result of farm amalgamations and other factors, such as the fall-out from the 2001 outbreak of foot and mouth disease, the number of commoners actively exercising grazing rights fell substantially. On a selection of upland commons across England surveyed in 2007, the proportion of active graziers was generally less than one-half of the total number of rights holders registered under the CRA.[7] Some rights were transferred to new owners but others ceased to be used (or were sometimes bought and mothballed by government agencies),[8] helping to depress stock numbers on the common.

On the Lake District fells a succession of agri-environment schemes provided financial compensation to commoners who agreed to cut grazing levels in the interests of ecological recovery.[9] Commoners in Eskdale, for example, agreed to remove 40 per cent of their stock in a bid to promote the regeneration of heather under a ten-year management scheme from 1995, and a later agreement on those parts which were SSSIs resulted in a further 40 per cent reduction after 2004.[10]

Driven by English Nature (and its successor, Natural England), the schemes aimed to reduce stocking levels to around 0.5 ewes per hectare, a level of grazing which was deemed necessary to allow habitat recovery on the fells. This was often achieved by the removal of all sheep from a common across the winter months, allowing a grazing density higher than 0.5 ewes/ha in the summer.[11] As a result, substantial reductions in sheep numbers occurred on most Lake District commons, cutting into the inflated numbers generated by headage payments (see Table 1). Other aspects of the conservation drive towards habitat recovery in the Lake District included blocking drainage ditches to repair the condition of blanket bogs and the re-introduction of cattle on some commons, with the intention that their less selective browsing would lead to an overall improvement of the sward.[12]

---

[6] Natural England, *Grazing Regimes for Nature Recovery*, pp. 17–18.

[7] Figures were 33 per cent on East Stainmore (Westmld); 40 per cent at Haslingden (Lancs.); 36 per cent at Peter Tavy (Devon); 25 per cent at Brendon (Som.); and 21 per cent on the Black Mountain (Heref.): Pastoral Commoning Partnership, *Trends in Pastoral Commoning* (Carlisle, 2009), pp. xxxii, xxxiv, xxxix, xliv, xlix, li, lvii.

[8] For examples, see *Contested Common Land*, pp. 105, 130–1; below, p. 220.

[9] The Environmentally Sensitive Area scheme (1993–2004); Sheep and Wildlife Enhancement Schemes (2003–06) and Higher Level Stewardship scheme (2006–14).

[10] *Contested Common Land*, p. 105.

[11] Natural England, *Grazing Regimes for Nature Recovery*, pp. 22–30.

[12] Ibid., pp. 32–3, 47.

Table 1. Changes in number of ewes grazing selected Lake District commons following the introduction of agri-environment schemes.

Common	Before 1993	Environmentally Sensitive Area scheme (1993)	Higher Level Stewardship scheme (2006)	% reduction since 1993
Bassenthwaite	1,700	1,197	850	50%
Buttermere	3,790	2,110	2,100	45%
Derwent	7,460	4,830	4,061	46%
Langstrath	5,595	3,438	2,500	55%
Matterdale	2,013	1,509	1,450	28%
Mungrisdale	7,389	5,560	3,900	47%
St Johns	3,571	3,100	1,640	54%

Data courtesy of Julia Aglionby, Foundation for Common Land.

The impact of the sudden and sharp reduction in grazing, both on traditional shepherding and on the ecological condition of Lake District commons, was not without controversy. Commoners complained that the reduction in sheep numbers led to a breakdown in heafing, as sheep moved onto ground vacated or undergrazed by neighbouring flocks, making gathering and driving the common more difficult. Lower stocking rates led to the replacement of some good grazing by less palatable species, such as *Molinia*, and allowed red deer to move into areas vacated by sheep, reversing some of the impact of reduced sheep numbers on habitat recovery.[13]

The spread of bracken (*Pteridium aquilinum*), a process which had begun by the middle decades of the twentieth century, has been noticeable on commons across Britain. Multiple factors seem to have been involved, combining to reduce the extent to which the plant was kept in check. The reduction in cattle grazing probably played a part, as cattle break and bruise the tender shoots in the spring in a way which sheep do not. The end of bracken-gathering on most upland commons since the 1950s meant that dead bracken accumulated each year, protecting the rhizomes from frost in the winter – and the trend towards warmer winters has also played a part. Heavy grazing by sheep removed competitor species, allowing bracken to spread, a process then accelerated by reduced grazing levels under agri-environmental schemes, which has been noticed by commoners, both in the Lake District and on the moorlands of south-west England.[14]

---

[13] Ibid., pp. 49–50, 56–63; *Contested Common Land*, pp. 105–6; Pastoral Commoning Partnership, *Trends in Pastoral Commoning*, p. xxviii.

[14] C. N. Page, 'The history and spread of bracken in Britain', *Proceedings of the Royal Society of Edinburgh, Section B*, 81 (1–2) (1982), pp. 3–10; Pastoral Commoning Partnership, *Trends in Pastoral Commoning*, pp. xxviii, xlix, lii.

Elements of these changes were also seen on common grazings in the crofting areas of Scotland. At Galson, on the Isle of Lewis, for example, cattle numbers declined after the Second World War and the sheep stock grew, largely as a result of the increasing importance of store lambs as a cash crop. The focus on sheep also led to more intensive use of enclosed grassland, boosted by fertiliser inputs, and, in some communities, the abandonment of grazing on the commons. This, in turn, resulted in unrestricted heather growth, not only as the plants were no longer 'pruned' by grazing livestock but also because traditional burning to maintain a crop of young heather ceased.[15] More generally, a survey of crofting areas in 2001 concluded that only three-quarters of the shares in common grazings were still actively used, some crofters keeping their stock entirely on their enclosed land. The number of graziers using each common was often small: over 70 per cent of common grazings had as few as two to four active graziers and only 11 per cent had five or more. Almost one-tenth were used by a single grazier, in effect converting a communal resource to private use. Grazing regimes were breaking down, as regulation by grazing committees became less effective. One result of these trends was that there was sometimes simultaneous overgrazing on parts of the common close to the crofts and undergrazing further away.[16] The cutting of peat – the principal source of domestic fuel in much of the Highlands and Islands until the later twentieth century – continued until the 1990s, but then declined rapidly. By 2001, peat was cut on only 40 per cent of common grazings and often by only a small number of crofters.[17]

A recent change on some upland commons has been an increase in woodland as part of a growing national drive to extend woodland cover. Planting schemes have become more frequent on commons across upland Britain, despite the obstacles inherent in planting trees on common land: the need to secure the agreement of both the owner and those with common rights and the legal restrictions on fencing commons. In England and Wales, most planting schemes are driven by conservation aims, to restore some native woodland. On the common grazings of the Scottish Highlands and Islands, tree planting was encouraged by statutory provision in 1991, which allowed grazings committees to receive payment for creating woodland on common land.[18]

Moorland

Moorland commons in northern England have a different history. Dominated by heather and peat, they embrace a multiplicity of ecologies, from wet peat bog supporting sphagnum moss, cotton grass and bog myrtle, to drier moors blanketed with heather

---

[15] F. Rennie, 'Human ecology and concepts of sustainable development in a crofting township', *Folk Life*, 46 (2007), pp. 44–7.

[16] K. M. Brown, 'New challenges for old commons: the role of historical common land in contemporary rural space', *Scottish Geographical Journal*, 122 (2006), pp. 116–18.

[17] Rennie, 'Human ecology and concepts of sustainable development', p. 46; Brown, 'New challenges for old commons', p. 116.

[18] The Crofter Forestry (Scotland) Act 1991.

or grass. The story of these moorlands across the past few centuries is of management by controlled burning to encourage the growth of heather.[19]

Across the nineteenth and twentieth centuries, moor burning (or 'swaling') intensified, in order to produce a monoculture of heather to support populations of red grouse (*Lagopus lagopus*) for sport. Grouse (traditionally termed 'moorcock' or 'moor game') had been hunted for many years before the fashion for shooting the birds on the wing gained popularity among the aristocracy and gentry in the later eighteenth century. By the 1770s and 1780s moors in the Yorkshire Pennines and the Derbyshire Peak District were being let for shooting. As moorland commons in the Peak District and parts of the Yorkshire Dales were enclosed, landowners often acquired vast allotments of moor in lieu of their manorial rights and, by purchasing others, consolidated control over broad areas of grouse moor which were no longer subject to common rights. However, some grouse moor commons survived, particularly in the North York Moors and northern Pennines. Where this was the case, the desire of the landowner to reap the benefits of intensive grouse shooting led some to buy up farms with common rights, in order to gain control of the grazing interests and to control grazing through tenancy agreements, reducing livestock numbers in the interests of grouse shooting.[20]

Management of grouse moors became more intensive after the arrival of the breech-loading shotgun in the 1860s, which heralded the age of competitive slaughter in the later nineteenth and early twentieth century. Rotational burning of heather ensured a steady and ample supply of young heather for the grouse; wetter moorland was drained by digging ditches (or 'grips'); and gamekeepers embarked on campaigns to exterminate predators, notably raptors.[21] The characteristic landscape of grouse moors – a patchwork of strips or blocks of heather of different ages, with shooting cabins and lines of grouse butts – was a product of that distinctive management regime.

After the heyday of grouse shooting in Edwardian times, intensive management of some grouse moors waned, in part because of fluctuations in the grouse population as a result of disease. At the same time, sheep numbers increased, leading to a reduction in heather through more intensive grazing. In the Kinder-Bleaklow area of the Peak District, for example, sheep numbers increased threefold between 1930 and 1976, contributing to a decline in the acreage of heather moorland, which fell by 36 per cent between 1913 and 1980.[22] A combination of changes in burning regimes,

---

[19] For moorlands and their history, see I. G. Simmons, *The Moorlands of England and Wales: An Environmental History 8000 BC – AD 2000* (Edinburgh, 2003). See also above, pp. 75–6.

[20] E.g. Harkerside Moor (Yorks. N.R.): W. Swales, 'Commons in the civil parish of Grinton' (TS report for 'Building Commons Knowledge' Project, 2013).

[21] See A. Done and R. Muir, 'The landscape history of grouse shooting in the Yorkshire Dales', *Rural History*, 12 (2) (2001), pp. 195–210; Simmons, *Moorlands of England and Wales*, pp. 139–40, 244–7; D. Hey, 'The grouse moors of the Peak District', in P. S. Barnwell and M. Palmer (eds), *Post-Medieval Landscapes* (Macclesfield, 2007), pp. 68–79.

[22] P. Anderson and D. W. Yalden, 'Increased sheep numbers and the loss of heather moorland in the Peak District, England', *Biological Conservation*, 20 (1981), pp. 203–6.

THE CHANGING FACE OF COMMON LAND SINCE 1860

Figure 36. Peat restoration at Buckstones on Marsden Moor, Yorkshire. Volunteers and National Trust rangers building wooden dams to block gullies in order to reduce erosion, 2008.

heavy grazing by sheep and the long-term effects of moorland drainage had led to widespread degradation of heather moorland by the 1990s. Without regular burning, heather became leggy and bracken and scrub species invaded; heavy grazing led to the replacement of heather by grasses and exacerbated peat erosion; the drying of peat as a result of 'gripping' increased the risk of erosion and wildfires and reduced biodiversity by destroying wetter habitats.[23] Peatlands also suffered damage as a result of atmospheric sulphur dioxide pollution, to which sphagnum moss – the dominant 'sponge' species, holding water – was particularly susceptible.[24]

Since the mid-1990s initiatives to restore moorland habitats have resulted in active manipulation of the ecology of moorland commons. The desire for ecological diversity, restoration of heather, repair of areas suffering from erosion, and recognition of the role played by moorland peat in carbon storage have led to interventions driven by government funding. The principal actions have included a substantial reduction in grazing, blocking 'grips' and gullies to reduce erosion and restore wetland ecosystems, and actively replanting sphagnum moss. On drier moorlands regular controlled burning has been promoted, as it is seen as key to maintaining heather moorland, by not only

---

[23] Simmons, *Moorlands of England and Wales*, pp. 221–32, 243–51.
[24] Ibid., p. 185.

promoting heather growth but also keeping bracken at bay and preventing trees and scrub from gaining a foothold.

Restoring peat has involved determined interventions on moorland commons. On Marsden Moor in the south Pennines, for example, severely eroded peat gullies have been dammed to reduce the flow of water in an attempt to prevent the peat from drying out (Figure 36). On Bowes Moor (Yorks. N.R.), a 11,015-acre (4,458-ha) regulated pasture which is an SSSI, a wide-ranging programme of interventions from 2007 included blocking drains, systematic heather burning, reductions in grazing, controlling the spread of rushes (*Juncus* spp.) and tree planting.[25] Later interventions, after an ecological assessment of the Moor in 2015–16, included further reductions in grazing, with almost complete off-wintering of sheep; re-seeding heather on areas under threat from the heather beetle; and ending the rotational burning of blanket bog.[26] These examples illustrate the tightly-directed and closely-monitored management in the interests of conservation which has been seen across many upland commons since the 1990s.

LOWLAND GRAZING COMMONS

Among the commons of lowland England, the New Forest (Hants) stands out as an area in which pasture rights have continued to be exercised widely to the present day. The largest tract of surviving common land in lowland Britain, its unique legal structures and institutions – notably the Verderers' Court, which upheld the interests of the commoners – and the survival of a smallholding economy in which common rights were an integral resource, ensured that active pastoral commoning continued, though grazing intensity and the exercise of other common rights have been subject to marked swings since the late nineteenth century. The number of active commoners declined from the 1920s, as did the livestock turned out to graze. Overall, numbers of both ponies and cattle fell from peaks in the 1880s to reach a nadir in the 1940s: almost 3,200 ponies were grazed in 1885; only 571 in 1940. After the Second World War, both cattle and pony numbers recovered quickly to regain late nineteenth-century levels. Despite a dip in the 1980s, the upward trend in the number of ponies continued, with over 4,800 being grazed on the forest in 2010, whereas the number of cattle fluctuated, standing at over 3,000 in the mid-1990s but only 2,200 in 2010. The exercise of other common rights declined. Pannage, for which 5,000–6,000 pigs were turned out in good mast years in the nineteenth century, had dwindled by the 1960s but lingered on: 547 pigs were turned out in 2010. Turf-cutting for fuel, which had seen perhaps 1.25 million turves cut annually in the 1890s, had died out by the

---

[25] Natural England, *Protecting England's Natural Treasures: Sites of Special Scientific Interest* (NE306, 2011), p. 37.

[26] *Bowes Moor SSSI Site Restoration Plan, 2018–2028*, http://publications.naturalengland.org.uk/file/6030598561071104.

mid-twentieth century, and the annual harvest of bracken for bedding declined from the 1940s, almost to extinction.[27]

The face of the New Forest commons also changed as a result of organised attempts, under the auspices of the Forestry Commission, to improve the quality of grazing in the 1950s, by burning, drainage and re-seeding. Heath burning to improve the pasture, which can be traced back to the eighteenth century in the New Forest, came under stricter control by the 1950s, when selected sections were burnt annually, not only to encourage fresh growth of heather and gorse but also to prevent tree seedlings from becoming established on open heathland. Drainage of the forest's mires also accelerated. A total of twenty-seven drainage schemes were carried out between 1923 and 1930 and a further ninety-six in a major drainage programme between 1965 and 1986, driven in part by a desire to restore the grassland of the open 'lawns' which provided some of the best grazing. The third strand of the campaign to improve the pastures took the form of reclamation by re-seeding patches of grassland on better drained sites. Around 1,300 acres (530 ha) were ploughed, fertilised and re-seeded in the decade after 1941, much of it under the Pastoral Development Scheme of 1944–52, when, in most cases, crops were taken for a few years before the reclaimed plots were put down to grass again.[28] The middle decades of the twentieth century thus saw repeated efforts to improve the forest commons without enclosure, increasing their economic efficiency at a time when maximising agricultural productivity was a driving force.

The forest's ecological value became increasingly prominent from 1959, when the Forestry Commission and the Nature Conservancy Council formally agreed that it should be managed with the status of a national nature reserve. Further layers of environmental protection followed, culminating in the forest's designation as a National Park in 2005, bringing increased management for conservation ends, notably in the restoration of natural river channels and valley mires.[29]

Grazing continued on some other lowland commons, especially in the more pastoral west, though the numbers of graziers and livestock tended to decline steeply. By the 1990s, sheep numbers on the Malvern Hills were one-sixth of the level they had been before 1960 and the common was devoid of cattle, while grazing had almost completely ceased in Ashdown and Epping Forests, for example.[30] Of the thirty-one registered commons on the Gower peninsula, near Swansea, only fourteen had active graziers by 2018, the numbers having dropped significantly since registration. Of these, eight commons had only two active graziers and five a single grazier each; only one, Cefn Bryn Common (five active graziers), had more. As a result, grazing pressure had dropped to the level where most of the commons were undergrazed. Bracken

---

[27] C. R. Tubbs, *The New Forest: History, Ecology and Conservation* (Lyndhurst, 2001), pp. 119, 124–33, 278–81; J. Ivey, 'Census of the New Forest Commoners 2011' (https://www.realnewforest.org/wp-content/uploads/2018/11/Final-census-report-August-2011.pdf), paras 6.2.2, 6.3.2, 6.3.3.

[28] Tubbs, *New Forest*, pp. 259–61, 269–77.

[29] Ibid., pp. 32–5; H. Cook, *New Forest: The Forging of a Landscape* (Oxford, 2018), pp. 193–9, 209–10.

[30] Pastoral Commoning Partnership, *Trends in Pastoral Commoning*, pp. 88, 90, 105.

and scrub cover expanded: in 1985 it was said that bracken had increased threefold since 1950, the spread being attributed specifically to a reduction in grazing by heavy horses since the war. As grazing reduced, active management sought to control the spread of bracken and scrub by controlled burning of heather and grass and cutting and rolling bracken.

Proximity to the growing urban area of Swansea and increasing tourist numbers also impinged on the commons and acted as disincentives to active grazing. From the 1960s, commoners suffered loss of livestock on the commons through collisions with vehicles and attacks by dogs, and fly-tipping became a nuisance – in 1960 one commoner removed over thirty oil drums, 'a tea chest full of turkey entrails' and 'another full of bones' from one of the streams. Other changes to the face of the Gower commons included the proliferation of invasive exotic species, notably rhododendron, Himalayan balsam and Japanese knotweed.[31]

The potential for conflict between the different values assigned to common land was laid bare elsewhere, when practices associated with grazing collided with conservation ideals. At Ewyas Harold (Heref.), the common, which was largely open grassland in the 1940s, had been colonised by bracken and gorse and become partly wooded by the 1990s. Periodic attempts were made to clear areas for grazing, including by burning off gorse. By the 1960s the amenity value of the common came to be voiced. Concepts of scenic beauty and public access for recreational use did not always sit easily with the scrub clearance and burning which were deemed vital to protect the grazing value of the common. Undergrazing and scrub growth could be seen as the result of neglect and management failure – or as fortuitously beneficial changes which enhanced the 'wild' look of the common. As conservation came to the fore, additional complexity was added to these understandings of value: regeneration of woodland scrub was viewed as detrimental to the species-rich flora of the common's traditionally open aspect, for example.[32]

In the Cotswolds, the grassy common at Cranham (Glos.) was traditionally burnt to remove dead grass and encourage new growth, and to prevent invasion by scrub. Burning went hand-in-hand with grazing. After the Second World War, regular burning ceased but informal burning, on the edge of legality, continued for some time, challenging both conservation bodies and new, non-farming residents. As 'rural gentrifiers' moved into the village from the 1960s, objections to traditional use of the common grew: they disliked the keeping of pigs and hens as well as the burning, which was seen as destructive and dirty. As one local put it, the newcomers 'didn't see it [the common] as a useful thing but as a recreational thing … its meaning has changed'. Parts of the common were notified as an SSSI in 1954 and a commons management committee was established in 1984, involving the Nature Conservancy Council. Burning no longer had

---

[31] S. Brackenbury and G. Jones, *Gower Commons: Successional Health Check* (2018) (at http://efncp.org/download/GowerCommonsreport2018.pdf); Gower Commons Association website: https://www.gowercommons.org.uk/gower-commons-management-methods/mechanical/.

[32] P. Parkes, 'A pasture in common: a twentieth-century environmental history of Ewyas Harold Common (Herefordshire)', *Rural History*, 16 (1) (2005), pp. 111–32.

a place on a common which became part of the Cotswolds Commons and Beechwoods National Nature Reserve.[33]

'AMENITY' COMMONS

The dominant trend in the history of most common land in lowland England across the twentieth century was a decline in traditional use. Many were abandoned as an agrarian resource, resulting in the regeneration of scrubland and wood, as grazing, fuel gathering and the digging of sand, gravel or clay ceased. Concurrently, the informal, customary uses of commons, which had little legal basis and were often viewed as 'nuisances', also declined, not least because of pressure from those in authority to suppress them, both in a drive to 'tidy up' common land and, more recently, in the interests of nature conservation. Lowland commons have thus seen a transition from an absence of control – uncontrolled vegetation change; unregulated informal exploitation – to increasingly close management to protect their ecological character.

Untidy, informal uses were widespread by the later nineteenth century, particularly on common land close to towns, as a growing population took advantage of the lack of manorial control on many lowland commons. The Inclosure Commissioners' reports tell of a host of uses by the 'lower orders' which lay outside or at the margins of the law: gathering turf, gorse and heather for firing; taking wood for garden fences and pea sticks; turning out donkeys and ponies to graze; digging sand, gravel or clay; encroaching on the margins of commons; and indulging in less 'respectable' recreations than those leading the battles to save commons for public enjoyment usually anticipated.[34] The Select Committee on Open Spaces, investigating London commons in 1865, highlighted the problems of unregulated gravel-digging and gorse-burning, piles of cinder and waste, and the 'bad characters' drawn to common land.[35] Similar rhetoric characterised the battles over the rump of Mousehold Heath on the outskirts of Norwich, which culminated in its regulation for use as a public park in 1884. Byelaws forbidding clay-digging, gamblers and gypsies, brawling and fighting and other uncouth behaviour sought to extinguish the rough plebeian culture with which the Heath had long been associated.[36]

Regulation of commons thus put pressure on informal uses and semi-legal practices, which increasingly came to be viewed as 'trespasses'. Some continued into the mid-twentieth century, especially the use of common land by the travelling community.

---

[33] C. J. Griffin and I. Robertson, 'Moral ecologies: conservation in conflict in rural England', *History Workshop Journal*, 82 (2016), pp. 38–43.

[34] A. Howkins, 'The commons, enclosure and radical histories', in D. Feldman and J. Lawrence (eds), *Structures and Transformations in Modern British History* (Cambridge, 2011), pp. 129, 134–7; A. Howkins, 'The use and abuse of English commons, 1845–1914', *History Workshop Journal*, 78 (2014), pp. 120–3.

[35] See B. Cowell, 'The Commons Preservation Society and the campaign for Berkhamsted Common, 1866–70', *Rural History*, 13 (2) (2002), p. 148.

[36] N. MacMaster, 'The battle for Mousehold Heath 1857–1884: "popular politics" and the Victorian public park', *Past & Present*, 127 (1) (1990), pp. 117–54 (quotation at p. 131).

Byelaws explicitly forbade gypsies from camping on some commons and the Law of Property Act 1925 balanced increased public access by banning camping or the drawing up of vehicles or caravans on common land, thus outlawing travellers from using commons without permission.[37] Nevertheless, 'deep-rooted' gypsy and tinker encampments remained, for example, on Colney Heath (Herts.) and in Kent (at Hosey Common near Sevenoaks and Free Heath at Lamberhurst) in the 1960s.[38] They were seen as a problem, 'a nuisance on a common, smothering it with litter' and causing 'profound annoyance'.[39] Further legislation in the 1960s, effectively, sought to remove travellers from commons.[40]

In parallel with these restrictions on informal use, economic and technological change since Victorian times reduced reliance on the agrarian resources of lowland common land, so that formal common rights gradually fell into abeyance on many commons. Grazing declined on commons in the southern and eastern counties of England, especially those near towns where there was pressure from semi-legal uses. Fuel-gathering also dwindled as wood and turf were replaced by coal and coke as domestic fuels and as open hearths were superseded by gas fires and central heating. Moreover, rural industries such as potteries and brick-making, which had extracted raw materials from common land, declined. The face of common land slowly changed: pits became ponds; bracken and gorse spread and took hold, followed by trees, leading in many cases to full woodland cover (Figure 37). The chronology of abandonment stretched back into the nineteenth century but accelerated after the Second World War.

Some commons had ceased to be used by mid-Victorian times. The land at Hurstbourne Tarrant (Hants), set out at enclosure in 1820 as a 'perpetual common', was described in 1874 as 'an almost impenetrable jungle of brambles, gorse and thorn bushes, with open glades in which certain persons have common rights', but these were 'not of much value to them'. It was still derelict and overgrown when it was requisitioned by the War Agricultural Executive Committee in 1942 and reclaimed for arable use.[41] By the early twentieth century the situation at Medmenham (Bucks.) was probably typical of many small commons in south-eastern England. A scrap of common land there, known as the Common Moor, lay unused by the 1920s, when it was noted that grazing rights had ceased to be exercised, 'as the grazing very largely consists of thistles and tin cans', and the common had been 'abandoned to the rabbits and rats'.[42]

It is generally agreed that the decline in grazing accelerated after the Second World War. Requisitioning, whether for military or agricultural use, could cause permanent ecological change. Where ancient pasture or heath was ploughed, or where land was

---

[37] L. W Chubb, 'The Law of Property Act, 1925 (Provisions for the Protection of Commons)', *Journal of the Commons and Footpaths Preservation Society*, 1 (1) (1927), pp. 9, 11.
[38] D. R. Denman *et al.*, *Commons and Village Greens* (London, 1967), p. 310; Hoskins & Stamp, p. 148.
[39] Denman *et al.*, *Commons and Village Greens*, p. 309.
[40] Caravan Sites and Control of Development Act 1960 (c.62, sec. 23); Caravan Sites Act 1968 (c.52).
[41] L. E. Tavener, *The Common Lands of Hampshire* (Southampton, 1957), p. 51.
[42] A. H. Plaisted, *The Manor and Parish of Medmenham, Buckinghamshire* (London, 1925), p. 312.

Figure 37. Nettlebed Common, Oxfordshire. Woodland colonisation of clay pits, disused by c.1900, which had supplied raw materials for the local brick, tile and pottery industries.

churned up by military vehicles, both the physical structure and chemical composition of soils were disrupted. Even where common land management was reinstated, the vegetation had changed.[43] At a time when the economics of commoning were in flux, this added to the difficulties of resuming traditional patterns of use. The snapshot of the state of common land in England in the 1950s, provided by returns made to the Royal Commission on Common Land, thus captured a moment of transition.[44] Some lowland commons were noted as being 'fully used', especially where management structures survived. More numerous, however, were the commons – often smaller ones – which were little used and turning to scrub: 'woodland and bushes, unused agriculturally' (Naphill, Hughenden, Bucks.); 'wet, scrub-covered, derelict' (Crostwick, Norf.), for example.[45]

The changes in use, both formal and informal, were thus multi-faceted. They can be illustrated by local memories of Frensham Common (Surrey), collected in 1997.[46] The heathland common, covering around 1,000 acres (400 ha), was, as one resident

---

[43] As traced at Lakenheath (Suff.): G. Crompton and J. Sheail, 'The historical ecology of Lakenheath Warren in Suffolk, England: a case study', *Biological Conservation*, 8 (1975), p. 311. I am grateful to Graham Bathe for highlighting these points.

[44] As recorded in the gazetteer in Hoskins & Stamp, pp. 247–350.

[45] Ibid., pp. 251, 301.

[46] Summaries of interviews conducted in 1997 by Clare Simkin as part of the 'Reminiscences of Surrey Heathland' survey for the Surrey Heathland Project (courtesy of Jackie Lake, Surrey County Council, 2013).

put it, both a 'playground' and a 'larder' for the local community in the first half of the twentieth century. Grazed, largely by cattle, until after the Second World War, the common also produced heather honey, some of which was sold commercially, from beehives set on the heath by local people. The common also yielded other resources until the middle decades of the century: heather, turf and dead wood (for fuel); fir cones and gorse (as kindling); bracken (for litter); moss (for hanging baskets); and limited amounts of sand and gravel.

The Second World War initiated major change. Frensham Common was used for military training, including tank manoeuvres, during the war, which resulted in an ecological transformation, as the ponds were drained (to avoid them being used as landmarks by enemy aircraft); scrub was cleared for paratroop manoeuvres; trees were flattened and the ground churned up by tanks. When the army left after the war, traditional exploitation of the common did not return and scrub and woodland spread rapidly. Older residents were aware of an increase in bracken and gorse and stated that the woodland cover, mostly birch and pine ('fir'), had grown dramatically since the 1950s. The spread of woodland on lowland heaths was also exacerbated by the collapse in the number of rabbits after the myxomatosis epidemic of 1953–55. Open heathland had provided an ideal habitat for rabbits, which had continued to graze after livestock grazing ceased; the decimation of rabbits then led to unchecked growth of scrub and trees.[47]

Ecological considerations played an increasing role in the management of lowland commons from the 1950s. Many were recognised by the state as being of high nature value and designated for protection as SSSIs (from the 1950s), Special Protection Areas (for birds, under the Wildlife & Countryside Act 1981) or Special Areas of Conservation (under the European Union's Habitats Directive, 1992). The multiple layers of legislative protection were often given concrete expression in the management of commons as nature reserves, whether at national or local level. Patterns of management on nature reserve commons tended to display similar features, including an explicit conservation objective, improved public access, and, on many commons, the reintroduction of grazing in an attempt to keep down invasive scrub. As early as the 1950s, when scrub was invading ungrazed commons, it was recognised that grazing was 'the most suitable mowing machine' for commons which were 'essentially public open spaces'.[48]

The recent history of Roydon Common, near King's Lynn (Norf.), illustrates these themes. Valued as an example of a lowland mixed valley mire system, it carries multiple conservation designations: SSSI (notified 1954), SAC (since 1995) and a wetland of international importance under the Ramsar Convention (since 1993). Traditional uses of the common are thought to have petered out before the Second World War: peat-cutting may have continued until the 1920s and grazing until the 1930s. The common

---

[47] See A. G. Crosby, 'A disappearing landscape: the heathlands of the Berkshire, Hampshire and Surrey borders', *AgHR*, 66 (2) (2018), p. 197; Crompton and Sheail, 'Historical ecology of Lakenheath Warren', p. 308. The impact of myxomatosis was also noted on Merrow Downs, near Guildford: https://merrowresidents.org.uk/merrow-downs.

[48] *RCCL Rep.*, para. 109 (p. 39).

Figure 38. Roydon Common, Norfolk. Members of Gaywood Valley Conservation Group clearing gorse, 2019.

was used for military training during the 1950s. Purchased by Norfolk Wildlife Trust in stages between 1963 and 1993, it was then managed to enhance its conservation value. Grazing became central to maintaining both the mire and the dry heath and direct interventions included rotational peat stripping to maintain areas of open water, mowing of rank vegetation, controlled burning of the dry heath to promote *Calluna*, and active control of invasive scrub by cutting (see Figure 38). The restoration of what were perceived as desirable eco-systems thus drove management of the common from the 1990s.[49]

Comparable manipulation of the vegetation cover occurred on nature reserves elsewhere. In 1980, Sussex Wildlife Trust bought Ebernoe Common, an area of wood pasture near Petworth, where grazing had ceased, leading to an expansion of scrub and tree cover. The Trust embarked on work to restore the wood pasture, opening up glades, cutting back bracken and bramble, clearing ponds of invasive reedmace, and reintroducing grazing with both ponies and rare breed cattle.[50] Skipwith Common (Yorks. E.R.) and Epworth Turbary (Lincs.) are further examples of active management to restore the desired ecology through clearance of woodland and scrub and re-introduction of grazing to help prevent regeneration of trees and maintain open heath.[51]

---

[49] B. Boyd, *Roydon Common Management Plan, April 2010–March 2015* (Norfolk Wildlife Trust, n.d.).
[50] https://sussexwildlifetrust.org.uk/visit/ebernoe-common/reserve-profile.
[51] https://www.escrick.com/the-estate/outdoor-and-conservation/skipwith-common; https://friendsofskipwithcommon.org.uk/history/. For Epworth, see below, p. 233.

The resulting managed landscapes on nature reserve commons are a far cry from the untidy, unruly world traditionally associated with lowland commons, where those who had little sought out the resources of common land to help make ends meet. Many lowland commons today could be described as carefully curated, semi-wild open spaces, oases of wildlife protected both for their inherent ecological value and for public enjoyment.

URBAN COMMONS: 'MUNICIPALISATION'

Transforming the landscape for public enjoyment took a different form on common land in the vicinity of towns. The dominant process here was the conversion of untidy commons, often scarred by extractive industry and dotted with pits and ponds from the era of rapid urbanisation since the eighteenth century, into public spaces expressing municipal civic ideals.

Where commons belonged to the freemen of ancient boroughs or cities, the decline of grazing across the nineteenth century provided opportunities to reconfigure the benefit of common land to the townspeople. At Marlborough (Wilts.), for example, the corporation had received income from burgesses putting cattle onto the common since the sixteenth century, extending the right to all inhabitants of the town in 1836. However, a decline in income from grazing during the later nineteenth and early twentieth century led the corporation to raise funds by licensing other activities on the common, such as agricultural shows, military manoeuvres and organised games.[52] At Lincoln all common rights on the city's three commons were extinguished by Act of Parliament in 1915, compensation having been paid to the commoners and freemen, to enable the corporation to convert large parts for recreational use, building sports grounds and playgrounds, golf courses and a racecourse.[53]

A prolonged legal battle was required to convert Mousehold Heath, on the outskirts of Norwich, into a park, as the city sought to wrest control of the common from the inhabitants of Pockthorpe, the working-class suburb on its edge, who had attempted to exclude other users from the 1840s. In 1844 they unilaterally set up a committee to exercise monopolistic control over the common, specifically over clay-digging and brick-making. In 1857 the Dean and Chapter of Norwich, which owned the common, offered it to Norwich town council for use as a 'People's Park'. After almost a quarter of a century of wrangling, matters came to a head in a court case over ownership of the Heath, culminating in a hearing in Chancery in 1883 which found in favour of the city. The following year, a local act established a board of conservators and made provision for the improvement of the Heath, including drainage, tree planting, the laying out of sports grounds, and how the new park should be policed. Norwich's unemployed were taken on as a labour force to fill holes, smooth rough areas, soften the edges of old gravel pits, prepare plots for tree planting and excavate a new road. By the end of the century, the brickfields and gravel pits had gone, parts of the Heath

---

[52] *VCH Wilts.* XII, p. 207.
[53] Hoskins & Stamp, pp. 114–15.

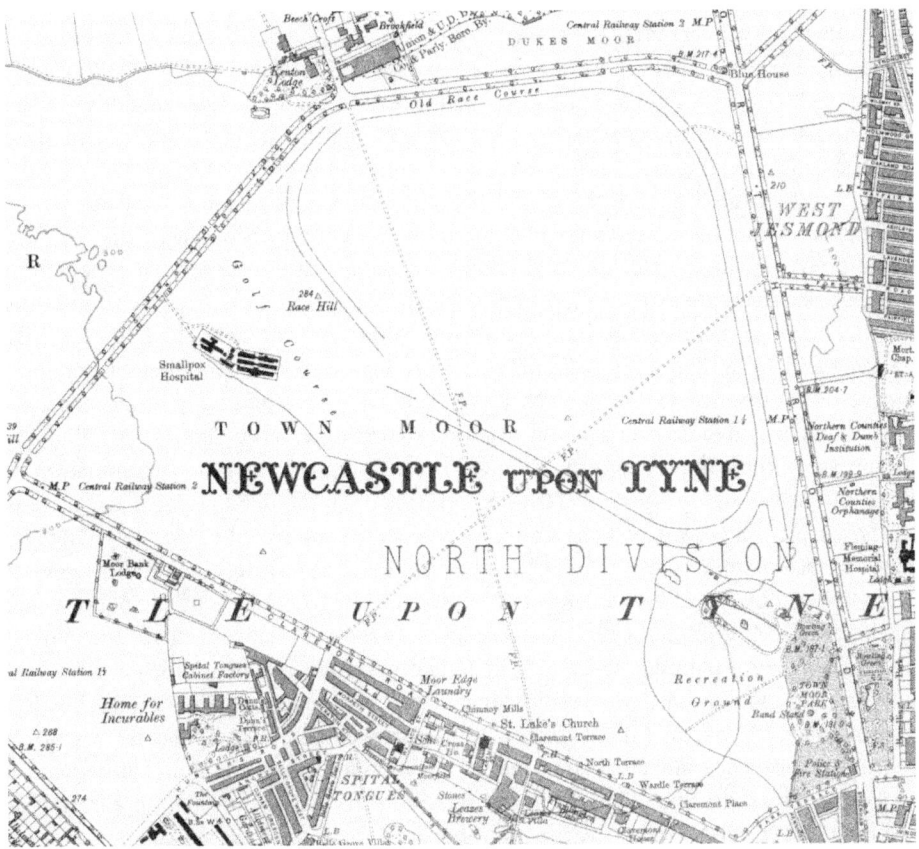

Figure 39. Town Moor, Newcastle upon Tyne. Several features of urban commons are shown: the old racecourse, golf course and isolation hospital, and the formal garden and recreation ground of Town Moor Park. (OS Six-Inch map, Durham 2, revised 1913–14).

had been planted, the network of paths had been rationalised and playing fields had been laid out. The Heath retained its largely open aspect and its character as rough, broken ground but some of the accoutrements of municipal parks (such as a bandstand and refreshment rooms) were added. As Neil MacMaster put it in his detailed study of the battle over the Heath, the park had become a 'sanitized zone' where 'restrained and decorous behaviour' was expected, though elements of 'deviant' plebeian leisure activities continued to take place until the early twentieth century.[54]

Similar intentions lay behind attempts to 'improve' the Town Moor at Newcastle upon Tyne. Proposals in 1861–62 to make the Moor 'more conducive to the health and recreation of the inhabitants', by building drives and rides, cricket and drill grounds and a gymnasium, met with opposition: 'liberty to stroll where you will, and not suffer confinement to harsh gravel walks' was greatly valued. In the end, the Newcastle upon Tyne Improvement Act 1870 allowed the corporation to take two sections of the

---

[54] MacMaster, 'Battle for Mousehold Heath', pp. 117–54.

common of up to 35 acres (14 ha) apiece to create public parks, resulting in the creation of Castle Leazes Park (with bandstand, lakes, walks and planting) and Town Moor Park (which included a formal garden and also a recreation ground). The remainder of the Moor remained open space where traditional uses (grazing by cattle and the holding of fairs) continued (Figure 39).[55]

On the metropolitan commons, the process of claiming common land for public recreation in the middle decades of the nineteenth century brought to the fore the question of just how 'wild' the land should be. In an early instance, an ornamental urban park was created to tame a common which had been the site of protest, and thus help to expunge memories of political dissent. A few months after the large Chartist gathering in 1848, Kennington Common was reported to be both an environmental and a social nuisance. Overlooked by a polluting vitriol factory, its 'stunted herbage' was 'trodden and soiled by a troop of cows belonging to a neighbouring milkman'. The pond on the common and the ditches running across it were 'an accumulation of black offensive muddy liquid' and 'the cemeteries of all the dead puppies and kittens of the vicinity'. By day it was the haunt of 'idle youths occupied in low gambling'; by night a place of immorality.[56] Under the promptings of a local clergyman, the common was enclosed by Act of Parliament in 1852, specifically to create a public park, which opened in 1854. Winding walkways were laid out around a more formal central oval, shrubberies were planted, seats installed. The park had a bandstand, fountain and an open-air 'gymnasium', converting empty open land into a public garden covering approximately 17 acres (7 ha), patrolled by wardens and locked at night (Figure 40).[57] More than a century and a half later, the taming of Kennington Common has been read as a desire to sanitise public space in order to stifle dissent,[58] and as 'a colonisation of working class political space' by the bourgeoisie.[59]

Later, nature was given a freer hand. The tone was set by the Wimbledon and Putney Commons Act 1871 which required the conservators to preserve, as far as possible, the 'natural aspect and state of the commons' and to protect the vegetation ('turf, gorse, heather, … shrubs and brushwood', as well as trees).[60] Retaining wildness was thus a key part of the campaign to save common land around the capital. In the looming battle to preserve Tooting Common in 1863, the *Daily News* had fretted about the prospect of losing 'a delightful little piece of gorse and heather shadowed with elms' to become 'a melancholy circle of eligible villas, with nothing but prosaic "green" in

---

[55] E. M. Halcrow, 'The Town Moor of Newcastle upon Tyne', *Archaeologia Aeliana*, 4th ser. 31 (1953), pp. 158–61; OS Six-Inch map, Northumberland sheet 97 NE (revised 1894–95).

[56] *The Builder*, 7 (27 January 1849), p. 44.

[57] HLE, no. 1000816; OS 1:2,500 plan, London sheet LV (surveyed 1871); *Town Commons*, p. 74; K. Navickas, 'Kennington Common, protest and public space', in *Kennington 1848: Another Look* (Friends of Kennington Park, 2019), p. 38.

[58] J. Kelly, 'Kennington Common, the Occupy movement and the freedom of assembly', *History Workshop: Histories of the Present*, 3 November 2011, online at https://www.historyworkshop.org.uk/kennington-common-the-occupy-movement-the-freedom-of-assembly/.

[59] S. Szczelkun, *Kennington Park: The Birthplace of People's Democracy* (London, 2018), p. 14.

[60] Wimbledon and Putney Commons Act 1871 (34 & 35 Vict., c. cciv), sec. 36.

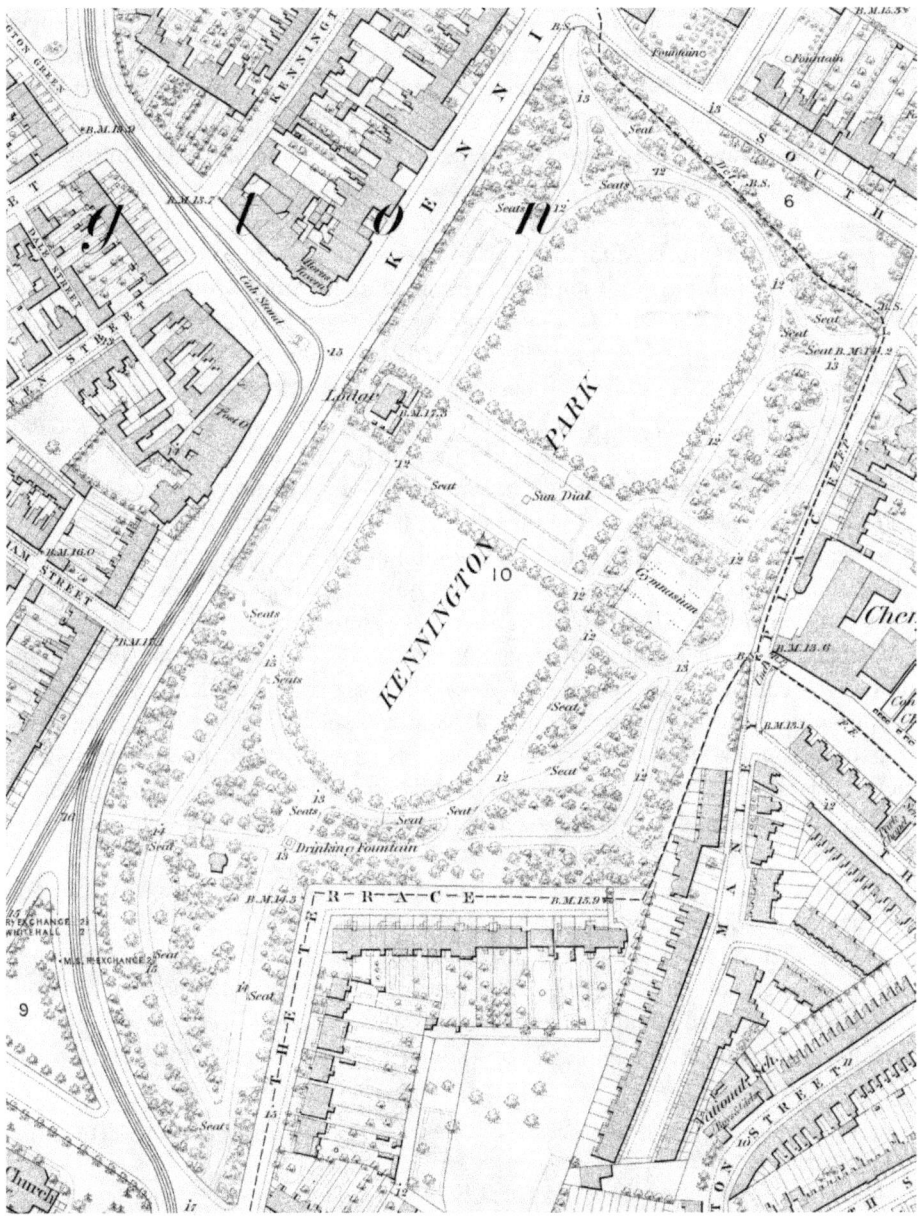

Figure 40. Kennington Park, London. The common, which had been the site of radical protests from the 1790s to the Chartist gathering in 1848, was transformed into an urban park in the 1850s (OS 1:2500 plan, London 55, surveyed 1871).

the centre'.[61] In the event, once its future was assured, the Metropolitan Board of Works intervened to 'improve' the landscape of Tooting Common from the 1870s, while seeking to retain much of its natural character: gravel paths were laid, avenues of trees planted, the ground levelled in places and an artificial pond created – but the rough ground and furze bushes remained. The Board resisted pressure to install the infrastructure for organised sports, rejecting a proposal to create a cricket pitch in 1873 and withdrawing permission to play golf on the common in 1894. Only in 1936 were sports facilities built.[62]

Of all sports, golf was the one most closely associated with common land in the later nineteenth century. Numerous golf courses were laid out in the decades either side of 1900, when passion for the game spread south from Scotland, becoming a familiar element of the landscape of commons in England, especially those close to towns and suburbs.[63] Among the earliest were those on Wimbledon Common, where a regimental golf club was given permission to play in 1865; Clapham Common (Surrey) and Crookham Common (Berks.), both established in 1873; and Coldham's Common (Cambs.), home to Cambridge University Golf Club from 1875.[64] The number grew rapidly, exploding in the 1890s as courses colonised commons near towns, large and small. As in Scotland, coastal dunes were used as golf links, from Alnmouth and Newbiggin (Northumb.), to Aberdovey (Merion.) and Westward Ho! (Devon),[65] while other courses were laid out on open ground on the skirts of the hills, as at Wooler Common (Northumb.) in the Cheviot Hills (1893), Rodborough Common (Glos.) in the Cotswolds (1904) and Meldon Common (Devon), on the edge of Dartmoor (1908). Many of the early courses were short-lived, not least because golfers did not always co-exist happily with other users of common land, whether walkers and picnickers or grazing livestock. From a golfer's perspective, the hazards on an urban common might include 'perambulators, nursery-maids, footballers, children playing games [and] lamp posts'.[66] As a result, some courses moved to new locations on private land before the First World War.

Of those which endured, some were municipal courses, like that in Meyrick Park, Bournemouth, which claimed to be the first in England. The park, which opened in 1894, was created from one of five turbary allotments set aside by the Christchurch enclosure award of 1802 for the inhabitants of surrounding villages. The turbaries continued to be used communally for much of the nineteenth century, not only for turf-digging (which declined) but also as a source of honey from hives placed on them,

---

[61] K. Layton-Jones (ed.), *The Common Story: A History of Tooting Common* (Wandsworth, 2019), p. 47, quoting *Daily News*, 26 November 1863, p. 4.

[62] Layton-Jones, *The Common Story*, pp. 53–6, 105–7.

[63] The following account draws on the wealth of information about individual golf courses gathered by John and Marie Llewellyn on their website: www.golfsmissinglinks.co.uk. For courses on urban commons, see *Town Commons*, p. 65.

[64] R. Browning, *A History of Golf: The Royal and Ancient Game* (London, 1990), pp. 91–2, 95.

[65] Golf courses on common land in the 1950s are recorded in the gazetteer in Hoskins & Stamp.

[66] Description of the course at Blackheath (Kent) in *Manchester Courier & Lancashire General Advertiser*, 20 January 1908 (reproduced at www.golfsmissinglinks.co.uk).

until, in the decades either side of 1900, they were annexed by the expanding town and converted into public parks.[67] Meyrick Park, the first to be opened, had a bowling green and playing fields, as well as the golf course, which it took one hundred men, twenty horses and a scarifier three months to create from a stretch of 'heather, furze and pine wood'.[68]

Private golf clubs wishing to play on common land needed the agreement of the owner of the common. In 1887 Guildford Golf Club agreed to pay the Earl of Onslow one shilling a year for the use of part of Merrow Downs, and they gained permission to construct putting greens there two years later; it was not until 1901 that they entered into a formal lease for thirty years.[69] The Royal West Norfolk Golf Club, which converted the dunes between the salt marsh and the sea on the common at Brancaster into a course in the late nineteenth century, made a formal agreement with the lord of the manor and the parish council (as representative of the commoners) in 1902.[70]

Other clubs secured control over common land by purchase. At Crowborough (Sussex), where a primitive course had been laid out on common land at the Beacon in 1895, the club purchased the manorial rights – and hence ownership of the common – in 1906. At Blackpan and Lake Commons, near Sandown (Isle of Wight), where a course had been established in 1900, the club first gained control of most of the grazing rights and later bought the commons outright.[71]

The early courses involved only minimal landscaping: natural features (pits and ditches; gorse bushes) – as well as other users of the common – formed part of the challenge for those playing golf. Over time, the increasingly manicured landscape of fairways and greens, and the desire to limit access to members of a club, often led to restrictions. On Merrow Downs, for example, limitations on the public's rights of access over the golf course were imposed in 1932, forbidding walking or riding which would cause damage to the greens and fairways.[72] At Crowborough, public access was confirmed in 1936, when the club issued a deed of declaration under the terms of the Law of Property Act 1925 to allow the public to take 'air and exercise' on the common, but the inherent conflict between golfing and other uses of common land, specifically questions of liability for injuries to members of the public, resulted in the club revoking the agreement in 2013.[73] Tensions between golfing and public access to common land thus rumble on.

* * *

---

[67] The legal tussles behind the transfer of the turbary commons are outlined in Eversley, pp. 270–1.
[68] T. Burton-Page, 'Bournemouth's biggest garden', *Dorset Life* (February 2017).
[69] https://merrowresidents.org.uk/merrow-downs.
[70] *Contested Common Land*, p. 167.
[71] Hoskins & Stamp, pp. 155, 284, 325; https://www.cbgc.co.uk/history; https://www.ssgolfclub.com/clubhouse/history/.
[72] https://merrowresidents.org.uk/merrow-downs.
[73] https://www.crowboroughcommon.org/history.

One theme which has run through this discussion of the changing face of commons across Britain since the later nineteenth century has been an evolving debate about how 'wild' common land should be. On upland commons this has played out in attempts to negotiate sustainable levels of use between the extremes of overgrazing and 're-wilding'; on lowland commons in attempts to reintroduce active use and management of common land to achieve conservation and recreational ends; on urban commons, a general acceptance that the land itself should be, to some degree, taken in hand and that its uses should be decorous and free from the wild, plebeian lack of control viewed as a problem on town commons before the late-Victorian decades. The degree of direct human intervention in the landscape of commons has thus varied widely. Common grazings in the Highlands of Scotland and upland grazing commons in northern England and Wales appear on the surface to remain 'natural', perhaps more than 'half-wild'. On many lowland commons in England the hand of conservation management is more obvious; these commons possess an air of self-conscious half-wildness, with paths and cleared spaces, and sometimes of wildlife parks with exotic rare breeds. Some town commons are green spaces of managed part-wildness, while others have become more fully domesticated, as municipal gardens.

PART II: A KALEIDOSCOPE OF COMMON LANDSCAPES: EIGHT CASE STUDIES

The following brief cameos aim to illustrate some of the themes introduced in the preceding chapters by sketching the history of individual commons, focusing on their management and the evolution of their landscapes since the early modern period. They have been chosen to illustrate the diversity of common land in Britain, both environmental (rural and urban, mountain, heathland, scrub and wetland) and institutional (from different forms of statutory regulation to what almost amounted to a free for all), and include crofters' common grazings in Sutherland, mountain commons in the Lake District and Snowdonia, lowland commons in Co. Durham, Herefordshire and the New Forest, turbary allotments in Lincolnshire, and Wimbledon Common, the urban common which played a key role in the history of metropolitan common land. The case studies (see Figure 41) are arranged broadly geographically, from north to south.

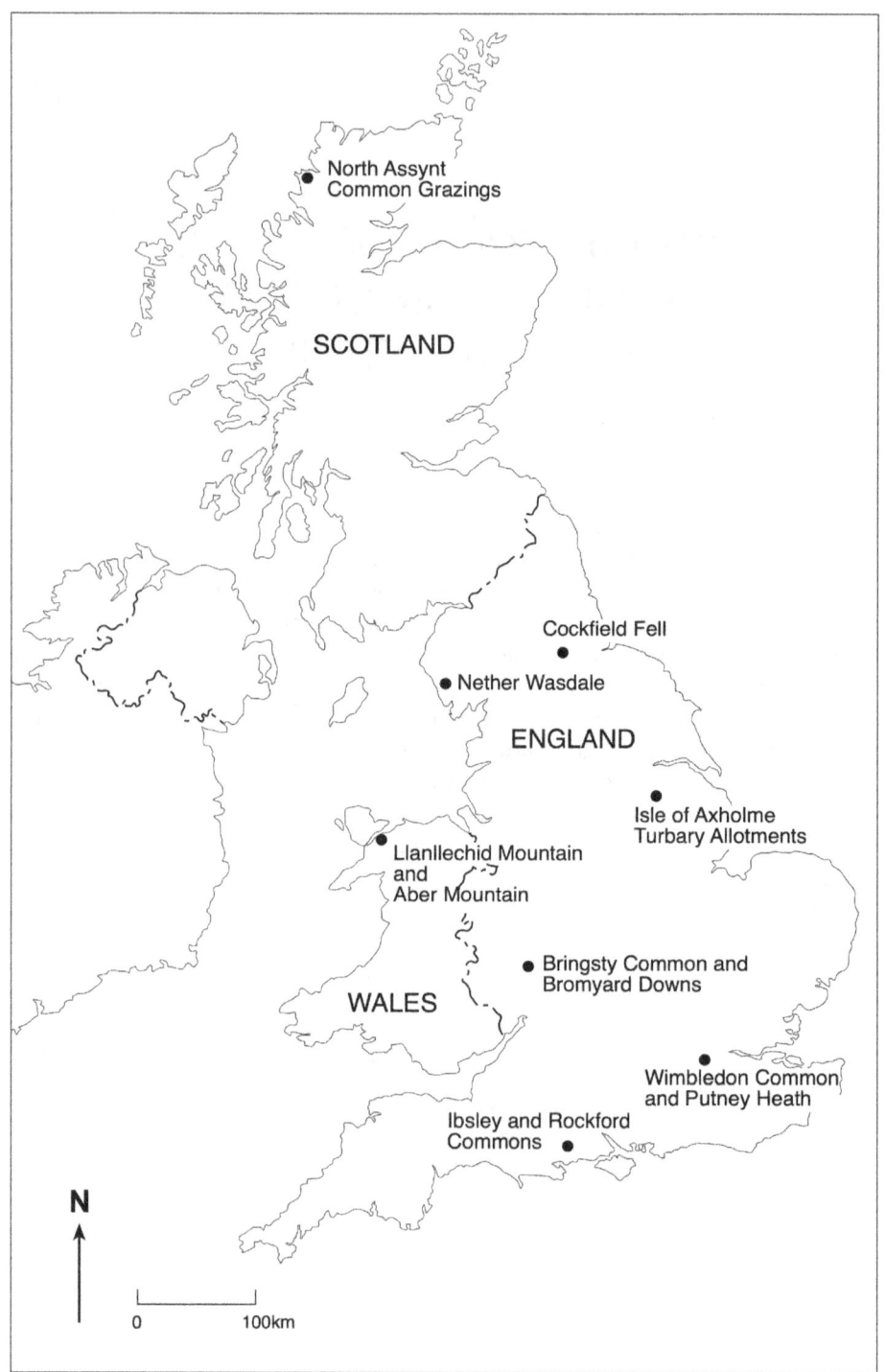

Figure 41. Location of case study commons.

CHAPTER 9

NORTH ASSYNT COMMON GRAZINGS, SUTHERLAND

Crofting Register Common Grazing numbers: Clachtoll (CG 232); Stoer and Balchladich (CG 118); Clashmore and Raffin (CG 186); Culkein (CG 87); Achnacarnan (CG 103); Clashnessie (CG 235); Culkein Drumbeg (CG 90); Drumbeg (CG 89); Nedd (CG 150).

THIS GROUP OF NINE contiguous common grazings belonging to crofting townships along the coast north of Lochinver, in the north-west Highlands of Scotland, was part of the Dukes of Sutherland's vast estates from 1757 until 1913. Most of the grazings consist of an ice-scoured plateau at around 100–150m above sea level, containing rocky knolls and wet depressions with countless lochans, typical of the 'cnockan and lochan' landscapes underlain by Lewisian gneiss (Figure 42). The Stoer peninsula, on the ancient Torridon sandstone, is gentler and smoother, but more exposed, ground. Surveying the Assynt estate in 1774, John Home sketched pithy pen portraits of the pastures. Those belonging to Clachtoll were 'Rugged rocky Hills interspersed with patches of Moss mostly coverd with Heath including Braes, Dens and hollow Slacks yielding grassy pasture with meadow Grass along the Burns'.[1]

Home's survey enables the boundaries of the modern common grazings to be compared with those of their eighteenth-century precursors (Figure 43). In 1774 the land was parcelled out between eleven farms, most in shared tenancies and containing multiple households (twenty in the most populous farm, Clashnessie). At Stoer, where there were fourteen families, the rent was divided between eleven of the tenants, for example.[2] Each farm was centred on small areas of ploughland around the settlements near the coast and there were smaller cultivated patches at shieling sites scattered across the farms' territories. The bulk of each farm consisted of the open grazings – 'Hills, Moss and rocky Muirish Pasture' in Home's shorthand description – shared by the tenants of the farm. This, and patches of natural woodland also used as grazing ground, accounted for the overwhelming majority (on average 84 per cent) of each farm's territory.[3]

---

[1] R. J. Adam (ed.), *John Home's Survey of Assynt*, Scottish History Society, 3rd ser. LII (Edinburgh, 1960), p. 12.
[2] Ibid., pp. l, 68–9.
[3] Ibid., pp. 5–6, 10–21, 39–45. The proportions (excluding the acreage accounted for by lochs) ranged from 74 per cent at Balchladich to 91 per cent at Nedd and Oldany.

Figure 42. Stoer common grazing, Assynt, Sutherland. 'Cnockan and lochan' landscape, looking east towards the mountains of Assynt.

From the late eighteenth century, the conversion of inland farms into large-scale sheep ranches and the consequent removal of sub-tenants from them, led to migration to the coastal townships where livings could be supplemented by fishing. By the 1840s the townships of northern Assynt were congested and the estate factors sought to ease pressure by sponsoring emigration and reorganising the townships into crofts.[4] Congestion persisted, however, the common grazings often becoming overstocked and settled by landless cottars, so that land hunger in the crofting districts became a major issue by the 1880s. A 'bitter history' unfolded in Assynt, centred on Clashmore on the Stoer peninsula, where the estate's removal of tenants in order to reclaim land for a model farm in the 1870s led to confrontations and unrest, culminating in dyke-breaking in 1887–88.[5] The crofters' agitation for more land ultimately proved successful, when they were awarded enlargements to their common grazings in 1888 under the terms of the crofting legislation of 1886.

Although parts of the framework of eighteenth-century farm boundaries across the wild hills and mosses are still visible in the map of modern common grazings, the

---

[4] M. Bangor-Jones, 'Settlement history of Assynt, Sutherland', in J. A. Atkinson, I. Banks and G. MacGregor (eds), *Townships to Farmsteads: Rural Settlement Studies in Scotland, England and Wales*, British Archaeological Reports, British Ser. 293 (Oxford, 2000), pp. 211–26.

[5] A. Tindley, *The Sutherland Estate, 1850–1920: Aristocratic Decline, Estate Management and Land Reform* (Edinburgh, 2010), pp. 140–66.

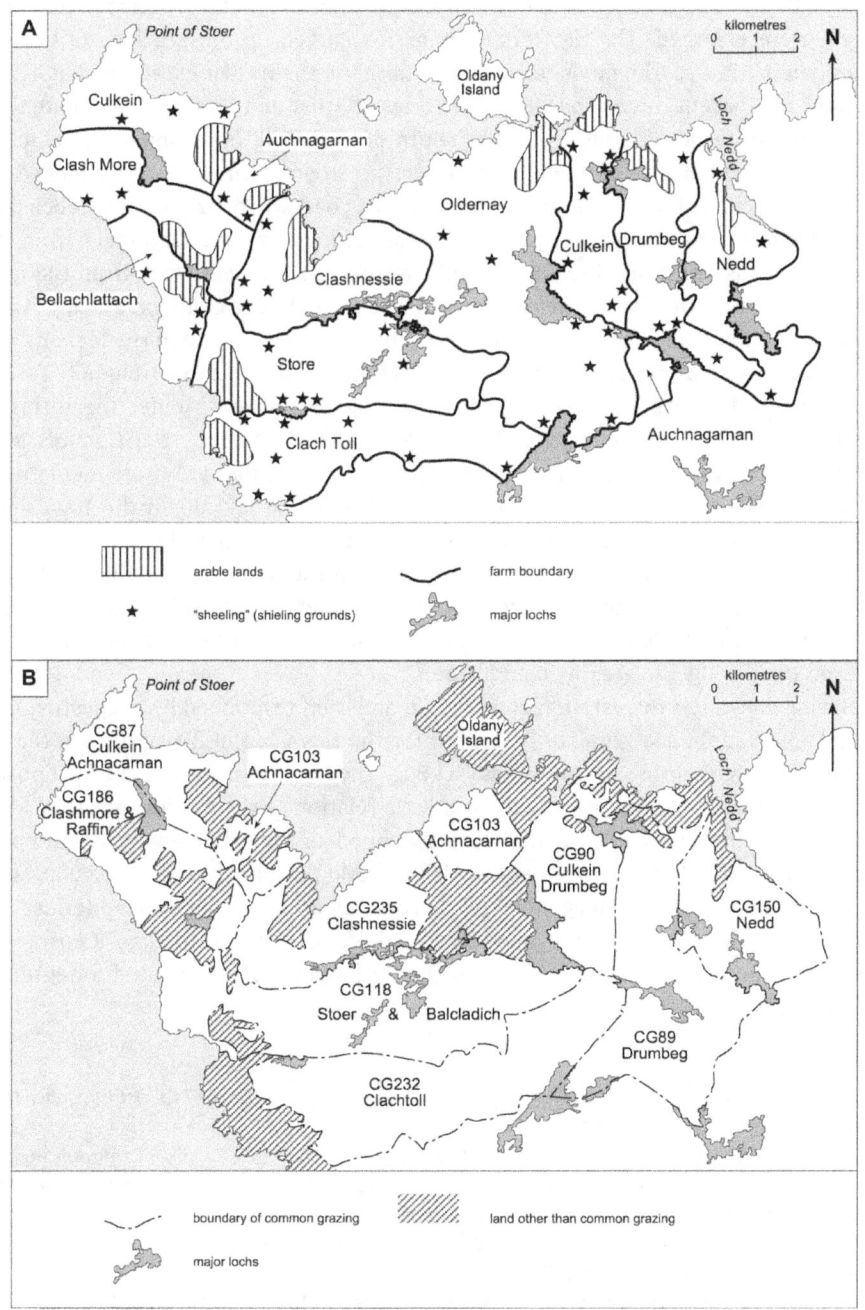

Figure 43. North Assynt, Sutherland: (A) farm boundaries, cultivated areas and shieling grounds recorded on John Home's survey of 1774; (B) boundaries of the modern common grazings attached to each crofting township.

modern boundaries date from 1888 when the grazings of most townships in northern Assynt were enlarged. The Crofters Commission carved up the grazings of Oldany, described in 1774 as 'the most commodious farm' on the Assynt estate, and assigned sections to adjacent townships.[6] The territories of Stoer and Clachtoll were extended eastwards to include Oldany's grazings south of Loch Poll, for example. A detached shieling ground belonging to Achnacarnan on the Stoer peninsula was exchanged for another detached block of common grazing on the coast which had formerly been part of Oldany farm. Drumbeg township gained part of its grazing enlargement from the lands of the distant farm of Achmore, while Nedd's enlargement came from the farm of Ardvar. Parts of the boundaries between the newly enlarged common grazings were demarcated physically, by wire-fenced march dykes running between the lochans.[7]

The new framework laid out by the Crofters Commission was the prelude to formal regulation and management by township grazing committees, under the terms of the Common Grazings Regulation Act of 1891, administered by the Commission.[8] In 1898, Nedd was the first township in the area to bring forward draft regulations, their proposals being limited to five brief clauses. These laid down the township's souming in relation to the rent paid; spelt out sums to be paid by other livestock on the common grazing (16s yearly per horse, with the horses 'belonging to distant Townships habitually on our Grazing' charged 20s; and 'Overstock' at the rate of 10s for each cow and 2s 0d for each sheep); and required cottars to cut peat only where allowed to do so by the grazing committee.[9]

Having consulted the estate factor, the Commission responded by suggesting that Nedd should adopt the regulations agreed for the township of Blairmore, on the far side of the neighbouring parish of Eddrachillis. They replaced the crofters' proposals with a set of nine regulations, which bore little relation to the original proposals and became the core of a common set of rules applied to the other townships in north Assynt from 1910.[10] The decades either side of 1900 not only saw the formulation of rules providing for close management of the common grazings, but also modernisation of their infrastructure by building new peat roads, fences and sheep dips.[11] Centralised control by the Crofters Commission and the Sutherland Estate ensured a degree of uniformity in the management of the grazings.[12]

---

[6] *Report of the Crofters Commission ... for the period from 10th December 1887 to 31st December 1888* [C.5634], pp. 133–40, HC (1889), vol. LX.

[7] As required by the Commission: *Report of Crofters Commission 1887–88*, p. xi. Examples include the dykes linking the lochans south from Gorm Loch Mor and north from Loch Crocach: OS Six-Inch maps, Sutherland 58 and 59, 1903 revision.

[8] Crofters Common Grazings Regulation Act 1891 (54 & 55 Victoria, c.41).

[9] Scottish Land Court, RN 913, p. 2.

[10] Ibid., pp. 5-6. They differed in omitting clauses 4, 6, 9 and 10 of the 1910 regulatory template.

[11] NRS, AF 42/1705, AF 42/4665, AF 42/6787: peat roads, Drumbeg (1903), Clachtoll (1908–09), Clashnessie (1909); AF42/2672: dipping tank for townships of Clashmore, Raffin, Culkein, Achnacarnan (1905).

[12] The following account is based on grazing regulations, 1898–1933, in Scottish Land Court, RN 913 (Nedd), RN 996 (Stoer), RN 1001 (Culkein Drumbeg), RN 1002 (Drumbeg), RN 1003

Although the 1910 regulations differed slightly between the townships, they provided a common framework under ten headings:

1. The souming for each share of the township's common grazings was spelt out in numbers of sheep, with a standard set of equivalents: a horse for eight sheep; a cow for five sheep. Horses were only to be grazed by substituting them for part of a crofter's entitlement to graze cattle or sheep.
2. If a crofter were unable to maintain his full soum, the grazing committee could grant permission to other crofters to graze excess stock, on payment of a sum which would be paid over to the 'undersoumed' crofter.
3. The grazing committee had power to engage herds or shepherds to manage stock on the common grazing and to levy the herds' wages from the crofters.
4. Souming was to be adjusted annually in November for winter grazing on the crofts. No horses or sheep were to be kept on land within the township dykes between seedtime and harvest and all sheep were to be removed from the crofts each spring on a date to be fixed by the committee.
5. The committee were to fix dates of gatherings, for marking, clipping, weaning and dipping. No crofter was to gather stock on the grazings except on those dates.
6. The committee were to have the 'entire management' of bulls and tups (rams) to service the township's stock, with liberty to buy and sell them. Crofters were only to keep tups approved by the committee.
7. The committee were to ensure that the crofters kept dykes, fences and drains in repair.
8. Newly opened peat banks were to have a minimum breadth of 3 feet, with a free outlet for water, and peat was to be cut 'in a regular manner', leaving an even bed and replacing the turf, sward uppermost.
9. Heather burning was to be regulated by the committee and the estate factor.
10. No one was to disturb stock on the common grazing and no one but the shepherd was to take a dog onto the common except on gathering days.

The 1910 suite of regulations provided a template which, with some tweaking, continued to govern the use of the common grazings across the twentieth century, as revised rules were confirmed in 1933, 1958 and between 1988 and 2001. Some additional clauses were added. In 1911–12 the grazing committees were made responsible for ensuring that government sheep dipping requirements were upheld, and were empowered to raise funds for necessary expenditure from the crofters.[13] The 1933 regulations ordered stock to be delivered annually to the committee for counting, required animals on the common grazings to be marked to show ownership and the committee to keep a register of marks, and ordered that young cattle and

---

(Clachtoll), RN 1004 (Clashmore), RN 1009 (Culkein Achnacarnan), RN 1015 (Balchladich) and RN 1211 (Clashnessie); and Crofting Commission grazing regulations for Assynt townships, 1958, 1988–2001.

[13] Scottish Land Court, RN 996, RN 1009, RN 1015.

horses not required for work were to be kept on the common grazings in summer and autumn. They also contained new provisions suggesting that the crofts' inbye land was increasingly being used as enclosed pasture. Cattle, sheep and lambs which could not be kept on the common grazings 'by ordinary herding' were to be kept on the crofts, and a crofter who wished to reserve the whole of his croft for his sole use across the winter months was entitled to do so, subject to certain conditions.

Table 2. North Assynt common grazings.

Township	Original common grazing			Grazing enlargement		
	Extent	No. of shares	Soum	Extent	No. of shares	Soum
Clachtoll	691 ha	29	19 sheep/share	318 ha	20	8 sheep/share
Stoer & Balcladich	537 ha	20	25 sheep/share	206 ha	19	11 sheep/share
Clashmore & Raffin	443 ha	26	16 sheep/share	42 ha*	21	*
Culkein	344 ha	25	9 sheep/share	25 ha*	15	*
Achnacarnan	132 ha	15	10 sheep/share	232 ha	15	12 sheep/share
Clashnessie	432 ha	21	23 sheep/share	124 ha	20	5 sheep/share
Culkein Drumbeg	373 ha	19	16 sheep/share	103 ha	16	5 sheep/share
Drumbeg	504 ha	20	17 sheep/share	448 ha	16	13 sheep/share
Nedd	328 ha	15	20 sheep/share	176 ha	13	10 sheep/share

* Grazing enlargements at Clashmore & Raffin consist of three enclosed parcels only one of which (24 ha) is soumed, at the rate of one sheep/share; that at Culkein consists of five arable enclosures and 12 ha of enclosed outrun, which is not soumed.
Source: Scottish Land Court and Crofting Commission, Common Grazings Regulations, 1933–2001.

The first clause in each set of township regulations spelt out the souming rates, both on the original township grazings and on the grazing enlargements granted in 1888 (see Table 2). Soums were expressed in numbers of sheep per share, the standard equivalency formulae laid down in 1910 being applied. The enlargements could not be fully integrated into the township's common grazings, as in most cases not all crofters had applied for shares in them, so the number of shares was less than on the core of the grazings. The soums, which had become fixed by 1933, gave stocking rates typically of a little over one sheep per hectare (mean: 1.31).

The basis of souming and the appropriate souming rates evolved across the early twentieth century. The crofters initially expressed soums in a variety of forms. The more western townships of Clachtoll, Balchladich and Clashmore specified a number of animals 'for each croft' in their regulations of 1910 (the implicit assumption being that each croft constituted an equal share of the grazings, which became increasingly inaccurate as crofts were amalgamated or divided). By contrast, from Clashnessie eastwards the soum was determined by the rent paid for the croft, expressed as 8 sheep per £1 rent and 2 cows per full croft at Culkein Drumbeg and Drumbeg, for example. By 1933 all the soums were expressed as sheep per share. In some townships the soums fixed then differed from earlier soumings. At Clachtoll the soum was 30 sheep per share on the original township grazing and 6 per share on the enlargement in 1928 but 22 and 8 sheep per share respectively in 1933. At Clashnessie, a soum of 26 sheep per share in 1928 had been reduced to 20 in 1933 but was then revised upwards to 23 sheep per share a few months later after representations by the crofters. The Commission commented that the revised souming was 'a very full one'.

Across the second half of the twentieth century, the changing use of the Assynt common grazings reflected aspects of the profound socio-economic upheaval seen in the crofting areas more generally: a steep fall in the resident population (Assynt's population halved between 1931 and 1951); the end of the traditional crofting economy, as arable cultivation ceased and cattle were replaced by sheep; a reduction in the number of active graziers and of communal traditional management, such as the systematic muirburn of heather and bracken; and the decline of peat-cutting, almost to extinction, from the 1960s.[14]

In 1993 the North Assynt estate was bought by the crofting community and vested in the Assynt Crofters' Trust.[15] The Trust's policies affected the common grazings, as they sought to diversify the economic benefit to be derived from them, by increasing income from tourism (notably loch fishing) and by embarking on woodland planting and a hydro-electric scheme. Under the terms of the Crofter Forestry (Scotland) Act 1991, 794 ha of native woodland had been planted by 2001, most of it on the common grazings, in schemes promoted by individual townships through their grazing committees. The hydro-electric scheme at Loch Poll, capturing water from the inland lochans, began to generate electricity in 2000.[16] This further modified the face of the common grazings at a time when the number of livestock using them was declining.

As with common land across Britain, the common grazings in Assynt are now valued as a national resource, both as recreational space, especially for hill walking

---

[14] I. MacPhail, 'Land, crofting and the Assynt Crofters Trust: a post-colonial geography?' (PhD thesis, University of Wales, Lampeter, 2002), pp. 94–7; information from Carol MacRae, Clachtoll (2021).

[15] The process is charted in detail in MacPhail, 'Land, crofting and the Assynt Crofters Trust', pp. 251–396.

[16] Ibid., pp. 441–515 *passim*.

and fishing, and for their conservation value. Loch Poll and Gorm Loch Mor are among the seven lochs forming the Assynt Lochs SSSI.[17] In recent years, threats to the ecology of the grazings have included the impact of uncontrolled muirburns on vegetation, especially juniper woodland, and of deer numbers on woodland regeneration.[18]

---

[17] Assynt Lochs SSSI: Scottish Natural Heritage Site Code 1713.

[18] For the impact of muirburns, see https://www.assyntwildlife.org.uk/assynt-wildlife-publications-list/assynt-muirburn-project/; for tensions between the Assynt Crofters' Trust and Scottish Natural Heritage over proposed culling of deer, see R. Mackay and V. Clements, 'SNH must heed the lessons of Assynt', *Am Bratach*, 318 (April 2018), pp. 6–7.

CHAPTER 10
NETHER WASDALE COMMON, CUMBERLAND

Cumberland CL 59.

THE FELL COMMON AT Nether Wasdale, a scattered hill farming community on marginal land on the western edge of the Lake District, provides an example of an upland grazing common which continued to be managed by a manor court until the 1930s. Nether Wasdale Common (Figures 44 and 45), covering 4,994 acres (2,021 ha) and accounting for 58 per cent of the land surface of the civil parish, consists of rough, mountainous ground carrying acidic soils on the volcanic rocks of the central Lake District. It rises steeply from the northern shore of Wast Water, stretching back into the higher fells to the summit of Haycock (797m) on the watershed with Ennerdale. The common includes the remote Stockdale valley, drained by the upper reaches of the River Bleng. Its resources were those typical of commons on the Lake District fells: grazing (summer pasture for cattle; year-round grazing for heafed Herdwick sheep); bracken, cut under the common right of estovers (which remained important until the twentieth century); and peat for fuel.

Nether Wasdale was part of the private forest of Copeland, belonging to the medieval barony of Egremont. When the forest was partitioned between heiresses in 1338, Nether Wasdale became part of the 'Middleward', along with the township of Kinniside and the wastes of Stockdale Moor, a seigniorial agistment ground lying between them, over which both townships possessed grazing rights. Nether Wasdale Common was bounded on the east by the 'deer fence' of Bowderdale, a section of the fells retained as private pasture by the lords of the barony, which had been enclosed by the 1540s.[1] Nether Wasdale descended as part of the Percy estates in western Cumberland to the Wyndham family, later Lords Leconfield and Egremont. In 1979 the common, along with the estate's other Lake District commons, passed to the National Trust in lieu of death duties.

In 1578 the forty-three holdings in Nether Wasdale each had appurtenant rights to 'sufficient common' on the fell. Three individuals living outside the manor, in neighbouring lowland communities, also had grazing rights, termed 'greslands', each of which gave the right to graze a fixed number of livestock (four, five or six beasts)

---

[1] A. J. L. Winchester, *Landscape and Society in Medieval Cumbria* (Edinburgh, 1987), pp. 84, 91; *Harvest*, pp. 22, 96–7.

Figure 44. Herdwick sheep on Nether Wasdale Common, Cumberland. The common extends back into the fells behind the craggy face of Buckbarrow.

on the common.[2] Like the agistment ground of Stockdale Moor, these rights in gross gave lowland farms access to summer grazing on the fells.

The 'greslands' were stinted rights and there are hints that stinting might have applied more generally at an early date. In 1547, each holding in Nether Wasdale was recorded in terms of a small acreage of land with pasture for a defined number of cattle, typically between three and six.[3] In 1578, one tenant who held a 'decayed toft' in addition to his farm had a stinted grazing right of four 'beastgates' which had been attached to the toft.[4] However, by the later sixteenth century, the grazing rights appear otherwise to have been governed by the rule of levancy and couchancy. The non-specific phrase 'sufficient common', used to describe the rights in 1578, implies that they were based on the rule, as does a regulation recorded in 1679, that any tenant in Nether Wasdale 'that tooke any goods [i.e. livestock] to couch upon the Common but what hee cold make apeare' was subject to a penalty of 6s 8d. The implication is that he had to show ('make apeare') the number of animals he had kept over the winter.

---

[2] Cockermouth Castle Muniments (formerly CAS, DLEC; hereafter 'CCM'), box 301, Percy Survey, Nether Wasdale.
[3] CCM, box 314/38.
[4] CCM, box 301, Percy Survey.

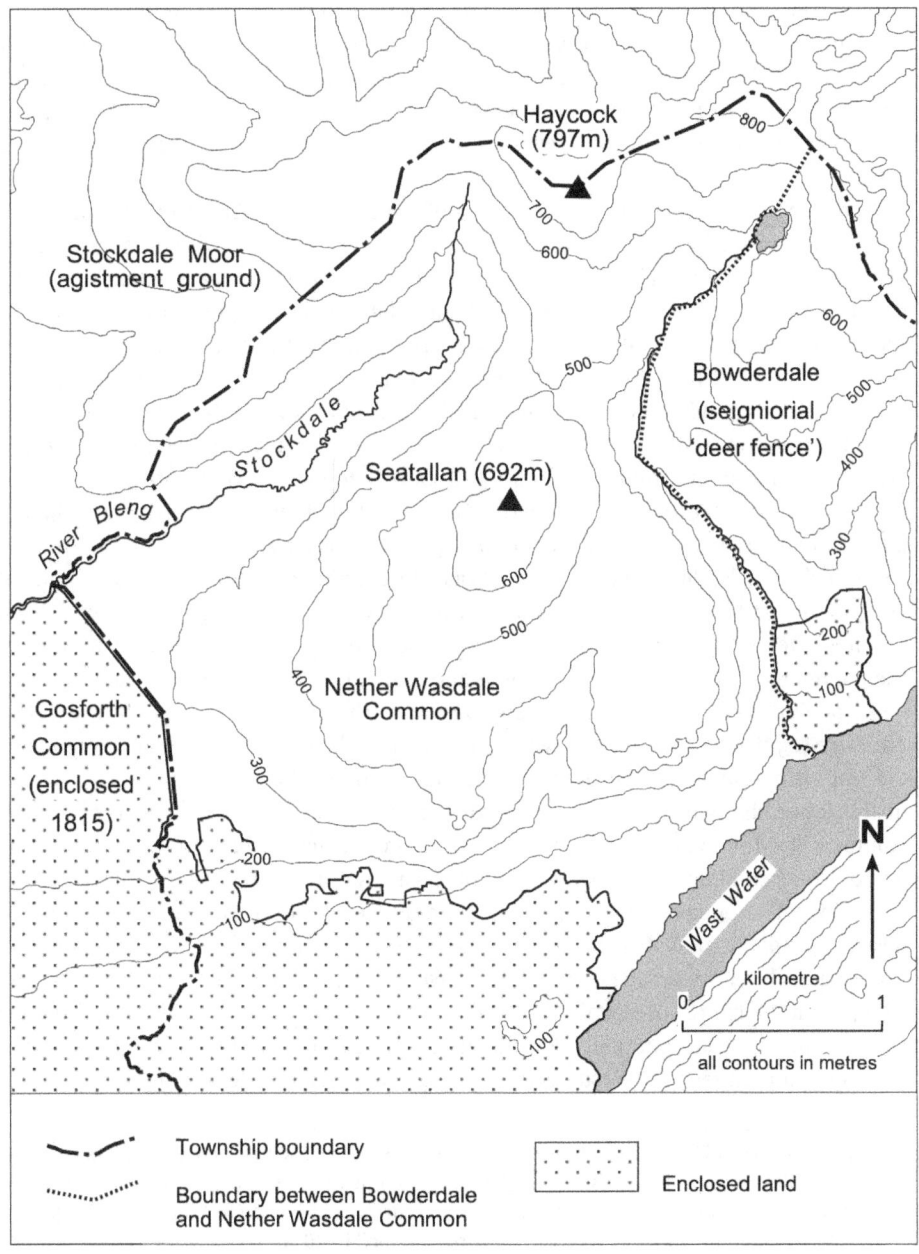

Figure 45. Nether Wasdale Common.

Use of the common was regulated by a manor court, usually meeting twice a year in spring and autumn until 1750 and once a year in spring thereafter. A set of rules ('good and ancient Customes … duely observed and performed by our ancient prede[ce]ssers') was put in writing in 1679 and surviving records preserve orders made by the court through to 1931. Original verdict sheets survive until 1858, later minutes of the court being entered into the back of the township vestry book from 1841 to 1898 and then, until 1931, in a new court book, which was retained locally, rather than in the estate office.[5]

Managing grazing rights occupied much of the court's time. Securing the common's boundaries with adjacent grazing grounds and preventing encroachments by 'foreign' livestock were perennial problems. The earliest surviving court record, for 1595, included the presentment of a Nether Wasdale farmer for bringing foreign oxen into the township and a slanderous complaint that men gathering stock from Nether Wasdale Common had driven cattle off the neighbouring Gosforth Common.[6] The eastern boundary with the leased-out fells belonging to Bowderdale was also porous, complaints being made in 1729 that forty or fifty sheep regularly escaped onto Nether Wasdale Common and that, in winter, 400–500 sheep trespassed onto the common when snow drove them off the higher fells in High Bowderdale.[7] Encroachments by livestock from neighbouring commons persisted even after other commons had been enclosed, leading eleven Nether Wasdale commoners to enter into a bond of association in the early nineteenth century to defend their rights against illegal grazing.[8] Defective boundaries along the enclosures adjoining the western edge of the common continued to exercise the manor court in the twentieth century.[9]

Managing legal grazing rights also consumed the court's energies. By the 1760s effective regulation appears to have been creaking. The rule of levancy and couchancy did not sit happily with the practice of sending young sheep to winter on pastures in the lowlands, which technically broke the rule when they were returned to the common the following spring. In 1763 the manor court forbade any tenant in the manor from sending sheep away to winter and reiterated the rule of levancy and couchancy. The penalty of 39s 11d (at the highest level that most manor courts could impose) probably indicates the seriousness with which the jury viewed the problem. An apparently abortive attempt to introduce stinting seems to have been made in 1769, when the court ordered that no tenant was to put more than twenty sheep to the common for every 6d rent paid.[10] By the nineteenth century the high numbers of sheep grazing common land in Wasdale were recognised as a problem, one commentator

---

[5] Verdict sheets 1679–1858 are in CCM, box 94. The vestry book is recorded in a newspaper report (*West Cumberland Times*, 13 April 1895, p. 3) but its subsequent history has not been traced. Nether Wasdale Court Book, 1899–1931, survives in private hands; a digital copy was kindly provided by the clerk to Wasdale parish council in 2021.
[6] CCM, box 299/27, Nether Wasdale court, 23 July 37 Elizabeth.
[7] CCM, box 94, petitions, Anthony Gunson against Henry Viccars, 1729.
[8] CCM, box 94, miscellaneous file, undated agreement [post-1794].
[9] Nether Wasdale Court Book 1899–1931, 26 May 1921, 3 June 1926, 8 June 1931.
[10] CCM, box 94, Nether Wasdale court verdict, 1769.

claiming that 'many Tenements in Nether Wasdale turn out many more sheep to the fell than they can possibly winter at home'.[11] Here, as elsewhere in Cumbria, the manor court appears to have struggled to prevent overgrazing.

Limiting the numbers grazing the common was only one aspect of the management of pasture rights. The rules put down in writing by the manor court at Nether Wasdale in 1679 were typical of those employed in the uplands to foster 'good neighbourhood' on the shared resources of the fells. They included detailed herding regulations:

- 7^{ly} if any tenant doe keep any unlawfull cure [*i.e. cur*] that is to byte mens [goods] or to take life from them haveinge warrninge to put the cure away and doe not is to be fined & to make sattisfaction to the suferer

- 8^{ly} if any tenant take any mo[r]e goods to the pasture then is right hee is to be fined vi^s viii^d neither ought any tenant to take any goods to couch or stafeheird upon the pastur upon the like paine

- 9^{ly} if any tenant to hounde and beat of goods from his sheep heafe unto anoether mans hee is to be fined vi^s viii^d for every default

- 10^{ly} if any tenant doe couch or heafe any sheep but in his heafe belonginge to his tenement hee is fineable

- 11^{ly} if any tenant doe drive his sheep through anoether mans sheepp heafe hee is fineable

- 12^{ly} if any tenant bringe downe thire sheep into anoether mans downefall but by strise [*i.e. stress*] of weather they or hee are to be fined and the[y] are to carrie them back againe as the snowe thawes and to followe it upon the like paine of vi^s viii^d every default.[12]

The communal basis of the exercise of rights was reinforced by the requirement that all rams were to be removed from the common by St Luke's Day (18 October), to control the timing of lambing, and that each commoner was to send a man to drive the common each September when all livestock grazing there were gathered in and any 'foreign' livestock were impounded in the manorial pinfold.[13] The annual 'drift' of the common in September continued into the twentieth century, the appointment of able-bodied men to carry it out being one of the few recurring items of business in the final decades of the court.[14]

---

[11] TNA, IR18/716, question 11; E. A. Straughton, *Common Grazing in the Northern English Uplands, 1800–1965* (Lampeter, 2008), p. 120.

[12] CCM, box 94, Nether Wasdale byelaws, 29 September 1679.

[13] Ibid.

[14] Nether Wasdale Court Book 1899–1931. For much of the nineteenth century, the date nominated for driving the common was 19 September, probably representing 'Lady Day in Harvest' (8 September), 'old style' (i.e. pre-1752 calendar change), suggesting that it had coincided with the annual drift of Stockdale Moor which took place then: CCM, box 94, Nether Wasdale verdicts, 7 May 1811, 9 May 1857; *West Cumberland Times*, 13 April 1895, p. 3. For Stockdale Moor, see *Harvest*, p. 96. The date of the Nether Wasdale drift had changed

As on other Lake District commons, each farm in Nether Wasdale had its own heaf on the fells as the grazing ground for its flock and a specified route (or 'downfall') along which to drive sheep to and from the heaf, fragmenting the common into areas assigned to individual farms. In cases of dispute, the court would reiterate the location of a holding's heaf, as in 1733, when it recorded, 'We find Gailsick Tenement Heave in Midlefell betwen Standey Gill and Great Riggfoot. Wee find Strands Tenement Heave to be in the Low Birck Cragg.'[15] As late as 1912, the court's concern over 'trespass of sheep' on the common may have related to a breakdown in heafing: it ordered those driving the common that year to 'take particular notice whether any sheep in undue numbers were found off their proper heath'.[16]

As well as the sheep heafs, one section of the common, the Stockdale valley, was reserved for cattle during summer months – they had to be brought down to land closer to the farms by Michaelmas (29 September) and were not to be kept on a farm's sheep heaf across autumn and winter.[17] The court also attempted to control the exploitation of bracken, in 1746 forbidding the mowing and burning of bracken before 12 September. This was later amended, by an order repeated annually from 1843 to 1845, that no bracken was to be cut before 1 September.[18]

How the common was managed in the decades after 1931, when the court book ends, has not been ascertained. A commoners' association was founded in 1985, the year that part of the common was notified as an SSSI, which suggests that its foundation may have been prompted by the need for a corporate voice when communicating with government agencies.[19]

Under the Commons Registration Act 1965, initial registrations were made by eighteen rights holders, grazing rights being registered for 8,535 sheep or equivalents. The equivalency formulae varied but were typically 9 sheep rights for a mare and foal, 6 for a horse, 6 for a cow and calf, 4 for a cow, stirk or bullock, and 2 geese for a sheep right. There were also 13 registrations of rights to estovers (or bracken); 9 for taking stone and 5 for turbary (or turves).[20] Later amendments to the register reflect attempts to reduce grazing pressure. In 1999 and 2002 the Countryside Commission and the National Trust severed a total of 841 sheep rights from the land to which they had been attached, converting them into rights in gross and, in effect, preventing them from being exercised.[21]

As elsewhere in the Lake District fells, agri-environmental schemes reduced stocking rates on Nether Wasdale Common in the early twenty-first century. The common entered a ten-year Environmentally Sensitive Area (ESA) agreement in 2001,

---

to 20 September by 1896; in 1915 it was changed to 18 September and in 1928 to 'some day' between 18 and 25 September.

[15] CCM, box 94, Nether Wasdale verdict, 18 April 1733.
[16] Nether Wasdale Court Book 1899–1931, 23 May 1912.
[17] CCM, box 94, Nether Wasdale byelaws, 29 September 1679; order, 23 October 1749.
[18] Ibid., 2 April 1746, 6 May 1843. The order was repeated later, in the court records preserved in the vestry book covering the years 1845–94: *West Cumberland Times*, 13 April 1895, p. 3.
[19] Information from David Diamond and Julius Manduell, Nether Wasdale Commoners (2021).
[20] Commons Register, Cumberland CL 59, rights section, entries 1–18.
[21] Ibid., entries 26, 28.

which capped livestock numbers at 1.5 ewes/hectare, giving a notional limit of 3,190 ewes, though actual sheep numbers were higher, as they included perhaps 2,000 younger sheep. When the ESA agreement expired in 2011, the common was placed in a Higher Level Stewardship scheme, which reduced stocking levels further (to a maximum of 1.2 ewes/hectare) and also re-introduced some cattle grazing and tree planting on four small areas on the edges of the common.[22] As on other upland grazing commons, national conservation priorities now steer the management of Nether Wasdale Common.

---

[22] Information from Simon Webb, Natural England (2021).

CHAPTER 11
COCKFIELD FELL, CO. DURHAM

Co. Durham CL 8.

COCKFIELD FELL COMPRISES 557 acres (225 ha) of open pasture on the eastern flanks of the north Pennines at around 250m above sea level. Heavily scarred by industry, it remains an actively grazed stinted pasture, managed by field reeves under the terms of the Inclosure Act 1845. The common is remarkable for its palimpsest of relict features, not only a rich legacy of industrial archaeology but also at least three banked and ditched enclosures, probably of Romano-British date. A striking aerial photograph, taken in low light in November 1971, revealed the full complexity of the multi-period landscape of the fell. Its publication by Brian Roberts in 1975 ultimately resulted in the bulk of the common being scheduled as an ancient monument, said to be the largest scheduled monument in England.[1]

The common consists of a stretch of grassland with patches of bracken and gorse, sloping north from the village of Cockfield down to the River Gaunless which forms the parish boundary. It is underlain by Carboniferous coal measures, capped by glacial till, but much of the surface is disturbed ground, the grassed-over legacy of the fell's industrial past. Industrial remains are numerous and various (Figures 47 and 48). Coal-mining, recorded from the fourteenth century, has left the common pockmarked by collapsed shafts and subsidence, ranging from shallow bell-pits, where a seam outcropped at the western end of the common, to the heads of the deeper shafts of nineteenth-century collieries. Several sandstone quarries had been opened by the 1850s, while the most dominant landscape feature, the long, deep quarry trench (now largely filled in) following the igneous intrusion of 'whinstone' and its associated spoil heaps, dates from the later nineteenth century.[2] Other sites of extractive industry on the common included a coke oven and brickworks, one recorded in 1811, a second by 1857.[3] Associated with the industrial exploitation of the fell are the remains of the

---

[1] B. K. Roberts, 'Cockfield Fell', *Antiquity*, 49 (193) (1975), pp. 48–50; HLE, no. 1002314. I should like to record my thanks to Brian Roberts for the loan of a photocopy of the memoranda book of the Cockfield Field Reeves, 1857–1944 (hereafter 'Cockfield Stint Bk'), without which this account could not have been compiled. The copy is now in Durham Record Office, D/X 2117 (add.) (accession no. 10434).

[2] OS Six-Inch maps, Durham 41 (surveyed 1857) and 41SE (revised 1896). Quarrying whinstone may have begun in the 1860s: the 'Blue Stone' quarry on Cockfield Fell was to be let from 1865: *Durham County Advertiser*, 11 November 1864.

[3] Roberts, 'Cockfield Fell', p. 49; OS Six-Inch map, Durham 41 (surveyed 1857).

Figure 46. Cockfield Fell, Co. Durham. Hen houses and pigeon lofts on the common close to the village. Taken during the closed month of April when all livestock are removed from the common. On the right is the fenced-off air shaft of a nineteenth-century colliery.

Bishop Auckland, Haggerleases & Barnard Castle branch of the North-Eastern Railway, opened in 1863, with a station on the common, a series of tramways, and rows of cottages at the railway station and beside one of the tramways at Fell Houses. Most of the industrial activity had ceased by the time of the First World War, though the whinstone quarry and a couple of collieries continued to operate.[4] The fell was being used as a convenient dumping ground for waste disposal by the early twentieth century and the village's sewage works (at two successive locations) were situated on the common.[5] As on many other commons across the country, part of the fell was used as a rifle range, permission being given in 1888 to a volunteer battalion of the Durham Light Infantry.[6]

As open land backing onto the village, the fell came to be used as communal space by villagers. In 1885 a committee was appointed to lay out a recreation ground,[7] but less formal activities also took place, such as the game of pitch and toss on the common on a Sunday in 1894, for which fourteen miners were prosecuted for betting

---

[4] OS Six-Inch map, Durham 41 (revised 1914–19). Millfield Grange colliery closed in 1911; Holy Moor colliery in 1929; New Copley colliery all but closed after the First World War but some mining continued until the 1960s. For the history of these collieries, see Durham Mining Museum website (www.dmm.org.uk), colliery numbers m040, h040, n019.

[5] Barnard Castle Rural District Council was given permission to site sewage tanks on the common in 1905 and its rubbish tips there needed fencing in 1911: Cockfield Stint Bk, ff. 124–5.

[6] Cockfield Stint Bk, f. 123.

[7] Ibid.

Figure 47. Cockfield Fell: LIDAR image, 2018. A palimpsest of ground disturbance: at least three enclosures, probably of prehistoric date (labelled a–c), are clearly visible through the legacy of later extractive industry. Much of the pock-marking comes from coal-mining; railways and tramways are clearly visible, as is the long, deep trench of the whinstone quarry.

on the Sabbath.[8] In the twentieth century, village residents erected drying posts, hen houses and lofts ('crees') for homing pigeons, a colourful scatter of structures on parts of the fell close to the village, which became a distinctive feature of the common, their number and location being controlled by the field reeves (Figure 46).

Like commons elsewhere in the industrial north, Cockfield Fell also served as a meeting place for political and religious gatherings in the nineteenth century. Methodist camp meetings were held on the common in the 1820s and still took place there in the 1970s. As many as 3,000 people were said to have attended one such Primitive Methodist ('Ranter') gathering in July 1823, newspaper reports claiming that the days degenerated into 'drinking and fighting' in the evenings.[9] In 1874 the Durham Franchise Association held a large meeting of around 1,500–2,000 miners on Cockfield Fell, pressing for the extension of the vote to working men. Colliery bands with banners held aloft converged on the village and moved in procession to the fell, where a wagon had been placed as a dais for the speakers.[10] Another mass meeting was organised on the common during the Durham miners' strike five years later.[11]

---

[8] *Northern Echo*, 1 December 1894, p. 1.
[9] *Durham County Advertiser*, 12 July 1823, 15 July 1826.
[10] *Northern Echo*, 13 July 1874, pp. 3–4.
[11] Ibid., 1 May 1879, p. 1.

Though industrial remains dominate the landscape, Cockfield Fell remained a grazing ground despite the inherent problems caused by extractive industry. Until the 1860s properties in Cockfield had an 'unlimited right of common' on the fell, suggesting that grazing was governed by the usual rule of levancy and couchancy.[12] An abortive attempt at enclosure was made in 1847 but change came when the common was regulated as a stinted pasture in 1868 under the Inclosure Act 1845.[13]

The award regulating the common determined that there should be 1,100 stints on the fell, each giving the right to graze one sheep. A scale of equivalents allowed a cow or other fully-grown beast to be grazed for every 5 sheep stints, a horse and foal for 8 stints and 10 geese for 6 stints. As lord of the manor, the Duke of Cleveland was allocated sixty-nine stints (one-sixteenth of the whole) and he and John Bowes of Streatlam Castle received a further 389.5 stints as the principal landowners. The remainder was divided between forty-four other commoners, a majority of whom were allocated fewer than 10 stints. The number of stintholders had almost doubled by 1910 (to eighty-four, excluding the two principal owners), presumably indicating that allocations had been split when properties were divided. In 1941 the figure was 78, of whom 62 held fewer than 10 stints, 25 having only 1, 1.5 or 2 stints each.[14] This suggests that the common had become a pasture largely for villagers rather than local farmers, though stints were frequently sub-let. By then, not all stints were exercised: 938 stints were 'occupied' in 1939, a number which dropped to 862 (78 per cent of the full 1,100 stints) by 1940.[15]

After regulation, the fell was managed by a committee of field reeves, appointed annually.[16] They oversaw grazing and appointed a shepherd, who inspected all stock before they were put on the common, each stintholder contributing towards his salary. The work of the field reeves was not without dispute. Questions over financial arrangements were raised with the Board of Agriculture in 1911 and 1914 and a more serious rift flared up in 1931 when a group of about ten dissatisfied stintholders set up a self-elected committee in opposition to the field reeves. Led by Obadiah Blenkinsopp, a former miner, the committee appointed its own shepherd and attempted to collect the 'Shepherd Rate or Shed Rent' from the commoners, until proceedings were taken against them.[17]

Initially, the common was closed to grazing for the winter half-year, but the closed period was reduced in 1884 and the common was open all year by 1934.[18] The types

---

[12] See, for example, sale notices in *Durham Chronicle*, 7 June 1828, 27 March 1830.

[13] A meeting to discuss enclosure, which had been proposed to the Inclosure Commission, was held in 1847 (see *Durham County Advertiser*, 12 November 1847). A copy of Cockfield Regulated Pasture Award, 16 April 1868, is in Cockfield Stint Bk, ff. 91–112.

[14] Cockfield Stint Bk, ff. 87–9 (1910), 118–19 (1941).

[15] Ibid., f. 126.

[16] The following account is based on notes from meetings of the field reeves, 1869–1940, in Cockfield Stint Bk, ff. 122–6.

[17] TNA, MAF 25/91, especially J. Ingram Dawson, solicitor, Barnard Castle, to Ministry of Agriculture, 7 May and 29 May 1931.

[18] In 1869 the common was stinted on 13 May and cleared on 23 November; in 1884 the grazing period was extended to February.

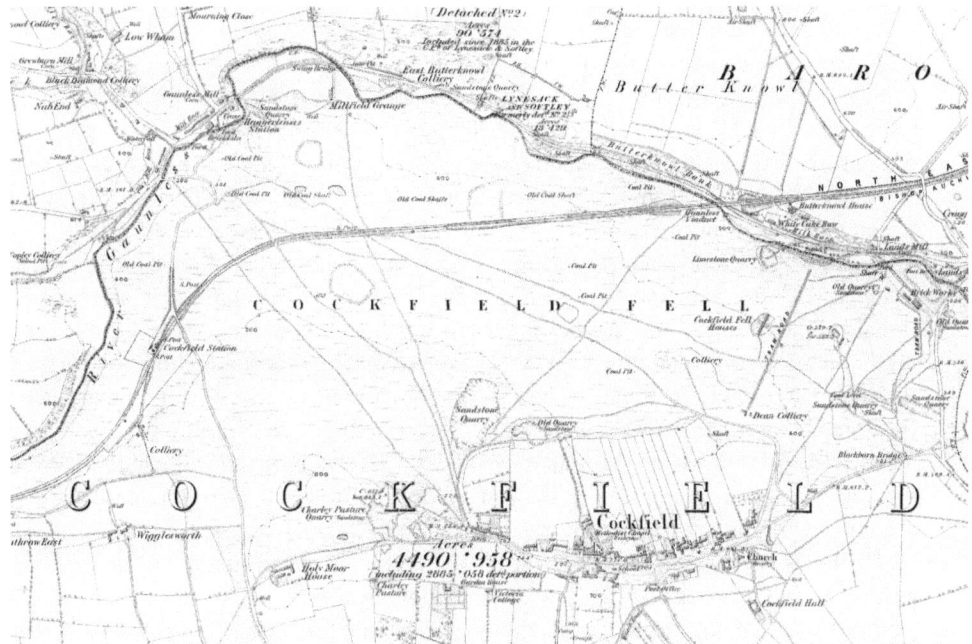

Figure 48. Cockfield Fell in 1857 (OS Six-Inch map, Durham 41, surveyed 1857).

of livestock which could be grazed were expanded, probably reflecting the increased holding of stints by villagers without land: pigs were allowed from 1883, at the rate of one pig for two sheep stints (as long as they were ringed), and goats (as long as they were tethered) from 1916.

The regulation award of 1868 contained a critical flaw from the stintholders' perspective. As was usual, the award confirmed to the lord of the manor the mineral rights under the regulated pasture but, unlike most awards, explicitly gave him the right to work minerals 'without paying for any damage to the surface which may thereby be done'.[19] Although the field reeves did obtain payment for damages from some colliery workings, the lack of obligation to put right damage to the pastures was blamed for the 'horrible state' the fell was in by 1944, when the value of the grazings was said to have been reduced by 'at least one half'.[20]

The face of the common changed after the demise of mining, quarrying and associated industries after the Second World War. It continued to be managed as an agrarian resource by the field reeves, the active graziers increasingly being local farmers rather than villagers. Only 562 of the 1,100 stints were registered under the CRA, many of the smaller stintholders in village properties failing to register their rights. The stint owners as a body registered 22 stints and these, together with the balance of unregistered stints, have since provided flexibility, allowing the field

---

[19] Cockfield Stint Bk, f. 97.
[20] Ibid., ff. 120–1 (letter from J. Ingram Dawson, solicitor, Barnard Castle, April 1944).

reeves to adjust grazing numbers annually by allocating rights up to the maximum of 1,100 stints. A majority of the 51 initial registrations were for small numbers of stints and were attached to houses in the village: 39 were for fewer than 10 stints, 23 of them for fewer than 5. However, a majority of the registered stints (295.5 stints; 53 per cent of the total) were held by six local farms. From the 1980s, a trade in stints resulted in many being detached from properties to become registered as rights in gross and led to some further concentration of stints in the hands of the larger farms.[21]

By the 1960s, if not before, a closed period was re-introduced during the month of April. The common continues to be grazed by sheep with some cattle and horses, the stintholders' fees now paying for a fell warden rather than a shepherd. Sheep predominate, the six main flocks having acquired informal heafs on different parts of the common through their natural hefting instinct. Grazing patterns were disrupted by the foot and mouth disease epidemic in 2001, resulting in a deterioration in the quality of the pasture, since when the field reeves have actively improved and maintained the grazing by regular liming during the April closed period and by rolling bracken and attempting to prevent the spread of gorse.

The fell is also valued as an open space by the local community, as well as drawing visitors from further afield to view its archaeological and industrial remains. It has suffered some of the problems shared by other commons close to populous areas, including fly-tipping, sheep worrying by dogs, and 'off-roading' by motorcycles and other vehicles. Despite these issues, the tired and battered common of the industrial era is now a successfully regulated pasture and amenity open space.[22]

---

[21] Data from analysis of Commons Register, Co. Durham CL 8.
[22] I am most grateful to Joanne Bainbridge and Stuart Heddle, Cockfield Field Reeves, for sharing their knowledge of the recent history of the fell in conversation in 2021.

CHAPTER 12
ISLE OF AXHOLME TURBARY ALLOTMENTS, LINCOLNSHIRE

Lincolnshire CL 2 (Epworth Turbary) and CL 8 (Belton Low Closes Turbary).

THE TURBARY GROUNDS ALLOCATED to village communities when wetlands surrounding the Isle of Axholme in the Humberhead Levels were enclosed in 1803 are examples of the perpetuation of shared use of common land as a result of Parliamentary enclosure. Two of the plots set aside then to supply domestic fuel for local people remain registered as common land.

Before enclosure and drainage, the open-field villages along the ridge of higher land on the Isle of Axholme were surrounded by wet carr lands, particularly on the western side stretching towards the River Torne.[1] These spacious commons, cut by natural creeks and drainage dykes, provided pasture for large numbers of livestock, the grazing enriched by silt from regular winter flooding. The commons also yielded the assortment of fen resources typical of wetland areas: turf and peat for fuel, clay, hay (in parts), fish and wildfowl. Hemp and flax cultivation was widespread on the Isle and the commons also offered scope for digging pits and ponds in which to 'ret' or steep the plants in order to extract the fibre.[2] The commons were thus so integral to the economy of the villages on the Isle that the resistance of villagers to the loss of large blocks of their commons to the 'Participants' in Vermuyden's drainage scheme of the 1620s is not surprising. Serious rioting occurred from 1628 to 1634 and again during the Civil War when sluices were destroyed to flood the newly-reclaimed land and to prevent Royalist troops from reaching the staunchly Parliamentarian Isle.[3] The resources of the commons also attracted migrants: it was said in 1675 that the area's liberal turf-cutting rights drew 'multitudes of the poorer sort' from adjacent counties to settle there.[4] Despite Vermuyden's activities, around 12,000 acres (4,850 ha) of wetland waste, known collectively as 'The Isle Commons', survived until they were enclosed and drained under an act of 1795.

---

[1] For the landscape history of the Isle, see K. Miller, *The Isle of Axholme Historic Landscape Characterisation Project* (Leeds, 1997).
[2] J. Thirsk, 'The Isle of Axholme before Vermuyden', *AgHR*, 1 (1) (1953), esp. pp. 21–2. Digging pits and ponds on the commons for steeping hemp, line and flax was forbidden within half a mile of a public highway by the Isle of Axholme Enclosure Act 1795 (35 Geo. III, c.107), p. 59.
[3] K. Lindley, *Fenland Riots and the English Revolution* (London, 1982), pp. 26–32, 72–9, 146–57.
[4] Miller, *Isle of Axholme Historic Landscape Characterisation*, p. 29.

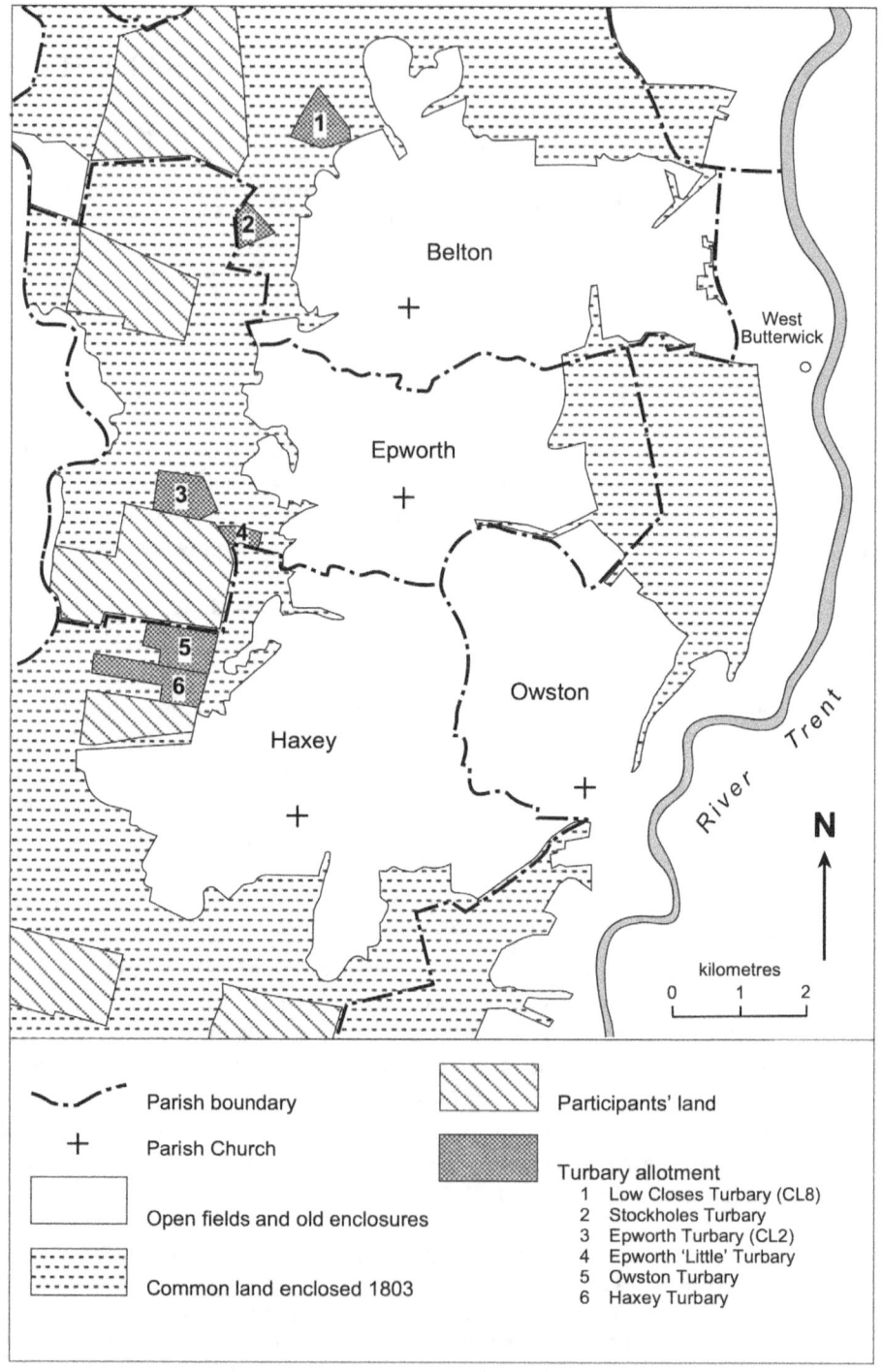

Figure 49. Isle of Axholme, Lincolnshire: turbaries and extent of former common land. Source: Lincolnshire Archives, EPWORTH PAR/17/1.

The Isle of Axholme Enclosure Act specified that the commissioners were to divide the wastes between the four parishes of Epworth, Haxey, Belton and Owston and to allocate to each parish one or more allotments of up to 100 acres (40 ha) 'for a Turbary … to be for ever thereafter held and enjoyed for the Purpose of digging Turves for the Use and Benefit of the Inhabitants', subject to regulations to be laid down by the commissioners.[5] The award of 1803 made six turbary allotments, two apiece for Belton and Epworth and one each for Haxey and Owston (one-third of Owston's subsequently being transferred to West Butterwick when it became a separate parish in 1841).[6] All were on the western side of the Isle, Owston's 100 acres being at a distance from the bulk of the parish, next to the 100-acre plot allotted to Haxey on Haxey North Carr (Figure 49). Epworth's turbary ground lay in two adjacent parts, Epworth 'Big' Turbary covering 78.5 acres (32 ha)[7] beside the road across the carrs to Wroot; the smaller turbary of 21.5 acres (9 ha) beside Skyers Dyke, nearby. At Belton the land allocated also lay in two allotments, Low Closes Turbary of 61.5 acres (25 ha)[8] and Stockholes Turbary of 38.5 acres (16 ha). The award restricted each inhabitant to an annual quota of no more than three wagon loads of material from the turbaries, under penalty of 20s per load to be paid to the overseers of the poor. The products which might be taken were listed as 'land, soil, earth, peats, turves, sand, whins and sods', reflecting the mixture of sand and peat in the turbary allotments and the diversity of resources they could yield.[9]

How long the turbaries continued to be exploited communally is unclear. By the 1820s, Haxey Carr (the east end of Haxey Turbary) and the two smaller turbaries at Epworth and Belton had begun to be settled and were let by the parish authorities as small (1- to 2-acre (0.5–1.0-ha)) plots to poor inhabitants, who built cottages and used their land for market gardening, creating clusters of cottage settlement, the rents of which generated income for poor relief.[10] Owston Turbary, inconveniently located for the village, was let as farmland by 1838 but it and part of Haxey Turbary had gone out of cultivation because of waterlogging by c.1930. The rental income from these turbaries was being applied for the provision of coal to the parishioners by the early twentieth century.[11] Peat-digging on Epworth 'Big' Turbary had ceased by the early twentieth century and it was described as

---

[5] Isle of Axholme Enclosure Act 1795 (35 Geo. III, c.107), pp. 4–5, 30–1, 38, 42–3, 54.

[6] Lincolnshire Archives, EPWORTH PAR/17/1; TNA, MAF 25/221, 'Turbaries in the Isle of Axholme' (TS report dated 13 December 1938) (hereafter 'Turbaries report, 1938'), p. 5.

[7] When the allotment was registered as common land, the acreage was recorded as 82.346 acres (33.3 ha): North Lincolnshire Council, Commons Register, CL 2, p. 3.

[8] When the allotment was registered as common land, the acreage was recorded as 64.028 acres (25.9 ha): North Lincolnshire Council, Commons Register, CL 8, p. 1.

[9] Lincolnshire Archives, EPWORTH PAR/17/1.

[10] Sections of Haxey and Epworth Little turbaries were being enclosed by 1820–21; plots on Stockholes Turbary were being let by 1835: 'Turbaries report, 1938', pp. 4–5. The three turbaries were fully divided, with cottages on most plots, by 1885: OS 1:2,500 plans, Lincolnshire XVII.14 (Stockholes), XXV.6 (Epworth), XXV.10 (Haxey).

[11] 'Turbaries report, 1938', p. 5.

Figure 50. Epworth Turbary, Isle of Axholme. The bird hide on the margins of the wooded perimeter overlooks the central open area, maintained by active scrub clearance and grazing.

'rough marsh land' in 1938 and 'derelict scrub' by the 1950s.[12] On the eve of the Second World War, Lincolnshire (Lindsey) County Council explored, without success, means of bringing the former turbaries into cultivation: their dereliction and the nominal rents they yielded for local purposes were considered to be 'most unsatisfactory' in an area of rich farmland. Uncertainty over the status of property rights on the turbaries appears to have thwarted these moves.[13]

Epworth 'Big' Turbary (CL 2) and Belton Low Closes Turbary (CL 8) were registered as common land under the CRA, though no common rights were claimed.[14] Attempts by the Ramblers Association to register Haxey Turbary and Owston Turbary (as CL 102 and CL 115, respectively) failed and the provisional registrations were withdrawn. The histories of the two turbaries registered as common land differed greatly. Belton Low Closes Turbary had been let for grazing by 1910 (or possibly earlier). By the 1950s most of it was a well-used pasture, fenced and regularly grazed; the remainder was

[12] Ibid., p. 4; Hoskins & Stamp, *Common Lands*, pp. 115, 297.
[13] TNA, MAF 25/221, E. W. Scorer, clerk to Lincolnshire (Lindsey) County Council, to Ministry of Agriculture, 19 and 21 December 1938; 'Turbaries on the Isle of Axholme' (TS report dated 4 January 1939).
[14] North Lincolnshire Council, Commons Register, CL2, CL 8.

marsh.[15] Once turbary rights had fallen into disuse, the parish appears to have decided to use the allotment for the good of the community by allowing the grazing to be let by the Belton Private Roads and Drains Committee, which applied the income to the maintenance of occupation roads and drains and the repair of fences. The enclosure award had made no provision for the ownership of the turbary allotment and the matter was resolved in 1972 by a commons commissioner's decision, which did not accept a claim to ownership by the Private Roads and Drains Committee and placed it under the care of the local authority as provided for by section 9 of the CRA.[16]

By contrast, Epworth Turbary (Figure 50) had become wet scrubland by the time it was acquired by the Lincolnshire Naturalists' Trust (now Lincolnshire Wildlife Trust) in 1958. Notified as an SSSI in 1951, its conservation value lay primarily as a wetland habitat with surviving raised peat bog and fen. The common had been largely treeless until around 1920, containing dangerous areas of bog. However, the deepening of the nearby Skyer's Drain resulted in a lowering of the water table, improving the drainage of the turbary and leading to a rapid expansion of tree cover. Birch scrub invaded the wet heath and fenland areas from the 1920s, covering much of the turbary by the 1970s. Since then, the common has been actively managed, in an attempt to restrict the woodland area to the outer fringes, with programmes of scrub clearance and pond digging from 1977 to foster the wetland habitats of the open central area. Summer grazing by Galloway cattle and native breeds of sheep was introduced on the fenced open areas from the 1990s, in order to limit scrub regeneration.[17] It is now a nature reserve, with waymarked paths and bird hides.

---

[15] CCD, Humberside: Belton Low Closes Turbary (CL 8), 24/U/1; Hoskins & Stamp, p. 297.
[16] CCD, Humberside: Belton Low Closes Turbary (CL 8), 24/U/1.
[17] G. Trinder, *Epworth Turbary Nature Reserve: Its Management and Wildlife since 1977* (privately printed, 2014), with further information from Dave Bromwich, Lincolnshire Wildlife Trust, 2021.

CHAPTER 13

LLANLLECHID MOUNTAIN AND ABER MOUNTAIN, CAERNARVONSHIRE

Caernarvonshire CL 3 (Aber) and CL 42 (Llanllechid).

THESE UPLAND GRAZING COMMONS, in the north-west corner of the Snowdonia National Park, cover a block of mountainous territory falling steeply from the summit of Carnedd Llewelyn (1,064m) down to the Ogwen valley and the narrow coastal strip to the east of Bangor. Divided by the watershed along the crest of the hills between Moel Wnion and Carnedd Gwenllian, their combined extent covers over 10,550 acres (4,270 ha), of which Llanllechid Mountain (CL 42) accounts for 6,126 acres (2,479 ha) and Aber Mountain (CL 3) 4,425 acres (1,790 ha). The mountain slopes are dominated by acid grassland, with areas of blanket peat and heather moorland, and rock and scree on the highest parts. The recent histories of the two commons are intertwined, as will be seen; the focus here is on Llanllechid Mountain, which Dudley Stamp described as 'an almost unique example of a true common',[1] by which he seems to have meant an unmanaged common, exhibiting aspects of a Hardinesque 'tragedy'.

Evidence of past human activity abounds on both commons (Figure 52). Legacies of prehistoric settlement are widespread in the remains of groups of huts and associated enclosures across the lower slopes, while reminders of resource exploitation in the historic period survive in disused stone quarries and trial levels from lead mining.[2] Tangible evidence of the exercise of common rights is also abundant. Sheepfolds are numerous, especially on Llanllechid Mountain, most of them simple folds but several taking the form of strikingly complex, multicellular structures (Figure 51). These probably reflect the large number of small graziers putting sheep on the common, the flock of each commoner being sorted from a central gathering area into cells belonging to individual farms. It has been suggested that the folds date from the expansion of sheep-farming during the eighteenth century: several are recorded on maps of c.1810.[3]

---

[1] Hoskins & Stamp, p. 229.
[2] Royal Commission on the Ancient & Historical Monuments in Wales (RCAHMW), *An Inventory of the Ancient Monuments in Caernarvonshire, Volume I: East* (London, 1956), pp. 7–16 (Aber parish) and 138–51 (Llanllechid parish).
[3] RCAHMW, *Inventory of Caernarvonshire I*, p. lxxvii. Examples include those at Gyrn (SH 648 688), beside Afon Llafar (SH 649 653), on the south side of Afon Caseg (SH 656 661) and either

Figure 51. Aber Mountain with multicellular sheepfold beside Afon Anafon.

Peat-digging in turbary grounds on wet saddles high in the hills also left a legacy of manmade features, notably the 'peat stools' (*ystolion mawn*), platforms of large stones beside the turbary grounds, on which peat was stacked to dry.[4]

Llanllechid and Aber lay in the medieval hundred of Uchaf which covered the five northern parishes of the forest of Snowdon. In 1352 the hundred was in the hands of the Crown, apart from the manor of Aber which had been granted away in 1280. Most of the mountain land in the hundred had the status of Crown wastes, except for that portion belonging to the manor of Aber, which was, in effect, manorial waste.[5] In Llanllechid parish, the Crown granted the mineral and sporting rights over the wastes to Lord Penrhyn on a long lease in 1784.[6] The lease created a divided interest in Llanllechid Mountain, which may have contributed to the lack of regulation of common rights when pressure on the resources of the common grew in the first half

---

    side of Afon Anafon on Aber Common (SH 681 711 (see fig. 50) and SH 689 710).

[4] RCAHMW, *Inventory of Caernarvonshire I*, p. lxxviii. Turbary grounds are marked on E. Owen's plan of Llanllechid Mountain in 1866: see fig. 51.

[5] The manorial waste did not, however, include all the common land: the northern section around Foel Ganol belonged to the landowners of the parish: National Library of Wales, Aber tithe map, 1848, parcel 48.

[6] O. Owen Roberts, *Crown Property in North Wales, its Management and Appropriation* (London, 1849), pp. 28–30. The 1784 lease is in Bangor University Archives & Special Collections [hereafter 'BUASC'], PFA/1/310.

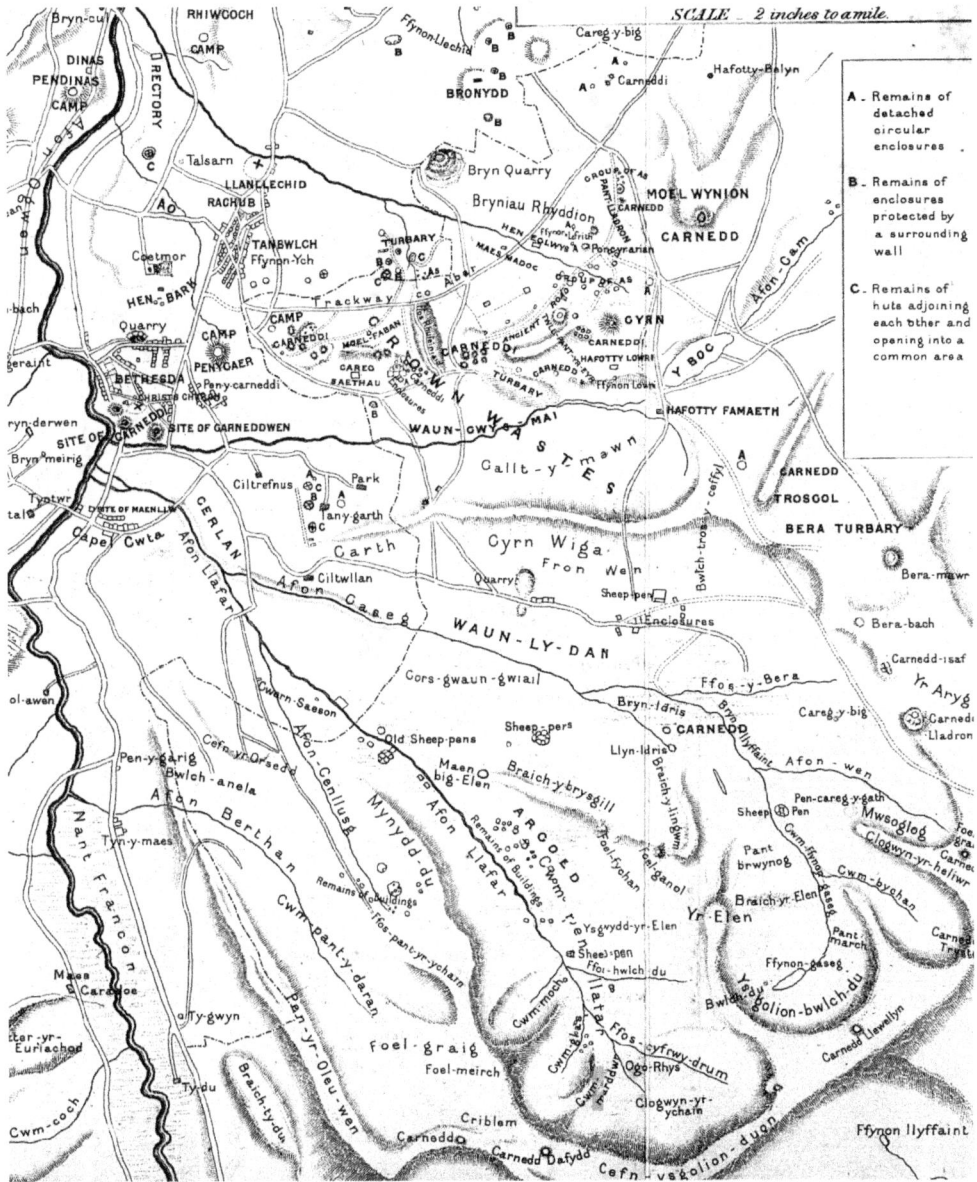

Figure 52. Llanllechid Mountain: Elias Owen's map of 'ancient remains' on the common, 1866. The map gives a vivid impression of the layers of human activity on the common: prehistoric huts and enclosures, trackways, quarries, sheep pens and turbaries. A host of minor place-names, many of which are not recorded on OS maps, are a reminder of how impoverished the portrayal of common land often is on modern maps. Source: *Archaeologia Cambriensis*, 3rd ser. no. L (April 1867), opp. p. 102.

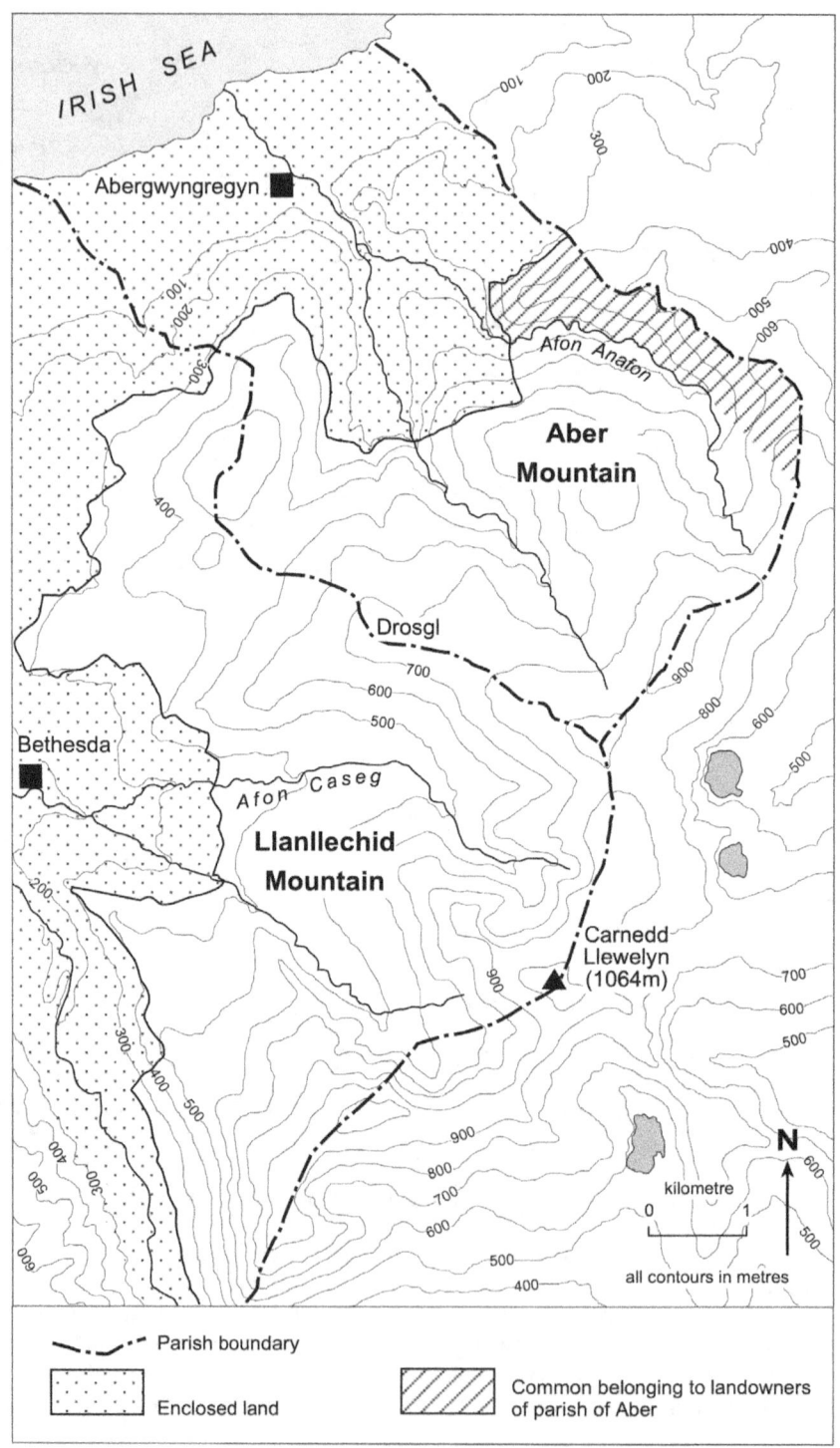

Figure 53. Llanllechid and Aber Mountains, Caernarvonshire.

of the nineteenth century. Penrhyn's successor, E. G. D. Pennant, obtained outright ownership of Llanllechid Mountain from the Crown in 1858.[7] The manor of Aber was also acquired by the Penrhyn estate in the mid-nineteenth century, so that the Penrhyn interest extended to both commons. Both Llanllechid Mountain and Aber Mountain came into the hands of the National Trust when it acquired the Penrhyn Castle estate in 1951.[8]

Grazing rights on the mountain wastes of Llanllechid were notably liberal. In 1802 it was said that 'every farmer' in Llanllechid parish had 'an unlimited and exclusive right of pasturage' on the parish wastes.[9] As slate-quarrying expanded, the new settlement of Bethesda grew from the 1820s, resulting in a rapid increase in the parish's population, from 3,075 in 1831 to 8,291 by 1881, which placed increasing pressure on the common. By 1839 the Bethesda cottagers were turning to the common as a source of fuel, 'paring the greensward' and thus damaging the pasture. Despite warnings to desist, around twenty individuals continued to cut turf and the Penrhyn estate had difficulty in finding a legal remedy to prevent the damage.[10]

By the 1840s the parish vestry oversaw the use of the common, laying out parameters for the exercise of common rights. In 1845 it issued a notice warning people not to damage the surface of the pasture by cutting sods and resolved to hire a bailiff to enforce the regulations on the common. It also attempted to limit peat-cutting, accepting that occupiers of houses who did not possess common rights were nevertheless to be allowed to take peat on payment of 6d per day's cutting, but limiting the amount to as much peat as one man could cut over two days. Selling peats was forbidden.[11]

The vestry of 1845 also laid down (or perhaps reiterated) a stint on the common: farmers could have three sheep for each acre of farmland they held and were to pay 1s 0d to the 'Bailiff of the Commons' for each sheep over that number, a sum which was raised to 2s 0d in 1846. Control of the common lay with the commoners themselves, through a committee appointed by the vestry (described in 1846 as 'the Committee men appointed to Superintend the Commons of Llanllechid'), which was doubled in size in 1849. Concern over turf-cutting surfaced again in 1849 and 1857, but the focus of the vestry's discussions increasingly turned to limiting the numbers of stock grazing the common.[12]

By 1851 control of grazing on the common seems to have broken down and the common was becoming overstocked. As well as the legitimate rights of those holding land in the parish of Llanllechid, illegal grazing was rife. Several categories of people who had no formal right were nevertheless turning stock onto the common in summer:

---

[7] BUASC, PFA/3/116.
[8] Information from Gethin Evans, Senior Estate Manager, The National Trust, who generously shared his knowledge of these commons.
[9] W. Williams, *Observations on the Snowdon Mountains* (London, 1802), p. 133.
[10] BUASC, PENHR/728–9.
[11] Gwynedd Archives, XB14/47, file entitled 'Llanllechid Mountain Pasture', TS copies of vestry meeting minutes, 1845–83: 13 March and 8 May 1845.
[12] Ibid., 8 May 1845–14 May 1857.

Figure 54. Lower slopes of Llanllechid Common, with the slate-quarrying settlement of Bethesda on the left.

quarrymen and labourers occupying cottages and gardens in the parish but not otherwise holding land; other residents who occupied no land 'in the usual way' but rented pasture in winter for sheep which they then put to the common in summer; and people from outside the parish. Some commoners rented or assigned their rights to others, and some bought large stocks of sheep in spring which they then grazed on the common in summer.[13] Long use enabled these graziers to claim rights by prescription.

The vestry's response was to reiterate the stint of three sheep per acre in 1850 and again in 1864 and it also attempted to clarify associated matters. In 1849 it minuted that no one was to put cattle other than their own on the common and spelt out that one pony could be grazed in lieu of twelve sheep. It also forbade the sub-letting of grazing rights, a practice which had been 'greatly abused', suggesting that a previous ruling in 1846 had proved ineffective. That regulation had stated that a farmer could only let his or her share of the common 'on the particular spot' where they or their ancestors 'used to pasture sheep on', suggesting that, as was common in Wales, each flock had its known and accepted sheepwalk. In 1857 the fines for animals found trespassing were set at 5s 0d for a horse or pony, 3s 0d for a cow or ox and 1s 0d for each sheep or donkey.[14] Sporadic attempts were made by the Penrhyn estate to tackle illegal grazing in the 1860s

---

[13] BUASC, PENRH/730.
[14] Gwynedd Archives, XB14/47, vestry meeting minutes, 24 March 1846–7 April 1864, *passim*.

and 1870s, including calling meetings of commoners, threatening to impound livestock and to give tenants notice to quit. In 1876 the exasperated agent complained that he was having 'a great deal more trouble than I should have had' from tenants in Llanllechid who persisted in overstocking the common.[15]

The situation did not improve. By 1930, it was said that Llanllechid Common was 'overstocked and without any control', the problem being that anyone residing in the parish could 'take what stock they like on the common', whether or not they held agricultural land. A farmer from Llandegai, outside the parish, had even taken the step of purchasing a ruined house in the parish, simply in order to acquire grazing rights on the common.[16] An attempt had been made in the early years of the twentieth century to uphold the regulations laid down by the vestry the previous century, when Lord Penrhyn paid a shepherd to ensure that the stint was adhered to, but at a parish meeting held in 1912 his right to police the common was challenged and different understandings of which householders had common rights surfaced. Lord Penrhyn's agent declared that only people who held 'parcels of land adjoining the common' had rights, while others claimed that all the parishioners of Llanllechid were entitled to graze stock on the common. After that meeting, any vestige of regulation seems to have evaporated.[17]

Uncontrolled grazing remained a persistent problem across the 1930s and 1940s. Drawing up a scheme of regulation under the terms of the Commons Act 1899 was mooted in 1932 and again in 1948 but nothing came of these suggestions. Despite the existence of a 'Llanllechid Mountain Sub-Committee' and a flurry of correspondence between the local authorities in 1948, no further action seems to have been taken.[18] In the 1950s, Stamp stated that some 140 commoners ran around 17,000 sheep and 60–80 ponies on Llanllechid Common.[19]

The lack of regulation on Llanllechid Mountain put pressure on the adjacent common in the parish of Aber. On the unfenced mountain slopes, sheep frequently strayed across the parish boundary. Several hundred sheep from Llanllechid and Llanfairfechan (the parish on the north-east side of Aber) were grazing on Aber Mountain when numbers were recorded between 1939 and 1952 and the legal status of such intercommoning became an issue when rights were registered under the CRA. The Aber Graziers' Committee claimed that only farms in Aber parish had grazing rights on the common, whereas farmers in the adjacent parishes claimed to have acquired rights by prescription through long usage. From the 1920s (if not earlier) until the

---

[15] BUASC, PENRH/1802, nos. 221–4 (July 1863); PENRH/1807, nos. 187–8, 192, 196. (August 1876)
[16] Gwynedd Archives, XB14/47, correspondence, 1930–48: Clerk of Ogwen RDC to Ministry of Agriculture, 16 December 1930.
[17] Ibid., Clerk, Ogwen RDC to Commons, Open Spaces & Footpaths Preservation Society, 4 July 1932.
[18] Ibid., L. Chubb, Secretary, Commons, Open Spaces & Footpaths Preservation Society to E. Roberts, Ogwen RDC, 6 July 1932; Clerk, Caernarvonshire County Council to Clerk, Ogwen RDC, 27 January 1948, and to Clerk, Bethesda UDC, 17 April 1948.
[19] Hoskins & Stamp, p. 229.

1950s, payments were claimed by the Aber estate from those from outside the parish whose sheep were found when the common was driven each year. The gatherings were overseen by a manorial constable (from 1954 described as the 'Estrays Bailiff and Mountain Watcher'), who claimed a 'fine' of 1s 6d for each sheep, though these were often not paid. The payments could be interpreted as showing that the graziers from Llanllechid and Llanfairfechan were grazing their stock on Aber Mountain by licence or agistment and the issue turned on whether paying the fines prevented the graziers from establishing rights by prescription. In at least one case, a flock had an established *cynefyn* (the north Welsh term for a heaf or sheepwalk), suggesting that they were not simply straying onto Aber Common. The commons commissioner's decision in 1977 was that prescriptive rights had been acquired, despite the claims for payment.[20]

Registration under the CRA exposed the highly unusual status of grazing rights on Llanllechid Mountain. As Ednyfed Hudson Davies, MP for Conway, put it, inhabitants of the parish had traditionally had unrestricted grazing rights on the common by virtue of residence, rather than tenure of land. Since inhabitancy was a prerequisite, these were not rights in gross. If each commoner were to register their rights separately, these would in future be tied to existing houses, preventing residents of houses built in future from possessing rights, which would be 'out of keeping with the rights enjoyed at present'. Hudson Davies suggested that the only way to secure the grazing rights was for Llanllechid parish council (which, he pointed out, had 'always been viewed as the administrator of the common') to register the rights in trust for the parishioners.[21]

Consequently, in 1968 the parish council made a block registration of grazing rights for 25,000 sheep, 500 ponies and 100 cattle, as well as rights of turbary, estovers and piscary. A further twelve individual registrations (including one for 9,000 ewes with followers, 180 ponies and 40 cattle, attached to Penrhyn Estate property in the parish) resulted in grazing rights totalling no fewer than 38,005 sheep, 735 ponies and 175 cattle being registered.[22] Giving a notional stocking rate of over 15 sheep per hectare, excluding other livestock, these were clearly inflated figures. However, the highly unusual block registration allowed the parish council to apportion grazing rights between parishioners, thus offering some control over stocking levels.

By the mid-twentieth century, grazing pressure on the commons was affecting their ecology and leading to a deterioration in the quality of the vegetation. Heather was declining, as heavy grazing broke stands of the plant into scattered patches, to be replaced by grassland, while bracken spread up the lower slopes as the heather retreated. The changes were exacerbated by moor burning, which had been practised until the 1950s by shepherds seeking to promote grass growth: it was thought that Welsh Mountain sheep and Cheviots throve better on grassland. Severe burning could

---

[20] CCD, Gwynedd: Unenclosed Mountain Land – Aber (CL 3), 50/D/45.
[21] Letters, E. Hudson Davies to A. Evans, Bethesda UDC (26 March 1967) and I. Davies, MP (9 May 1968). Copies kindly supplied by Gethin Evans, 2021.
[22] Commons Register, Caernarvonshire CL 42, rights section.

lead to incipient soil erosion on the steep slopes, as occurred after a burn in the late 1940s on Craig Braich-ty-du.[23]

Stocking levels remained very high in the 1990s, by which time there was evidence of severe overgrazing on Llanllechid Common, especially on the lower ground close to the access tracks onto the common. Despite efforts by the Graziers' Association (a body of local councillors and farmers, successor to the Mountain Sub-Committee of the 1940s), effective regulation of the common appears to have been absent, as not all active graziers were members of the Association. In 1996, over 20,000 sheep grazed the common in the summer months, a rate of nine sheep per hectare, which was considered to be 'grossly excessive'. Although most graziers removed their stock during the winter, those without access to enclosed winter grazing could not, with the result that an average of 2,400 ewes remained on the common between November and March. The conclusion of the Farming and Rural Conservation Agency's survey of the common that year was that no stock should graze the common over the winter months and that summer stocking levels should be reduced by around one-half.[24] As well as sheep, Llanllechid and the adjacent commons were home to a herd of around 150 semi-feral ponies.[25]

In contrast to the adjacent Aber Mountain, where an effective commoners' association enabled the common to be entered into the Welsh government's *Glastir* agri-environmental scheme, grazing rights on Llanllechid Mountain continued to be a source of contention into the twenty-first century. Attempts by the parish council to allocate grazing rights according to the acreage of land held and to impose a limit of 1,000 sheep per grazier met resistance. In 2009 a proposal to introduce a scheme involving removal of sheep from the common for the five winter months failed, as some graziers felt excluded and consensus could not be reached. Trespass by illegal grazing remained a problem.[26]

---

[23] D. A. Ratcliffe, 'The vegetation of the Carneddau, North Wales: I. Grassland, heaths and bogs', *Journal of Ecology*, 47 (2) (1959), pp. 371–413.

[24] C. Whitworth, K. Jones and R. Evans, *Survey of the Grazing Practice and Farming Systems on Holdings with Access Rights to Llanllechid Common: Results and Recommendations* (Cardiff, 1997).

[25] Noted in the Welsh government's explanatory booklet on the agri-environmental *glastir* scheme: https://gov.wales/sites/default/files/publications/2020-02/glastir-commons-general-rules-booklet-2020-2021.pdf.

[26] Information from Gethin Evans, 2021.

CHAPTER 14

BRINGSTY COMMON AND BROMYARD DOWNS, HEREFORDSHIRE

Herefordshire CL 14 (Bringsty Common) and CL 15 (Bromyard Downs).

THESE TWO COMMONS, LYING little more than a mile apart on the sandstone hills of north-east Herefordshire, illustrate many of the themes in the history of common land in lowland England. Despite their proximity to each other, their characters differ. Bringsty Common (Figure 55) covers 229 acres (93 ha) of broken land, straddling the boundary between Whitbourne and Linton parishes. It is a landscape of rolling hillsides and hidden dells, partly wooded; some parts are clogged by bracken and bramble, others are open grassy slopes. Bromyard Downs (Figure 56), covering 282 acres (114 ha), is a curving sweep of hillside to the east of the medieval borough and market town of Bromyard, rising to the crest of the ridge at *c*.200m above sea level, which forms the parish boundary. The common contains more open land than Bringsty, with large areas of grassland and some patches of surviving heathland, as well as bracken and scrub. Their contrasting ecologies were apparent by the seventeenth century, when the road from London to Aberystwyth (the modern A44) passed through 'Furrs & Fern' on Bringsty Common, while the Downs were referred to as 'Bromiard heath', perhaps suggesting that the heathland was formerly more extensive.[1]

In the era of medieval colonisation, Bringsty and the neighbouring smaller common at Badley Wood (56 acres; 23 ha) were surviving woodlands on rising ground on the western edge of Whitbourne parish. By the sixteenth century both were common grazings, all the tenants of the manor having common of pasture in them 'without number' (*sance nombre*), implying that the rule of levancy and couchancy applied.[2] The woods continued to provide pannage for pigs in the later sixteenth and early seventeenth century and in 1562 the manor court had sought to protect woodland by amercing those who felled trees and removed wood without licence from Bringsty, Badley Wood and Bromyard Downs.[3]

---

[1] J. Ogilby, *Britannia* (1675), Plate 2.
[2] HARC, AA59/A/2 (Butterfield's Survey, 1577), f. 133.
[3] Ibid., f. 116v; AM33/8/3, Whitbourne court, 2 April 1619; AM33/9/8, Whitbourne court, 16 October 1622; Glamorgan Record Office, CL Manorial Box 4, Bromyard Foreign court (Whitbourne, Norton, Linton), 22 April 1562.

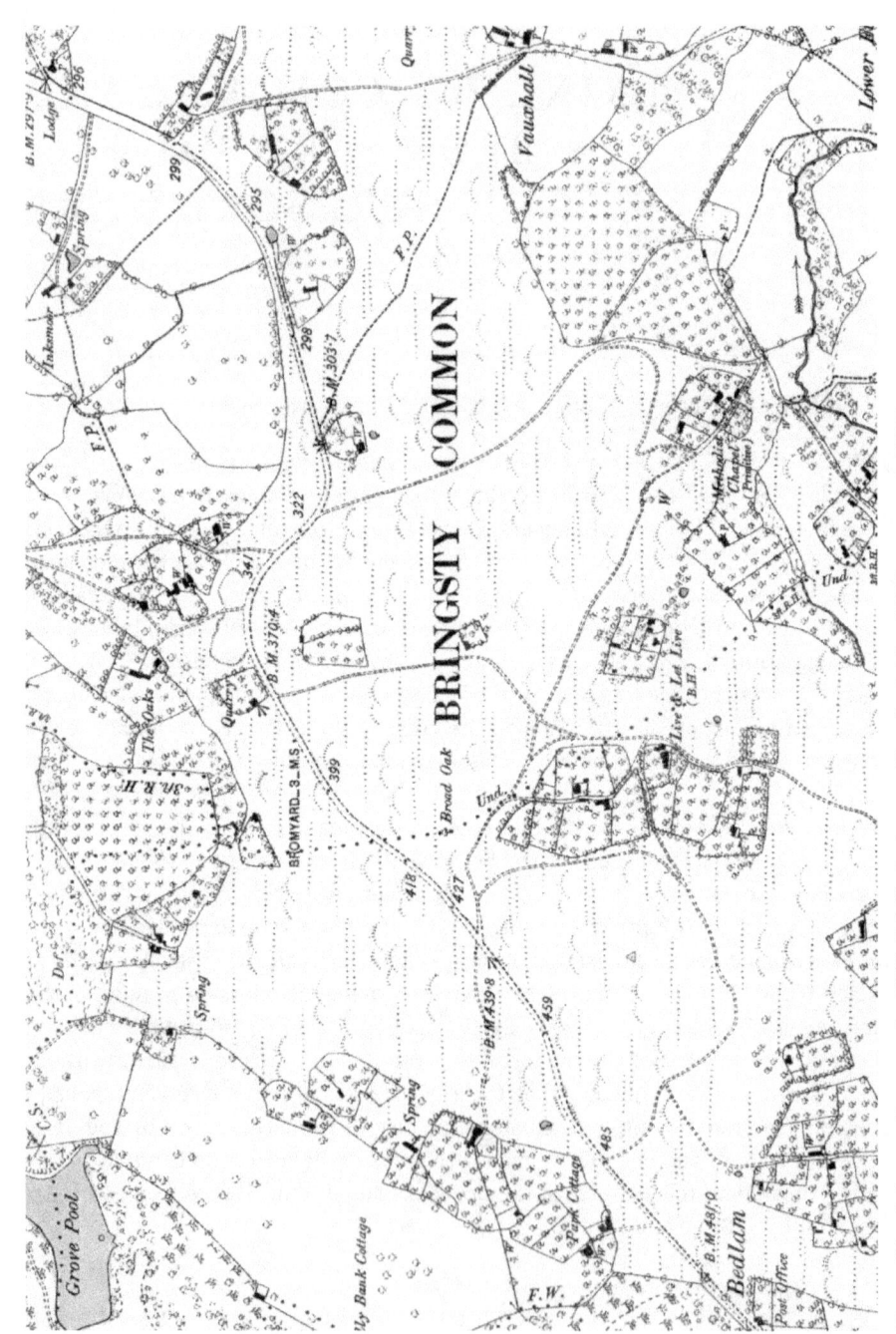

Figure 55. Bringsty Common in 1885 (OS Six-Inch map, Herefordshire 21NE, surveyed 1885).

Grazing pressure was also evident on the Downs. By 1555, a limit had been placed on the number of goats which might be grazed on the common: men were presented for putting more than four goats on the Downs that year.[4] In 1562 John Nokes of Cradley (several miles south of Bromyard) was guilty of 'Staffedryving' cattle to Bromyard Downs where they oppressed the common, while in 1605 a local man was charged with overburdening the Downs with his sheep and pigs.[5] By the nineteenth century both commons were largely open, the woodland cover presumably having been reduced by continued grazing.

Other resources taken from the commons included gorse and bracken, the latter continuing to be harvested for litter until the mid-twentieth century. Pressure on bracken is implied by an order of 1622, which set St Bartholomew's Day (24 August) as the date after which 'fearne' could be cut on Bringsty.[6] There was some small-scale quarrying on Bromyard Downs in the nineteenth century.

As elsewhere in Wales and the Marches, the commons were colonised by cottages from the sixteenth century (Figure 57). On Bromyard Downs, cottage-building was concentrated in a cluster where the lane from the town reached the common, while on Bringsty and Badley Wood the cottages were more widely dispersed, each with its attached patch of orchard forming a small island of enclosure on the common. Four cottages were held under lease in the woods of Bringsty and Badley Wood by 1576.[7] By 1605 more had been built without being declared to the manor court. In that year, and again in 1622, the court attempted to limit cottage encroachments by ordering enclosures taken from the common on Bringsty and Badley Wood to be thrown open and, in 1622, forbidding further enclosure.[8] In 1798, twenty-seven leasehold cottages on Bringsty, held of the bishop of Hereford as lord of the manor, were transferred to Whitbourne parish, becoming 'parish houses', providing housing or rental income to support the poor. Some occupants claimed the cottages as their own, leading the vestry to take steps to ensure that the parish's ownership was acknowledged.[9]

The scattered cottage community was largely agricultural. In 1841 the heads of households on Badley Wood and Bringsty were overwhelmingly agricultural labourers, though they also included paupers, a carpenter and a bricklayer, shoemakers and a horsebreaker.[10] Living on the margins of the parishes, the cottagers formed distinct communities. Those on Bringsty were served by a Methodist mission which held open-air meetings on the common in the 1830s, before a Primitive Methodist chapel

---

[4] HARC, AM33/5, Bromyard Foreign court (Norton), date illegible and 4 October 1555.
[5] Glamorgan Record Office, CL Manorial Box 4, Bromyard Foreign court (Linton), 22 April 1562, 8 October 1605.
[6] HARC, AM33/9/3, Whitbourne court, 8 May 1622.
[7] HARC, AA59/A/2, f. 137.
[8] Glamorgan Record Office, CL Manorial Box 4, Bromyard Foreign court (Linton), 16 April 1605; Whitbourne court, 17 April and 9 October 1605; HARC, AM33/9/8, Whitbourne court, 16 October 1622.
[9] P. Williams, *Whitbourne: A Bishop's Manor* (privately printed, 1979), pp. 145–6.
[10] On Badley Wood Common, 19 of the 25 householders were farm labourers, as were 22 out of 34 on the part of Bringsty Common in Whitbourne parish: TNA, HO 107/419/18, ff. 17–23.

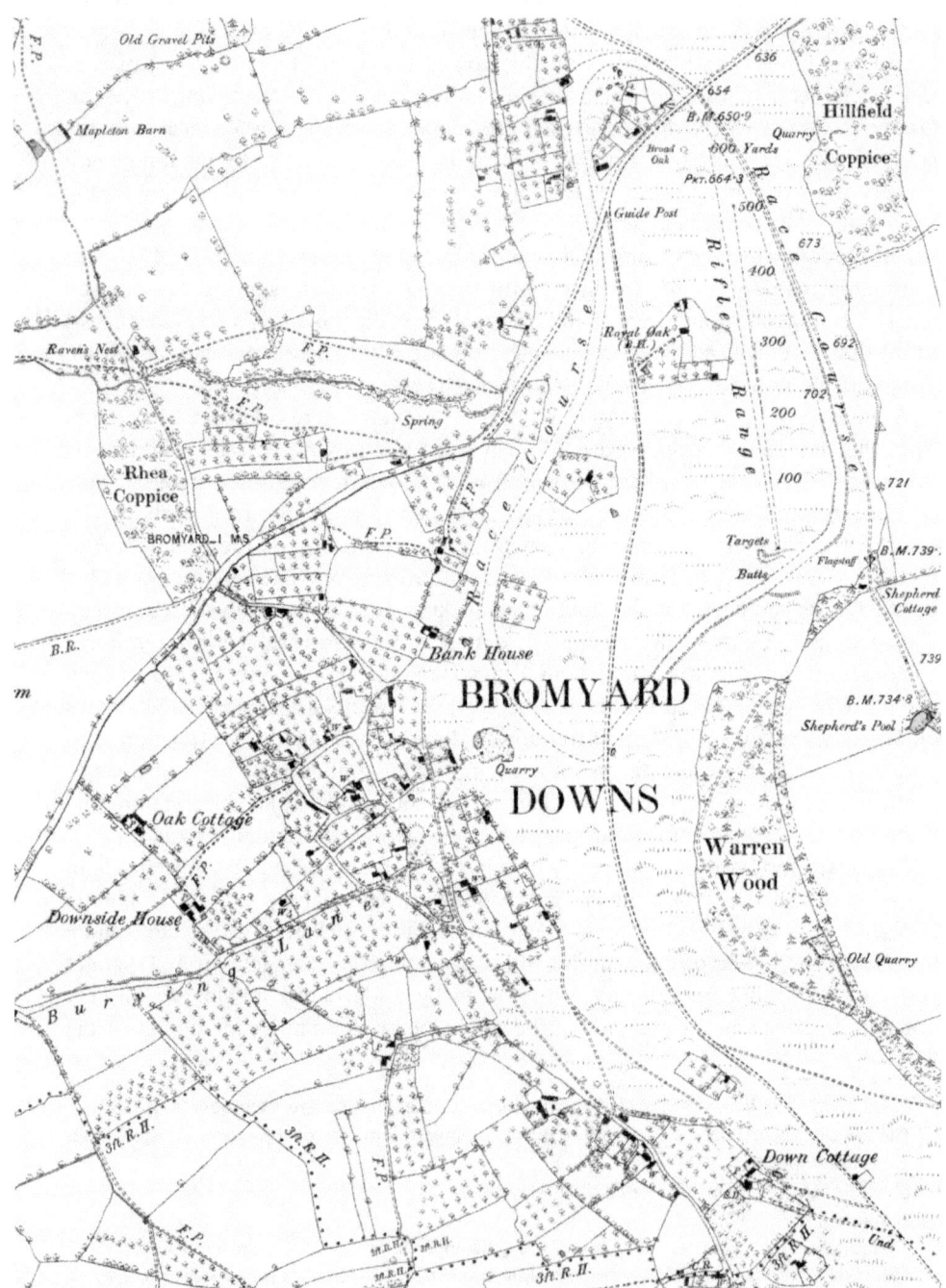

Figure 56. Bromyard Downs in 1885 (OS Six-Inch map, Herefordshire 21NW, surveyed 1885).

Figure 57. Cottage on Bringsty Common. One of the numerous cottages, set in small enclosures, which dot the bracken and scrub of the common.

was built in 1861.[11] The cluster of cottages on the edge of Bromyard Downs had a Wesleyan Methodist chapel (built 1886) and Anglican services were held in the golf clubhouse on the common by the 1920s, until a small plot was enclosed from the common for a mission church and recreation room in 1924–25. After its completion, the vicar of Bromyard wrote that 'the cottagers are uniting in a quite surprising way' to involvement in the social activities and religious services, suggesting that they continued to be viewed as a distinct community.[12]

From the nineteenth century use of the commons for recreational and other non-agrarian purposes grew, Bromyard Downs acquiring the sporting and military activities characteristic of common land adjacent to towns. Horse racing was recorded there from 1810. According to local tradition, a racecourse was laid out by soldiers returning from the Napoleonic wars, the first race meeting being in 1820; the last in 1900.[13] When the Herefordshire Rifle Volunteer Corps were raised in 1860, the Bromyard company trained on a rifle range laid out on the common; analysis of ammunition

---

[11] Williams, *Whitbourne*, p. 158.
[12] TNA, MAF 25/110, J. F. Stephen Pritchitt, vicar of Bromyard, to Ministry of Agriculture, 25 June 1924, 4 December 1925.
[13] https://bromyarddowns.co.uk/community/; http://www.greyhoundderby.com/Bromyard%20Racecourse.html.

Figure 58. Bromyard Downs in July. Part of the meadow grass has been cut for hay.

recovered from the range suggests that it had been abandoned by 1890.[14] A golf course was laid out in 1895 at the northern end of the common, overlapping with the racecourse, and flourished until *c*.1940.[15] Recreational use of both commons expanded in the early twentieth century, Bringsty Common becoming a favoured destination for cyclists from the Birmingham area, the 'Live and Let Live' public house on the common becoming well-known. By the 1920s, the commons were said to be 'simply alive' with picnicking motorists on Bank Holiday weekends.[16]

The need for a scheme of management had been raised in 1897, when a group of freeholders mooted that the commons might be regulated, presumably under the Inclosure Act 1845, in order to prevent encroachments and to protect the commoners' rights. The division of the commons between parishes and manors (both were partly in manors belonging to the Ecclesiastical Commissioners and partly in the manor of Clater and Hodgbatch) was cited as a reason for difficulty in vesting authority under

---

[14] N. Baker and T. Hoverd, *Bromyard Downs Rifle Range Report*, Herefordshire Archaeology Report No. 356 (Herefordshire Council, n.d. [2016]), pp. 8, 18–19. However, military use seems to have continued for some years: a 'sham fight' on the Downs and Bringsty was being planned in 1902: *Bromyard News*, 24 July 1902, p. 4.

[15] https://www.golfsmissinglinks.co.uk/ (under Bromyard Broad Oak), which states that the course closed in the 1930s; the information board on Bromyard Downs (2021) gives the closure date as 1942.

[16] *Bromyard News*, 9 August 1923, p. 2; 24 April 1924, p. 3.

a single body.[17] Nothing came of the initiative, regulation being deferred until 1951, when the Downs, Bringsty and Badley Wood were regulated by Bromyard Rural District Council by a scheme under the Commons Act 1899.[18]

During the Second World War, 31 acres (12.5 ha) of the Downs were requisitioned by the County Agricultural Executive Committee and were ploughed, proving to be productive agricultural land. After the war, when de-requisitioning was contemplated and the regulation scheme was introduced, Bromyard Rural District Council sought to ensure that the cultivated land should not be allowed to revert to 'rough bracken'. Their strategy included purchasing the manorial rights from the Ecclesiastical Commissioners in 1953, in order to gain greater control.[19] Parts of the commons, 'in a deplorable state, overgrown with bracken and practically of no value to the commoners', should be used for housing, they suggested, to help preserve good agricultural land which would otherwise have to be used.[20] John Knott, Vice-Chairman of Bromyard Rural District Council and one of the drivers behind the Council's proposals, urged a comprehensive set of measures: a statutory commoners' committee with powers to determine who had common rights, to improve the carrying capacity of the common by levelling, manuring and draining, and to levy a rate from the commoners, based on numbers of livestock turned out, to cover costs. 'Subject to the overriding interests of PRODUCTION', he wrote, the aim should be 'to preserve the rights of the public at large to the Commons for reasonable recreation and ammenity'.[21]

On the return of the requisitioned land in 1955, the Bromyard Downs Commoners Committee (which had come into being since 1951) took the initiative in improving the common, with a view to enhancing the 'grazing, agricultural and pleasure purposes of the Downs'. In 1956 the committee cleared a 12-acre (5-ha) plot, ploughed it for rape and turnips and undersowed it with grass; a second plot was being cleared in 1958.[22] These actions led to local protest, ostensibly because the committee, which consisted mainly of farmers and stockbreeders, had failed to consult the smaller property owners who had common rights and was displacing them by filling the common with sheep. The changing face of the common ('levelling and bulldozing the beauty spot'; ploughing and fencing; blocking footpaths; clearing trees; removing seats) also provoked criticism. Opposing views of the value of the Downs are exposed in the response of one member of the committee to these complaints. 'Is it not better to cultivate the downs than leave them for "Brummies" to despoil with litter and debris at weekends and [to have] bracken growing on good land?', he asked rhetorically.[23]

---

[17] TNA, MAF 25/110, E. L. Cave, Bromyard, to Secretary, Board of Agriculture, 7 December 1897.
[18] TNA, MAF 25/110, Scheme for regulation, 2 August 1951 (approved by minister, 1 October 1951).
[19] TNA, MAF 25/110, J. B. Senior, clerk to Bromyard RDC, to Ministry of Agriculture, 10 April 1951; conveyance, 2 September 1953 (copy courtesy of Bringsty Common Manorial Court, 2021).
[20] TNA, MAF 25/110, J. B. Senior to MAF, 9 April 1952.
[21] Ibid., J. E. Knott, Birchyfield, Bromyard, to Minister of Agriculture, 10 December 1951 (emphasis and spelling in MS retained).
[22] *Bromyard News*, 29 March 1956, p. 3; 19 June 1958, p. 4.
[23] *Kington Times*, 12 June 1959.

Although wartime cultivation and continuing grazing ensured that much of Bromyard Downs retained its open, grassland character (Figure 58), military training on Bringsty Common and the consequent disruption to grazing patterns appear to have led to an expansion in scrub by the 1950s. John Knott had painted a bleak picture in 1951: Bringsty and Bromyard commons, he wrote, were 'six hundred acres of excellent rolling land, covered entirely, with the exception of some green strips leading to cottages, by impenetrable seas of bracken and the whole tenanted by a few scraggy sheep'. Sporadic bracken fires in springtime left 'huge black patches of burnt sticks'.[24] Despite these comments, local memory suggests that grazing by sheep, cattle and horses continued on Bringsty into the 1960s, keeping the sward short and preventing encroachment by scrub. Bracken continued to be mown each autumn as litter for livestock and poultry.[25]

Registrations under the CRA suggest continuing active exercise of common rights. On Bringsty Common 69 provisional registrations of grazing rights were made (for sheep, cattle, horses, donkeys, poultry and goats), though 12 were subsequently cancelled and other initial claims were modified. Rights of estovers (or bracken-cutting) were included in 47 registrations, pannage in 33 (though most of these were cancelled before confirmation), turbary (or turf-cutting) in 12 and rights in the soil in 6.[26] Many of the grazing rights were rationalised by commons commissioners' decisions in 1978, which imposed a standard equivalency formula of 8 sheep rights to 1 beast; 4 sheep to 1 donkey and 1 sheep to 1 goat.[27] Several of the provisional registrations reflected the traditional cottage economy, specifying rights to run poultry and to take particular produce from the common. The rights registered for Rose Cottage, for example, were to gather bracken, gorse or bushes; to take turf and tree loppings; and to have free range for 50 poultry on the northern part of the common.[28] On Bromyard Downs, 86 grazing rights were registered under the CRA, as were 26 rights of estovers, some specifically for bracken and gorse, and 9 rights of turbary. Again, grazing rights were regularised by a commons commissioner's decision in 1976.[29]

Registration heralded a revival in the active management of Bringsty Common. In 1971 a committee, known as the Bringsty Common Manorial Court, was established to manage the common, in part because it straddled two parishes and thus two local authorities. Composed of residents and those with common rights, the committee's work initially focused not on grazing rights but on amenity matters, such as clearing

---

[24] TNA, MAF 25/110, J. E. Knott, Bromyard, to Minister of Agriculture, 17 December 1951, later quoted by Archer Baldwin, MP for Leominster: *Hansard*, House of Commons, 14 May 1954, col. 1636. Cf. Hoskins & Stamp, p. 285.
[25] Information from Linda James, Bringsty Common, 2021.
[26] Herefordshire Council, Commons Register, CL 14.
[27] CCD, Hereford & Worcester: Bringsty Common (CL 14), 215/D/22–49.
[28] Herefordshire Council, Commons Register, CL 14, rights section, no. 37. Similar rights occur in entries nos. 14, 30, 31, 56 and 60.
[29] CCD, Hereford & Worcester: Bromyard Downs (CL 15), 215/D/50–87.

rubbish, controlling rabbits, licensing catering vans and cutting firebreaks.[30] Both Bringsty and the Downs had become such tourist honeypots that in 1972 Herefordshire county planning authorities proposed creating a country park on the commons, complete with car parks and campsite, toilet blocks and a viewing platform. The plan provoked vigorous opposition from locals and was swiftly dropped.[31]

A major theme in the recent history of the commons has been the decline and cessation of grazing since the 1970s, hastened on Bringsty by the increased risk to livestock from motor traffic on the unfenced A44 road. It was said that around 600 sheep grazed the common in the 1970s, but that the number declined to around 140 by the late 1980s and to perhaps 30 or so by the time of the 2001 foot and mouth disease outbreak; grazing ceased when the last few sheep were removed c.2009.[32] As grazing numbers declined, scrubland spread, giving parts of the common a densely wooded character akin to that of the nearby Badley Wood Common, which became a thicket of secondary woodland. On Bromyard Downs, some grazing also continued until the dislocation caused by foot and mouth disease in 2001.[33]

Undergrazing had thus become an issue on both commons by the late twentieth century, allowing bracken and scrub to spread unchecked at a time when the commons' conservation and recreational value was growing. Bringsty was designated as a Special Wildlife Site by the Herefordshire Nature Trust in 1990 – its rich bird life and butterfly and insect populations being particularly noteworthy – and the common was put under a twenty-year Countryside Stewardship Scheme in 1997.[34] In 2011 some new common grazing rights were registered under the terms of the Commons Act 2006, explicitly because the common was considered to be undergrazed.[35]

On Bromyard Downs, the cessation of grazing threatened habitat diversity in the species-rich grassland areas and surviving patches of heath. Active management included grass-cutting and haymaking to prevent encroachment by scrub, and the management plan drawn up for the Bromyard Downs Common Association and the Herefordshire Wildlife Trust in 2015 contemplated re-introducing grazing to maintain the grassland ecology.[36] Like many lowland commons, both Bringsty and Bromyard Downs are examples of 'amenity commons', now managed as recreational open spaces and valued for their ecological and cultural heritage.

---

[30] Evidence of early minute books, courtesy of Nigel Shaw.
[31] *Birmingham Daily Post*, 23 October 1972, p. 12; 11 December 1972, p. 5.
[32] Information from Derek Brookes and Tom Fisher, Bringsty Common Manorial Court (2021).
[33] H. Welsh, *Bromyard Downs Common Management Plan 2015–2025*, http://www.bromyarddowns.co.uk/media/1640/bromyard-downs-10-yr-management-plan-simplified-version-2016.pdf, pp. 5-6.
[34] https://brockhamptongrouppc.org.uk/the-parish/bringsty-common/.
[35] Herefordshire Council, Decision Notice, 27 October 2011, re. applications 2010/RIGHT/002-004.
[36] Welsh, *Bromyard Downs Common Management Plan*, esp. pp. 6, 9, 12.

CHAPTER 15

IBSLEY COMMON AND ROCKFORD COMMON, NEW FOREST, HAMPSHIRE

IBSLEY COMMON (932 ACRES; 377 ha) and Rockford Common (*c*.460 acres; *c*.185 ha)[1] were part of the arc of common land abutting the historic northern and western boundaries of the New Forest, brought within the limits of the modern forest by the New Forest Act 1964. The two commons lay open to the forest wastes in Linwood bailiwick, so that their histories can only be understood in relation to the history of the forest. The manors of Rockford (in Ellingham parish) and Ibsley descended together from the sixteenth century and were bought by the family of Lord Normanton in 1825, becoming part of the Somerley estate.[2] The National Trust acquired the majority of both commons in 1999.

Most of the commons consist of dry heath on a plateau at around 60–70m above sea level. Their western edges, abutting the enclosed land in Ibsley and Ellingham, lie where the ground falls away to the Avon valley. The commons are bisected by Dockens Water and its wet valley mire, with most of Ibsley Common lying to the north and Rockford Common to the south (though the manorial and parish boundary cuts across the terrain, ignoring the valley). The underlying geology is Eocene sands and clays, capped on the plateau by river terrace gravels, on which leached podzol soils carry a cover of heather, with areas of bracken and gorse. Rockford Common has a more wooded character than Ibsley, with scattered clumps of pine, patches of birch scrub and some oak, many of the trees probably having colonised from adjacent woodland in the forest.[3]

Writing in 1905, Heywood Sumner noted how, although the forest landscape seemed to include the heather-clad plateau of Ibsley and Rockford commons, the forest's legal limits followed a line across the open heath coinciding approximately with the eastern limits of Ibsley and Ellingham parishes (Figure 60), defined by 'low grey posts, furred

---

[1] Acreages are based on Somerley Estate sales particulars, 1919 (copy in HRO, 67M99/PX21). The estate owned the whole of Ibsley Common and 415 acres (representing all but *c*.50 acres) of Rockford Common.
[2] *VCH Hants* IV, pp. 579–80.
[3] British Geological Survey 1:50,000 Map, England & Wales Sheet 314 (Ringwood) (2004); J. H. Lavender and C. R. Tubbs, 'Report on the Ecology of Rockford Common, Hampshire (1965)', pp. 2–7 (TS report in HRO, H/CL5/1p/18/14/2).

Figure 59. Ibsley Common, Hampshire, viewed across the valley of Dockens Water. Whitefield Plantation is on the skyline.

with lichen, & hidden with ling'.[4] Until 1964, that invisible boundary across the heath separated manorial from forest wastes, the common rights regimes differing on either side. As Sumner put it, his rights as a freeholder in Ibsley allowed him to turn beasts onto Ibsley Common without payment, to dig sand, gravel and soil on the common and to take from it as much turf, gorse, bracken or heather as required for his own use; in other words, to exercise the usual common rights of pasture, estovers and turbary, and of common in the soil, on the manorial waste.[5] By contrast, on the forest beyond the stakes, common rights were attached to specific holdings. They allowed grazing only on payment of *per capita* marking fees, and some holdings also had rights to pannage (again on payment per pig), to a certain number of cords of firewood, or to digging specified numbers of turves. Common of turbary was sometimes interpreted loosely, to include cutting 'fern, heath and furze', and some properties had common of marl (the right to take calcareous clay from established pits in the forest).[6]

A recurring theme in the history of the forest was a grumbling incompatibility between the commoners' interests and the Crown's priorities, which saw the forest

---

[4] H. Sumner, *Cuckoo Hill: The Book of Gorley* (London, 1987), pp. 19–20.
[5] Ibid., pp. 22–3, confirmed by Somerley Estate sales particulars, 1919, p. [2], para. 2.
[6] Sumner, *Cuckoo Hill*, pp. 22–3; C. R. Tubbs, *The New Forest: History, Ecology and Conservation* (Lyndhurst, 2001), esp. pp. 113–16.

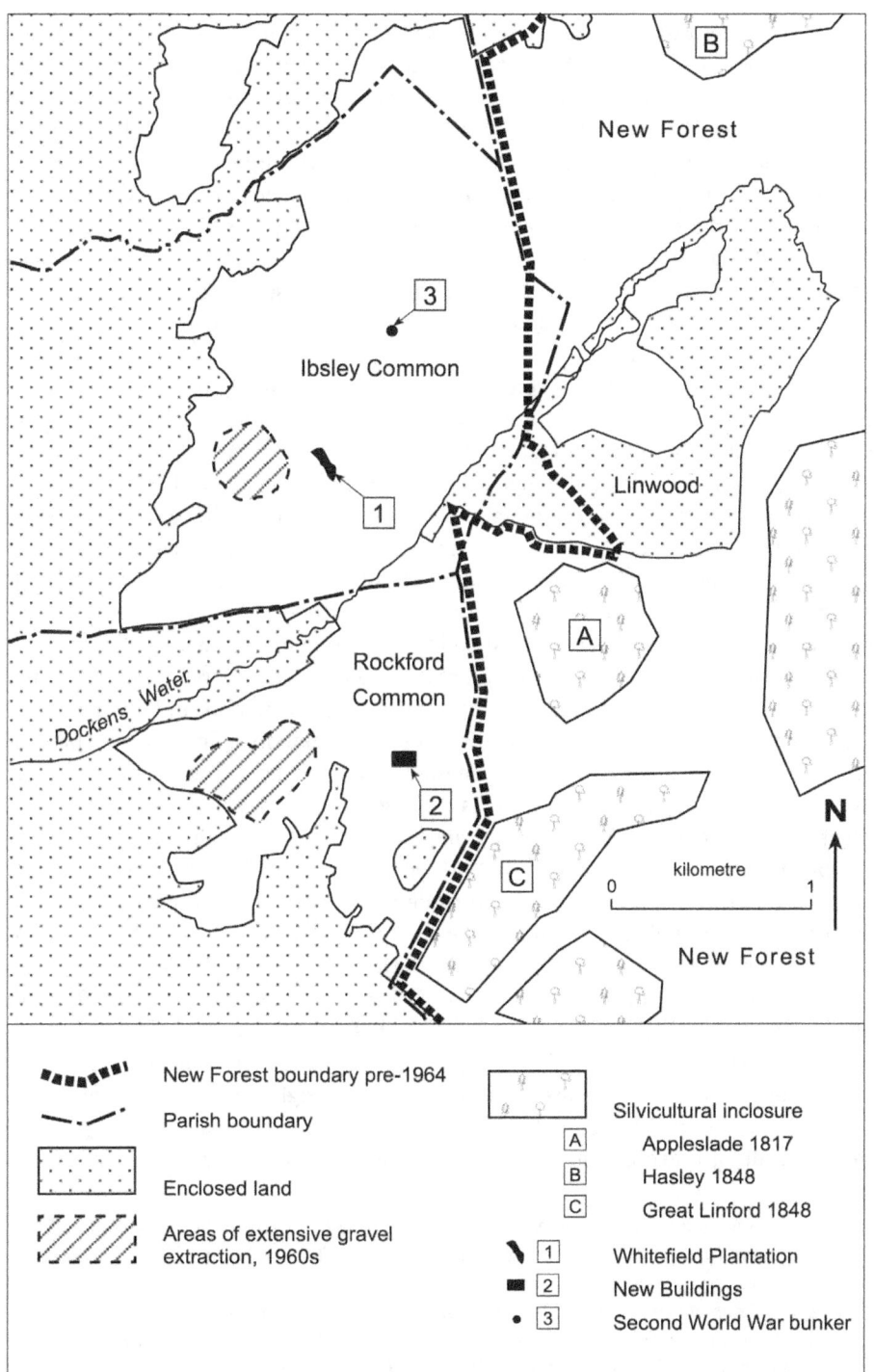

Figure 60. Ibsley and Rockford commons.

first as hunting ground and then, from the seventeenth century, as a source of timber. By the nineteenth century, the state's increasing desire to use the New Forest for timber production resulted in tensions with the commoners. Legislation in 1698, 1808 and 1851 allowed a substantial increase in the acreage of enclosed land for forestry plantations, putting greater pressure on grazing on the open heaths. In a gesture intended to mitigate this, the Deer Removal Act 1851 relinquished the Crown's right to keep deer on the open ground of the forest in exchange for the right to enclose a further 10,000 acres (c.4,050 ha).[7] As a result of these acts, fences were thrown around parts of the forest, creating a series of forestry enclosures, including Appleslade (enclosed 1817), Great Linford and Hasley (both 1848), close to the boundary with Ibsley and Rockford commons.[8]

The increased pressure on common rights as a result of the drive for timber, combined with the growing awareness of the forest's value as recreational space for the nation at large, provoked resistance and led eventually to the New Forest Act 1877, which not only prevented further enclosure for plantations but also put in place structures to protect common rights, by reinstating the ancient Verderers' Court to regulate use of the forest commons.[9] A scale of fees payable for each animal grazed on the forest, for pigs exercising a right of pannage, and for turves cut on the commons was specified, in effect confirming the commoners' rights and laying down the framework under which the forest commons continue to be managed.

Rights on the forest wastes were not restricted to smallholders within the bounds of the forest but extended to certain properties in adjacent manors. In 1670 the lords of the manor of Ibsley claimed on behalf of their tenants common of pasture and pannage and liberty to cut turf and heath on the forest wastes, as did three landowners in Rockford. The claimants paid small sums of 'lease fee' and 'month money' and, in some cases, oats and eggs in kind.[10] When claims were prepared for the register of rights compiled after the Deer Removal Act 1851, eighteen landholdings and thirty cottages on the Somerley estate in Ibsley parish made them. They included pasture rights for 30 horses, 112 horned cattle, and 803 sheep (750 of which were accounted for by just two farms); pannage for 182 pigs; 147 loads of turf for fuel annually; 40 loads of heath or furze and 22 loads of fern. The cottagers' claims were restricted to turf (90 loads) and pannage (for 32 pigs). While some claimants paid forest dues and 2s 6d for a 'fern ticket', others, including the cottagers, paid nothing.[11] Evidence gathered in the process of compiling the claims suggests that not all rights were actually exercised. Evans' Farm, Ibsley (200 acres; 80 ha) claimed a right to 12 loads of turf from the forest but did not exercise it. Nor did a 10-acre (4-ha) smallholding, despite a claim

---

[7] H. Cook, *New Forest: The Forging of a Landscape* (Oxford, 2018), pp. 157–9; P. Readman, *Storied Ground: Landscape and the Shaping of English National Identity* (Cambridge, 2018), pp. 158–64.
[8] Cook, *New Forest*, pp. 150–1.
[9] Readman, *Storied Ground*, pp. 163–4, 184–5; Cook, *New Forest*, pp. 161–2.
[10] *Abstract of Claims Preferred at a Justice Seat held for the New Forest ... AD 1670 with a Return made by Commissioners acting under the Acts of the 39 & 40 Geo. 3, cap. 86 and 41 Geo. 3, cap. 108 as to Incroachments &c. in the said Forest* (London, 1853), pp. 8–9, 14, 29–30, 32, 120, 209, 289.
[11] HRO, 21M57/E864, bundle 3 (summary of claims).

for 6 loads of turf, having all it needed from Ibsley Common.[12] Evans' Farm turned out 30 head of a herd of 40 cattle, 8 horses and 30 or 40 pigs, but none of its flock of 250 sheep, despite claiming a right to do so; and had 7 loads of fern, 3 of heath and 3 of furze. The farmer sought permission to cut the litter from the keeper, 'who tells him where to cut it'. The holding paid forest dues totalling 7s 5d, part of which was a payment in lieu of half a bushel of oats.[13]

Claims from the Somerley estate were consolidated and nine other claims for properties in Ellingham parish (which included the island of enclosures inside the forest boundary at Linwood) were allowed. Rights on the forest confirmed by the commissioners included pasture rights attached to most of the land in Ibsley and Ellingham parishes, and rights of turbary (for twelve messuages), pannage (a few properties) and fuel wood (for two properties) in Ellingham, but not in Ibsley.[14] The forest commons clearly formed an integral part of the resources available to the inhabitants of Ibsley and Rockford.

The boundary between manorial and forest wastes was also permeable when it came to the exploitation of another resource – the carpet of flowering heather. As on heathlands elsewhere in Hampshire and Dorset, honey production formed part of the local economy on the heather-clad commons of the New Forest. Both Ibsley and Rockford commons preserve tangible evidence of this in the form of small, low, banked enclosures known as 'bee gardens', built to protect straw beehives from the grazing livestock.[15] The date of those on Ibsley and Rockford commons is not known, but over sixty such enclosures were presented at the New Forest swainmote court in 1635, the majority of the fifty-five presentments coming from the western bailiwicks (see Figure 61). Almost all were very small enclosures, typically containing 1 perch of ground (equivalent to 5.5 yards square, assuming that statute measure was used), to house groups of hives ('beestalls'). Those presented were mainly yeomen or husbandmen from the local farming communities (including two men from Rockford), the number of hives in some of the bee gardens suggesting commercial honey production: a group of 7 bee gardens in Fritham bailiwick held 50 hives; another group in Linwood had 35. The standard fines of 5s 0d for each presentment are probably to be interpreted as licence fees for the small encroachments which enabled the exploitation of a valuable heathland resource.[16]

Lying outside the forest until 1964, Ibsley and Rockford commons also possessed features which differentiated them from the forest commons. As manorial waste, control over them lay ultimately with the lord of the manor. Small plantations of pine on Ibsley Common, at Whitefield and Dorridge, are thought to have been created by the Earl of Normanton around 1835, not as forestry plantations but to improve

---

[12] Ibid., bundle 2: nos. 67a, 71.
[13] Ibid., bundle 2: no. 67a.
[14] *New Forest Register of Decisions on Claims to Forest Rights* (London, 1858), nos. 719–27 (Ellingham parish), 1126 (Earl of Normanton).
[15] Sumner (*Cuckoo Hill*, p. 25) noted three at Chibden Bottom on Ibsley Common.
[16] D. J. Stagg, *A Calendar of New Forest Documents: The Fifteenth to Seventeenth Centuries* (Hampshire County Council, 1983), nos. 653–707.

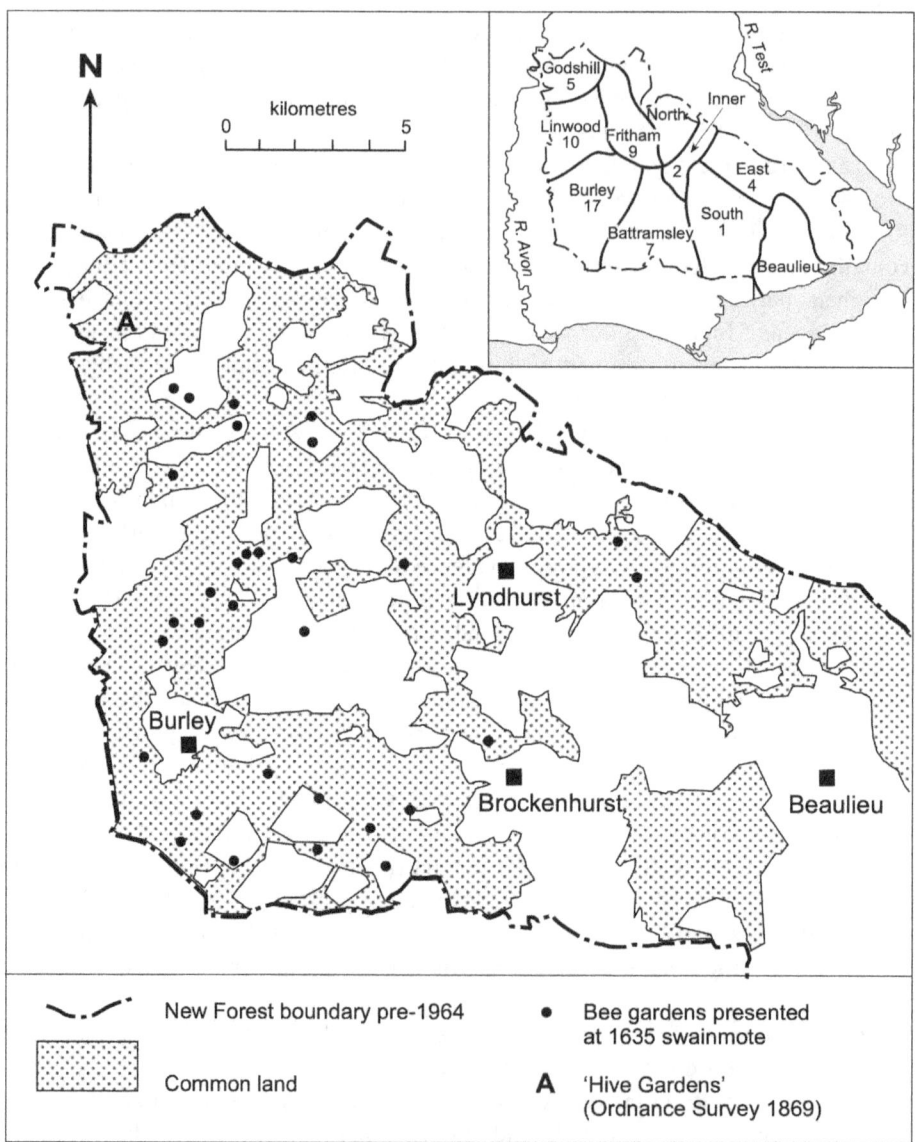

Figure 61. The New Forest: bee gardens recorded in 1635 in relation to common land. Approximate locations of bee gardens have been identified from minor place-names on the Drivers' map (*A Plan of His Majesty's Forest, called the New Forest* ... 2nd edn, 1814) and early OS maps. The inset shows the number of presentments in each bailiwick. Source: D. J. Stagg, *A Calendar of New Forest Documents: The Fifteenth to Seventeenth Centuries* (Hampshire County Council, 1983), nos. 653–707.

the view of the heathland skyline from his residence at Somerley on the other side of the Avon valley.[17] Another aspect of seigniorial exploitation is hinted at by pillow mounds on Rockford Common, which suggest the presence of rabbit warrens on the heath. Some are aligned with earthen banks marking temporary enclosures, probably of eighteenth- or early nineteenth-century date (some containing evidence of plough ridges), which have subsequently reverted to the common.[18]

Rockford Common also exhibited an aspect of community use found widely on lowland commons elsewhere. A small section was taken in c.1835 for two pairs of parish poor houses. Set in a rectangular enclosure, which provided generous gardens, the New Buildings, as they were known, were of cob construction with thatched roofs. In 1841, each housed a labouring family with lodgers (foster children, a young woman and her baby, elderly paupers). They continued to be occupied for over a century but had fallen into ruin by the 1960s and the site was later redeveloped for a private house.[19]

The late nineteenth and twentieth centuries saw both short-lived military use and longer-term land use changes. When large military manoeuvres took place in the New Forest over three weeks in the summer of 1895, the largest camp, housing 8,000 men, was on the edge of Rockford Common, just inside the forest.[20] The common was again used for a camp during manoeuvres in August 1908, when a storm blew down the field hospital there.[21] During the Second World War, both commons fell within the New Forest Training Area, despite at that time lying outside the forest boundary.[22] Several structures were built on Ibsley Common in connection with the RAF station at Ibsley (which opened in 1941 and closed in 1947). They include a polygonal blast wall for the wooden tower of a Direction Finding Station, a bunker and the footings of an accommodation building.[23]

Of greater impact on the landscape was large-scale gravel-digging in the mid-twentieth century. Comparatively small sand and gravel pits had been opened on the western margins of both commons by 1870,[24] but the scale of extraction expanded greatly in the 1960s. Gravel was stripped to a depth of up to 6 metres from around 40 acres (16 ha) on the western side of Rockford Common and a slightly smaller acreage

---

[17] Sumner, *Cuckoo Hill*, p. 25.

[18] A. Young, *The Aggregate Landscape of Hampshire* (Cornwall County Council Historic Environment Service, 2008), pp. 62–4: PDF version (2011) at https://archaeologydataservice.ac.uk/archiveDS/archiveDownload?t=arch-1062-1/dissemination/pdf/cornwall2-74457_1.pdf.

[19] A. H. Pasmore, 'Enclosure at New Buildings, Rockford Common', *Hampshire Field Club Newsletter*, 37 (Spring, 2002), pp. vii–ix.

[20] *St James's Gazette*, 18 July 1895, p. 7. Reports of the manoeuvres include *London Daily News*, 31 August 1895, p. 5.

[21] *Army & Navy Gazette*, 8 August 1908, p. 12; *Daily Mirror*, 28 August 1908, p. 3.

[22] New Forest Training Area map, 1943, at https://nfknowledge.org/contributions/the-new-forest-training-area-map-1943/#map=10/-1.58/50.87/0/24:0:0.6|39:1:1|40:1:1.

[23] https://nfknowledge.org/contributions/ibsley-hf-df-station-overview/#map=10/-1.75/50.89/0/24:0:0.6|39:1:1|40:1:1.

[24] OS Six-Inch maps, Hampshire 62 and 70 (1872 edn, surveyed 1870–71).

Figure 62. Ponies grazing on Rockford Common.

on Ibsley Common, lowering the land surface and leaving flat-bottomed depressions flanked by steep, gorse-clad sides.[25]

Pastoral use of the commons also changed. It seems likely that grazing declined across the first half of the twentieth century. In the first decade of the century, the commoners were carrying out controlled burning of the heath with the approval of the lord of the manor, to improve the quality of grazing by destroying leggy heather and gorse. After unauthorised and uncontrolled fires sprang up following a burn on Ibsley Common in March 1906, the Gorley, Ibsley and Rockford commoners met as a body in 1907 to discuss the systematic burning of heather and agreed to meet annually in February to plan each year's burning.[26] Grazing was presumably then at a level to justify such organised improvement of the sward. By the 1950s, however, there were very few active commoners and few common rights were exercised,[27] circumstances which may have facilitated the boundary change in 1964, which brought Ibsley, Rockford and other adjacent commons within the perambulation of the forest. The 1964 act was prompted in part by the need to create clearer physical boundaries around the forest commons when cattle grids were being constructed to restrict livestock to the

---

[25] See papers for the 1966 public inquiry into gravel extraction on Rockford Common: HRO, H/CL5/1p/18.
[26] Sumner, *Cuckoo Hill*, pp. 67–81.
[27] L. E. Tavener, *The Common Lands of Hampshire* (Southampton, 1957), p. 85.

commons and prevent them from straying along roadside verges to inhabited areas. Unless the adjacent manorial commons were treated as part of the forest, the open boundary between them would have defeated the object of securing the boundaries of common land in the forest.[28] The act also brought grazing rights over the adjacent commons under the auspices of the verderers. Marking fees were introduced, initially (until 2025) at reduced rates: one-eighth of the normal fee for bovine stock; half the fee for other animals.[29] Although other common rights were not brought into the machinery of forest administration, Ibsley and Rockford commons, grazed by ponies and herds of cattle (Figure 62), are now effectively an integral part of the New Forest pastoral commoning system.

---

[28] Tubbs, *New Forest*, pp. 94–6.
[29] 'The Commons Agreement 1964' (Agreement between verderers and commoners at the time the bill was going through Parliament. Copy courtesy of Sue Westwood, Clerk to the Verderers, 2021).

CHAPTER 16

WIMBLEDON COMMON AND PUTNEY HEATH, SURREY

WIMBLEDON COMMON WAS PIVOTAL in the battles over metropolitan commons in the 1860s, its transformation from manorial waste to a playground, 'the pearl of London's open spaces',[1] forming a central strand in its history. The debates over the future of the common played a prominent part in the revolution in attitudes to common land in the mid-nineteenth century – and in the 1970s the imaginary litter-recycling 'Wombles of Wimbledon Common' immortalised, through story and song, the place of common land in modern urban life. With the nearby open space of Richmond Park, Wimbledon Common and the adjacent Putney Heath form one of the largest of London's green lungs, surrounded by the urban areas of Putney, Wimbledon, Kingston and Richmond.

Wimbledon Common and Putney Heath comprise 1,140 acres (460 ha) of woodland and open ground. They form a fairly level plateau of river gravels at *c.*52m above sea level, capping the London Clay, which outcrops on the western slopes of the common, where the land drops to the valley of the Beverley Brook. Together, the commons represent the bulk of the manorial waste of the manor of Wimbledon[2] and also include a small area which was part of the waste of the manor of Battersea and Wandsworth; the Earls Spencer were lords of both manors from the eighteenth century.

Records of the manor court make it possible to reconstruct the use and regulation of the common from 1462 to the mid-seventeenth century.[3] From the earliest records, there is evidence of pressure on the common – from those without common rights overburdening the common with livestock; from unringed pigs churning up the soil; from those taking fuel illicitly or excessively. The common's fuel resources, in particular, not only firewood but also gorse ('furze') and bushes, were in high demand. In the decade after 1500 men were presented for cutting more fuel (namely '*firses et bushes*') on the common 'than seems necessary or fitting'; their number included

---

[1] W. Johnson, *Wimbledon Common: Its Geology, Antiquities and Natural History* (London, 1912), p. 281.
[2] The manor also included smaller areas of common land at Putney Lower Common and Barnes Common and at East Sheen Common and Palewell Common in Mortlake parish.
[3] [P. H. Lawrence], *Extracts from the Court Rolls of the Manor of Wimbledon extending from 1 Edward IV to AD 1864* (London, 1866); hereafter '*Wimbledon Ct R.*'.

a brewer, who took 'furze, thorns and bushes' in excess to burn in his brewhouse.[4] Regulations aimed at reducing demand for fuel were imposed in the 1520s, when bakers, brewers and undertenants ('undersettes') were forbidden from taking wood or furze from the common.[5]

By custom, grazing rights were limited to copyholders ('virgate holders').[6] In the mid-sixteenth century the court placed differential limits on the number of animals copyholders and cottagers could turn out on the common: in 1559 it ordered that copyholders could graze no more than 5 cattle and 25 sheep, 1 horse and 5 pigs for each virgate, whereas cottagers were limited to 3 cattle, 1 horse and 2 pigs. The same court also imposed limits on fuel: 5 cartloads of wood for each virgate of land held; 2 cartloads for cottagers.[7] Continuing pressure on resources led to reductions in those limits. Cottagers in Putney were limited to one cow and a heifer or one mare with a colt in 1564, while in 1576 fuel rights were reduced for a three-year period to two cartloads of wood for each virgate annually and one cartload for each cottage.[8] In order to preserve resources as population expanded, the courts ordered that recently-built cottages should have neither grazing nor fuel rights.[9]

Reiterations of these restrictions (or tinkering with their limits) across the later sixteenth and seventeenth centuries suggest continuing pressure on the common, as the court struggled to preserve both resources and order. Commons keepers (*supervisores communiorum*) were appointed from 1610 to control access to firewood, instituting a regime, recalled in the nineteenth century, whereby the keepers declared the common open at Michaelmas (29 September), allowing commoners to cut the oak pollards for fuel across the winter months, until it was closed again at Lady Day (25 March).[10]

In the eighteenth century, the pressures on Putney Heath and Wimbledon Common changed character, as fashionable residences were built around their margins. Small sections of the common were enclosed by licence across the second half of the century,[11] and some unlicensed encroachments reflect the change in the social tone of the common, as when Percival Lewis, a wealthy sugar merchant, railed in

---

[4] Ibid., pp. 62–7.
[5] Ibid., pp. 76–7 (1521: no baker or brewer to take wood or furze), 80–1 (1527: no 'undersettes' to carry or draw wood).
[6] Ibid., pp. 24–5 (1468), 57 (1494).
[7] Ibid., pp. 114–19.
[8] Ibid., pp. 126–9, 140–2.
[9] Ibid., pp. 146–7 (1582: re. cottages built within twenty years in Mortlake or East Sheen), 184–5 (1609: re. cottages 'lately' built), 230–1 (1655: licence to build a cottage 'without benefit of common').
[10] 'Overseers and supervisors of the common woods' at Mortlake were appointed in 1610; in 1676 two surveyors of the commons were appointed for each of Putney, Wimbledon and Mortlake: *Wimbledon Ct R.*, pp. 186–8, 242. For the system for regulating the cropping of pollards before they were felled in 1812, see Eversley, pp. 65–6.
[11] *Wimbledon Ct R.*, pp. 314–15 (licensed enclosure 1757), 319–26 (1761), 332 (1762), 345–6, 352–3 (1780s), 367–403 (1790s).

and enclosed a pond near his mansion on Putney Heath in 1745.[12] The new villas put particular pressure on the sward of the commons – George Lord Hobart was said to have taken 4,000 turves from the commons in Putney without authority in 1802. Despite an attempt in 1783 to prevent turf-stripping without licence and to require those who obtained permission to do so to sow grass seed on the ground from which they had taken turves, it was reported in 1810 that householders freely cut turf 'for the improvement of their gardens and pleasure grounds'.[13]

By 1800, order on the common was beginning to break down, notwithstanding the manor court's repeated attempts to regulate its use. In 1796, the court noted that 'many encroachments are daily committed' against the orders concerning gravel-digging and taking turf; several pollards had been felled and taken away; people without common rights were turning cattle onto the common. The orders governing the use of the common were to be printed and posted in public places and read out in church and rewards offered for information leading to the conviction of offenders.[14] Pressure on fuel resources continued, illicit woodcutting leading to legal action in 1806 and tight rules governing furze cutting being imposed in 1810.[15] 'Great numbers' of the ancient oak pollards were felled in 1812, so that little wood remained on the common by the mid-nineteenth century.[16] Small-scale encroachments were made by putting up buildings,[17] and other 'nuisances' included heaping broken tiles and rubbish on the common, tipping 'night soil and other filth' and polluting a well on Putney common.[18]

Gravel-digging became a major destructive activity on the commons by the first half of the nineteenth century. Gravel could only be taken by licence from the manorial officers, generating income for the lord of the manor, a proportion of which was used to fund charity schools in the parishes in the decade after 1802.[19] The licensing system was abused, however: in 1810 the common keepers reported that some 'take just what quantity they like and sell it to persons at a low rate in the same manner as stolen goods'.[20] Brickmaking also took place, using the clays which outcropped on the western side of the common, where the lord of the manor had a large brick kiln at Brickfield Cottage by the 1860s.[21]

Licensed exploitation of the common and exercise of formal common rights were by no means the only activities which drew people to Wimbledon Common in the

---

[12] Ibid., p. 306.
[13] Ibid., pp. 346, 421, 491.
[14] Ibid., p. 375.
[15] Ibid., pp. 440, 485–7.
[16] Eversley, pp. 65–6.
[17] *Wimbledon Ct R.*, pp. 482 (1809), 535 (1818), 559–62 (1829–30), 578–81 (1835–36).
[18] Ibid., pp. 521–2 (1814), 589 (1829), 597 (1844).
[19] In 1802 one-sixth of the surplus income from the common was to go to the schools; the proportion was increased to one-quarter in 1810, but the payments were suspended the following year and then revoked: *Wimbledon Ct R.*, pp. 418, 489–90, 500, 507.
[20] Ibid., p. 484.
[21] Johnson, *Wimbledon Common*, pp. 75–6.

eighteenth and early nineteenth centuries. As a large open space in proximity to London and increasingly surrounded by built-up areas, the common was a public place, attracting many of the gatherings described in Chapter 4. It also gained fame through royal, aristocratic and military presence, both formal (regimental reviews by George III in 1774, and by Prince Albert in 1849, for example)[22] and clandestine, as the location of duels involving public figures, events which continue to form part of the common's popular history.[23]

Mentions of Wimbledon Common and Putney Heath in newspaper reports in the first half of the nineteenth century bring to life the range of activities on the common before the imposition of the new order in the 1860s.[24] Military reviews brought large crowds: when the Prince of Wales reviewed 10,000 men of the horse and foot regiments on the common in 1802, 'Carriages of every description were to be seen around the heath for several miles in circuit', the throng inevitably bringing pickpockets, who were 'as active as usual'.[25] A different spectrum of metropolitan society would presumably have been attracted to the bare-knuckle prize fights which were taking place regularly on Wimbledon Common by 1800 and drawing scrums of followers (and the ubiquitous pickpockets).[26] Gypsy encampments were a feature of the common, particularly along the open boundary between Wimbledon and Putney, where they could readily cross into the neighbouring parish when accosted by parish officers.[27] An attempt to hold races on the common in 1846 was stamped on by the steward of the manor because, being so close to the metropolis, they would 'draw a very large concourse of people', including 'many disreputable characters'.[28] The savage stabbing and robbery of John Smith, an elderly dairyman, when he went to the common to fetch home his cows at

---

[22] *Police Gazette (or Public Hue and Cry)*, 25 March–8 April 1774, p. 3; 29 April–13 May 1774, p. 4; *Morning Post*, 28 June 1849, p. 6.

[23] Duels in the earlier nineteenth century included the fatal duel in 1838 when C. F. Murfin was killed: *London Courier & Evening Gazette*, 27 August 1838, p. 4; that in 1840 which resulted in the trial and acquittal of Lord Cardigan: *Sun* (London), 17 February 1841, pp. 1–2; and the intended duel between Prince Louis Napoleon and Count Leon, prevented by police action, also in 1840: *Bell's New Weekly Messenger*, 8 March 1840, p. 6. Other duels on Wimbledon Common were reported in *Evening Mail*, 23 January 1804, p. 3; *Globe*, 1 September 1819, p. 3; *Morning Chronicle*, 20 September 1824, p. 3; *Evening Mail*, 15 February 1832, p. 4; *Morning Post*, 26 August 1837, p. 3.

[24] The following paragraph is based on searches for 'Wimbledon Common' and 'Putney Heath' in the British Newspaper Archive: https://www.britishnewspaperarchive.co.uk/ (searched 10 November 2020).

[25] *Morning Post*, 21 July 1802, p. 3.

[26] Examples of reports of boxing matches on the common are: *Evening Mail*, 15 December 1802, p. 3; *St James's Chronicle*, 15 February 1803, p. 4; *British Press*, 16 February 1803, p. 4; *Morning Chronicle*, 17 June 1818, p. 3; *Globe*, 31 August 1819, p. 4; *Morning Advertiser*, 4 May 1822, p. 3; and *Morning Chronicle*, 17 September 1823, p. 3; and an abortive attempt to hold a fight, disrupted by the appearance of a magistrate, in *Star* (London), 19 March 1828, p.4.

[27] *Star* (London), 21 March 1831, p. 4; *County Chronicle, Surrey Herald & Weekly Advertiser for Kent*, 27 July 1841, p. 3.

[28] *Morning Post*, 16 July 1846, p. 7.

4.00 a.m. one July morning in 1836 is a reminder both that the common continued to be an agrarian resource and that it could be an unsafe place.[29]

Despite being fringed by fashionable villas along Parkside and in Putney, the common was in a poor state by the middle decades of the nineteenth century, ravaged by over-exploitation and suffering from the nuisances of poor drainage, rubbish heaps and the presence of 'undesirables'. At the same time, common land in the vicinity of London was beginning to be valued as open space. When a furze fire on Putney Heath in 1854 caused so much damage that it was said that 'the appearance of the heath had been destroyed',[30] the concern over the aesthetics of the common perhaps indicates a growing appreciation of the open landscape among wealthy local residents. In 1859 a rumour of plans to enclose Wimbledon Common began to circulate, provoking a strong reaction. *Punch* resorted to ironic hyperbole, claiming that, for some in the metropolis, demolishing St Paul's Cathedral 'would be a less grievous spectacle than the heather and blackberry bushes of the common [being] replaced by turnips and mangold wurzel, or, worse still, by eligible residences, principally stuccoed villas'.[31]

It is not surprising, therefore, that when, in 1864, Earl Spencer proposed what would, in effect, have been the enclosure of the commons (even though his intention was that part should become a public space), his plans met with stiff opposition, triggering a sequence of events which led to the preservation of Wimbledon Common and Putney Heath as recreational open space.[32] Spencer wished to sell the northern one-third of the commons for housing and to convert the remaining 680 acres (275 ha) into a fenced and tended urban park, in which he intended to build himself a residence. He sought to achieve his plans through a private bill which came before Parliament in 1865. The proposals met with staunch resistance from the commoners and neighbouring residents, among whose number were wealthy and educated figures, including 'many able lawyers', who formed a committee to oppose the plans. Moreover, Spencer's proposals prompted the House of Commons to establish a committee to consider how to preserve the metropolitan commons as recreational spaces, ensuring that the case of Wimbledon received scrutiny there. The Parliamentary committee advised against enclosure and fencing of the common, and Spencer's bill was dropped. After legal action brought against Spencer by the Wimbledon residents and commoners' committee, which sought to demonstrate that his freedom to act was curtailed by the commoners' rights, agreement was reached in 1870, whereby Spencer would convey the commons to trustees for the public in exchange for an annuity of £1,200, representing his average annual receipts from the common, principally from gravel extraction. The provisions were embodied in the Wimbledon and Putney Commons Act 1871, which vested ownership of the commons in eight conservators, five elected by local ratepayers and three appointed by government.[33] Spencer's annuity and the

---

[29] *St James's Chronicle*, 4 August 1836, p. 4.
[30] *London Daily News*, 7 June 1854, p. 7. Examples of earlier fires are recorded in *Morning Post*, 5 September 1835, p. 4; *The Atlas*, 7 August 1847, p. 7.
[31] *Punch*, 18 June 1859 (quoted in *Surrey Comet*, 25 June 1859, p. 5).
[32] The following account is based on Eversley, pp. 19–22, 66–70.
[33] Local Act, 34 & 35 Vict., c. cciv.

conservators' other expenses were to be raised by a rate levied on properties within three-quarters of a mile of the commons.

One impediment to recreational use was the presence of rifle ranges across much of the common, where the National Rifle Association held its annual volunteer camp, under Earl Spencer's patronage, from 1860. As well as the target butts, flag staffs, ricochet huts and watch boxes of the ranges themselves, the association built a magazine store, skittle ground and croquet ground around the 'Iron House', to the south of the Kingston Road, which formed its headquarters (Figure 63).[34] The ranges were explicitly protected by the 1871 act, which allowed the Association to fence a large part of the common between May and August each year for the camp. Opposition from adjoining landowners and residents – and the inherent incompatibility of firing ranges and public recreation – ultimately led the Association to move its base to Bisley Common in 1890. An offshoot of the presence of the rifle volunteers on the common was the London Scottish Golf Club, one of the earliest golf clubs in England, founded in 1865, its course being the forerunner of the golf course on Wimbledon Common today.[35]

Since the later nineteenth century, the face of the common has changed substantially. The 1871 act enabled the conservators to modify the landscape by draining and improving the common (but only as far as necessary for health and recreation), making ornamental ponds, planting trees and shrubs and making temporary enclosures.[36] In the century and a half since the act, active management has resulted in gravel pits becoming ponds, rides and footpaths proliferating, and vegetation being to some extent tamed and controlled. Queen's Mere, the largest of the ponds, was a deliberate artefact, created by enlarging and damming a natural bog in the jubilee year of 1887.[37] Military use during both world wars involved the construction of a variety of temporary structures as well as disturbance of the ground surface. The open ground known as The Plain became an airfield from 1915 to 1918, and in the Second World War, during which the common was bombed, it was used for training, with an army camp, an ammunition dump and defensive structures, including pill boxes and concrete anti-tank 'dragons' teeth'.[38] Further modification of the surface of the common took place in the 1960s, when spoil from roadworks on the A3 was dumped on the plateau to the north of the Windmill, forming an artificial hill 10 metres above the original ground surface.[39]

Across the twentieth century, the common's ecology underwent dramatic change. Woodland survived on the western slopes of the common in the mid-nineteenth century but much of the plateau was open ground, largely devoid of trees. In 1912,

---

[34] For full extent of ranges, see OS Six-Inch map, Surrey 7 (1874 edn, surveyed 1865).

[35] The complex early history of the golf clubs at Wimbledon is summarised in R. Browning, *A History of Golf: The Royal and Ancient Game* (London, 1955, repr. 1990), pp. 90–2.

[36] Wimbledon & Putney Commons Act 1871, sec. 39.

[37] Johnson, *Wimbledon Common*, p. 91.

[38] Military use of the common during the world wars is summarised in https://www.wpcc.org.uk/latest-news/news/post/87; https://www.wpcc.org.uk/latest-news/news/post/175.

[39] T. Drakeford et al., *Wimbledon Common: 100 Years of Change* (Wimbledon, 2012), p. 21.

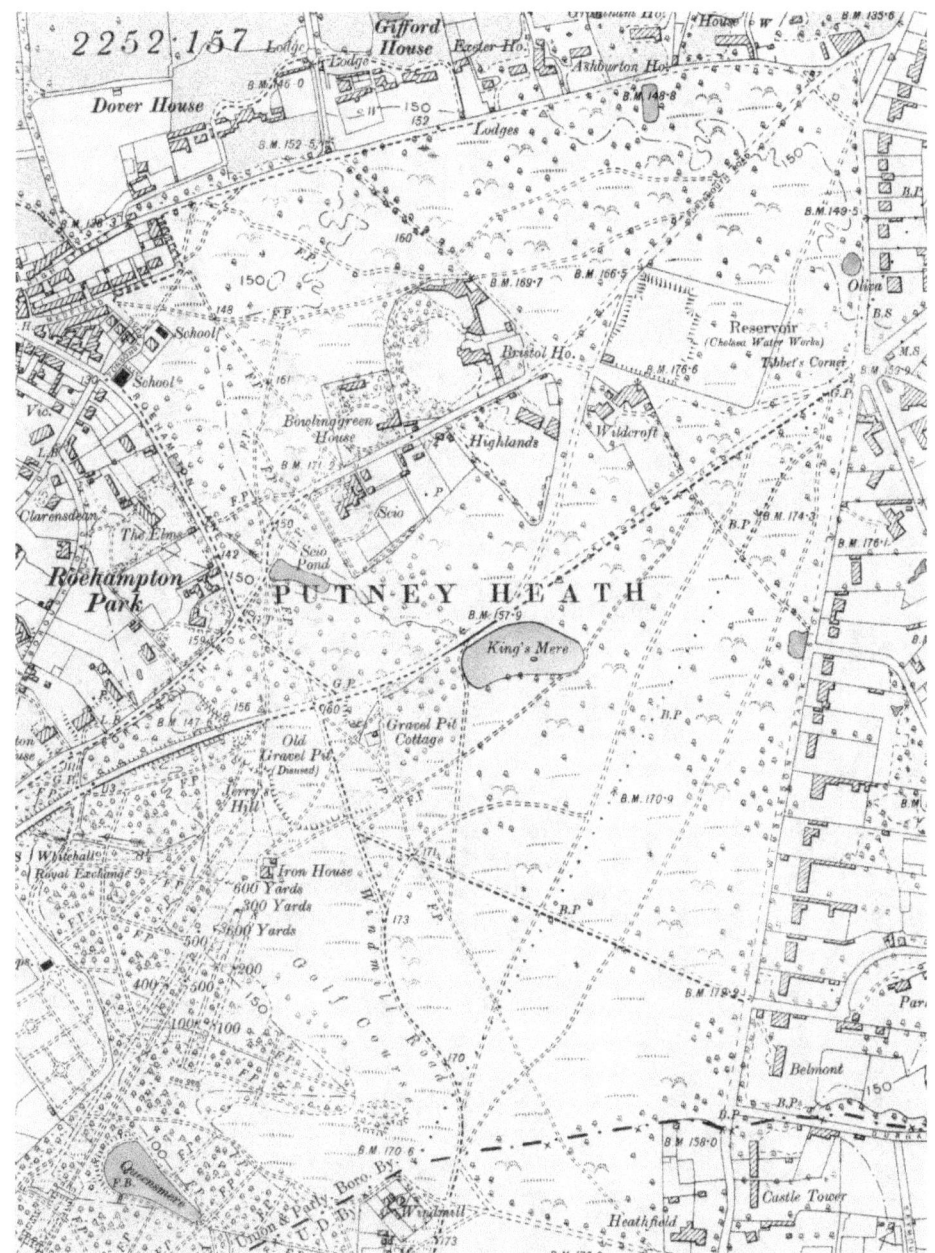

Figure 63. Putney Heath in the 1890s, showing rifle ranges and associated structures, golf course and disused gravel pits. By that date, woodland was beginning to spread to much of the common. Note the villas lining the north and east sides of the heath (OS Six-Inch map, Surrey 7NW, published 1899).

Figure 64. Wimbledon Common. A path through woodland, worn bare by heavy use, between Queensmere and the Windmill.

the bare eastern side of the common was partly heathland with 'scattered clumps of gorse, with rather infrequent bushes of broom'.[40] Since then, natural regeneration in the absence of grazing has clothed much of the common with secondary woodland dominated by oak and birch, the main exception being the acid grassland of The Plain. The common was notified as an SSSI in 1986 for its surviving heathland and acid grassland habitats, which modern management seeks to preserve and restore.[41]

Wimbledon Common and Putney Heath have become managed urban spaces. Recreational pressure can be considerable, especially on warm summer days: it was said that 30,000 visitors gathered on Wimbledon Common and Putney Heath over the August Bank Holiday weekend in 1956.[42] Order continues to be maintained on the common by uniformed keepers, employed by the conservators, who patrol the common (mounted on horseback since after the Second World War) and police its use. The 1871 act specified that the conservators were to 'preserve, as far as may be, the natural aspect and state of the commons' and also to preserve the existing vegetation.[43] Despite the numerous modifications to the face of the commons since 1871, the aim of conserving natural 'wildness' remains key to their modern management.

---

[40] Johnson, *Wimbledon Common*, p. 237.
[41] Drakeford et al., *Wimbledon Common*, pp. 50–61.
[42] *RCCL Rep.*, para. 95 (p. 34).
[43] Wimbledon & Putney Commons Act 1871, sec. 36.

CONCLUSION: COMMON GROUND

THE BULK OF THIS book has focused on the multiple meanings assigned to common land in Britain and how these have played out in the landscape across the centuries. Evolving conceptions of rights in land lie at the heart of the cultural context, shaping the shifting attitudes to commons. In drawing together this historical survey, this chapter begins by sketching out a history of common land, using these changing perceptions as a lens through which to view the story of commons in Britain. It takes a broad view, as a full picture of common land reaches beyond the shared use of agrarian resources, to embrace the wider place of commons in so many aspects of life.

Alan Everitt's memorable phrase, that common land is 'half-wild country',[1] has run as a thread throughout this book and gets to the heart of the ambiguities which lay behind perceptions of common land. Commons are neither one thing nor the other, neither fully wild, nor fully tamed landscapes; neither no man's land nor fully private property; neither exclusively agrarian resource, nor unfettered public space. They were full of paradoxes and, thus, difficult to pigeonhole. 'Half-wildness' implies an inherent tension between tameness and wildness and also a restlessness: the multiple interests in common land and the different meanings and values assigned to it by different players have resulted in a fluid balance between the processes of taming and wilding across the centuries.

Multiple interests and shifting values are a theme which is prominent in much of the literature on commons. Contested rights surface repeatedly in tensions over who should be able to use common land and for what purposes. Uncertain boundaries and disputed ownership of common land recur, especially across the medieval period; the limit of common rights, both in terms of who could exercise them and how much resource could be taken, was a perennial issue across the early modern centuries; tensions between customary users of commons and those with formal property rights re-surface across the nineteenth and twentieth centuries; and the balance between private and public interests continues to be contested in the twenty-first century.

Those tensions spring from a paradox which lies at the heart of common land in Britain, namely that both English and Scots law define this communally-used land in terms of private property rights. Most common land has been privately owned and common

---

[1] A. Everitt, 'Common land', in J. Thirsk (ed.), *The English Rural Landscape* (Oxford, 2000), p. 210.

rights belong to individuals and are usually possessed by virtue of being attached to land held by the possessor. However, that linkage between rights and land also connected commons to communities, so that, although rights were private, they were not, in a sense, fully independent of the settlements and communities by which a common was used. Even though the law attempted to confine property rights to individuals, the sense of communal 'ownership' of common land persisted through the early modern period, both in customary exploitation of resources by those without formal property rights and in community use of the space afforded by commons. From the nineteenth century, private property rights were further constrained by a growing sense that commons were a public asset and should be used in the wider national interest. Taking the long view, the evolution of common land since the Middle Ages reflects the interplay between communal and individual interests but does not, as has sometimes been claimed, point inexorably towards privatisation and loss of the communal interest.

The fragmentary evidence from the early medieval centuries hints at the existence of rights, perhaps tribal in origin, which enabled multiple settlements to share access to resources over a wide area. From around the tenth century the older patterns tended to fragment as manorial lordship developed, a key transition occurring when wastes came to be vested in the feudal lords of individual settlements. In the absence of manorial lordship in royal forests, earlier patterns of shared use often persisted on forest wastes. The notion of 'the common pasture of the vill' and the assumption, stated explicitly in the Statute of Merton (1236), that common wastes lay within the boundaries of a manor, show that many commons had become the exclusive preserve of individual settlements by the thirteenth century. Intercommoning between manors, sitting uneasily with such a norm, declined, spilling over into disputes over boundaries, as areas of waste came to be appropriated by individual landowners, though it survived in the concept of commonty in Scotland.

Once the waste had become vested in an individual lord, it was they who ultimately had the power to decide how it should be used. Merton should be seen as a measure to mitigate that power at a time when most resources were exploited communally and multiple interests in land were the norm. By enshrining communal use of the waste in law, Merton confirmed the unique status of common land which survives in English law to the present. In Scotland, by contrast, communal use continued but the basis of that use was by grant or favour of the heritor, whose permission could be withdrawn.

If English law vested ownership of common land in the lord of the manor, the exercise of common rights gave farmers and villagers much of the day-to-day possession of a common. Although the manorial court was a seigniorial institution, its structures enabled the users of a common to build a body of local customary law to regulate the exploitation of resources. For most practical purposes, the management of common rights lay in the hands of the commoners.

Once the boundaries of a common had become certain, questions over the limits of different interests continued to surface, especially during the seventeenth and eighteenth centuries. The theoretical tidiness of rights held within the structures of the law often masked an untidy reality which made commons flashpoints where the claims of those with different interests collided. As property rights became more formalised, custom came to be disputed and the rights of the landless to the resources of common land became issues of contention and debate. As a result, the association between common land and the poor and powerless became a dominant theme in the history of commons in the post-medieval centuries. Inhabited by groups on the margins of society, who scraped a living from the resources of 'half-wild' land, commons came to be perceived by those in authority as disorderly places, where activities on or beyond the fringes of legality and morality took place. To the masterless men and cottagers of the early modern period they offered independence and comparative freedom from those in power.

In a wider sense of 'ownership', the use of common land as communal public space in the medieval and early modern world had many facets. Commons were places where the gentry and aristocracy convened, whether for sport (notably horse racing) or public display (such as military musters), but they were also places where plebeian masses could congregate, at fairs and for rougher sports, reinforcing a perception of commons as wild places of freedom and unruliness. Commons also became theatres of dissent, at times challenging the authorities on both political and religious fronts. Briefly, in the utopian idealism of the Diggers of the mid-seventeenth century, common land became the focus of challenge to the very idea of the private ownership of land by individuals.

The history of commons in the modern world can be read in terms of changing responses to 'wildness'. Several facets of modernity – the rejection of tradition, the triumph of individualism and the rise of capitalism and the market economy – helped to create conditions which led to the demise of many commons in the eighteenth and nineteenth centuries, while the increasing role of the nation state became a major driver of changes on common land from the twentieth.

In the heyday of improvement in the century 1760 to 1860, common land was viewed not only as half-wild waste but also as the haunt of half-wild people; on both fronts, it needed to be taken in hand, converted into private property, and reclaimed for productive use by making a 'desert' bloom, so that it no longer provided a living for its undesirable, indolent inhabitants. The success of the improvement movement resulted in the loss of so much common land that attitudes changed, abruptly and within comparatively few years, in the middle decades of the nineteenth century. Common land was no longer waste land in need of reclamation but open space deserving to be preserved for the nation's benefit. Communal interest had been redefined in terms of a wider public good.

The changed value of common land brought to the fore the question of how wild it ought to be, the late-Victorian concern for decorum extending to the use of commons. Formal regulation by boards of conservators and the conversion of some commons into municipal parks sought to purge them of 'nuisances', which (especially on commons near towns) included indecorous behaviour, and it sometimes involved some taming of the common's physical face as well.

Across the twentieth century, common land increasingly came to be viewed as a resource to be used for the national good. This was most clearly seen during the two world wars and the Cold War, when large tracts of the open spaces provided by common land were appropriated for military use, as training grounds, army bases and airfields. The view that commons were under-utilised land which could be put to better use led to more fertile commons being requisitioned and ploughed up for the war effort. It also fed into the national planning debates over the best use of land in modern society which lay behind the appointment of the Royal Commission on Common Land in the 1950s. While the Commission's focus was on public access and traditional economic exploitation of commons, conceptions of the value of common land were already changing. By the later twentieth century, the national interest was increasingly expressed in terms of nature conservation. The dominant concern became to protect commons as precious remnants of nature, in need of conservation in the face of either over-intensive use (mainly in upland areas) or neglect (mainly in the lowlands). Increasingly active management was introduced, powered by agri-environmental policy and conservation designations, in an attempt to balance the demands of agrarian use, recreational pressure and biodiversity. As a result, the face of much common land today is the product of deliberate intervention, aimed at maintaining or restoring (or even creating) desirable ecological characteristics – the right sort of 'wildness', so to speak.

* * *

It could be said that commons increasingly became communal land across the twentieth century: ownership shifted from the private sphere to the public, as increasing numbers of commons were vested in public bodies, whether local authorities or the National Trust; the public now has a right of recreational access on common land; and many commons are protected for their environmental value and managed in the public interest for nature conservation. The greater clarity of property rights resulting from registration under the CRA and the power of public bodies and government agencies to decide what is in the public interest have removed many of the messy, fuzzy ambiguities which characterised common land in the past. Yet, despite the weight of legalistic bureaucracy, common land retains an almost primeval attraction. The encounter with wildness gives commons an otherness, separating them from the everyday modern world, as does their distinctive legal character. The fact that there is no single controlling interest over common land is a chink in the armour of the exclusive property rights which dominate modern life, allowing a glimpse of an alternative in which land is the inheritance of all people.

Commons are ultimately shared spaces, which transcend social divisions. In a tract opposing enclosure in 1812, Thomas Wilkinson of Yanwath (Westmld) made the striking claim that 'The *Common* and the *Grave-yard* are almost the only places that I know of, where the rich and the poor are in partnership together.'[2] Despite turning a blind eye to the persistent tensions over the use of common land (between the powerful and the powerless and between informal users and those with formal property rights), Wilkinson was hinting at a deeper, persistent truth, that commons were, indeed, common ground.

---

[2] T. Wilkinson, *Thoughts on Inclosing Yanwath Moor and Round Table* (Penrith, 1812), p. 37.

They continue to evoke strong feelings, including a passionate attachment which seems to be deeply embedded in the national psyche.

Recent years have seen a surge in the celebration of common land, in projects combining nature conservation and restoration with a desire to raise awareness of the rich heritage, both natural and cultural, of commons.[3] Recapturing the history of individual commons has often played a part in inculcating a sense of community ownership and shared heritage – something which has been particularly evident on urban commons.[4] Across the country commons are being re-claimed by local communities and celebrated as communal open space, often with funding from the Heritage Lottery Fund (now National Lottery Heritage Fund). Local groups have researched the histories of metropolitan commons at Tooting Bec and Wandsworth (the latter celebrating the 150th anniversary of the Wandsworth Common Act 1871).[5] At Bromyard (Heref.) child actors have recreated episodes from the common's twentieth-century past;[6] at Brockdish (Norf.) local residents have prompted their parish council to take charge of a small scrap of riverside common, 'covered in brambles, nondescript scrub and nettles', and to manage it for wildlife conservation and recreation – 'a place to pause and enjoy the river'.[7]

Space, freedom to roam, community 'ownership', engagement with the natural world, spiritual refreshment – these are only part of the meaning of common land in twenty-first-century Britain. Many commons continue to be actively used as an agrarian resource and the culture of commoning and the commoners themselves increasingly fascinate modern urban society. The practices associated with communal grazing provide a link with the past, a continuity which gives actively grazed common land the character of living heritage. Pastoral commoning can seem to provide a glimpse of sturdily independent rural communities governing their own affairs. The collaborative culture of grazing on common land and the role of commoning tradition in fostering a strong sense of community identity are increasingly recognised as possessing a cultural value as well as a practical benefit. When the Lake District was inscribed as a World Heritage Site, its distinctive 'agro-pastoral traditions', centred on sheep farming on common land, were identified as the key drivers in creating and maintaining the region's unique landscape.[8] More generally, the work of the Foundation for Common Land in fostering collaborative management of common land seeks to harness the culture of commoning to raise public awareness and achieve conservation objectives.[9]

---

[3] The aims of the Chilterns Commons Project, 2011–15: see https://www.chilternsaonb.org/about-chilterns/chilterns-commons-project/commons-project-news.html.
[4] For example, the multi-disciplinary 'Wastes and Strays' project involving several universities: see https://research.ncl.ac.uk/wastesandstrays/.
[5] For the Tooting Common Heritage Project, see https://www.tootingcommon.co.uk/history; for Wandsworth: https://www.wandsworthcommon.org/history-blog.
[6] 'The Common People Project': see http://www.bromyarddowns.co.uk/about/.
[7] E. Murphy, 'Brockdish Common, Norfolk: historical research for present-day community benefit', *The Local Historian*, 51 (1) (January 2021), pp. 47–56.
[8] See the nomination document at www.lakesworldheritage.co.uk.
[9] At the time of writing, the 'Our Common Cause' project, coordinated by the Foundation, is central to this approach: https://foundationforcommonland.org.uk/our-common-cause.

In the face of contested interests in common land, its successful management requires connectedness, reciprocity and trust among commoners. Where they are found, those attributes become part of the local farming culture and help to create a distinctive sense of place where actively grazed commons survive.[10] This is especially true in the particular context of the New Forest. In the nineteenth-century campaigns to protect the forest from an expansion of silviculture, the commoners came to be seen as the guardians of the wider interest of the people as a whole in the land of England.[11] New Forest commoners continue to have a strong commitment to commoning and its traditions, experiencing it as part of their heritage which fosters social ties and a close-knit forest community. When asked why they continue to turn out animals to graze, references to 'family tradition', commoning being 'in my blood' and an inherent feature of 'a community I love being part of' suggest that the way of life created by commoning is paramount in their minds.[12]

Perhaps the most visible expression of the communal culture of pastoral commoning is driving a common to gather in the animals grazing there. It is a timeless practice which fascinates modern society as an expression of the otherness of traditions on common land. As practised on the fell commons of northern England, it sets the scene in James Rebanks' best-selling autobiography, *The Shepherd's Life* (2015), and has been celebrated in song, such as 'Gathering Day' by the Moonbeams.[13] In the very different environment of the New Forest, the mounted drifts, in which commoners ride out to gather in the ponies on the commons, have veered towards becoming a spectator sport, to the extent that the verderers now have to discourage the public from congregating to watch.[14] Continuity of tradition on common land has the power to bridge worlds, bringing modern, urban society a fleeting experience of an older way of life.

As long ago as 1877, Octavia Hill claimed that common land could teach the nation the value of shared possessions, 'in which separate right is subordinated to the good of all; each tiny bit of which would have no value if the surface were divided amongst the hundreds that use it'. Common land, she continued, gave a share of the country 'to be inherited by the poorest citizen', creating a 'solemn joyful fellowship', binding people together through 'common memory, or common cause, or common hope'.[15] A sense of communal 'ownership' of common land has refused to die, despite reiterations of

---

[10] L. Mansfield, 'Hill farming identities and connections to place', in I. Convery, G. Corsane and P. Davis (eds), *Making Sense of Place: Multidisciplinary Perspectives* (Woodbridge, 2012), pp. 67–77.

[11] P. Readman, *Storied Ground: Landscape and the Shaping of English National Identity* (Cambridge, 2018), p. 183.

[12] J. Ivey, 'Census of New Forest Commoners 2011' (at www.realnewforest.org), paras 4.3.2, 4.3.6, 4.4.

[13] J. Rebanks, *The Shepherd's Life* (London, 2015), especially pp. 6–21; The Moonbeams, 'Gathering Day', on *This Land* (2018), an album celebrating the environment and rural life in the Yorkshire Dales: https://www.themoonbeamcollective.co.uk/moonbeam-music-1.

[14] https://www.newforest-life.com/New-Forest-Drift.html.

[15] O. Hill, 'The future of our commons', in her *Our Common Land and other short essays* (London, 1877), pp. 205–6.

the legal status of commons as private land. In the twenty-first century, the half-wild country of common land remains important to the inhabitants of a crowded island, not only as an agrarian resource, as recreational space and for its conservation value, but for its intrinsic connotations of being 'common ground' in which all have an interest.

SELECT BIBLIOGRAPHY

SPACE DOES NOT ALLOW the inclusion of a full bibliography of all the sources cited in this book. The following pages list works relating directly to common land and its history and provide details of the principal sources used to compile the case studies in Part II. Other sources consulted are cited in the footnotes.

PRIMARY SOURCES

Statutes (only general acts relating directly to common land are listed)
1236 Statute of Merton
1285 Statute of Westminster II
1401 Moorburning (Scotland) https://www.rps.ac.uk/trans/1401/2/15
1424 'Of murbyrning eftir Marche' (Scotland) https://www.rps.ac.uk/trans/1424/22
1540 The Horses Act (32 Hen. VIII, c.13)
1543 Act for the Preservation of Woods (35 Hen. VIII, c.17)
1549 Improvement of Commons Act (3 & 4 Edward VI, c.3)
1593 'Regarding the common good of burghs' (Scotland) https://www.rps.ac.uk/trans/1593/4/58
1609 Burning of Moor Act (7 Jas. I, c.17)
1695 Division of Commonties Act (Scotland) www.legislation.gov.uk/aosp/1695/69
1845 Inclosure Act (8 & 9 Vict., c.118)
1866 Metropolitan Commons Act (29 & 30 Vict., c.122)
1876 Commons Act (39 & 40 Vict., c.56)
1886 Crofters Holdings (Scotland) Act 1886 (49 & 50 Vict., c.29)
1891 Crofters Common Grazings Regulation Act 1891 (54 & 55 Vict., c.41)
1899 Commons Act (62 & 63 Vict., c.30)
1925 Law of Property Act (c.20)
1965 Commons Registration Act (c.64)
1991 The Crofter Forestry (Scotland) Act (c.18)
2000 Countryside and Rights of Way Act (c.37)
2006 Commons Act (c.26)

Manuscript Sources for the Case Study Commons

Bangor University Library, Archives and Special Collections

PENRH/1802, 1807, 1809: Penrhyn Castle estate letter books, 1862–63, 1876–77, 1878
PENRH/728–730: cases for counsels' opinion, Llanllechid Common, 1839, 1851
PFA/1/310: Letters patent: lease for three lives of hundred of Uchaf to Richard Lord Penrhyn, 1784
PFA/3/116: Conveyance of waste lands in hundred of Uchaf (Llanllechid Mountain) to Edward Gordon Douglas Pennant of Penrhyn Castle, 1858

Cockermouth Castle Muniments (formerly Cumbria Archive Service, DLEC)

Box 94: Nether Wasdale byelaws, 1679; court leet verdicts, 1679–1858 and other papers

Commons Commissioners' Decisions (at www.acraew.org.uk)

Gwynedd: Unenclosed Mountain Land – Aber (CL 3), 50/D/45
Hereford & Worcester: Bringsty Common (CL 14), 215/D/22–49
Hereford & Worcester: Bromyard Downs (CL 15), 215/D/50–87.
Humberside: Belton Low Closes Turbary (CL 8), 24/U/1

Commons Registers

Cumbria County Council: Cumberland CL 59 (Nether Wasdale Common)
Durham County Council: Co. Durham CL 8 (Cockfield Fell)
Gwynedd County Council: Caernarvonshire CL 42 (Llanllechid Mountain)
Herefordshire Council: Herefordshire CL 14 (Bringsty Common)
North Lincolnshire Council: Lincolnshire CL 2 (Epworth Turbary), CL 8 (Belton Low Closes Turbary)

Crofting Commission, Inverness

Common grazings regulations, north Assynt, 1958, 1988–2001

Durham Record Office, Durham

D/X 2117 (add.) (accession no. 10434): 'Cockfield Stint Book': photocopy of memoranda book of the Cockfield Field Reeves, 1857–1944

Glamorgan Record Office, Cardiff

CL Manorial Box 4: Bishopric of Hereford court rolls, 1562–91, 1604–05, 1636

Gwynedd Archives, Caernarfon

XB14/47: Ogwen Rural District Council records: file entitled 'Llanllechid Mountain Pasture' including TS copies of vestry meeting minutes, 1845–83; correspondence re. Llanllechid Common, 1930–48

SELECT BIBLIOGRAPHY 285

Hampshire Record Office, Winchester
21M57/E863: 'New Forest Rights', 2 vols, undated [*c*.1850]
21M57/E864: papers re. rights in New Forest claimed by Somerley Estate, 1850s (3 bundles)
67M99/PX21: Somerley Estate sales particulars, 1919
H/CL5/1p/18/1–22: papers re. public inquiry into gravel extraction, Rockford Common, 1966

Herefordshire Archive and Records Centre, Hereford
AA59/A/2: Butterfield's Survey, 1577
AM33/5, AM33/8–9: Bishopric of Hereford court rolls, 1554–55, 1616–22

Lincolnshire Archives, Lincoln
EPWORTH PAR/17/1: Isle of Axholme enclosure award, 1803

The National Archives, Kew
MAF 25/91, Cockfield Fell, correspondence and papers, 1897–1931
MAF 25/110, Bringsty Common and Bromyard Downs, correspondence and papers, 1897–1952
MAF 25/221, Isle of Axholme Turbaries, correspondence and papers, 1938–39

National Library of Scotland, Edinburgh
NLS Estate Plans, Dep. 313/3585: John Home's Survey of Assynt, 1774

In private hands
Nether Wasdale Court Book, 1899–1931, inscribed 'Manor of Netherwasdale'

Scottish Land Court, Edinburgh
Common grazings regulations, 1898–1933: RN 913 (Nedd), RN 996 (Stoer), RN 1001 (Culkein Drumbeg), RN 1002 (Drumbeg), RN 1003 (Clachtoll), RN 1004 (Clashmore), RN 1009 (Culkein Achnacarnan), RN 1015 (Balchladich) and RN 1211 (Clashnessie)

Printed Primary Sources

Abstract of Claims Preferred at a Justice Seat held for the New Forest ... AD 1670 with a Return made by Commissioners acting under the Acts of the 39 & 40 Geo.3, cap. 86 and 41 Geo. 3, cap. 108 as to Incroachments &c. in the said Forest (London, 1853)
Adam, R. J. (ed.), *John Home's Survey of Assynt*, Scottish History Society, 3rd ser. LII (Edinburgh, 1960)
Anon., *Some Account of a very Seditious Book, lately found upon Wimbledon Common* (London, 1794)
A Plan of His Majesty's Forest, called the New Forest, in the County of Southampton ... from surveys undertaken by Thos. Richardson, Wm. King and Abm. and Wm. Driver ... MDCCLXXXIX (2nd edn, 1814)

Barron, D. G. (ed.), *The Court Book of the Barony of Urie in Kincardineshire, 1604–1747*, Scottish History Society XII (Edinburgh, 1892)

Beckerman, J. S., 'The articles of presentment of a court leet and court baron, in English, c.1400', *Bulletin of Institute of Historical Research*, 47 (1974), pp. 230–4

Bishton, J., *General View of the Agriculture of the County of Salop* (Brentford, 1794)

Blyth, W., *The English improver improved* (London, 1653 edn)

Bracton, H., *De Legibus et Consuetudinibus Angliae*, translated by S. E. Thorne (Cambridge, Mass., 1977), at Bracton Online: https://amesfoundation.law.harvard.edu/Bracton/index.html

Clark, J., 'On commons in Brecknock', *Annals of Agriculture*, XXII (1794), pp. 632–8

Cunningham, W. (ed.), 'Common rights at Cottenham and Stretham in Cambridgeshire', *Camden Miscellany, Vol. XII*, pp. 173–287, Camden Society, 3rd ser. XVIII (London, 1910)

Dalrymple, J., *An Essay on the Husbandry of Scotland with a Proposal for the Improvement Thereof, by a lover of his country* (Edinburgh, 1732)

Dickinson, W. C. (ed.), *The Court Book of the Barony of Carnwath, 1523–1542*, Scottish History Society, 3rd ser. XXIX (Edinburgh, 1937)

Domesday Book, 35 county volumes, ed. J. Morris (Chichester, 1973–86)

E. G., 'Waste Land's Improvement', dated October 1653 (BL, Thomas Tract, E715 (18)), printed in J. Thirsk and J. P. Cooper (eds), *Seventeenth-Century Economic Documents* (Oxford, 1972), pp. 135–40

Evans, E., 'Arwystli and Cyfeiliog in the sixteenth century: an Elizabethan inquisition', *Montgomeryshire Collections*, 51 (1949–50), pp. 23–37

Fitzherbert, J., *The Boke of Surveyeng and Improume[n]tes* (London, 1523)

Gilpin, W., *Remarks on Forest Scenery and other Woodland Views ... illustrated by the scenes of New-Forest in Hampshire* (London, 1794)

Hallam, H. E., 'The fen bylaws of Spalding and Pinchbeck', *Lincolnshire Architectural and Archaeological Society*, 10 (1963), pp. 40–56

Hartlib, S., *Samuel Hartlib, his Legacie or an Enlargement of the Discourse of Husbandry used in Brabant and Flaunders ...* (London, 1651)

[Lawrence, P. H. (ed.)], *Extracts from the Court Rolls of the Manor of Wimbledon extending from 1 Edward IV to AD 1864* (London, 1866)

Lawton, G. (ed.), *Church Lawton Manor Court Rolls, 1631–1680*, Record Society of Lancashire & Cheshire 147 (Lancaster, 2013)

MacDowall Bankton, A., *An Institute of the Laws of Scotland in Civil Rights, Book II* (Edinburgh, 1751)

Mackintosh, W., *An Essay on Ways and Means for Inclosing, Fallowing, Planting &c.* (Edinburgh, 1729)

Maxwell Morison, W., *The Decisions of the Court of Session from its First Institution to the Present Time* (Edinburgh, 1801)

Neilson, N. (ed.), *A Terrier of Fleet, Lincolnshire, from a Manuscript in the British Museum* (London, 1920)

New Forest Register of Decisions on Claims to Forest Rights by the Commissioners acting under the Act of 17th & 18th Victoria, Chapter 49 (London, 1858)

Norden, J., *The Surveiors Dialogue* (London, 1618)

Ordnance Survey Six-Inch (1:10,560) County Series maps, 1840s onwards (accessed via https://maps.nls.uk)

Owen Roberts, O., *Crown Property in North Wales, its Management and Appropriation* (London, 1849)

Plymley, J., *General View of the Agriculture of Shropshire* (London, 1803)

Purton, R. C. (ed.), 'A Description of ye Clee, ye L'dships, Comoners and Strakers adjoined, made about 1612, 10 Jac.', *Transactions of the Shropshire Archaeological Society*, 2nd ser. 8 (1896), pp. 195–8

'Reminiscences of Surrey Heathland': summaries of interviews conducted in 1997 by Clare Simkin for the Surrey Heathland Project (courtesy of Jackie Lake, Surrey County Council, 2013)

Report of the Crofters Commission ... for the period from 10th December 1887 to 31st December 1888 [C. 5634], HC (1889), vol. LX

Sharpe France, R., 'Two custumals of the manor of Cockerham, 1326 and 1483', *Transactions of the Lancashire & Cheshire Antiquarian Society* 64 (1954), pp. 38–54

Short, B. (ed.), *The Ashdown Forest Dispute 1876–1882: Environmental Politics and Custom*, Sussex Record Society 80 (Lewes, 1997)

Slack, W. J. (ed.), *The Lordship of Oswestry, 1393–1607* (Shrewsbury, 1951)

Special report of Inclosure Commissioners, 1863

Stagg, D. J. (ed.), *A Calendar of New Forest Documents, 1244–1334* (Hampshire County Council, 1979)

—— *A Calendar of New Forest Documents: The Fifteenth to the Seventeenth Centuries* (Hampshire County Council, 1983)

Stenton, D. M. (ed.), *Rolls of the Justices in Eyre*, Selden Society 53 (London, 1934)

Stuart, J. (ed.), 'Extracts from the court books of the baronies of Skene, Leys, and Whitehaugh, 1613–1687', *Miscellany of the Spalding Club V* (Aberdeen, 1852), pp. 215–38

Swales, W., 'Commons in the civil parish of Grinton' (TS report for 'Building Commons Knowledge' Project, Newcastle and Lancaster Universities, 2013)

Tusser, T., *Five Hundred Points of Good Husbandry*, introduced by G. Grigson (Oxford, 1984)

Vancouver, C., *General View of the Agriculture of Hampshire and the Isle of Wight* (London, 1813)

Wilkinson, T., *Thoughts on Inclosing Yanwath Moor and Round Table* (Penrith, 1812)

Williams, W., *Observations on the Snowdon Mountains* (London, 1802)

SECONDARY LITERATURE

Adams, I. H., *Directory of Former Scottish Commonties*, Scottish Record Society, new ser. 2 (Edinburgh, 1971).

—— 'The legal geography of Scotland's common lands', *Revue de l'Institut de Sociologie*, 2 (1973), pp. 259–332.

Aitchison, J. W. and Hughes, E. J., 'The common lands of Wales', *Trans IBG*, 13 (1) (1988), pp. 96–108

Aitchison, J., Crowther, K., Ashby, M. and Redgrave, L., *The Common Lands of England: A Biological Survey* (Aberystwyth, 2000)

Allen, R., 'The battle for the commons: politics and populism in mid-Victorian Kentish London', *Social History*, 22 (21) (1997), pp. 61–77

Anderson, P. and Yalden, D. W., 'Increased sheep numbers and the loss of heather moorland in the Peak District, England', *Biological Conservation*, 20 (1981), pp. 195–213

Anon., 'The armed forces on Dartmoor: a brief history', at https://assets.publishing.service.gov.uk/government/uploads/system/uploads/attachment_data/file/33309/armed_forces_ondartmoor_brief_history.pdf

Ault, W. O., 'Village by-laws by common consent', *Speculum*, 29 (1954), pp. 378–94

—— 'Village assemblies in medieval England', *Album Helen Maud Cam*, vol. I (Louvain, 1960), pp. 13–35

—— *Open Field Husbandry and the Village Community: A Study of Agrarian By-Laws in Medieval England*, Transactions of the American Philosophical Society, new ser. 55, pt 7 (Philadelphia, 1965)

Bailey, M., *The English Manor c.1200–c.1500* (Manchester, 2002)

Baker, A. R. H. and Butlin, R. A. (eds), *Studies of Field Systems in the British Isles* (Cambridge, 1973)

Baker, N. and Hoverd, T., *Bromyard Downs Rifle Range Report*, Herefordshire Archaeology Report 356 (Herefordshire Council, n.d. [2016])

Bangor-Jones, M., 'Settlement history of Assynt, Sutherland', in J. A. Atkinson, I. Banks and G. MacGregor (eds), *Townships to Farmsteads: Rural Settlement Studies in Scotland, England and Wales*, British Archaeological Reports, British ser. 293 (Oxford, 2000), pp. 211–26

Barnwell, P. S. and Roberts, B. K. (eds), *Britons, Saxons and Scandinavians: The Historical Geography of Glanville R. J. Jones* (Turnhout, 2011)

Barrett, J. R., *The Making of a Scottish Landscape: Moray's Regular Revolution, 1760–1840* (Croydon, 2015)

Barrow, G. W. S., 'The uses of place-names and Scottish history: pointers and pitfalls', in S. Taylor (ed.), *The Uses of Place-Names* (Edinburgh, 1998), pp. 54–74

—— *The Kingdom of the Scots: Government, Church and Society from the Eleventh to the Fourteenth Century*, 2nd edn (Edinburgh, 2003)

Beckett, J. V., *A History of Laxton: England's Last Open-Field Village* (Oxford, 1989)

Bil, A., *The Shieling 1600–1840: The Case of the Central Scottish Highlands* (Edinburgh, 1990)

Birrell, J., 'Common rights in the medieval forest: disputes and conflicts in the thirteenth century', *Past & Present*, 117 (1987), pp. 22–49

Birtles, S., 'Common land, poor relief and enclosure: the use of manorial resources in fulfilling parish obligations 1601–1834', *Past & Present*, 165 (1999), pp. 74–106

Bonfield, L., 'What did English villagers mean by "customary law"?', in Z. Razi and R. Smith (eds), *Medieval Society and the Manor Court* (Oxford, 1996), pp. 103–16

Bonser, K. J., *The Drovers. Who They Were and How They Went: An Epic of the English Countryside* (London, 1970)

Bowden, M., Brown, G. and Smith, N., *An Archaeology of Town Commons in England: 'A very fair field indeed'* (Swindon, 2009)

Bowen, J. P., 'Cottage and squatter settlement and encroachment on common waste in the 16th and 17th centuries: some evidence from Shropshire', *Local Population Studies*, 93 (2014), pp. 11–32

—— '"The struggle for the commons": commons, custom and cottages in Shropshire during the sixteenth and seventeenth centuries', in J. P. Bowen and A. T. Brown (eds), *Custom and Commercialisation in English Rural Society: Revisiting Tawney and Postan* (Hatfield, 2016), pp. 96–117

Bowen, J. P. and Martin, J., 'The "Big Freeze" of 1962–3: the loss of livestock, the issue of fodder supply and the problem of the commons in two upland hill farming regions of England and Wales', *AgHR*, 64 (2) (2016), pp. 226–60

Boyd, B., *Roydon Common Management Plan, April 2010–March 2015* (Norfolk Wildlife Trust, n.d.)

Boyle, J., 'The second enclosure movement and the construction of the public domain', *Law and Contemporary Problems*, 66 (1–2) (2003), pp. 33–74

Brackenbury, S. and Jones, G., *Gower Commons: Successional Health Check* (2018) at http://efncp.org/download/GowerCommonsreport2018.pdf

Broad, J., 'The smallholder and cottager after Disafforestation – a legacy of poverty?', in J. Broad and R. W. Hoyle (eds), *Bernwood: The Life and Afterlife of a Forest* (Preston, 1997), pp. 90–107

—— 'Housing the rural poor in southern England, 1650–1850', *AgHR*, 48(2) (2000), pp. 151–70

—— 'Boundary settlements and overlapping jurisdictions: marginal communities and Little Londons', in R. W. Hoyle (ed.), *Histories of People and Landscape: Essays on the Sheffield Region in Memory of David Hey* (Hatfield, 2021), pp. 170–92

Brookes, S., 'On the territorial organisation of early medieval Hampshire', in A. J. Langlands and R. Lavelle (eds), *The Land of the English Kin* (Leiden, 2020), pp. 276–93

Brooks, C. W., *Law, Politics and Society in Early Modern England* (Cambridge, 2008)

Broun, D., 'Statehood and lordship in "Scotland" before the mid-twelfth century', *Innes Review*, 66 (1) (2015), pp. 1–71

Brown, K. M., 'New challenges for old commons: the role of historical common land in contemporary rural space', *Scottish Geographical Journal*, 122 (2006), pp. 109–29

Buck, S. J., *The Global Commons: An Introduction* (Washington DC, 1998)

Burnett, J., 'The sites and landscapes of horse racing in Scotland before 1860', *Sports Historian*, 18 (1) (1998), pp. 55–75

Chapman, J., 'Parliamentary enclosure in the uplands: the case of the North York Moors', *AgHR*, 24 (1976), pp. 1–17

—— 'The extent and nature of Parliamentary enclosure', *AgHR*, 35 (1987), pp. 25–35

—— 'Parliamentary enclosure in Wales: comparisons and contrasts', *Welsh History Review*, 21 (4) (2003), pp. 761–69

Chapman, J. and Seeliger, S., *Enclosure, Environment and Landscape in Southern England* (Stroud, 2001)

Chubb, L. W., 'The Law of Property Act, 1925 (Provisions for the Protection of Commons)', *Journal of the Commons and Footpaths Preservation Society*, 1 (1) (1927), pp. 7–13

Clark, G. and Clark, A., 'Common rights to land in England, 1475–1839', *Journal of Economic History*, 61 (4) (December 2001), pp. 1009–36

Cook, H., *New Forest: The Forging of a Landscape* (Oxford, 2018)

Coull, J. R., 'Crofters' common grazings in Scotland', *AgHR*, 16 (2) (1968), pp. 142–54

Countryside Commission, *Common Land: The Report of the Common Land Forum* (Cheltenham, 1986)

Cousins, E. F., with Honey, R., *Gadsden on Commons and Greens* (London, 2012)

Cowell, B., 'The Commons Preservation Society and the campaign for Berkhamsted Common, 1866–70', *Rural History*, 13 (2) (2002), pp. 145–61

Cox, S. J. B., 'No tragedy on the commons', *Environmental Ethics*, 7 (1985), pp. 49–61

Cressy, D., 'Trouble with gypsies in early modern England', *Historical Journal*, 59 (2016), pp. 45–70

Crocker, S., *Squatters and Social Crime: Encroachments in the New Forest in the Eighteenth Century*, Hampshire Papers, 2nd ser. 6 (Hampshire Field Club & Archaeological Society, 2018)

Crompton, G. and Sheail, J., 'The historical ecology of Lakenheath Warren in Suffolk, England: a case study', *Biological Conservation*, 8 (1975), pp. 299–313

Crosby, A. G., 'A disappearing landscape: the heathlands of the Berkshire, Hampshire and Surrey borders', *AgHR*, 66 (2) (2018), pp. 171–98

Crouch, D. and McDonagh, B., 'Turf wars: conflict and cooperation in the management of Wallingfen (East Yorkshire), 1281–1781', *AgHR*, 64 (2016), pp. 133–56

Dallas, P., 'Sustainable environments: common wood pastures in Norfolk', *Landscape History* 31 (1) (2010), pp. 23–36

Darby, H. C., *The Medieval Fenland* (Newton Abbot, 1974 [1940])

—— *Domesday England* (Cambridge, 1976)

Davies, E., 'Hafod, hafoty and lluest: their distribution, features and purpose', *Ceredigion*, 9 (1) (1980), pp. 1–41

De Moor, T., *The Dilemma of the Commoners: Understanding the Use of Common-Pool Resources in Long-Term Perspective* (Cambridge, 2015)

De Moor, M., Shaw-Taylor, L. and Warde, P. (eds), *The Management of Common Land in North West Europe, c.1500–1850* (Turnhout, 2002)

Denman, D. R., Roberts, R. A. and Smith, H. J. F., *Commons and Village Greens* (London, 1967)

Devine, T. M., *Clanship to Crofters' War: The Social Transformation of the Scottish Highlands* (Manchester, 1994)

Di Palma, V., *Wasteland: A History* (London, 2014)

Dilley, R. S., 'The Cumberland court leet and the use of the common lands', *Trans CWAAS*, new ser. 67 (1967), pp. 125–51

—— 'The enclosure awards of Cumberland: a statistical list', *Trans CWAAS*, new ser. 100 (2000), pp. 225–39

Dodgshon, R. A., 'The landholding foundations of the open-field system', *Past & Present*, 67 (1975), pp. 3–29

—— *Land and Society in Early Scotland* (Oxford, 1981)

—— *From Chiefs to Landlords: Social and Economic Change in the Western Highlands and Islands, c.1493–1820* (Edinburgh, 1998)

Done, A. and Muir, R., 'The landscape history of grouse shooting in the Yorkshire Dales', *Rural History*, 12 (2) (2001), pp. 195–210

Drakeford, T., Frampton, D., Haldane, P., Sutcliffe, U. and Wills, D., *Wimbledon Common: 100 Years of Change* (Wimbledon, 2012)

Dunsford, H. M. and Harris, S. J., 'Colonization of the wasteland in County Durham, 1100–1400', *Economic History Review*, 2nd ser. 56 (2003), pp. 34–56

Dyer, C., *Lords and Peasants in a Changing Society: The Estates of the Bishopric of Worcester, 680–1540* (Cambridge, 1980)

—— 'Conflict in the landscape: the enclosure movement in England, 1220–1349', *Landscape History*, 28 (2006), pp. 21–33

Edwards, M., 'Sheep Farming on the Lake District Fells: adapting to change' (TS report, revised 2017)

Edwards, P., *The Horse Trade of Tudor and Stuart England* (Cambridge, 1988)

Everitt, A., 'Common land', in J. Thirsk (ed.), *The English Rural Landscape* (Oxford, 2000), pp. 210–35

Eversley, Lord [George Shaw Lefevre], *Commons, Forests and Footpaths* (London, 1910)

Fairhall, D., *Common Ground: The Story of Greenham* (London, 2006)

Faith, R., *The English Peasantry and the Growth of Lordship* (London, 1997)

Fleming, A. *The Dartmoor Reaves: Investigating Prehistoric Land Divisions*, 2nd edn (Oxford, 2008)

Foot, W., 'The impact of the military on the agricultural landscape of England and Wales in the Second World War', in B. Short, C. Watkins and J. Martin (eds), *The Front Line of Freedom: British Farming in the Second World War* (Exeter, 2006), pp. 132–42

Ford, A.-M., 'On common ground', in *Our Common Heritage: A Collection of Six Essays about the Social History of Chiltern Commons* (Chilterns Conservation Board, 2015), pp. 70–83

Fox, A. W., *A Lost Frontier Revealed: Regional Separation in the East Midlands* (Hatfield, 2009)

Fox, H. S. A., 'Approaches to the adoption of the Midland system', in T. Rowley (ed.), *The Origins of Open Field Agriculture* (London, 1981), pp. 64–111

—— 'The people of the Wolds in English settlement history', in M. Aston, D. Austin and C. Dyer (eds), *The Rural Settlements of Medieval England* (Oxford, 1989), pp. 77–101

—— *Dartmoor's Alluring Uplands: Transhumance and Pastoral Management in the Middle Ages* (Exeter, 2012)

Frazer, B., 'Common recollections: resisting enclosure "by agreement" in seventeenth-century England', *International Journal of Historical Archaeology*, 3 (2) (1999), pp. 75–99

French, H. R., 'Urban agriculture, commons and commoners in the seventeenth and eighteenth centuries: the case of Sudbury, Suffolk', *AgHR*, 48 (2) (2000), pp. 171–99

—— 'Urban common rights, enclosure and the market: Clitheroe Town Moors, 1764–1802', *AgHR*, 51 (1) (2003), pp. 40–68

—— 'The governance of urban common lands in England, 1500–1840', working paper (December 2017), at https://www.researchgate.net/publication/321685425

Gelling, M., *Place-Names in the Landscape: The Geographical Roots of Britain's Place-Names* (London, 1984)

Gibson, R., *The Scottish Countryside: Its Changing Face, 1700–2000* (Edinburgh, 2007)

Gilbert, J. M., *Hunting and Hunting Reserves in Medieval Scotland* (Edinburgh, 1979)

Gorman, M., *Saving the People's Forest: Open Spaces, Enclosure and Popular Protest in Mid-Victorian London* (Hatfield, 2021)

Grantham, J., *The Regulated Pasture (a History of Common Land in Chipping Norton)* (printed privately, 1997)

Gray, H. L., *English Field Systems* (Cambridge, Mass., 1915)

Grigg, D. B., *The Agricultural Revolution in South Lincolnshire* (Cambridge, 1966)

Griffin, C., 'Enclosure from below? The politics of squatting and encroachment in the post-Restoration New Forest', *Historical Research*, 91 (252) (2018), pp. 274–95

Griffin, C. J. and Robertson, I., 'Moral ecologies: conservation in conflict in rural England', *History Workshop Journal*, 82 (2016), pp. 24–49

Griffiths, E., 'Draining the coastal marshes of north-west Norfolk: the contribution of the le Stranges of Hunstanton, 1605–1724', *AgHR*, 63 (2015), pp. 221–42

Groves, N., 'From Berkhamsted to battlefield: WW1 training trenches on Berkhamsted Common', in Chilterns Conservation Board, *Our Common Heritage: A Collection of Six Essays about the Social History of Chiltern Commons* (2015), pp. 84–98

Halcrow, E. M., 'The Town Moor of Newcastle upon Tyne', *Archaeologia Aeliana*, 4th ser. 31 (1953), pp. 149–64

Haldane, A. R. B., *The Drove Roads of Scotland* (Edinburgh, 1952)

Hale, W. G. and Coney, A., *Martin Mere: Lancashire's Lost Lake* (Liverpool, 2005)

Hall, D., *The Open Fields of Northamptonshire* (Northampton, 1995)

Hardin, G., 'The tragedy of the commons', *Science*, new ser. 162 (3859) (1968), pp. 1243–8

Harris, B. and Ryan, G., *An Outline of the Law Relating to Common Land* (London, 1967)

Harris, L. E., *Vermuyden and the Fens: A Study of Sir Cornelius Vermuyden and the Great Level* (London, 1953)

Harrison, C., 'Manor courts and the governance of Tudor England', in C. Brooks and M. Lobban (eds), *Communities and Courts in Britain 1150–1900* (London, 1997), pp. 43–59

Hart, C. E., *Royal Forest: A History of Dean's Woods as Producers of Timber* (Oxford, 1966)

Healey, J., 'The political culture of the English commons, *c.* 1550–1650', *AgHR*, 60 (2) (2012), pp. 266–87

Hearnshaw, F. J. C., *Leet Jurisdiction in England, Especially as Illustrated by the Records of the Court Leet of Southampton* (Southampton, 1908)

Herbert, N., 'The squatter and rural settlement in the Georgian Age: Woolridge Common, Hartpury', *Transactions of the Bristol & Gloucestershire Archaeological Society*, 133 (2015), pp. 175–206

Hey, D., 'The grouse moors of the Peak District', in P. S. Barnwell and M. Palmer (eds), *Post-Medieval Landscapes* (Macclesfield, 2007), pp. 68–79

Hill, O., 'The future of our commons', in her *Our Common Land and other short essays* (London, 1877), pp. 175–206

Hindle, S., '"Not by bread only"? Common right, parish relief and endowed charity in a forest economy, *c.*1600–1800', in S. King and A. Tomkins (eds), *The Poor in England 1700–1850: An Economy of Makeshifts* (Manchester, 2003), pp. 39–75

—— *On the Parish? The Micro-Politics of Poor Relief in Rural England c.1550–1750* (Oxford, 2004)

Hodgson, R. I., 'The progress of enclosure in County Durham, 1550–1870', in H. S. A. Fox and R. A. Butlin (eds), *Change in the Countryside: Essays on Rural England 1500–1900* (London, 1979), pp. 83–102

Hoskins, W. G. and Stamp, L. D., *The Common Lands of England and Wales* (London, 1963)

Houston, R., 'Custom in context: medieval and early modern Scotland and England', *Past & Present*, 211 (2011), pp. 35–76

Howell, D. W., *Land and People in Nineteenth-Century Wales* (London, 1977)

Howkins, A., 'The commons, enclosure and radical histories', in D. Feldman and J. Lawrence (eds), *Structures and Transformations in Modern British History* (Cambridge, 2011), pp. 118–41

—— 'The use and abuse of the English commons, 1845–1914', *History Workshop Journal*, 78 (2014), pp. 107–32

Hoyle, R. W., 'Disafforestation and drainage: the Crown as entrepreneur?', in R. W. Hoyle (ed.), *The Estates of the English Crown, 1558–1640* (Cambridge, 1992), pp. 353–88

—— 'Introduction: custom, improvement and anti-improvement', in R. W. Hoyle (ed.), *Custom, Improvement and the Landscape in Early Modern Britain* (Farnham, 2011), pp. 1–38

Hoyle, R. W. and Spencer, C. J., 'The Slaidburn poor pasture: changing configurations of popular politics in the eighteenth- and early nineteenth-century village', *Social History*, 31 (2) (2006), pp. 182–205

Huggins, M., *Horse Racing and British Society in the Long Eighteenth Century* (Woodbridge, 2018)

Hunter, J., *The Making of the Crofting Community* (Edinburgh, 1976)

Hurle, P., *The Forest and Chase of Malvern* (Chichester, 2007)

Ibbetson, D., 'Custom in medieval law', in A. Perreau-Saussine and J. B. Murphy (eds), *The Nature of Customary Law* (Cambridge, 2007), pp. 151–75

Inui, H., 'The creation and administration of post-enclosure poor lands in English parishes, c.1630–1840', *AgHR*, 69 (2) (2021), pp. 192–212

Ivey, J., 'Census of the New Forest Commoners 2011', report at https://www.realnewforest.org/wp-content/uploads/2018/11/Final-census-report-August-2011.pdf

Jarman, A. L., 'Customary rights in Scots law: test cases on access to the land in the nineteenth century', *Journal of Legal History*, 28 (2) (2007), pp. 207–32

—— 'Urban commons: from customary use to community right on Scotland's bleaching greens', in A. Lewis, P. Brand and P. Mitchell (eds), *Law in the City: Proceedings of the Seventeenth British Legal History Conference, London 2005* (Dublin, 2007), pp. 319–45

Johnson, W., *Wimbledon Common: Its Geology, Antiquities and Natural History* (London, 1912)

Jones, G., *Trends in Common Grazings: First Steps towards an Integrated Needs-Based Strategy* (European Forum for Nature Conservation & Pastoralism, 2011)

Jones, R. and Page, M., *Medieval Villages in an English Landscape: Beginnings and Ends* (Macclesfield, 2006)

Jones Pierce, T., *Medieval Welsh Society* (Cardiff, 1972)

Kelly, J., 'Kennington Common, the Occupy movement and the freedom of assembly', *History Workshop: Histories of the Present*, 3 November 2011, at https://www.history workshop.org.uk/kennington-common-the-occupy-movement-the-freedom-of-assembly/

Knox, S. A., *The Making of the Shetland Landscape* (Edinburgh, 1985)

Land Use Consultants, *Agricultural Management of Common Land in England and Wales* (DEFRA, 2005)

Langton, J., 'Medieval forests and chases: another realm?', in J. Langton and G. Jones (eds), *Forests and Chases of Medieval England and Wales, c.1000 to c.1500* (Oxford, 2010), pp. 14–35

Langton, J. and Jones, G. (eds), *Forests and Chases of Medieval England and Wales, c.1000 to c.1500* (Oxford, 2010)

Layton-Jones, K. (ed.), *The Common Story: A History of Tooting Common* (Wandsworth, 2019)

Leslie, M. and Raylor, T., *Culture and Cultivation in Early Modern England: Writing and the Land* (Leicester, 1992)

Lindley, K., *Fenland Riots and the English Revolution* (London, 1982)

Lloyd, J., *The Great Forest of Brecknock* (London, 1905)

Loux, A. C., 'The Great Rabbit Massacre: a "comedy of the commons"? Custom, community and rights of public access to the Links of St Andrews', *Liverpool Law Review*, 22 (2000), pp. 123–55

MacCuish, D. J., 'Crofting legislation since 1886', *Scottish Geographical Magazine*, 103 (2) (1987), pp. 90–4

MacDermot, E. T., *The History of the Forest of Exmoor*, revised edn (Newton Abbot, 1973)

McDonagh, B., 'Landscape, territory and common rights in medieval East Yorkshire', *Landscape History*, 40 (2) (2019), pp. 77–100

MacMaster, N., 'The battle for Mousehold Heath 1857–1884: "popular politics" and the Victorian public park', *Past & Present*, 127 (1990), pp. 117–54

Macnair, A. and Williamson, T., *William Faden and Norfolk's 18th-Century Landscape* (Oxford, 2010)

Maitland, F. W. and Baildon, W. P., *The Court Baron*, Selden Society IV (London, 1891)

Mansfield, L., 'Hill farming identities and connections to place', in I. Convery, G. Corsane and P. Davis (eds), *Making Sense of Place: Multidisciplinary Perspectives* (Woodbridge, 2012), pp. 67–77

Martin, E., 'Greens, commons and tyes in Suffolk', in A. Longcroft and G. Jobey (eds), *East Anglian Studies* (Norwich, 1995), pp. 167–78

Mayall, D., *Gypsy-Travellers in Nineteenth-Century Society* (Cambridge, 1988)

Miller, K., *The Isle of Axholme Historic Landscape Characterisation Project* (Leeds, 1997)

Moody, D., 'Godshillwood and Woodgreen: a squatter settlement on the edge of the New Forest, 1600–1840', *Hampshire Studies 2016* (*Proceedings of Hampshire Field Club Archaeological Society*, 71), pp. 126–47

Murota, T. and Takeshita, K. (eds), *Local Commons and Democratic Environmental Governance* (New York, 2013)

Murphy, E., 'Brockdish Common, Norfolk: historical research for present-day community benefit', *The Local Historian*, 51 (1) (January 2021), pp. 47–56

Natural England, *Bowes Moor SSSI Site Restoration Plan, 2018–2028*, at http://publications.naturalengland.org.uk/file/6030598561071104

Natural England Lake District Team, *Grazing Regimes for Nature Recovery: Experience from 25 Years of Agri-Environment Agreements in the Lake District's High Fells* (Kendal, 2020)

Navickas, K., 'Moors, fields and popular protest in South Lancashire and the West Riding of Yorkshire, 1800–1848', *Northern History*, 46 (1) (2009), pp. 93–111

—— *Protest and the Politics of Space and Place, 1789–1848* (Manchester, 2016)

—— 'Kennington Common, protest and public space', in *Kennington 1848: Another Look* (Friends of Kennington Park, 2019), pp. 34–9

Neeson, J. M., *Commoners: Common Right, Enclosure and Social Change in England, 1700–1820* (Cambridge, 1993)

Neilson, N., *Customary Rents*, Oxford Studies in Social and Legal History II (Oxford, 1910)

O'Donnell, R., *Assembling Enclosure: Transformations in the Rural Landscape of Post-Medieval North-East England* (Hatfield, 2015)

Oldrey, D., Cox, T. and Nash, R., *The Heath and the Horse: A History of Racing and Art on Newmarket Heath* (London, 2016)

Oosthuizen, S., *Landscapes Decoded: The Origins and Development of Cambridgeshire's Medieval Fields* (Hatfield, 2006)

Ostrom, E., *Governing the Commons: The Evolution of Institutions for Collective Action* (Cambridge, 1990)

—— *Understanding Institutional Diversity* (Princeton, 2005)

Overton, M., *Agricultural Revolution in England: The Transformation of the Agrarian Economy 1500–1850* (Cambridge, 1996)

Owen, E., 'Arvona antiqua: ancient remains, hafottai etc', *Archaeologia Cambriensis*, 3rd ser. L (April 1867), pp. 102–8

Page, C. N., 'The history and spread of bracken in Britain', *Proceedings of the Royal Society of Edinburgh, Section B*, 81 (1–2) (1982), pp. 3–10

Pannett, D., 'Commons of the Stiperstones mining district', *Shropshire History and Archaeology (Transactions of the Shropshire Archaeological & Historical Society)*, 95 (2020), pp. 61–82

Pantos, A., '"On the edge of things": the boundary location of Anglo-Saxon assembly sites', in D. Griffiths, A. Reynolds and S. Semple (eds), *Boundaries in Early Medieval Britain* (Oxford, 2003), pp. 38–49

—— 'The location and form of Anglo-Saxon assembly places: some "moot" points', in A. Pantos and S. Semple (eds), *Assembly Places and Practices in Medieval Europe* (Dublin, 2004), pp. 155–80

Parkes, P., 'A pasture in common: a twentieth-century environmental history of Ewyas Harold Common (Herefordshire)', *Rural History*, 16 (1) (2005), pp. 111–32

Parry, M. L., *Climate Change, Agriculture and Settlement* (Folkestone, 1978)

Parton, A. G., 'Parliamentary enclosure in nineteenth-century Surrey: some perspectives on the evaluation of land potential', *AgHR*, 33 (1985), pp. 51–8

Pasmore, A. H., 'Enclosure at New Buildings, Rockford Common', *Hampshire Field Club Newsletter*, 35 (Spring 2002), pp. vii–ix

Pastoral Commoning Partnership, *Trends in Pastoral Commoning* (Carlisle, 2009)

Petit, S. and Watkins, C., 'Pollarding trees: changing attitudes to a traditional land management practice in Britain 1600–1900', *Rural History*, 14 (2) (2003), pp. 157–76

Pettit, P. A. J., *The Royal Forests of Northamptonshire: A Study in Their Economy 1558–1714*, Northants Record Society XXIII (1968)

Phillips, A. D. M., *The Underdraining of Farmland in England during the Nineteenth Century* (Cambridge, 1989)

Pinches, S., 'From common right to cold charity: enclosure and poor allotments in the eighteenth and nineteenth centuries', in A. Borsay and P. Shapely (eds), *Medicine, Charity and Mutual Aid* (Aldershot, 2007), pp. 35–53

Porter, J., 'Waste land reclamation in the sixteenth and seventeenth centuries: the case of south-eastern Bowland, 1550–1630', *Transactions of the Historic Society of Lancashire & Cheshire*, 127 (1978), pp. 1–23.

Quartermaine, J. and Leech, R. H., *Cairns, Fields and Cultivation: Archaeological Landscapes of the Lake District Uplands* (Lancaster, 2012)

Rackham, O., *The History of the Countryside* (London, 1986)

Ratcliffe, D. A., 'The vegetation of the Carneddau, North Wales: I. Grassland, heaths and bogs', *Journal of Ecology*, 47 (2) (1959), pp. 371–413

Readman, P., 'Preserving the English landscape, 1870–1914', *Cultural & Social History*, 5 (2008), pp. 197–218

—— *Storied Ground: Landscape and the Shaping of English National Identity* (Cambridge, 2018)

Rees, W., *The Great Forest of Brecknock: A Facet of Breconshire History* (Brecon, 1966)

Reid, N., 'Five centuries of dispute: the common lands of St Andrews', *Scottish Archives*, 21 (2015), pp. 30–43

Rennie, F., 'Human ecology and concepts of sustainable development in a crofting township', *Folk Life*, 46 (2007), pp. 39–57

Richardson, F., 'The enclosure of the commons and wastes in Nantconwy, North Wales, 1540–1900', *AgHR*, 65 (1) (2017), pp. 49–73

Rigby, L., *The History of Stoke Common: A Poor's Fuel Allotment Charity* (Stoke Poges, 1975)

Ritvo, H., *The Dawn of Green: Manchester, Thirlmere and Modern Environmentalism* (London, 2009)

Roberts, B. K., 'Field systems of the West Midlands', in A. R. H. Baker and R. A. Butlin (eds), *Studies of Field Systems in the British Isles* (Cambridge, 1973), pp. 188–231

—— 'Cockfield Fell', *Antiquity*, 49 (193) (1975), pp. 48–50

Roberts, B. K. and Barnwell, P. S., 'The multiple estate of Glanville Jones: epitome, critique, and context', in P. S. Barnwell and B. K. Roberts (eds), *Britons, Saxons and Scandinavians: The Historical Geography of Glanville R. J. Jones* (Turnhout, 2011), pp. 25–128

Roberts, B. K. and Wrathmell, S., *Region and Place: A Study of English Rural Settlement* (London, 2002)

Roberts, M. J. D., 'Gladstonian Liberalism and environment protection', *English Historical Review*, 128 (2013), pp. 292–322

Rodgers, C. P., Straughton, E. A., Winchester, A. J. L. and Pieraccini, M., *Contested Common Land: Environmental Governance Past and Present* (London, 2011)

Roebuck, P., 'Cattle-droving through Cumbria after the Union: the stances on the Musgrave estates, 1707–12', *Trans CWAAS*, 3rd ser. 12 (2012), pp. 143–58, and follow-up note in 3rd ser. 13 (2013), pp. 256–9

Ross, A., 'Scottish environmental history and the (mis)use of soums', *AgHR*, 54 (2006), pp. 213–28

Rowley, T., *The Shropshire Landscape* (London, 1972)

Royal Commission on Common Land, *Report of Royal Commission on Common Land 1955–1958* (Cmnd. 462, 1958)

Royal Commission on the Ancient & Historical Monuments in Wales, *An Inventory of the Ancient Monuments in Caernarvonshire, Volume I: East* (London, 1956)

Russell, E. and R. C., *Old and New Landscapes in the Horncastle Area* (Lincoln, 1985)

Rymer, L., 'The history and ethnobotany of bracken', *Botanical Journal of Linnean Society*, 73 (1976), pp. 151–76

Scottish Government, *Economic Report on Scottish Agriculture 2010* (Edinburgh, 2010)

Searle, C. E., 'Customary tenants and the enclosure of the Cumbrian commons', *Northern History*, 29 (1993), pp. 126–53

Shannon, W. D., 'Approvement and improvement in the lowland wastes of early modern Lancashire', in R. W. Hoyle (ed.), *Custom, Improvement and the Landscape in Early Modern Britain* (Farnham, 2011), pp. 175–202

—— 'The survival of true intercommoning in Lancashire in the early-modern period', *Agricultural History*, 86 (2012), pp. 169–91

Sharp, B., 'Common rights, charities and the disorderly poor', in G. Eley and W. Hunt (eds), *Reviving the English Revolution: Reflections and Elaborations on the Work of Christopher Hill* (New York, 1988), pp. 107–37

Shaw-Taylor, L., 'Labourers, cows, common rights and Parliamentary enclosure: the evidence of contemporary comment, c.1760–1810', *Past & Present*, 171 (2001), pp. 95–126

—— 'The management of common land in the lowlands of southern England circa 1500 to circa 1850', in M. De Moor, L. Shaw-Taylor and P. Warde (eds), *The Management of Common Land in North West Europe, c.1500–1850* (Turnhout, 2002), pp. 59–85

Short, B., 'Conservation, class and custom: lifespace and conflict in a nineteenth-century forest environment', *Rural History*, 10 (2) (1999), pp. 127–54

Short, C. and Winter, M., 'The problem of common land: towards stakeholder governance', *Journal of Environmental Planning and Management*, 42 (5) (1999), pp. 613–30

Silvester, R., 'The commons and the waste: use and misuse in mid-Wales', in I. D. Whyte and A. J. L. Winchester (eds), *Society, Landscape and Environment in Upland Britain* (Birmingham, 2004), pp. 53–66

—— 'Landscapes of the poor: encroachment in Wales in the post-medieval centuries', in P. S. Barnwell and M. Palmer (eds), *Post-Medieval Landscapes* (Macclesfield, 2007), pp. 55–67

Simmons, I. G., *The Moorlands of England and Wales: An Environmental History 8000 BC – AD 2000* (Edinburgh, 2003)

Siraut, M., *Exmoor: The Making of an English Upland* (Chichester, 2009)

Skipp, V., *Crisis and Development: An Ecological Case Study of the Forest of Arden, 1570–1674* (Cambridge, 1978)

—— 'The evolution of settlement and open-field topography in North Arden down to 1300', in T. Rowley (ed.), *The Origins of Open Field Agriculture* (London, 1981), pp. 162–83

Slack, P., *The Invention of Improvement: Information and Material Progress in Seventeenth-Century England* (Oxford, 2015)

Smith, B., *Toons and Tenants: Settlement and Society in Shetland, 1299–1899* (Lerwick, 2000)

Smout, T. C. (ed.), *Scottish Woodland History* (Edinburgh, 1997)

Snell, K. D. M., *Annals of the Labouring Poor: Social Change and Agrarian England, 1660–1900* (Cambridge, 1985)

Straughton, E. A., *Common Grazing in the Northern English Uplands, 1800–1965* (Lampeter, 2008)

Sumner, H., *Cuckoo Hill: The Book of Gorley* (London, 1987)

Szczelkun, S., *Kennington Park: The Birthplace of People's Democracy*, 3rd edn (London, 2018)

Tankard, D., 'The regulation of cottage building in seventeenth-century Sussex', *AgHR*, 59 (1) (2011), pp. 19–35

Tate, W. E., *The English Village Community and the Enclosure Movements* (London, 1967)

—— *The Parish Chest: A Study of the Records of Parochial Administration in England*, 3rd edn (Chichester, [1969] 1983)

Tate, W. E. (ed. M. Turner), *A Domesday of English Enclosure Acts and Awards* (Reading, 1978)

Tavener, L. E., *The Common Lands of Hampshire* (Southampton, 1957)

Taylor, C., 'Fenlands', in J. Thirsk (ed.), *The English Rural Landscape* (Oxford, 2000), pp. 167–87

Thirsk, J., 'The Isle of Axholme before Vermuyden', *AgHR*, 1 (1) (1953), pp. 16–28

—— (ed.), *The Agrarian History of England and Wales, Vol. IV, 1500–1640* (Cambridge, 1967)

—— 'Field systems of the East Midlands', in A. R. H. Baker and R. A. Butlin (eds), *Studies of Field Systems in the British Isles* (Cambridge, 1973), pp. 232–80

—— *The Agrarian History of England and Wales, Vol. V, part I* (Cambridge, 1984)

—— 'The Crown as projector on its own estates, from Elizabeth I to Charles I', in R. W. Hoyle (ed.), *The Estates of the English Crown, 1558–1640* (Cambridge, 1992), pp. 297–352

—— (ed.), *The English Rural Landscape* (Oxford, 2000)

Thompson, E. P., 'Custom, law and common right', in his *Customs in Common* (Harmondsworth, [1991] 1993), pp. 97–184

Thompson, F. M. L., 'The second agricultural revolution, 1815–1880', *Economic History Review*, new ser. 21 (1968), pp. 62–77

Thomson, W. P. L., *Orkney: Land and People* (Kirkwall, 2008)

Tindley, A., *The Sutherland Estate, 1850–1920: Aristocratic Decline, Estate Management and Land Reform* (Edinburgh, 2010)

Tomlinson, R. W., 'A geography of flat-racing in Great Britain', *Geography*, 71 (3) (1986), pp. 228–39

Trinder, G., *Epworth Turbary Nature Reserve: Its Management and Wildlife since 1977* (privately printed, 2014)

Tubbs, C. R., *The New Forest: History, Ecology and Conservation* (Lyndhurst, 2001)

Turner, M., *English Parliamentary Enclosure: Its Historical Geography and Economic History* (Folkestone, 1980)

Victoria County Histories, searched through British History Online (www.british-history.ac.uk)

Vinogradoff, P., *Villainage in England* (Oxford, 1892)

—— *The Growth of the Manor* (London, 1905)

Virgoe, J., 'Thomas Fleetwood and the draining of Martin Mere', *Transactions of the Historic Society of Lancashire and Cheshire*, 152 (2003), pp. 27–47

Waddell, B., *Landscape and Society in the Vale of York, c.1500–1800*, Borthwick Paper 120 (York, 2011)

—— 'Governing England through the manor courts, 1550–1850', *The Historical Journal*, 55 (2) (2012), pp. 279–315

Ward, C., *Cotters and Squatters: Housing's Hidden History* (Nottingham, 2002)

Warde, P., 'The idea of improvement, c.1520–1700', in R. W. Hoyle (ed.), *Custom, Improvement and the Landscape in Early Modern Britain* (Farnham, 2011), pp. 127–48

Warde, P. and Williamson, T., 'Fuel supply and agriculture in post-medieval England', *AgHR*, 62 (1) (2014), pp. 61–82

Watson, C. E., 'The Minchinhampton custumal and its place in the story of the manor', *Transactions of the Bristol & Gloucestershire Archaeological Society*, 54 (1932), pp. 203–384

Welsh, H., *Bromyard Downs Common Management Plan 2015–2025*, http://www.bromyarddowns.co.uk/minutes-byelaws/

Whittington, G., 'The common lands of Berkshire', *Transactions & Papers (IBG)*, 35 (1964), pp. 129–48

Whitworth, C., Jones, K. and Evans, R., *Survey of the Grazing Practice and Farming Systems on Holdings with Access Rights to Llanllechid Common: Results and Recommendations* (Cardiff, 1997)

Whyte, I. D., *Agriculture and Society in Seventeenth-Century Scotland* (Edinburgh, 1979)

—— 'Population mobility in early modern Scotland', in R. A. Houston and I. D. Whyte (eds), *Scottish Society, 1500–1800* (Cambridge, 1989), pp. 37–58

—— *Transforming Fell and Valley: Landscape and Parliamentary Enclosure in North West England* (Lancaster, 2003)

—— '"Wild, barren and frightful": Parliamentary enclosure in an upland county: Westmorland, 1767–1890', *Rural History*, 14 (1) (2003), pp. 21–38

—— 'Taming the fells: Parliamentary enclosure and the landscape in northern England', *Landscapes*, 6 (1) (2005), pp. 46–61

Whyte, N., 'The deviant dead in the Norfolk landscape', *Landscapes*, 4 (1) (2003), pp. 24–39

—— *Inhabiting the Landscape: Place, Custom and Memory, 1500–1800* (Oxford, 2009)

Williams, M., *The Draining of the Somerset Levels* (Cambridge, 1970)

—— 'The enclosure and reclamation of waste land in England and Wales in the eighteenth and nineteenth centuries', *Trans IBG*, 51 (1970), pp. 55–69

Williamson, T., *Shaping Medieval Landscapes: Settlement, Society, Environment* (Macclesfield, 2003)

—— *England's Landscape: East Anglia* (London, 2006)

—— 'Joan Thirsk and "The Common Fields"', in R. Jones and C. Dyer (eds), *Farmers, Consumers, Innovators: The World of Joan Thirsk* (Hatfield, 2016), pp. 35–48

—— 'How natural is natural? Historical perspectives on wildlife and the environment in Britain', *Transactions of the Royal Historical Society*, 29 (2019), pp. 293–311

Winchester, A. J. L., *Landscape and Society in Medieval Cumbria* (Edinburgh, 1987)

—— *Discovering Parish Boundaries*, 2nd edn (Princes Risborough, 2000)

—— 'Dividing lines in a moorland landscape: territorial boundaries in upland England', *Landscapes*, 1 (2) (2000), pp. 16–34

—— *The Harvest of the Hills: Rural Life in Northern England and the Scottish Borders, 1400–1700* (Edinburgh, 2000)

—— 'Village byelaws and the management of a contested common resource: bracken (*Pteridium aquilinum*) in highland Britain, 1500–1800', *Digital Library of the Commons*, http://hdl.handle.net/10535/1234

—— 'Vaccaries and agistment: upland medieval forests as grazing grounds', in J. Langton and G. Jones (eds), *Forests and Chases of Medieval England and Wales, c.1000 to c.1500* (Oxford, 2010), pp. 109–24

—— '"By ancient right or custom": the local history of common land in a European context', *The Local Historian*, 45 (4) (2015), pp. 266–85

—— 'Shielings and common pastures', in K. J. Stringer and A. J. L. Winchester (eds), *Northern England and Southern Scotland in the Central Middle Ages* (Woodbridge, 2017), pp. 273–97

Winchester, A. J. L. and Straughton, E. A., 'Stints and sustainability: managing stock levels on common land in England, c.1600–2006', *AgHR*, 58 (2010), pp. 30–48

Wmffre, I., 'Toponymy and land-use in the uplands of the Doethïe valley (Cardiganshire)', in H. James and P. Moore (eds), *Carmarthenshire and Beyond: Studies in History and Archaeology in Memory of Terry James*, Carmarthenshire Antiquarian Society Monograph Ser. 8 (2009), pp. 270–83

Wood, A., 'The loss of Athelstan's gift: the politics of popular memory in Malmesbury, 1607–1633', in J. Whittle (ed.), *Landlords and Tenants in Britain, 1440–1660: Tawney's Agrarian Problem Revisited* (Woodbridge, 2013), pp. 85–99

—— *The Memory of the People: Custom and Popular Senses of the Past in Early Modern England* (Cambridge, 2013)

Woodward, D., 'Straw, bracken and the Wicklow whale: the exploitation of natural resources in England since 1500', *Past & Present*, 159 (1998), pp. 43–76

THESES

Birtles, S., '"A green space beyond self-interest": the evolution of common land in Norfolk, *c*.750–2003', PhD thesis, University of East Anglia, 2003

Dilley, R. S., 'Common land in Cumbria, 1500–1800', MPhil thesis, University of Cambridge, 1972

—— 'Agricultural change and common land in Cumberland, 1700–1850', PhD thesis, McMaster University, 1991

Hodgson, R. I., 'Coalmining, population and enclosure in the Seasale colliery districts of Durham (northern Durham), 1551–1810: a study in historical geography', PhD thesis, Durham University, 1990

Kerner, F., 'Enclosure and survival: common land in the Buckinghamshire Chilterns *c*.1600–*c*.1900', PhD thesis, University of Lancaster, 2016

Lowdon, R. E., 'To travel by older ways: a historical-cultural geography of droving in Scotland', PhD thesis, University of Glasgow, 2014

MacPhail, I., 'Land, crofting and the Assynt Crofters Trust: a post-colonial geography?', PhD thesis, University of Wales, Lampeter, 2002

Moir, J., '"A World unto Themselves"? Squatter settlement in Herefordshire, 1780–1880', PhD thesis, University of Leicester, 1990

Newman, C., 'Mapping the late medieval and post medieval landscape of Cumbria', PhD thesis, University of Newcastle upon Tyne, 2014

WEBSITES

Association of Commons Registration Authorities of England and Wales: https://www.acraew.org.uk

British Newspaper Archive: https://www.britishnewspaperarchive.co.uk/

Common Land Research Resource (archive of the AHRC 'Contested Common Land' project, 2007–10): https://research.ncl.ac.uk/commons/about/

Digital Library of the Commons: https://dlc.dlib.indiana.edu/dlc/

Foundation for Common Land: https://foundationforcommonland.org.uk

International Association for the Study of the Commons: https://iasc-commons.org

Open Spaces Society: https://www.oss.org.uk

Wastes and Strays (Newcastle University urban commons project): https://research.ncl.ac.uk/wastesandstrays/wastesandstraysblog/

INDEX

Page numbers in **bold** indicate explanation of technical and obsolete terms. Page numbers in *italics* refer to illustrations and their captions.

Aber (Caern.) *see* Llanllechid
Aberdeenshire   71–2
agistment   33, **40**, 41, 42, 56, 146, 147, 215, 242
agri-environmental schemes   162, 184, 185–6, 220, 243
Aldbourne Chase (Wilts.)   88
almshouses   127
Alston Moor (Cumb.)   66, 70
Anglo-Saxon period   14, 23, 85
   see also extensive lordship, shire moors
Anstruther (Fife)   44
Appleby (Westmld)   93, 99
approvement   **26**, 27, 46, 130, 154
Arden (Warw.)   23, 27
Arwystli (Montgom.)   28, 40
Ashdown Forest (Sussex)   76, 77, 80, 83, 120, 133, 163 n.42, 165, 167, 168, 191
   common rights   36, 39 n.94, 73
Ashill (Norf.)   147
Assynt (Sutherland)   12, 207–14
Axholme, Isle of (Lincs.)   132, 150, 229–33

Badley Wood (Heref.)   245, 247, 251, 253
Bagshot (Surrey)   138, 176–7
Banham (Norf.)   36, 60
Banstead (Surrey)   99, 155

Barnby (Notts.)   28
Barnham Broom (Norf.)   *149*
barony courts *see* courts, seigniorial
Bassenthwaite (Cumb.)   *141*, *142*, 143, 186
battlefields   89
beacons   87–8, 99, 101
Beaulieu Rails (Hants)   121, 123
Bedfordshire   83
Bedwyn, Great (Wilts.)   150
beehives   196, 259, *260*
Berkhamsted (Herts.)   155, 179
Berkshire   148, 172, 175
Bernwood (Bucks.)   133, 146
Beverley (Yorks. E.R.)   97, 179
Black Country (Staffs.)   119, 123
Blackheath (Kent)   100, 101, 102, 108, 114, 202 n.66
Bladon (Oxon.)   59, 60
Bleathwood Common (Heref.)   125
Blyth, Walter   60–1
Bootle (Cumb.)   143
Borrowdale (Cumb.)   169
boundaries over common land   27, 45–50, 275–6
   county   17, 121
   hundred   85
   parish/township   13, 17, 22, 23, 25, 38, 42, 43, 87, 268
boundary markers   47–50

303

Bournemouth   202–3
Bowes Moor (Yorks. N.R.)   190
Bowland Fells (Lancs./Yorks. W.R.)   134, 143, 145
bowling/bowling greens   95, 96, 203
bracken ('fern')   28, 77–8, 191, 196, 215, 220, 252, 258–9
  spread of   181, 186, 189, 192, 228, 242, 251, 253
Brancaster (Norf.)   75, 147, 162, *176*, 203
Brecon Beacons   17, 139, 157, 180
Breconshire   124, 138
Brent, South (Devon)   33
brick-making   115, 120, 194, *195*, 198, 267
Bridestowe (Devon)   168
Bringsty Common (Heref.)   245–53
Bristol   96, 101
Bromyard Downs (Heref.)   97, 245–53, 279
Broseley (Shrops.)   119, 124
Bryncoch   29
Buckinghamshire   11, 17, 75, 102
Burgh-by-Sands (Cumb.)   168
Burton Agnes (Yorks. E.R.)   22, 26, 72
Bushey (Herts.)   75
byelaws governing resource use   51–2, 53–78, 160, 165, 193–4, 210–13, 218–20, 239–40, 247, 265–7

Cambridgeshire   14, 22, 37, 59, 69, 85, 150, 180
Cannock Chase (Staffs.)   41, 77
Cardiganshire   63
Carnwath (Lanarkshire)   68
  see also Libberton
Castleton (Derby.)   114, 134, 139
cattle (horned beasts)   39, 40, 59, 66, 72, 164, 190, 220, 258–9
  brands (marks)   64–5
  decline in grazing numbers   184, 187, 191, 196, 198, 213
  milk cows   57, 58, 112–13, 147, 200, 268
  re-introduction of   185, 197, 221, 233
  see also droving, fairs, stints

Cawston (Norf.)   113
Chartists   103–4, 200
Chester   88, 97
Cheviot Hills   15, 42, 202
Chiltern Hills   11, 17, 80, 90, 115, 166
Chippenham (Cambs.)   35
Chipping Norton (Oxon.)   106, *144*, 145, 150
Chobham (Surrey)   *174*, 176–7
Church Lawton (Ches.)   35
Cirencester (Glos.)   22
Clare, John   137, 153
clay/clay pits   31, 115, 138, 151, 154, 166, 193, *195*, 198, 229, 256
Clee Hills (Shrops.)   41, 66
Clitheroe (Lancs.)   44, 101
Clyne Common (Swansea)   178
Cobham (Surrey)   102
Cockermouth (Cumb.)   43
Cockfield (Dur.)   145, 223–8
Colchester (Essex)   89, 176
  Mile End Heath   97, 105
Coldingham (Berwickshire)   *24*
Comberton (Cambs.)   60
common good (Scottish burghs)   44–5
common grazings (in crofting areas)   9, *10*, 29, 31, 156, 158, 159–60, 187, 207–14
common land
  changing perceptions of   20, 108–9, 111, 128, 130–1, 153–9, 171, 269, 275, 277–81
  communal assemblies on   83–108, 277
  definition   1–3
  distribution and extent   9–13, 15–18
  ecology/vegetation   1–3, 17, 19, 137, 183–98, 200, 202, 204
    of case study commons   213–14, 228, 233, 242–3, 245, 251–3, 255, 270, 273
  licensed use   31–2, 40–1, 267
  location of (in relation to settlement)   12–13, 14, 15–18, 46–7

property rights in   21–45, 159–62, 275–6
recreational use   154, 156–7, 250, 270, 273
resources from   4, 27–8, 112–13, 115
  see also common rights
'wildness' of   20, 109, 200, 275, 277–8
common rights
  access to   34–6
  legal definitions   27–8, 29, 30, 33, 275–7
  regulation of   4–5, 51–81, 163–71
  see also estovers, pannage, pasture, piscary, soil, turbary
commoners' committees/associations   163–4, 167–71, 220, 243, 253, 269
Commons Act 1876   151, 155, 165
Commons Act 1899   167, 241, 251
Commons Act 2006   158, 161, 253
Commons Commissioners   160, 161, 162, 233, 242, 252
Commons Preservation Society   153, 154–6
Commons Registration Act 1965 (CRA)   160–2, 171, 185
  examples of rights registered   227, 232, 242, 252
  see also Commons Commissioners
commonty   30, 34, 71–2, 91, 107, 116, 136, *140*, 142, 276
Coniston (Lancs.)   60
conservation   20, 153, 157, 162, 183–97 *passim*, 214, 221, 233, 278
conservators, boards of   155, 164–5, 166, 167, 171, 198, 269–70, 273
coppice woodland   73–4, 145
cottage settlement on commons   115–23, 231, 247–9
cottagers
  common rights   34–6, 69–70, 74, 78, 252, 258, 266
  domestic economy   119–20
  impact of enclosure   112–13
  perceptions of   124–5

Cottenham (Lincs.)   65, 69
courts, seigniorial (manor courts, barony courts)   51–5, 118, 218–19, 276
  decline of   79–81, 163–4
  see also byelaws
Covenanters   106–7
Cranham (Glos.)   192
Crawley (Oxon.)   74
Crieff (Perthshire)   90, 91
crime   89–90, 95, 109, 268
Crofters Act 1886   159–60
Crofters Commission   159, 163, 210, 213
Crookham Common (Berks.)   180, 202
Crosby Garrett (Westmld)   165, 168
Crowborough (Sussex)   203
Cumberland   12, 87–8, 99, 135, 143
Cumbria   55, 56, 80, 115, 127, 166, 184–5
  common land, extent of   9, 17
  see also Cumberland, Lake District, Westmorland
Cumwhinton (Cumb.)   *53*
custom   27, 28, 33–7, 40, 42, 53–4, 62, 80, 113
Cwmdeuddwr (Radnorshire)   *62*
  see also Elan Valley
Cyfeiliog (Montgom.)   25, 28, 40
cytir   28–9, 64

Dartmoor   13, 19, 46 n.135, 164, 172, 202
  Commoners Council   171
  forest   39, 40, 47
  military use   177, 180
Dawley, Great (Shrops.)   119, 123
Dean, Forest of (Glos.)   73, 119, 121, 124
deer   39, 186, 214, 258
Dengie (Essex)   23
Derbyshire   119
Diggers   102, 277
Domesday Book   22, 27, 37, 41
donkeys (asses)   39, 167, 193, 240, 252
Dorset   88, 94

drainage
  fen/marsh   132–3, 229
  field   135, 191
  reversal ('re-wetting')   185, 189, 191
driving common land (to gather livestock)   55, 186, 211, 218–20, 242, 280
droving   56, 90–1, 94
Durham, County   9, 12, 76, 133, 135

Ebernoe Common (Sussex)   197
Eden Valley (Cumbria)   *18*, 99
Edgar, laws of   37
Edgerley (Shrops.)   *122*
Edmonton (Mddx)   64, 145
Elan Valley (Radnorshire)   175, 184
enclosure   11, 129, 132–45
  see also approvement
Enslow Hill (Oxon.)   102
Epping Forest (Essex)   112 n.3, 131, 155, 165, 166, 191
Epsom (Surrey)   85, 99
Epworth (Lincs.)   132–3, 197, 231–3
Eskdale (Cumb.)   61, 66, *78*, 169, 185
Eskrick (Yorks. W.R.)   74
Essex   14, 23, 102
estovers, common of   27, 28, 32, 68, 161, 162, 215, 220, 242, 252, 256
  regulation of   73–8
Everitt, Alan   3, 11, 111, 275
Ewyas Harold (Heref.)   192
Exmoor (Devon/Som.)   15, 39, 41, 46–7, *48*, 76
extensive lordship   23–6
extra-parochial wastes   121

fairs   90–5, 114
Falkirk (Stirlingshire)   89, 90, 91, 94
Fens
  boundaries in   46, 47
  common rights   21–2, 23, 25, 32, 37
  drainage   132–3
  poor allotments   150
  regulation of use   59, 65, 69

Fforest Fawr (Brec.)   40–1, 139, 168
Finchley (Mddx)   88, 90, 96, 131
firewood   68, 71, 73–4, 256, 266
Fitzherbert, [John]   58, 60, 66, 130
forests, hunting   39–41, 47, 73, 105
  enclosure/disafforestation   133, 146
Frensham (Surrey)   179, 195–6
fuel   4, 27, 30, 35, 43, 113, 119, 187, 190, 194, 196, 239, 258–9
  regulation of resources   67–76, 265–7
  see also estovers, fuel allotments, turbary
fuel allotments   146–52
furze *see* gorse
Fylingdales (Yorks. N.R.)   46 n.135, 69, 76

Galloway   *70*, 95, 107
gallows   86–7, 109
Galson (Isle of Lewis)   187
game   31, 80, 162, 188, 258
  see also forests, grouse
Gateward's case   36
gathering livestock *see* driving common land
Geddington Chase (Northants.)   35–6
geese   35, 39, 64, 111–12, 147, 167, 220, 226
gibbets   87, 109
Gilpin, William   118, 124
goats   39, 113, 120, 124, 227, 247, 252
golf courses   96, 100, 198, 202–3, 250, 270
gorse (furze)   43, 44, 74–5, 120, 193, 252, 258–9, 265–6, 267, 269
  spread of   192, 194, 196, 197, 228
  see also fuel allotments
Gorsley (Glos./Heref.)   116, *117*, 118, 123
Gower Peninsula (Glamorgan)   169, 191–2
gravel digging   27, 138, 154, 155, 172, 193, 261, 267, 269
grazing regulations   210–13, 216–20
  see also byelaws
Greenham Common (Berks.)   180

INDEX

gross, rights in **27**, 216, 220, 228, 242
grouse 75, 76, 169, 188
Guildford (Surrey) 96
 see also Merrow Downs
Guisborough (Yorks. N.R.) 69, 70 n.122, 72
Gunolfsmoors (Lancs.) 25, 26
gypsies 95, 114–15, 166, 169, 193, 194, 268

Hackney (Mddx) 108, 154
Halstock Down (Devon) 59, 177
Hambleton (Yorks. N.R.) 97, 99, 100
Hampshire 94, 95, 114, 115, 180
 see also New Forest
Hampstead Heath (Mddx) 90, 96, 155
Hardin, Garrett 4–5
Harrington (Cumb.) 69
Hartlib, Samuel 111, 131
Haslemere (Surrey) 127
heafs **61**, 62, 66, 161, 186, 219, 220, 228
heather 19, 32, 75–6, 160, 185, 187, 188–90, 242, 255–6, 259
 see also moor-burning
herding regulations 66, 160, 212, 219
Herefordshire 116, 120, 123, 125
Heveningham (Norf.) 124
Heyford, Lower (Oxon.) 75
Highlands (Scottish) 12, 31, 47–8, 90–1, 187
Hill, Octavia 280
Holme-on-Spalding (Yorks. E.R.) 35
honey 196, 202, 259
horses 35, 53, 57, 210, 211, 220, 226, 266
 ponies 190, 193, 197, 241, 242–3
horse racing 95–100, 268
 see also racecourses
Horsell (Surrey) 169
Hoskins, W. G. 19, 179
hospitals 172, 172 n.86, 199
Hounslow Heath (Mddx) 88, 90, 131
hundreds 22, 85–6, 87, 88, 102, 236
Hurstbourne Tarrant (Hants) 73, 145, 194
Hutton, New (Westmld) 62

Ibsley (Hants) 255–63
improvement 54, 60, 79, 130–1, 136, 277
 see also drainage, enclosure
Inclosure Act 1845 134, 135, 151, 154, 164, 223, 226, 250
Inclosure Commission 116, 154, 193
Ingleby Greenhow (Yorks. N.R.) 70 n.122, 71, 72 n.136
Ingleton (Yorks. W.R.) *49*, 169
intercommoning 22–6, 30, 37, 39, 59, 64, 241
Inveroran (Argyll) 91

Juniper Hill (Cottisford, Oxon.) 125

Keithick (Perthshire) 34
Kelton Hill Fair (Galloway) 94–5
Kennington Common (Surrey) 86, 104, 108, 154, 200, *201*
Kersal Moor (Lancs.) 97, 100, 104
Killearn (Stirlingshire) 71
Killingworth (Northumb.) 97
Kingmoor (Cumb.) 97
Kirkby-on-Bain (Lincs.) 143
Knavesmire (York) 44, 86, 97

Lake District (Cumbria) 13, 19, 47, 153–4, 156, 184–6, 279
 common rights in 40, 56, 60, 69, 77–8
Lakenheath (Suff.) 77 n.169, 180
Lamberhurst (Kent) 167, 194
Lammermuir Hills (Berwickshire) 15, 42
Lancashire 22, 71, 72, 133
Langdale, Great (Westmld) 156, 157, 165, 169
Langwathby (Cumb.) 99
Latton (Essex) 94
Lawrence, Philip 36
Laxton (Notts.) 128, 181
Leicestershire, county boundary 17, 23, 46, 121 n.55
Leith (Midlothian) 97, 100
Leland, John 75

levancy and couchancy, rule of **33**, 56, 60, 61, 216, 218, 226, 245
Libberton (Lanarkshire) 56
Lincoln 97, 177, 179, 198
Lincolnshire 17, 21–2, 46, *47*, 65, 135
livestock *see* cattle, donkeys, geese, goats, horses, poultry, sheep
livestock management *see* driving common land, herding regulations, pasture
livestock numbers 184–6, 188, 190–1
  on case study commons 212–13, 220–1, 241, 242–3, 253, 258–9
Llanllechid (Caern.) 235–43
Llanwrthwl (Brec.) 63
local authorities 166, 167, 171, 233, 241
  see also parishes
London, commons in vicinity of 59, 64, 88, 90, 96, 154–5, 193
  see also names of individual commons
Long Mynd (Shrops.) 64, 168
Longridge Fell (Lancs.) 127, 134
Loweswater (Cumb.) 61, 69
Lyndhurst (Hants) 97, *98*, 179

Mackenzie, Sir Kenneth 160
Maelienydd (Radnorshire) 121
Magdalen Hill Fair (Hants) 93
Malmesbury (Wilts.) 44
Malvern Hills 166, 191
manors, rise of 23, 25–6
manor courts *see* courts, seigniorial
manorial waste 11, **26–7**, 29, 129, 236, 256, 259, 261
Marlborough (Wilts.) 75, 198
Marsden Moor (Yorks. W.R.) *189*, 190
marshes 4, 17, 22, 23, 162, 168, 180, 232–3
  reclamation 133
  stinting 59, 144
Martlesham (Suff.) 179
Masham Moor (Yorks. N.R.) 26
Medmenham (Bucks.) 194
Meigle (Perthshire) 34

Merrow Downs (Surrey) 19, 151 n.97, 196 n.47, 203
Merton, Statute of (1236) 26, 30, 38, 39, 46, 130, 276
Methodists 108
  Primitive 104, 108, 123, 225, 247
  Wesleyan 249
Metropolitan Commons Act 1866 155, 164, 165
Middlethorpe (Yorks. W.R.) 27
Midlands, English 14, 38, 51, 67, 116
  fuel allotments 147, 150
  pasture rights 56, 57, 58, 59
Mildenhall (Suff.) 38
military use of commons 88–9, 103, 168, *173–4*, 175-80, 196, 197, 198, 249, 261, 268, 270
Milverton (Som.) 38
Minchinhampton (Glos.) 73, 90, 163
mineral rights 31, 113, 138, 227, 236
moor-burning (muirburn) 71, 76, 188, 191, 213, 214, 242
Moota Hill (Cumb.) *84*, 85, 88, 99, 101
Mootlaw (Northumb.) *84*, 85, 88
Mousehold Heath (Norf.) 101, 102, 103, 193, 198–9
musters 88, 101, 102
Muthill, shire of (Perthshire) 25
Myddle (Shrops.) 31, 121

Nantconwy (Caern.) 33, 135
national parks 157
National Trust 156, 163, 189, 215, 220, 239, 255
nature reserves 191, 193, 196–8, 233
Nether Wasdale (Cumb.) 60, 215–21
Netherwitton (Northumb.) 66
Nettlebed (Oxon.) 166, *195*
New Forest (Hants) 40, 77, 156, 157, 166, 167, 177, 190–1, 255–9, *260*, 280
  boundary of 255, 262–3
  cottage settlement 115, 118, 120, 121, 124
Newark (Notts.) 97, 99

INDEX

Newby (Yorks. W.R.)   *49*
Newcastle upon Tyne: Town Moor   43, 66, 86, 93, 97, 172 n.86, 176, 199–200
Newmarket (Suff.)   97, 99
Nomans Land (Hants/Wilts.)   121
Norden, John   29, 124
Norfolk   23, 69, 74, 75, 87, 88, 133
  common land, extent of   12, *13*, 17
  commons and poor relief   125, 127
  fuel allotments   150, 151
  samphire rights   162
  stinted pastures   144, 146, 147
North York Moors   70–1, 76, 96, 139, 142, 148, 164, 188
Northamptonshire   11, 59, 73 n.142, 75, 102
Northumberland   24, 38
Nottinghamshire   114
  county boundary   23, 46

open fields   3, 9, 58, 65, 66
  enclosure of   129, 130, 133, 145, 147
Orkney   29, 61, 63
Ostrom, Elinor   5, 79
Oswestry (Shrops.)   29, 120
outfield cultivation   14–15
overgrazing   19, 60, 64, 80, 184, 187, 204, 218–19, 243
Oxenhope (Yorks. W.R.)   *137*
Oxfordshire   11, 74, 75, 88, 102, 166

pains *see* byelaws
pannage, common of   4, **27**, 32, 39, 40, 245, 252
  in New Forest   190, 256, 258, 259
Pardshaw Crag (Cumb.)   *105*, 106
parishes
  boundaries   13, 17, 23, 42, 87
  parish councils   161, 166–7, 169, 203, 242
  poor cottages   125, 247, 261
  vestry meetings   145, 239–40, 247
pasture, common of   **27**, 37–8, 39–41
  regulation of   33–4, 53, 55–67
  see also grazing regulations

Peak District (Derby.)   41, 114, 188
peat   19, 68–72, *70*, *139*, 142, 187, 189–90, 197
  on case study commons   210–11, 213, 236, 239
  see also fuel allotments, turbary, turf
Pennines   67, 91, 103–4, 188
  common land, extent of   12, 17
  enclosure   135, 139
  pasture rights   40, 41, 58
Penrith (Cumb.)   93
Pickering (Yorks. N.R.)   22, 139
pigs (swine)   27, 35, 39, 54, 64, 166, 190, 192, 227, 247, 265, 266
  see also pannage
Pinchbeck (Lincs.)   21, 52, 72
piscary, common of   **27**, 133, 242
place-names (on common land)   14, 17, 19, 45, 85–6, 87, 89, 96, 121, 146, *237*
plantations, woodland   138, 187, 213, 258, 259
Plumstead (Kent)   155, 177
political protest   100–4, 225
pollarding   74, 266, 267
poor
  allotments for   146–52
  poor relief, common land and   125–8
  see also cottagers, parishes
poultry   113, 192, 252
  see also geese
Prees (Shrops.)   35, 118
prehistoric sites   13–14, 48, 109, *225*, 235, *237*
Preseli Hills (Pembrokeshire)   157, 164
public institutions on common land   127, 171–2, 175
  see also hospitals, schools, water supply
Putney (Surrey)   59, 64
  Putney Heath   96, 155, 165, 265–73

Quakers   105–6
quarries/quarrying   31, 116, 119, 138, 223–4, *225*, 235, 239, 247

rabbits 45, 100, 194, 196, 253, 261
racecourses 96–100, 198, 249
Radnorshire 135, 181, 184
rams, control of 67, 160, 211, 219
recreational use see under common land
regulated pastures 145, 164–5, 167, 190, 226–8, 251
religious dissent 104–8
  see also Covenanters, Methodists, Quakers
Renwick (Cumb.) 68
requisitioning 175, 178–81, 194, 251
Rhuddlan (Flints.) 39
Rhynie (Aberdeenshire) 93
Richmond (Yorks. N.R.) 86, 99
rifle ranges 177, 224, 249, 270
Rockford (Hants) 255–63
Rodborough Common (Glos.) 108, 163–4, 202
Rombaldsmoor (Yorks. W.R.) 25
Rosley Hill Fair (Cumb.) 94, 95
Royal Commission on Common Land 61, 158, 169, 181, 278
Roydon Common (Norf.) 196–7, *197*
Rushmere Heath (Suff.) 168, *173*, 176
Rye (Sussex) 94

sand-digging/sandpits 31, 36, 115, 138, 151, 162, 193, 196, 231, 256, 261
Savernake Forest (Wilts.) 119
Scalby (Yorks. N.R.) 68, 70, 75 n.158, 76 n.165
Scales Moor (Yorks. W.R.) *49*, 60, 169
Scarisbrick (Lancs.) 72
scattald 30, 46, 136, 156
schools 127, 171, 172, 175, 267
Scotland 24, 46, 52, 66
  common land, extent of 9, *10*, 12, 15
  common rights, legal basis of 29–31, 33–4, 39, 57, 159–60
  enclosure 136, 138
  shielings 41–2
  urban commons 44–5

Sedbergh (Yorks. W.R.) 163
Sedgemoor (Som.) 89, 133, 150
servitude, rights of 30, 45, 136, 160
sheep 35, 39, 41, 58–60, 61–5, 94, 159
  numbers 184–7, 188, 191
  on case study commons 208, 210–13, 218–21, 226–8, 233, 235, 239–43, 251–3, 258, 266
sheep marks 64–5, 211
sheepwalks 61, *62*, 63–4, 136, 142–3, 161–2, 175, 240
  see also heafs
Sherwood Forest (Notts.) 76
Shetland 30, 46, 136, 156
shielings 41–2, 207, *209*, 210
  see also transhumance
shire moors 24–5
Shropshire 4, 119–20, 124, 125
Shute Hill (Devon) 88
Sinclair, Sir John 131, 147
Sites of Special Scientific Interest (SSSIs) 157–8, 162, 183, 185, 190, 192, 196, 214, 220, 233, 273
Skelton in Cleveland (Yorks. N.R.) 32
Skene (Aberdeenshire) 71
Skeoch Hill (Galloway) 106, *107*
Skipwith (Yorks. E.R.) 101, 165, 197
Skircoat Moor (Yorks. W.R.) 104
Snettisham (Norf.) 147, 151
Snowdonia 63, 139, 142
  see also Llanllechid
soil, common in the 27, 31
Somerset 57
  Levels 93, 133, 135, 136
soums/souming 57, 160, 210–13
Southern Uplands 47, 107
Spalding see Pinchbeck
Spencer, Earl 154, 155, 265, 269, 270
Spennymoor (Dur.) 25
sports 95–100, 198, 202
  see also golf, grouse, racecourses
squatter cottages see cottages
St Andrews (Fife) 44, 100

INDEX

Staffordshire   15, 108, 115, 119
stints/stinting   **34**, 44, 56–61, 152, 165, 216, 218, 226–8
  stinted pastures   57–8, 143–5, 147, 151, 164, 168
  see also soums
Stiperstones (Shrops.)   119
Stockbridge (Hants)   164
Stoke Poges (Bucks.)   113, 148, 178
Sudbury (Suff.)   64
Suffolk   14, 22, 57
Sugar Loaf Mountain (Mon.)   162
Surrey   46, 75, 138
  heaths   172, 176
Sussex   58

Tatham (Lancs.)   142, 145
Temple Sowerby (Westmld)   95
Thirlmere (Cumb.)   175
Thirsk, Joan   58, 67
Thornes (Yorks. W.R.)   34
Thornham (Norf.)   144, 162
Thornthwaite (Westmld)   67 n.105, 71, 72 n.136
Todmorden (Yorks. W.R.)   *103*, 104
Tooting (Surrey)   155, 200, 202, 279
Torrington, Great (Devon)   166 n.60
townships   34, 52
  see also vill
townships, crofting   160, 207–13
transhumance   41–2
Treales (Lancs.)   71
turbary, common of   **27**, 30, 32, 35, 139, 142–3, 161, 220, 236, 242, 252, 256, 259
  regulation of   68–72
  turbary allotments   148, 150–1, 202, 229–33
turf   35, 43, 68–72, 113, 166, 190, 239, 258–9, 267
  see also fuel allotments, peat, turbary
Tusser, Thomas   64

undergrazing   186, 187, 191, 192, 253
urban commons   42–5, 86, 97, 198–202, 204, 265–73
Urie (Kincardineshire)   72

Vermuyden, Cornelius   132, 133, 229
vills   22, 27, 37–8
  see also townships

Wales   25, 87, 90, 106, 108
  common land, extent of   9, 17
  common rights, legal basis of   28–9
  cottages   116, 121, 123
  Crown wastes   157, 236
  enclosure   135
  pasture rights   33, 40, 41, 61, 63, 65
  registrations under CRA   160 n.33, 161
Wallingfen (Yorks. E.R.)   22, 52, 69
Wall-with-Pipehill (Staffs.)   58
Wandsworth Common (Surrey)   155, 165, *170*, 172, 265, 279
wapentakes   88, 101–2
Warcop (Westmld)   25, 180
Warwickshire   75
water supply   175
Waterbeach (Cambs.)   69
Watermillock (Cumb.)   143
Wavendon Heath (Bucks.)   150
Weald (Kent/Sussex)   23, 119, 167
Wensleydale (Yorks. N.R.)   83, 165
Westminster II, Statute of (1285)   26, 130
Westmorland   12, 25, 101, 135
Wey Hill Fair (Hants)   *92*, 93–4
Wheeler End Common (Bucks.)   *126*, 128
Whillimoor (Cumb.)   25
White Down Fair (Som.)   93, 94
Whittlewood Forest (Northants.)   39, 64
Whitwell (Norf.)   151
Whixall (Shrops.)   118
Wicken (Cambs.)   69, 150
Wilkinson, Thomas   115, 278
Wilton (Roxburghshire)   *140*, 142

Wiltshire 59, 94
Wimbledon (Surrey) 34, 59, 67, 74
  Wimbledon Common 104, 154, 155, 165, 177, 202, 265–73
Wimbledon and Putney Commons Act 1871 200, 269
Wimblington (Cambs.) 60
Windermere (Westmld) 34, 73
Winfrith Heath (Dorset) 181
Woking (Surrey) 172, 175
Wolsingham (Dur.) 139
wooded commons 13, 19, 73–4, 119, 245
  see also coppice woodland, plantations, pollarding, woodland regeneration
Woodgreen (Hants) 116, 120, 121, 123
woodland regeneration 19, 192, 194–6, 233, 253
  see also plantations

Woolhope (Heref.) 125
Woolridge Common (Glos.) 121, 123
Woolwich Common (Kent) 175
workhouses *126*, 127
World Wars
  First 178–9
  Second *176*, 179–80, 196, 251, 261, 270
  see also requisitioning
Worlington Abergavenny (Suff.) 69
Wormley (Herts.) 34
Wychwood Forest (Oxon.) 73

Yardley (Warw.) 15, 27
Yateley Common (Hants) 180
York 44, 97, 179
Yorkshire 9, 59, 75, 76, 80, 89, 101
  Vale of York 12, 17
  Yorkshire Dales 76, 91, 188
  see also North York Moors, Pennines

Garden and Landscape History

Previously published

1. *Designs Upon the Land: Elite Landscapes of the Middle Ages*
Oliver H. Creighton

2. *Richard Woods (1715–1793): Master of the Pleasure Garden*
Fiona Cowell

3. *Uvedale Price (1747–1829): Decoding the Picturesque*
Charles Watkins and Ben Cowell

4. *Common Land in English Painting, 1700–1850*
Ian Waites

5. Observations on Modern Gardening, *by Thomas Whately:*
An Eighteenth-Century Study of the English Landscape Garden
Michael Symes

6. *The Landscape Studies of Hayman Rooke (1723–1806):*
Antiquarianism, Archaeology and Natural History in the Eighteenth Century
Emily Sloan

7. *Transhumance and the Making of Ireland's Uplands, 1550–1900*
Eugene Costello

8. *The Foldcourse and East Anglian Agriculture and Landscape, 1100–1900*
John Belcher

9. *Erasmus Darwin's Gardens: Medicine, Agriculture and the Sciences in the Eighteenth Century*
Paul A. Elliott

10. *Rediscovering Lost Landscapes: Topographical Art in north-west Italy, 1800–1920*
Pietro Piana, Charles Watkins and Ross Balzaretti

11. *Cottage Gardens and Gardeners in the East of Scotland, 1750–1914*
Catherine Rice

12. *Territoriality and the Early Medieval Landscape:*
The Countryside of the East Saxon Kingdom
Stephen Rippon

13. *"Turbulent Foresters": A Landscape Biography of Ashdown Forest*
Brian Short

www.ingramcontent.com/pod-product-compliance
Lightning Source LLC
Chambersburg PA
CBHW081824230426
43668CB00017B/2367